Withdrawn

A HISTORY OF THE
BRITISH CAVALRY

1816 to 1919
VOLUME I
1816 to 1850

A HISTORY OF THE
BRITISH CAVALRY

1816 to 1919

by

THE MARQUESS OF ANGLESEY

F.S.A.

VOLUME I
1816 to 1850

THE SHOE STRING PRESS, INC
HAMDEN, CONNECTICUT

Library of Congress Cataloging in Publication Data

Anglesey, George Charles Henry Victor Paget, 7th
    Marquis of, 1922–
    A History of the British cavalry, 1816–1919.

    Includes bibliographical references.
    CONTENTS: v. 1. 1816–1850.
    1. Great Britain.   Army.   Cavalry—History.
I Title.
UE57.A65   357'.1'0942   73–8663
ISBN 0–208–01404–7

Published in Great Britain 1973
by Leo Cooper Ltd., London
and in the United States of America
as an Archon Book
by The Shoe String Press, Inc.
Hamden, Connecticut
Printed in Great Britain

DEDICATED, WITH PERMISSION, TO
D. W. KING, ESQ.
O.B.E., F.L.A.
CHIEF LIBRARIAN OF THE MINISTRY OF DEFENCE
LIBRARY
THE MILITARY HISTORIAN'S
FRIEND AND MENTOR

CONTENTS

7

Contents

Contents

ILLUSTRATIONS

Illustrations

Illustrations

MAPS

ACKNOWLEDGMENTS

The dedication of this volume bears testimony to my gratitude for the ever willing and never failing help given me by the Library of the Ministry of Defence and its Chief Librarian. Other institutions without whose assistance I could not have proceeded include the London Library, the India Office Library (Mr S. C. Sutton, Chief Librarian, and Dr R. J. Bingle), the Library of the Royal United Service Institute for Defence Studies (Mr J. R. Dineen, Chief Librarian), the Royal College of Veterinary Surgeons' Wellcome Library (Miss B. Horder, Librarian), the Society for Army Historical Research and the National Army Museum.

To Mrs L. S. Bickford, Mr F. M. Delmar, Mr F. R. Hodge, Mr E. A. Lucas, Mr George Pearman, Lieutenant-Colonel W. H. Unett, and the Home HQ of the 14/20 King's Hussars I am very grateful for allowing me to see and quote from original papers in their possession.

Amongst the many people who have kindly answered my importunate questions, read through portions of the manuscript or given me invaluable advice (but who bear no responsibility for the results of their kindness) are Mr Brian Bond, Mr Hector Bolitho, Mr Roger Fulford, Professor H. T. Lambrick (Oriel College, Oxford) the late Mr T.D. McGuffie, Mrs Charles Morgan, Messrs Boris and John Mollo and Lieutenant-Colonel H. Moyse-Bartlett. To all of them and to my wife, whose patience has often been tried, I give my warm thanks.

Mrs H. St G. Saunders of Writer's and Speaker's Research has as always gone to extreme lengths to satisfy my appetite for facts and verification of sources, and Mrs Pat Brayne's speed and accuracy in typing and re-typing have never failed me. My gratitude to both knows no bounds.

To my publishers, Mr Leo Cooper and Mr Tom Hartman, I give special thanks for the care and trouble they have taken at all stages, and I am also grateful to Mr Patrick Leeson for producing such excellent maps.

A list of abbreviations used in the footnotes and in the
source notes (p. 308) appears on p. 302

'A soldier, cried my Uncle Toby,
interrupting the corporal, is no more
exempt from saying a foolish thing,
Trim, than a man of letters – But
not so often, an' please your
honour, replied the corporal.'

–STERNE, *Tristram Shandy*
(Book viii, chapter 19)

PREFACE

The cavalry is dead. Today, except for ceremonial purposes, for a squadron or two in the Angolan part of the Portuguese army and in the mountains of Switzerland, horsed soldiers are employed nowhere in the world. Yet half a century ago they were still an essential component of virtually every nation's land forces.

In the British army, indeed, one of the largest assemblies of cavalry ever seen was successfully engaged in the Middle East towards the end of the First World War. Others were concentrated at the same date behind the Western Front and took part in the final victorious advance which ended the conflict. Even the start of the Second World War saw numerous cavalry formations still in being. Some of these, notably those of the Polish army, went into action before being decimated or replaced by armoured units.

* * *

The objects of this present work – a more or less definitive history of the final phase of the British cavalry – are many. I wanted, for instance, to fill a gap by providing a chronicle of the use of the mounted arm in peace and war over the century which followed the defeat of Napoleon; to show in some detail how it fulfilled its policing functions at home and overseas, and how it played its part in the frequent small wars which were so characteristic a feature of the British Empire in its heyday.

* * *

There are obvious difficulties, especially when describing battles, in separating one arm from the others. This is most clearly demonstrated in the present case by the horse artillery, which so often worked closely with the cavalry. My approach to this special problem has been to avoid going into any detail, except where it was necessary for an understanding of the part played by the cavalry.

* * *

Preface

The question of what to leave out is always particularly harrowing for the writer who professes to be definitive. I have tried to steer between the tedium of a catalogue and the risk of being charged with omitting matters which might be considered worthy of inclusion. The tendency has been to concentrate in the case of military actions upon those which are well documented and to enter fully into those where an element of controversy or special interest appears. This has meant, of course, that certain minor engagements have not been mentioned at all, and that others have only been touched upon.

* * *

Another difficulty common to all military historians is the question of the accuracy of casualty figures, particularly in Indian campaigns. In nearly every engagement related in the present volume the figures given for killed and wounded amongst the enemy come from the British alone. They are almost certainly exaggerated, sometimes outrageously. Where, rarely, an Afghan or Sikh source quotes a figure it is at least equally suspect. Suspicion must also rest on nearly all the estimates, official and unofficial, of the numbers of the enemy engaged.

* * *

In prefacing this first volume of the work by an extended Prologue, I have tried to paint a very general picture of the history of cavalry, with particular reference (from the seventeenth century onwards) to the British cavalry, up to and inclusive of the Waterloo campaign. This part of the book does not pretend to be complete, nor is it based upon primary sources. It may appear to military historians unnecessarily lengthy, especially as regards the historical background to the wars of the eighteenth and early nineteenth centuries. For the general reader, however, I have felt that a more detailed resumé of the campaigns in which the cavalry regiments of the British army took part may be of use. Those readers whose general knowledge of these earlier periods is substantial are advised to omit the Prologue altogether.

* * *

The three volumes which are planned to follow the present one will be designed to be read independently of their companions, each seeking to present a more or less complete image of the period covered. The chief exception to this is that campaigns which took place in South Africa before 1850 have been excluded from the present volume. Instead they will be presented as a prelude to the larger conflicts in that part of the world which took place at later dates, and will therefore appear in a subsequent volume.

*　　*　　*

The 10th Hussars and the 12th Lancers went out to Portugal in 1827 as part of an expedition sent there by Canning in support of the Regency of Queen Isabella. Neither regiment saw action, and both were soon recalled. I have therefore not dealt with that episode. Nor have I discussed either the four-year post-Waterloo occupation of France or the three years spent in Canada by the 1st Dragoon Guards and the 7th Hussars during and after the Rebellion of 1838. In the latter period the two regiments were engaged in duties similar to those of peace-keeping in the industrial areas at home or in Ireland, though at times (see Fig. 16, facing p. 192) in much lower temperatures.

*　　*　　*

It would not have been possible to contemplate a work such as this without the indispensable backing of Sir John Fortescue's *History of the British Army*. Though he was not always accurate in details and sometimes unduly biased, his grasp of the broad sweep of events and his capacity for condensing a vast mass of facts into highly readable prose place all those who work in this field of history permanently in his debt.

*　　*　　*

In the spelling of Indian proper names I have been undogmatic, perhaps even at times erratic. For well-known places, such as Bhurtpore, I have usually preferred the more familiar and generally accepted forms to the more modern or scholarly. When quoting from contemporary accounts I have not altered the original spelling.

*　　*　　*

21

Preface

Except where I have thought them especially interesting, startling or amusing, I have resisted the temptation to describe details of the uniforms worn by officers and men. Numerous lavishly illustrated books dealing exclusively and fully with the subject have appeared in recent years.

A HISTORY OF THE
BRITISH CAVALRY
1816—1919

VOLUME I
1816–1850

'No faith and honour is found in men who follow camps.'

LUCAN, *De Bello Civili*, Bk. x, 1, 407

'Everyman thinks meanly of himself for not having been a soldier.'

DR SAMUEL JOHNSON, Boswell, *Life*, 1778

'At the same time that nothing can be more useful in the day of battle than a body of disciplined cavalry, nothing can be more expensive, and nothing more useless than a body of regular cavalry half and insufficiently disciplined.'

THE DUKE OF WELLINGTON in 1804
(Wellington (D), II, 679)

'I have always considered the cavalry to be the most delicate arm that we possess. We have few officers who have practical knowledge of the mode of using it, or who have ever seen more than two regiments together. . . . You will see the necessity of keeping the cavalry as much as possible *en masse*, and in reserve, to be thrown in at the moment when an opportunity may offer of striking a decisive blow.'

THE DUKE OF WELLINGTON in 1811
(Wellington (D), VII, 375)

PROLOGUE

'The history of the use of the horse in battle is
divided into three periods: first, that of the
charioteer; second, that of the mounted warrior
who clings to his steed by pressure of the knees;
and third, that of the rider equipped with stirrups.'

White, Lynn, *Medieval Technology
and Social Change*, 1962, p. 1

(i)

Cavalry from the earliest times to the end of the Civil War

The relative importance of cavalry and infantry has shifted through
the ages, but cavalry can be said to have been the predominant arm
from the time of Alexander the Great to the early fifteenth century.*

This came about as the result of certain technological inventions,
the chief of which was that of the foot-stirrup. Presumed to have
been invented in China, this revolutionary aid to horsemanship was
in common use there by the middle of the fifth century A.D. In
Western Europe it did not appear, it seems, until the beginning of
the eighth century.

It made possible for the first time speedy and powerful shock
combat. Before its advent the rider was always insecure in his seat.
To some degree the simple saddle provided stability, while bit and
spur helped to control his mount, but at best he was no more than a
rapidly moving bowman, swordsman or hurler of javelins. Without
stirrups, the spear, javelin or lance depended for its delivery solely
upon the strength of the rider's shoulder and biceps. With stirrups
he could deliver his blow using the combined weight of himself and
his charging horse. Equally, the mounted swordsman when taking
'a good broadhanded swipe at his foe, had only to miss to find himself on the ground.'[1] In short, the stirrup was an important invention
which welded horse and rider into a single unit capable of an

---

* A short-lived, localised re-birth of cavalry pre-eminence took place under
Frederick the Great (see p. 38). In fifteen of his twenty-two battles, the Prussian
cavalry can be said to have decided the day.

unprecedented violence. The Franks under Charles Martel and his sons in the eighth century were probably the first to realise its full significance in terms of shock combat.

*   *   *

In Europe, for a thousand years from the end of the western Roman empire, the art of war was little attended to in the chaos of the dark ages. The ascendancy of horse over foot, however, remained, and even grew. The teutonic feudal system, which spread over Christian Europe, gradually excluded all but the rich and powerful from the 'noble' trade of war. The concept of the common man as a warrior became obsolete. The disciplined infantry mass became a thing of the past. Only knights on horseback, encased in armour (a legacy from the Romans), engaged in combat. 'The feudal class of the European Middle Ages existed to be armed horsemen, cavaliers fighting in a particular manner which was made possible by the stirrup.'[2] The rabble of retainers which accompanied them on foot was no more than their maintenance staff, neither equipped nor required to fight.

The heyday of the armoured knight was reached under Charlemagne, who held his huge empire together through polygot armies, the nucleus of which was the heavy cavalry. By then the Latin word for soldier, *miles*, was already losing any meaning except that of noble horseman or knight. *Caballarius*, *chevalier* and *caballero*, which originally meant any horseman, had become, by the eleventh century, titles of nobility. This implied not only that none but nobles could be military horsemen, but also that every noble was, by definition, a military horseman.

Where, as in north-west Europe, infantry was to some degree still relied upon, it was ill-armed and powerless against armour-protected, mobile horsemen. Its sole resource when attacked in open country was the palisade, behind which, as at Hastings in 1066, it found static protection. Hastings was virtually 'the last attempt made for three centuries by infantry to withstand cavalry'.[3] Harold possessed no fighting horsemen. The only horses he had were used as transport, while the Norman force consisted mainly of cavalry assisted by archers and a few Flemish pikemen.

The institution of knight-service, which followed the Norman invasion, laid the foundation of the British cavalry. The English man-at-arms, who emerged over the next three centuries, was trained from youth in the handling of the lance, sword, dagger and shield, but his standard of horsemanship, compared with that of later ages, was low. This was due, perhaps, as much to the weakness of his bit and the unwieldiness of his saddle, as to the weight of his armour, which was not as great as is commonly supposed.

The basic administrative unit was the constabulary, consisting of as few as 25 or as many as 80 men-at-arms. In a campaign varying numbers of constabularies were grouped in a tactical formation known as a banner, commanded by a banneret. The usual method of going into battle was in a large unwieldy wedge-shaped mass of hundreds of closely-packed knights. The speed of a charge was almost certainly no more than a trot, and the room for manoeuvre slight. As time went on the wedge gave way to the *haie*, or thin line, which made speedier evolutions possible.

There were two lesser types of armed horsemen: the more lightly armoured pauncenars (from *panzer*, the German for coat of mail) who fought with a lance; and the light cavalry left over from pre-Conquest times, who originally patrolled the coasts. These were called hobelars from the hobbies or ponies they rode. They wore no body armour and were armed with swords. Their chief employment was in skirmishing and reconnoitring.

* * *

The total contempt which the chivalry of Europe showed for foot soldiers is nowhere better demonstrated than in the Crusades. For the two and a half centuries of their duration, infantry, as such, hardly existed. The lack of cohesion, central direction and tactical skill of the heavy cavalry of the Christian knights, 'who hated the very name of subordination',[4] when pitted against the light horse of the Saracens, was partly made up for by the self-contained protection of their armour, and partly by their religious fervour. Under a really distinguished leader, such as Richard the Lion Heart, they could accomplish great things, as witness his march from Joppa to Jerusalem, and his victory at Arsouf in 1191. Though, on occasion, the knights fought on foot, their resemblance to infantry proper was limited.

If the dark ages and the Crusades present a picture of the military art at its feeblest, something like the opposite can be said of the great Mongol invasion. Genghis Khan was, perhaps, the most formidable cavalry leader of all time. His highly organised armies, and those he bequeathed to his heirs, were almost totally devoid of infantry. The defeat of the heavy Polish cavalry at Lignitz by Subotai (a first-class general in his own right) in 1241, fourteen years after Genghis Khan's death, well illustrates how superior were the flexibility and mobility of the light and intangible Mongolians. It was their 'sudden and *unexpected* return to the charge'[5] when apparently in retreat – a manoeuvre calling for cool control – which most disconcerted the unwieldy Poles.

*   *   *

In Western Europe, meanwhile, the end of feudal chivalry, and with it the end for all time of cavalry as the predominant arm, came gradually into sight. Three nations, each employing different means, were the agents of this revolution in warfare. By the time the English, Swiss and Bohemian foot-soldiers had humbled the gallant, insubordinate men-at-arms of France, Austria and Germany, the conception of war as the 'noble' art in which the masses took only a menial part was becoming obsolete.

It was as much a social as a military revolution. The Hussite Bohemians, nationally roused to throw off their German yoke, found a man of genius in Jan Zizka. It was he who brought to perfection the tactics of the *laager* (anglicized to 'leaguer'). Against these, which consisted in the speedy formation of wagons into mobile forts, the German knights contended in vain. At the same time, and for nearly 200 years from the beginning of the fourteenth century, the free herdsmen of Switzerland, armed with pike and halberd, and formed in phalangeal order, nearly always got the better of the German and Austrian knights who came against them.

During the same period the gradual perfecting of the bow and crossbow gave the English an ascendancy over the chivalry of France.

'It is certainly not the least curious part of the military history of the period', wrote Sir Charles Oman, 'that the commanders who made such good use of their archery had no conception of the tendencies of their action. Edward the Black Prince and his father regarded themselves as the flower of chivalry, and would have been horrified had they realised that their own tactics were going far to make chivalrous warfare impossible. Such, however, was the case; that unscientific kind of combat which resembled a huge tilting match could not continue if one side persisted in bringing into the field auxiliaries who could prevent their opponents from approaching near enough to break a lance.'[6]

In the English wars against the Scots, the terrible slaughter of Edward II's 3,000 horsemen at Bannockburn in 1314 showed that by that date cavalry was already declining as the chief arbiter of battle. At Falkirk, in 1298, Edward I beat the infantrymen of William Wallace by a well-timed attack of archers and horsemen combined. Indeed the English were ahead of the rest of Europe in the blending of horse and foot. Baliol's and Beaumont's defeat of the Earl of Mar at Dupplin Muir in 1332 was an early example of the success which could attend an intelligent combination of bow, pike and lance.

The effect that the arrow missile, projected at speed, could have on armour was early demonstrated at the siege of Abergavenny in 1182. The Welsh arrows, it was said, pierced an oak door four fingers thick.[7] To defend himself against such penetration the knight was compelled to add plate armour to his mail shirt. This so increased his weight that he found it more difficult than ever to negotiate rough ground on horseback. His enemies, therefore, tried their best to meet him on such ground. Nor, however hard he tried, did the knight ever succeed in armouring his horse satisfactorily. At Poitiers in 1356 the French knights fought dismounted because ten years before, at Crécy, the English arrows had killed or maimed their horses. The knight deprived of his horse lost nearly all his tactical value.

The story was much the same at Agincourt where Henry V's 6,000 men, a large majority of whom were archers, vanquished a French army three or four times more numerous. The lightly armed yeomen of England had the unwieldy knights of France, again mostly dismounted, at their mercy. First they decimated them with their arrows, and then, in close combat, 'beat upon their armour with mallets, as though they were smiths hammering upon their anvils'.[8]

*   *   *

Though gunpowder, which was first used with any effect at Crécy, gradually revolutionised the art of war, it was not the cause of the fall from pre-eminence of cavalry. For many years the power of the bow was so much superior to the power of the handgun that the impact of the new weapons was only gradually realised. Three cavalry reforms, however, slowly materialised under the new conditions.

First, armour, after an initial period in which it had been enormously strengthened, grew lighter. Second, an attempt was made to unite shock and fire power by placing cavalry amongst the infantry.

This was first tried at the battle of Pavia in 1525, when the Marqués de Pescara inserted bodies of heavily armed musketeers in the intervals of his cavalry. His defeat of the French was thought to have been due to the success of this practice, which consequently gained ground for some years. It was a long time before it was realised that it was, in fact, fatal to deprive horsemen of the advantage which they derived from the speed of their mounts; that horsemen charging at a walk were more prominent targets than infantrymen, and that careful and steady aiming was more difficult from horseback than on foot. Third, the lance was increasingly replaced by portable fire-arms. The English lancers, for example, were first armed with pistols in 1599. In the long run, however, because they slowed down the speed of the charge, neither the mixing of horse and foot, nor the use of fire-arms by cavalry were developments which, in themselves, proved particularly successful.

As early as the second decade of the sixteenth century, Niccolo Machiavelli, in his *Art of War*, defined what might have been expected to be the role of cavalry in the age of gunpowder.

'It is right', he wrote, 'to have some cavalry to support and assist infantry, but not to look upon them as the main force of an army, for they are highly necessary to reconnoitre, to scour roads, to make incursions, and lay waste an enemy's country, to beat up their quarters, to keep them in continual alarm, and to cut off their convoys; but in the field battles, which commonly decide the fate of nations, and for which armies are chiefly designed, they are fitter to pursue an enemy that is routed and flying than anything else.'[9]

It is one of the surprises of modern warfare not only that the mounted arm was seldom confined to this limited rôle, but also that in a considerable number of European campaigns, for many years to come, cavalry sometimes still played the decisive part in battle. The chief reason, as has already been indicated, was that infantry fire-arms took a very long time to fulfil their early promise. For centuries the matchlock musket was the fire-arm most generally used. It was the least complicated, most trustworthy and easiest to maintain of available weapons, but it was slow-loading, and, especially in wet weather, uncertain. Its speed and efficiency were not materially improved until the percussion lock and cap, and the rifling of barrels, came into general use in the nineteenth century. In these circumstances, cavalry shock tactics enjoyed a success which would have astonished Machiavelli.

* * *

Gustavus Adolphus's victories in the Thirty Years' War (1618–1648) were partly due to his realisation that a reversion to shock tactics could make nugatory the power of the slowly delivered bullet. The Swedish King taught his horsemen, the depth of whose line he reduced from six to three or four, to eschew the universal habit of advancing cautiously upon the enemy, depending chiefly on the pistol. Instead, when he had softened up the opposing lines by artillery and musketry, he bade his horsemen ride forward, fire a single pistol volley and then charge home with the sword, coming to close quarters as soon as possible. It seems unlikely, though, that the charge was conducted at more than a sharp trot.

* * *

In Britain, meanwhile, for many years past, the art of war had been little studied. As elsewhere in Europe, the practice of hiring mercenaries when needed was followed to the detriment of the training of native troops. Organised bodies of horse scarcely existed. In Henry VIII's time, it is true, the Northern Horsemen, who for many years had helped to defend England's Scottish border, grew into a not inefficient force of light cavalry and did good service in France in the 1540s.

In the same reign steps had been taken to improve the English breed of horse, but in the century preceding the Civil War (1642–51) the mounted arm had suffered sad neglect. As the nation divided itself into two camps in preparation for the great struggle between King Charles I and his Parliament, the building up of fighting forces had to start from scratch.

It soon became clear that the majority of good amateur gentlemen-riders were for the King. This initial advantage was very valuable to the Royalist cause in the first few years of warfare. The ascendancy which early training in falconry and the chase gave Prince Rupert's horsemen, their quick eye for country and their superior mounts and equestrian prowess, proved especially useful in patrol work. It took some time before Cromwell was able to exploit their besetting sin of indiscipline. That he did so is one of the reasons why Parliament won the war.

Cromwell and Prince Rupert in their spirit and dash had much in common with Gustavus Adolphus. Cromwell, whose military career started at the age of forty-three, was perhaps the greatest cavalry leader of them all, for he combined fire, brilliance and energy with prudence, presence of mind and iron willpower. Prince Rupert, on the other hand, who had become a soldier at sixteen and was a veteran of twenty-three by the time he first met Cromwell in battle, lacked the restraining qualities of his adversary, while conspicuously possessing the others.*

At Edgehill in 1642, the Prince, who had fought for the Swedes two years before, showed at once that he had imbibed and even improved upon Gustavus Adolphus's system. Partly because his cavaliers were deficient in fire-arms, he made them attack without the customary preliminary pistol volley, thereby accelerating the speed of the charge. At Edgehill, too, as well as at Worcester a month earlier, the Roundheads had received the charge at the halt. Rupert, on the other hand, never allowed his men to await an attack, and the Parliamentary cavalry very soon learned the same lesson. Cromwell, who was a mere captain at Edgehill, at once saw that the Parliament must 'get men of spirit . . . that is likely to go on as far as gentlemen will go' if the courage, honour and resolution of the Cavaliers were to be matched. He therefore set about welding into a highly disciplined force the Puritan farmers and yeomen whose religious and social convictions had attached them strongly to the Parliamentary cause. His first success came in a skirmish near Grantham in May 1643, where his newly formed regiment routed an approximately equal number of Cavaliers. The charge was made at 'a pretty round trot' which for those days probably meant the very acme of shock action.

It is significant that Cromwell was not present at Roundway Down two months later. Had he been, the Royalists might not have won the most dramatic battle of the whole war, in which the superiority of the Cavaliers' morale crushed the as yet half-trained Parliamentary horse. Amongst these were Sir Arthur Hazelrigg's famous 'lobsters' (so called from the hardness of their shells), probably the last fully mailed body of horsemen to go into action in England. Though some of the Parliamentary cavalry commanders had been trained in the Swedish school, the Roundheads in this battle were

* In comparing the two men it should be remembered that Cromwell was only a subordinate commander throughout the First Civil War, while Rupert was Commander-in-Chief under the King.

still fighting in lines five or six deep, while the Royalists had adopted the three deep line. Within a year both sides had adopted it.

Three months after Roundway Down the battle of Winceby gave the Roundhead horse, through superior training and morale, their first great success over the Cavaliers. Though Cromwell's own part in the battle was not very distinguished, it vastly raised his reputation and that of his Ironsides. It was not until 10 months later, at Marston Moor, that both the superiority of Cromwell's horse and the skill of his generalship (in conjunction with that of Thomas Fairfax) blazed out. The cavalry on both sides were at their best and Marston Moor has rightly been described by the historian of the British army as the first great day of the English cavalry.[10]

It was also an interesting example of the period of transition through which the cavalry was passing. Opposed to Fairfax's old-fashioned lancers were Lord Goring's horsemen mingled with musketeers in the Swedish fashion, while the men of Cromwell faced those of Prince Rupert, each body equally well taught by their leaders in what came to be known as the New English School of Cavalry. But it was Cromwell alone, who, at the eleventh hour, had a fresh reserve at hand. It was he alone who could be certain that the harsh discipline imposed on his Roundheads would make them attend to the 'rally' as well as to the 'charge'.

In spite of the victory at Marston Moor, and the massive assistance of the Scots which had helped to make it possible, the Parliamentary cause suffered greatly from lack of central direction, and its army from mutiny and desertion. Constant bickering between its various commanders and committees developed into recriminations when it was seen that the first two-and-a-half years of war had left a stalemate. To put all these things right, Parliament took the historic decision to raise a New Model Army, with regular pay. Fairfax was given supreme command, and in due course Cromwell became the Lieutenant-General of Horse.

The cavalry of the New Model Army consisted of eleven regular regiments, each with six troops of 100 men, and one regiment of Dragoons, 1,000 strong. The regular cavalryman was armed with a sword, a pair of pistols and, later, a carbine. On his head he wore a light iron headpiece, known as a 'pot', and over his leather coat, a light cuirass, known as a 'back and breast'. The dragoon, or mounted infantryman, wore no armour, and as a rule fought on foot with a sword and a musket.

At Naseby in June 1645, the first large-scale battle fought by the

New Model Army, a decisive victory was won as much through Prince Rupert's over-impetuosity as by the Roundheads' superior timing and discipline.

Though it dragged on for two more years, the First Civil War was virtually over. The Second started when the King, throwing himself into the arms of the Scots, invaded England in July 1648. Cromwell marched from Pembroke, where he had been suppressing a Royalist rising, to Preston, where he beat the Scots. This speedy raid, and the relentless pursuit which followed, are cavalry epics comparable with those of the Third Maratha War, 1817–19 (see p. 194) and the Central Indian campaign of 1857–58.

Cromwell's first independent army command took him to Ireland. His ruthless campaign of 1649 was accomplished by four regiments of foot and only one of horse. It was followed by his masterly defeat of the Scottish Covenanters at Dunbar the following year. In this, the greatest action fought by an English army since Agincourt, the Scots were largely superior in cavalry. It is interesting to note that their front ranks were still equipped with the lance, a weapon generally considered obsolete at that date. The horse on both sides fought well. It was the faulty disposition of the Scots which gave Cromwell the victory. At Worcester exactly a year later he had overwhelming superiority in all arms, and the annihilation of the Scots was never in doubt. By the end of 1651 the New Model Army had achieved its object: it was master of the whole of Britain.

(ii)

British cavalry from the Standing Army until 1790

Soon after the restoration of the monarchy in 1660, Charles II decided to maintain four regiments of foot and three of horse.* These

* 'Throughout this reign and up to the end of the century it was still the custom for a trooper of Horse to bring his own troop horse on enlisting. If he could not do so the King provided him with a horse and if necessary stopped the price from his pay. It was never officially settled as to whether or not he was entitled

were formed in part from former units of the New Model, in part from those Royalists who had joined him in exile, and in part from specially raised troops. Within the first two years of the new reign the foundations were laid for what were to become in due course the four senior cavalry regiments of the British army: the 1st and 2nd Life Guards, the Royal Horse Guards (known from the colour of their uniform as 'the Blues'), and the 1st, or Royal, Dragoons.*

This small nucleus of a so-called standing army was not materially added to until James II in 1685, the year of his accession, used Monmouth's insurrection as an excuse to raise a further twelve infantry and eight cavalry regiments. Thus were born what eventually became the 1st to 6th Dragoon Guards, and the two senior hussar regiments, the 3rd King's Own and the 4th Queen's Own.† In 1678 three independent troops of dragoons, the first since the Restoration, were raised. Three years later these, with the addition of a further three troops, were made into a regiment which is now world famous as the Scots Greys. In 1689, a year after the Bloodless Revolution, a cavalry regiment, known as the Black Horse, was raised by the Earl of Devonshire from his Derbyshire tenantry. This in due course became the 7th Dragoon Guards. In the same year the Protestants of Northern Ireland raised troops to quell the Catholics of the South. Amongst these were two regiments of dragoons which evolved ultimately into the 5th Royal Irish Lancers and the 6th Inniskilling Dragoons. Both regiments took part in the battle of the Boyne in 1690.

In Europe, meanwhile, three great French generals, Condé, Turenne, and Luxembourg were proving that the revival of limited

to take his horse with him when he was discharged, the practice varying from regiment to regiment, but this was never allowed if the man had under a year's service. It was because the Horse originally found their own remounts that they received a higher rate of pay than Dragoons, who did not.' (Tylden, 8–9.)

* This regiment started as The Tangier Troop and was employed to garrison the fortress of Tangier which Charles II had acquired as part of the dowry of his Queen, Catherine of Braganza. On its return to England in 1684 it was converted into a regiment of dragoons.

† The word 'hussar' was in use in Hungary early in the fifteenth century, and meant a scout or spy. It seems to have been an Hungarian adaptation through old Serbian of the Italian *corsaro*, free-booter, which in turn derived from a Byzantine Greek word.

The earliest dragoons took their name from the 'dragon'. This was a short musket or carbine which suggested a fire-spouting dragon. It was carried in the middle of the sixteenth century by Marshal de Brissac's mounted foot, who seem to have been the first to be called dragoons.

shock-action, learnt from Gustavus Adolphus, often gave cavalry the decisive rôle in the seventeenth century. For example, Marshal Luxembourg at Leuze, in 1691, with only twenty-eight squadrons, overthrew seventy-five of the enemy's. In this battle the only British troops present were the Life Guards who comported themselves with distinction. For the rest of the war, which lasted from 1690 to 1697, and in which William III commanded the Grand Alliance against Louis XIV, the British cavalry played no great part. At Landen, in 1693, the King himself, near the end of the battle, tried to save his beaten infantry by throwing in six regiments of cavalry. These, the Life Guards, 1st, 3rd, 4th, 6th Dragoon Guards and Galway's Horse, charged the enemy many times with great intrepidity, but they could not stop what became a total rout.

For William's campaigns Parliament, often under protest, voted large armies. In these the only cavalry regiment which survived to the present time was Conyngham's Irish Dragoons, raised for the 1693 campaign, and later known as the 8th Hussars. In the following year the 7th Dragoons which had been raised in Scotland in 1689–90 took its place on the English Establishment. This regiment eventually became the 7th Hussars.

*   *   *

In the War of the Spanish Succession (1701–13) from a quarter to a third of the Allied and French armies were horse soldiers. The French believed that cavalry was the decisive arm, but they failed to make it so. Louis XIV's massed squadrons were taught to rely heavily on the horse-pistol volley fired at the halt. The sword was only to be used in the *mêlée*. Marlborough, on the other hand, eschewed the use of fire-arms by his cavalry, except in individual emergency, allowing each man no more than three pistol-rounds for a whole campaign. Yet his and Prince Eugene's great victories were won less by their cavalry than by the judicious co-operation of all arms, and by ensuring, particularly in the case of cavalry, that reserves were always to hand. The famous charge of eighty allied squadrons at Blenheim (1704) was made at no more than a fast trot, and not before the French were already broken. When sixteen British squadrons, Marlborough himself at their head, led the charge at Elixem in 1705, they rode forward at a trot, only a few of them, it is said, breaking into a gallop. At both Blenheim and Ramillies (1706), the Duke so manoeuvred his squadrons that, by the time they charged, their numbers were overwhelmingly superior to those of the enemy in their immediate front. The British horse, which formed but a small part of the 25,000 Allied cavalry at Ramillies, and had been scarcely engaged in the battle itself, conducted a classic pursuit which lasted till the early hours of the morning.

At Malplaquet, three years later, Marlborough, using much the same tactics as at Blenheim, overthrew Marshal Villars' cavalry with more than 30,000 Allied horsemen. In order to do so, and thereby complete a largely infantry victory, these massed squadrons, the Scots Greys prominent in the first line, had to pass through the French entrenchments as soon as the infantry had seized them, and then deploy in the plain beyond. There followed a long and bloody see-saw, perhaps the largest tussle of cavalry against cavalry in the eighteenth century. At length the magnificent horsemen of France gave way and the unexampled carnage of Malplaquet was over.

At no time in the course of the war did the British cavalry exceed 13,000 of which 6,000 were dragoons. Both under Marlborough and in Spain,* it proved itself efficient.

*   *   *

While, year after year, the great armies of the Grand Alliance were pitting themselves against the power of France, Charles XII of Sweden, great-great-nephew of Gustavus Adolphus, in his battles against Peter the Great of Russia, was exerting an important influence on the development of cavalry. The almost lunatic energy and astonishing impetuosity of the 'Alexander of the North', as he was aptly called, carried the principle of shock-action to new extremes. Charles XII placed a total prohibition upon the use of any form of protective armour, and absolutely forbade his horsemen the use of fire-arms. To him speed was everything, not only in the actual charge, but also in manoeuvring. He is said to have ridden two horses to death while putting a single regiment through its paces at a review. On another occasion he followed a Saxon army of 10,000 men for nine consecutive days without unsaddling, and when he overtook it charged with only two regiments of horse, completely routing infantry and cavalry, and capturing all the guns. He was finally beaten at Poltava in 1709 by Peter the Great who showed superior

* In 1710, General Stanhope, with only twenty-two squadrons, which included the Royals, charged and routed forty-two Spanish squadrons in a brilliant action in Almenara in Spain.

skill in a prudent and skilful expansion of the idea of mutual support between all three arms.

Marshal Saxe, who had fought under Marlborough, laid down, in his famous *Reveries*, principles for the organisation, tactics and armament of cavalry which, combined with the example of Charles XII, had their influence on both Frederick the Great and Napoleon. He was not against light armour, nor did he entirely eschew fire-arms, but above all, he taught the necessity for cavalry when charging and when pursuing to keep together.

*   *   *

It was Frederick the Great who, in an age of 'learned warfare in which ingenuity in manoeuvre was more prized than impetuosity in combat',[1] created the most efficient, vigorous and mobile cavalry of modern times. Fierce discipline, constant manoeuvring in large masses, and, above all, unremitting attention to the training of the individual soldier were the secrets of his success. Not until they had learned to ride 'as if they were centaurs, horse and man one entity; capable of plunging home, at full gallop, in coherent masses upon an enemy',[2] were the Prussian horsemen sent into action.

The chief disadvantage of large masses of horsemen, well closed together, and forbidden the use of carbines and pistols, was their vulnerability to artillery and infantry fire. To overcome this, Frederick created batteries of lightly equipped horse-drawn guns, their crews mounted like troopers. By reason of their speed, these were able to follow the movements of the cavalry, keep the enemy's guns and infantry at a distance, and help to pave the way for the charge. It was this innovation, more perhaps than any other in the age of gunpowder, which made it possible for cavalry to survive in the face of increasingly effective fire power. Before long batteries of horse artillery, or galloper guns as they were first called, were attached to cavalry formations in all the armies of Europe. In Britain the Royal Horse Artillery was founded in 1793. It quickly became the most efficient artillery in the army.

The Prussian cavalry, under Seydlitz and Ziethen, and especially Ziethen's incomparable 'Death's Head' Hussars, soon became the model for the world. Though practically invincible in battle, when it came to the minor functions of the mounted service, the Prussian cavalrymen often found themselves outwitted by the Hungarian hussars in the service of Austria. In outpost and reconnoitring work, and raids in the enemy's rear, these irregular regiments constantly disrupted the Prussian foraging operations, collection of intelligence and lines of communication. In the art of screening the movements of an army, they set an example sometimes emulated but seldom excelled.

*   *   *

For the best part of thirty years from the end of the War of the Spanish Succession, the British army engaged in no important active service. At the prospect of the Jacobite rising in Scotland in 1715, twenty-one regiments had been raised or resurrected. Of these, six cavalry regiments survived to become in due course the 9th Lancers, the 10th and 11th Hussars, the 12th Lancers and the 13th and 14th Hussars.

In 1742, 16,000 men, under Lord Stair, crossed to Flanders. These formed part of an Allied army assembled against the French in the War of the Austrian Succession. In the following year, with a misty notion of preventing a junction of the Bavarian and French armies, but chiefly because George II wished to secure his Electorate of Hanover, the Allies marched to the valley of the Main. About to be caught in a trap set by de Noailles, their plight was serious, when 28,000 Frenchmen made an unnecessary attack instead of patiently closing the trap. In the battle of Dettingen which followed, elements of ten British and a number of Hanoverian cavalry regiments took part in the victory. The 3rd Dragoons, only two squadrons strong, after suffering lengthy exposure to artillery fire, charged nine squadrons of the flower of the French cavalry, not once, but three times. Three-quarters of their men and horses and all but two of their officers were killed or wounded. Trooper Thomas Brown of the regiment performed one of the bravest acts of personal valour in the annals of the British horse. While trying to recover a regimental standard from the ground he lost two fingers from a French sabre cut. His horse at once bolted, carrying him into the enemy's lines. There he rode straight at, and killed, the Frenchman who was carrying off the standard. Securing it between his leg and saddle, he fought his way back to his own lines with seven wounds in face and body and three bullet holes through his hat, but with the precious standard safe. Immediately after the four-hour battle, the last in which a King of England took command of his army in person, Lord Stair, and it is said, apocryphally, Dragoon Brown, were created knights banneret in the field, an archaic revival the like of which has never since been seen.

Two years later, the young Duke of Cumberland, commanding the British, fought Marshal Saxe at the indecisive battle of Fontenoy, which was chiefly remarkable for the inability of the French Household Cavalry to overcome the deadly fire of the British infantry.

In Britain, meanwhile, the Young Pretender had landed in the Western Isles. With the support of the Highlanders he had begun his southward march. In Edinburgh, the only regular troops opposed to him were the raw, untrained men of the 13th and 14th Dragoons. Pistol shots from a few mounted rebels sufficed to send both regiments in panic retreat all the way to Preston. There the terror was soon renewed when a dragoon, falling into a disused pit, screamed for help. Thinking the Highlanders were upon them, his frightened comrades galloped on to Dunbar. This disgraceful flight, which came to be known as the 'Canter of Coltbrigg', may well have been a chief cause of the subsequent successes of Prince Charles Edward. It certainly led to the total defeat of General Cope in the ten minute slaughter at Prestonpans five days later where the two regiments of dragoons again gave way.

To meet the threat of the 'Forty-five', Cumberland was recalled from Flanders, thus effectively bringing that campaign to an end. Before he took command and restored the morale of the Royal troops, the 13th and 14th Dragoons had once again turned tail: at Falkirk Muir in mid-January 1746. From the large force with which just a year after the Pretender's first landing Cumberland finally smashed the rebellion at Culloden Moor, the 13th and 14th Dragoons were excluded.

In 1747, Cumberland returned to Europe to command the Allies in the final stages of the peculiarly futile war of the Austrian Succession. In the indecisive battle of Lauffeld on 2 July, John Ligonier, later, after Cumberland's defeat at Hastenbeck in 1757, to succeed him as Commander-in-Chief, led a brigade of cavalry which included the Greys and Inniskillings in a gallant charge against superior cavalry and infantry. The Greys lost 160 and the Inniskillings 120 men.

*   *   *

On the conclusion of the short-lived, uneasy peace which followed the Treaty of Aix-la-Chapelle in 1748, the army establishment was, as usual, promptly reduced. Seventeen regiments of cavalry and fifty-two of infantry were all that were left.

The struggle with France was soon resumed, but little that redounded to British credit occurred till the elder Pitt had grasped the reins. In 1756, under the fear of invasion from France, new infantry regiments were speedily raised, but instead of creating fresh cavalry ones, a light troop, wearing jockeys' caps and boots, was added to eleven of the existing dragoon regiments. The men and horses thus raised were trained and equipped to perform the sort of duties which were later carried out by every regiment, but which till then, had been the preserve of irregular horse, modelled upon the Hungarian hussars. This was an important step towards the removal of the concept of dragoons as mere mounted infantry.

Two years later, nine of these light troops were employed in two of Pitt's abortive expeditions against the coast of France, the first at St Malo and the second at Cherbourg. These were minute side-shows in the world-wide strategy to which the new Prime Minister now committed the country's armed forces.

In the Canadian, Indian and African theatres of war, cavalry played an insignificant part. Only in the defence of Hanover against French invasion were considerable mounted forces employed. In alliance with Frederick the Great, Pitt now placed the Hanoverian army under one of the Prussian King's finest generals, Prince Ferdinand of Brunswick. In June 1758, he added 6,000 British troops to Prince Ferdinand's force, including six cavalry regiments. These were the Blues, 1st and 3rd Dragoon Guards, Greys, Inniskillings and 10th Dragoons.

At Minden, on 1 August 1759, the British and Hanoverian infantry covered itself with immortal fame. A few squadrons of Prussian dragoons lent by Frederick the Great also behaved with great spirit. The British squadrons, however, remained inactive. In all the history of the British army no behaviour of a subordinate general has ever equalled that of their commander Lord George Sackville. As soon as Ferdinand saw that the infantry had broken the French cavalry, he sent for Sackville's squadrons on the right wing to make good the rout. Sackville disputed the order, moved forward a short distance and halted. Nor would he advance a step further, though three more aides-de-camp brought him peremptory orders to do so. Ferdinand in despair at last sent a fifth messenger to bring up Sackville's second line, commanded by the Marquess of Granby. Granby was about to obey when Sackville rode up and forbade him to do so.

Sackville was eventually court-martialled and declared unfit ever to serve again in any military capacity. What prompted this intelligent but inordinately conceited gentleman, who later became Minister-at-War, to act in such an extraordinary manner, it is impossible to say. Temporary cowardice and jealousy of Ferdinand have been advanced as reasons. Whatever the truth may be, he deprived the flower of the British cavalry of their share in a famous victory for British arms, and lost 'one of the greatest opportunities for cavalry in the whole of military history.'[3]

*   *   *

In the same year as Minden seven new cavalry regiments were raised. Of these, three survived. Elliott's Light Dragoons, which, retaining the original number of its precedence, became in due course the 15th Hussars, was the first to be raised for forty-four years. It was also the first to consist entirely of light troops, such as had been added to certain dragoon regiments three years before. There followed two further light regiments: Colonel John Burgoyne's, now the 16th Lancers, and Colonel John Hale's. This last, which eventually evolved into the 17th Lancers, was raised, it is said, at the sole expense of the officers, in the appropriate period of seventeen days. These new light regiments were known unofficially as 'hussars' because it was the original intention to employ them as irregulars. The troopers were trained to fire at the gallop. Their saddlery was specially light and their horses were nags or hunters. On their heads they wore helmets of lacquered copper, or leather, and beside their swords they carried a carbine and a pistol.

Early in 1760, the 15th Light Dragoons, together with six other cavalry regiments, were sent out to Germany as part of what was known as 'The Glorious Reinforcement'. Three days after their arrival, the 15th went into battle for the first time. In the action of Emsdorf on 16 July, the new regiment astonished the veterans by charging three separate times against formed French infantry, completely routing them. They lost 125 men and 168 horses, and had to be sent back to Hanover to reorganise, but the victory was complete.

This brilliant affair restored the cavalry's reputation, confirmed the value of light dragoons, and established the precedent, followed in so many subsequent engagements by Britain's light horse, of charging through and through, without a moment's hesitation.

Six days earlier, at Korbach, a squadron each of the 1st and 3rd

Dragoon Guards had saved the rearguard from annihilation by a desperate charge. Of ninety men who took part with the 1st, only twenty-four survived.

Yet these were but minor actions set beside the battle of Warburg on 31 July. Here, after a two hour trot in very hot weather, Granby, who had succeeded the lamentable Sackville, charged de Muy's cavalry with twenty-two British squadrons, supported by artillery. Granby, riding well out in front of the Blues, his own regiment, kept his two lines well in hand. As they passed from the trot to the gallop, his hat flew from his head, exposing to view a pate devoid of hair shining prominently in the sun, thus providing a model for generations of inn-sign painters, and giving birth to the phrase 'going for it bald-headed'. All but three of the French squadrons wavered and broke. By an exceedingly well-controlled movement, Granby immediately wheeled round upon the French infantry. This gave the three French squadrons which had held firm the chance to smash into the flank of the King's Dragoon Guards on the right of the first line. This regiment was saved in the nick of time by the Blues, and the three French squadrons were destroyed. The French infantry then broke and fled. Granby pursued with ten squadrons and the victory was complete.

At Kloster Kampen in October the British cavalry, unlike much of the rest of the British contingent, yet again behaved with valour and discipline. In spite of overwhelming numbers, the French failed to turn the retreat of the British infantry into a rout. This was largely due to a spirited charge by the 15th Light Dragoons, who emulated their dashing conduct at Emsdorf, and without question saved the Erbprinz of Brunswick's troops from disaster.

Two years later, after Spain had entered the war, the 16th Light Dragoons distinguished itself in a small affair at Valencia de Alcantara, destroying a Spanish infantry regiment after a forty-five-mile forced march. This was the regiment's first action. It is important, chiefly, since it brought into prominence John Burgoyne. In command of a cavalry regiment he was excellent. As a general he was a failure. This was proved fifteen years later when his career ended at Saratoga.

In the American War of Independence (1775–83) which finished with the Treaty of Versailles, the 16th and 17th were the only two British cavalry regiments which took part. Neither was given much opportunity to distinguish itself. Locally raised irregular horsemen, however, filled an useful rôle.

With the exception of the 19th Light Dragoons, which was raised specifically for service in India (see p. 63), the twenty-five regiments of cavalry on the establishment at the peace of 1763 remained at home till the opening of the Revolutionary War with France brought some of them again into the field thirty years later.

(iii)

British cavalry in the Revolutionary and Napoleonic Wars, 1793–1814

When, in 1793, a reluctant Britain was drawn into the conflict against Revolutionary France, the quality and quantity of her armed forces were pitiable. After ten years of peace, the army at home had dwindled to 17,000 men. Nevertheless, by the end of 1794 hasty recruiting and the hiring of German mercenaries had brought the establishment up to 265,000,* a figure which included 90,000 home defence troops.

The proportion of British units in the Allied armies which assembled in the Low Countries in 1793 was not large. In the following year the British cavalry element consisted of twenty-eight squadrons drawn from fourteen regiments, formed into three heavy brigades and one light. Some of these distinguished themselves in three brilliant little engagements at the end of April and beginning of May.

At Villers-en-Cauchies two squadrons of the 15th Light Dragoons and two of Austrian Hussars, all under the Hungarian Colonel Szentkereszty, found themselves confronting 3,000 of the French Revolutionary army in position. Being too far committed to retire, the commander of the Allied cavalry, General Otto, ordered Szen-

---

* Thirteen new regiments of Light Dragoons, numbered 21st to 33rd, were raised in 1794 and 1795. The 30th, 31st, 32nd and 33rd were disbanded the following year. The 22nd, 23rd, 24th and 28th were disbanded in 1802–3, whereupon the 25th, 26th, 27th and 29th, whose survival was chiefly due to their being overseas, were renumbered the 22nd, 23rd, 24th and 25th respectively (see p. 65). Of these the 23rd survived till 1817, the 24th and 25th till 1819, and the 22nd till 1820, in which year the 21st was also disbanded.

tkereszty to attack. The order was received with cheers. Officers and men of both regiments shook hands with each other, and crossed swords, swearing to charge home in mutual support. As they plunged forward, at the gallop, the *chasseurs à cheval* in their front wheeled outwards, unmasking a battery of guns. Behind these stood a mass of six infantry battalions, and beyond them again, more cavalry. All these broke before the onslaught. The 15th, their small numbers (7 officers and 180 men) precluding the taking of prisoners, inflicted terrible casualties on the infantry.

After dispersing a long line of fifty guns and ammunition wagons, the two British squadrons chased the enemy cavalry for four miles. They were halted at last by fire from the fortress of Bouchain. On their return, with hostile forces closing in on them (many of which mistook them for friends on account of their blue uniforms), they found re-formed bodies of infantry with guns, blocking their re-entry into Villers-en-Cauchies. In their rear they saw fresh troops from the fortress bearing down on them. Speedily 'changing front to the rear', they first checked their pursuers, and then, again reversing their front, galloped through the rest to their starting point. Here, at last, they were met and protected by Mansel's heavy brigade. These troops, though intended from the start as supports, had unaccountably lost their way. Had they arrived in time, the French force might well have been annihilated, and fifty guns captured. As it was, the 3rd Dragoon Guards, one of Mansel's regiments, managed to lose thirty-eight men to no good purpose.

The 15th lost thirty-one men and thirty-seven horses; the Austrians ten men and eleven horses. The French, for the most part raw levies, left 1,200 men on the field and lost three guns. This astonishing action serves to show that well mounted, highly trained light horsemen, led by resolute and skilful officers, could achieve miracles against overwhelming odds.

Two days later there followed what Fortescue has called, with a certain degree of exaggeration, 'the greatest day in the annals of the British horse'.[1] Under cover of fog, a French force of some 30,000 men surprised the Duke of York's army near Beaumont. The Duke, noticing that the enemy's left flank had been 'left in the air', sent off twelve British and six Austrian squadrons to turn it. By skilful use of the natural folds in the ground, this large force worked its way round, over a distance of nearly three miles, entirely undetected by the enemy. There followed a spectacular series of charges at the gallop, which rolled up the entire French corps – infantry, cavalry and artillery. Shock action, following a carefully planned surprise, has seldom had greater success. Mansel, who was killed at the head of his brigade, wiped out the disgrace of forty-eight hours before, and re-established the reputation of the heavy cavalry. In half an hour something like 5,000 Frenchmen were lost, and over 30 guns captured. The British and Austrian cavalry lost between them 15 officers and 384 men. Of the British, the Blues and the 3rd Dragoon Guards suffered the heaviest.

Exactly a fortnight later, at Willems, the Duke of York tried a turning movement similar to that which had succeeded so brilliantly at Beaumont. Led by General Harcourt, sixteen British and two Austrian squadrons worked their way round to the enemy's exposed right flank. This time the ground was sodden, and though level, much cut up by cultivation trenches. In consequence, the speed of the nine successive regiments which charged up to the French bayonets was not great. Further, for the first time since the revolution, the French infantry formed themselves into 'squares'. They held fast. The cavalry fell back frustrated. It was necessary to bring up artillery to assist them, and to launch a frontal attack with infantry, before the combination of all arms proved too much for the French. As they began to waver an officer of the Greys, galloping out in front of his brigade, rode straight at the largest of the three squares and overthrew nine men, thereby making a gap for his troopers to enter. Now, after some hours of stubborn resistance, the squares were finally broken.

Elsewhere, the Carabiniers (6th Dragoon Guards), outnumbered four to one, charged and overthrew their French namesakes. By this action they avenged the capture of one of their standards by the very same regiment thirty years before. The Carabiniers' casualties were the highest of all the regiments engaged. The total British losses did not exceed forty-two killed and missing, and eighty-two wounded. More than 400 French prisoners and 14 guns were taken, and perhaps as many as 1,000 men cut down. Not until Salamanca, eighteen years later, were the British cavalry again to break a French infantry square.

*　　*　　*

In his succession of European victories, Napoleon's strategic use of cavalry was masterly. Massive columns, thrust well ahead of the main army, kept him constantly and minutely informed of the enemy's dispositions and intentions. At the same time they served to screen his own movements, and to manoeuvre his victims into positions of his own choosing. When the battle was about to be joined, he usually withdrew his mounted troops to the rear and flanks of the army. He would then, like Marlborough, release them for shock action only when the enemy, softened up by artillery, was ripe for disruption.

It was the hardy, swift, ubiquitous Russian cossacks who first successfully challenged the Napoleonic cavalry. By preventing effective reconnaissance they wrested from the Emperor that freedom of movement which had been the basis of his achievements. In the campaigns of Leipzig and France in 1813 and 1814 the Russian cossacks contributed more to the destruction of the Grand Army than did the numerous regular regiments of the other Allies.

*　　*　　*

Between the disastrous end of the Netherlands campaign of 1795 and the opening of the Peninsular War in 1808 the British cavalry had little opportunity for distinguishing itself. Unlike the infantry, most of its regiments remained on the Home establishment. Those few which went abroad served in many different parts of the world. Detachments from ten light regiments, for instance, were despatched from time to time to the graveyard of the West Indies, a terrain particularly unsuited to mounted operations, while to Corsica, which is even more so, were sent the 12th Light Dragoons. The 7th, 11th, 15th and 18th Light Dragoons saw service in the virtually fruitless Helder campaign of 1799, in which Lord Paget (better known as Earl of Uxbridge and Marquess of Anglesey) first proved himself as a leader of horse. Five light regiments assisted in Abercromby's Egyptian campaign two years later, but for lack of horses achieved very little. Parts of one heavy and four light regiments took part in Whitelocke's mad-cap South American adventure of 1807. But in none of these side-shows was the cavalry very profitably employed.

*　　*　　*

Among the regular troops in Ireland when the French-aided rebellion of 1798 broke out were the 4th Royal Irish Dragoon Guards, which had been stationed in Ireland for no less than 100 years, with only two (1793–5) in England. Also in Ireland were the 5th Royal Irish Dragoons. This regiment, with distinguished service under

Marlborough behind it, had remained inactive on the Irish establishment for eighty-three unbroken years. For most of that time, like the 4th Dragoon Guards, it had been dispersed in troops and fractions of troops in widely separated towns and villages, its locally recruited troopers subject to very slight supervision by their officers. In such circumstances it is no surprise to find that in 1798 a number of recruits were discovered in a conspiracy with the rebels. The sad result was the disbandment of the regiment in the following year. It was not reinstated in the Army List till 1858. A part of another regiment, the Carabiniers (6th Dragoon Guards), with less excuse, for it had been in the country only two years, fled in panic when faced by a small French force landed in Ireland. This shameful affair came to be known as 'the Race of Castlebar'.

*　　*　　*

When, in 1808, Napoleon, having first occupied Portugal, interfered in the affairs of Spain, he turned an ally into an enemy. In answer to Spanish appeals for help, an army under Sir Arthur Wellesley landed in Portugal. It defeated General Junot in two infantry battles, Roliça and Vimeiro. Wellesley was then superceded by two senior generals of marked inferiority. He and they contracted the Convention of Cintra, by which the French were evacuated intact. This discreditable arrangement was execrated in England, and Sir John Moore was ordered to succour the Spaniards. He was given command of the largest army to be sent abroad since the days of Marlborough.

With 20,000 men he was to enter Spain from Portugal and to join forces at Valladolid, with Sir David Baird who was to land with 19,000 at Corunna. With Baird was Lord Paget in command of two cavalry brigades, consisting of the 7th, 10th, 15th and 18th Light Dragoons, and the 3rd Hussars, King's German Legion, numbering less than 2,500 sabres in all.

While Moore and Baird were marching to their rendezvous Napoleon was reinforcing his army. He speedily defeated two of the three Spanish armies, on whose co-operation the whole British effort depended, and occupied Valladolid. Moore, vastly outnumbered, was constrained to retreat.

Napoleon, however, instead of turning westward to fight the British, proceeded to march on Madrid. When Moore learned that the people of the capital had risen to defend it he felt bound to assist them. He therefore interrupted the retreat. Before continuing it he would try, as a diversion on behalf of Madrid, to defeat Soult's army of 20,000 which was all that had been left facing him in the north-west. Moore's and Baird's armies met at Mayorga on 20 December. So successful were the cavalry in masking the junction that Soult was quite unaware that it had taken place.

Early next morning there followed what Oman has described as 'perhaps the most brilliant exploit of the British cavalry during the whole six years of the [Peninsular] war'.[2] With the 10th and 15th Hussars and four horse artillery guns, Lord Paget set off to surprise 700 French cavalry in the town of Sahágun. The 10th were to form one arm of a pincer movement, the 15th the other. The 10th failed to arrive in time. Consequently the 15th alone attacked and utterly overthrew two French regiments. The charge, which was made at the gallop, uphill, over a ditch and across the roughest ground, was received at the halt. It was preceded by three cheers from the men and shouts of 'Emsdorf and Victory', showing that the regiment had not forgotten its first great triumph nearly fifty years before (see p. 42). A mere 200 Frenchmen escaped death or capture. The bridge was wrecked, and its baggage, money and plate taken. Only two men of the 15th were killed and twenty-three wounded.

Two days later, before his main attack against Soult could be launched, Moore learned that his great object had been achieved. Napoleon with 200,000 men was marching from Madrid to attack him. The Spaniards had been given a vital breathing space. On Christmas Eve, therefore, Moore resumed his epic retreat to Corunna.

Everything now depended on whether the French could be kept in ignorance of the withdrawal. For two days, the British cavalry so harassed Soult's outposts that he was convinced that a major assault was about to be launched against him. Napoleon therefore planned to destroy the British army by a three-pronged encircling movement. But when he moved in for the kill he found the trap empty. By extraordinary exertions, the cavalry had allowed the infantry to steal three vital marches on the enemy.

It now fell to Paget's five regiments, contending against thirteen of the French, to exert every nerve to keep the advance guard at bay for as long as possible. For four wearing days every troop was constantly in action from dawn to dusk. Some measure of their success can be gauged by the fact that Napoleon himself set down the British cavalry at double its actual strength.

At Benavente, on 29 December, the bridge over the Esla was

blown up just as the enemy approached it. It took General Lefebvre-Desnouettes, who commanded the élite of Napoleon's
cavalry, some time to find a ford. When at last he did so he was kept
in check by the 3rd Hussars, King's German Legion. Paget, meanwhile, brought up the 10th Hussars. These he concealed from view
until the French were in the act of charging down upon the Germans.
The 10th then crashed into the French flank. As they did so, the
French horsemen, utterly surprised, broke and made a dash for the
river. Some plunged into it, others were taken prisoner, including
Lefebvre-Desnouettes. The French did not again attempt a crossing
that day. Moore's infantry had gained further important hours.

For the rest of the retreat, through mountainous country, the
cavalry handed over the rearguard to the infantry. When Corunna
was eventually reached, there was no room on the transports for the
horses. Large numbers had to be destroyed. Thus ended for the
cavalry a campaign in which they had conducted screening and rearguard actions which soon became accepted models in the armies of
Europe.

*   *   *

The ascendancy which the British cavalry had established over the
French in the Corunna campaign, was largely maintained through
the five remaining years of the Peninsular War. Wellington made
skilful use of the mounted arm for reconnaissance and deception,
and for covering withdrawals, but tended to distrust the 'cavalry
spirit' as manifested by gallant but improvident charges in battle.

At Talavera, which ended the first of the campaigns following his
return to Portugal in April 1809, there took place one of those madly
heroic exploits which justified his fears. Towards the end of the
battle, the 23rd Light Dragoons, which had recently arrived from
India, advanced at a trot (together with the 1st German Hussars)
over ground traversed by a hidden water-course. They made the
mistake, while still some distance from the enemy, of breaking into
a canter. Consequently, when they came unexpectedly upon the
obstacle, they were thrown into great confusion and a number of
limbs and necks were broken. Undismayed but in considerable disorder, one part of the 23rd hurled itself against an infantry square,
while the other, outnumbered five to one, assailed a brigade of
chasseurs. Though these charges cut deeply into the enemy's flank,
they were certainly not worth the cost. The regiment lost 207 men
and 224 horses, nearly half its strength.

Earlier, at the battle of Oporto on 12 May 1809, Charles Stewart, who had been one of Paget's two brigadiers in 1808, and was now Wellesley's Adjutant-General, led one squadron of the 14th Light Dragoons in a charge against superior French infantry. About 300 prisoners were taken, but the losses of the 14th were heavy. Fortescue dubs this attack 'foolhardy',[3] yet Wellesley, in his General Order, specially commended the bravery of the regiment. It was perhaps regrettable, but not very unusual in those days, that a senior staff officer should put himself at the head of two squadrons.

In the late summer of 1810, Wellesley (who had become Lord Wellington after Talavera) confronted by Masséna's much superior army, withdrew to the lines of Torres Vedras. The retirement was covered by Anson's cavalry brigade with energy and skill.

When it came to following up Masséna's retreat from Portugal next year, many mistakes were made. The sheer incompetence of some of the senior cavalry officers was quite alarming. General Slade (who, three years previously, had been responsible for the 10th Hussars failing to reach Sahágun in time) and General Erskine, exasperated their brigades by dilatory and ill-judged movements whenever they were away from Stapleton-Cotton. Stapleton-Cotton, who commanded all the cavalry under Wellington, was certainly not brilliant, but he was far from incapable.

The fiasco at Campo Maior, north of Badajoz, on 25 March 1811, however, resulted from the incompetence of that astonishing man, Marshal Beresford, who had so skilfully built up the Portuguese army to fight beside the British. By interfering, on incomplete information, with a plan put into operation by General Long, commanding one light and one heavy brigade, he prevented the annihilation of 2,400 Frenchmen and 16 heavy guns. Five troops (about 200 men) of the 13th Light Dragoons, by a series of truly brilliant charges, against three times their number of French cavalry, had captured all the French guns, rallied admirably, and were pursuing, in excellent order, when Beresford, thinking them destroyed, withheld the heavy brigade on which Long was depending. Left on their own, the 13th first chased the enemy cavalry for nearly ten miles, then returned, still in good order, having suffered no very great losses. But, for lack of support, they had to relinquish all their prisoners, guns and other trophies, just at the moment when the whole French force was on the point of surrender. Nevertheless, the French casualties amounted to something like 500.

These are the bald outlines of the combat. It generated much bitter controversy for years to come. Wellington, on receiving Beresford's most untruthful report, which accused the 13th of getting out of hand, severely censured the regiment. He threatened to take away their horses and return them to Lisbon. When, later, he learned the truth, he made what unofficial amends his pride allowed him.

Three weeks later the 13th chased the remnants of the cavalry they had beaten at Campo Maior for nine miles, cut down numbers of them and took some 150 prisoners. This time, though the pursuit was just as headlong as on 15 March, Beresford commended them.

* * *

Throughout the northern campaign of 1811, the numbers of Masséna's cavalry far exceeded those of the British. In the general action of Fuentes de Onõro in early May, this discrepancy was strongly marked. At the critical moment of the battle, Wellington was forced to throw back his right wing. This entailed withdrawing two infantry divisions in face of the full weight of Masséna's attack, including 3,500 cavalry. The British horse, consisting of the Royals, the 14th and 16th Light Dragoons and the 1st German Hussars, numbered hardly more than 1,000. Yet, on horses already wearied by earlier exertions, they covered this excessively delicate movement, charging in small bodies of one, two and sometimes three squadrons at a time, with immense gallantry and skill. 'We were but scattered drops amid their host' wrote a subaltern of the 14th.[4] At one moment, when two horse artillery guns had lingered too long in the front, they were extricated from an enveloping swarm of cavalry by a squadron of the 14th and another of the Royals, who charged back to their rescue. It is true to say, with Fortescue, that the cavalry were 'the real heroes of Fuentes de Onõro'.[5] But there was one unfortunate blot. Holding a conviction that cavalry, unaided, could take a battery of artillery by a frontal, rather than a flank charge, Captain Knipe, 14th Light Dragoons, put it to the test. He was killed and his squadron decimated.

On 25 September in an engagement very similar in type to Fuentes de Onõro, but smaller in scale, 500 men of General Victor Alten's cavalry brigade took on five times their number at El Bodon. In successfully covering the infantry's retirement, as many as thirty or forty separate charges were made, always against superior numbers.

It was in this combat that the British cavalry first encountered the Polish 'lancers of the Vistula'.

It was probably Wellington's scathing rebuke to the 13th Light Dragoons after Campo Maior which prevented the action at Bienvenida (after his capture of Badajoz in April 1812), from being the model cavalry action it should have been. Engaged were nine regiments under Stapleton-Cotton. In the course of the engagement, the 5th Dragoon Guards, after a four-mile march, and greatly outnumbered, made two charges against the French cavalry. In the second they took the enemy in the flank, while the 16th Light Dragoons, leaping a wall in line, crashed at the gallop into the French front. Cotton then saw fit, so as to restore his formation, but without, it seems, sufficient reason, to halt the pursuit of the fleeing enemy. Consequently the French rallied, and had to be attacked again, this time by the 12th Light Dragoons in front and two squadrons of the 16th in the flank. The British lost 58 men to the French 200. This was the first considerable engagement in which General John Le Marchant, commanding a brigade, took part. He had recently arrived from England, and was soon to be the hero of Salamanca.

Before that great victory took place there occurred an incident which showed how much the sense of superiority which the British cavalry usually felt in the Peninsular War depended upon the quality of its leaders. At Maguilla, on 11 June, Slade, whose extensive series of past failures ought long ago to have excluded him from further command, with the 3rd Dragoon Guards and two squadrons of the Royals, pursued a single regiment of French dragoons for a dozen miles. Letting slip several favourable chances of closing, he eventually charged and overthrew them. He then continued the pursuit in the wildest manner, until another French regiment, about to come to the assistance of its harassed comrades, was seen on the right. A sudden panic seized the Royals and the 3rd Dragoon Guards. They turned and fled. 'For a few moments the extraordinary sight presented itself of two forces running away from each other.'[6] The French halted, turned and re-formed. The third squadron of the Royals, which had been kept in reserve, now charged and momentarily checked them, but the flight of the rest, in spite of their officers, continued for eight miles. Their casualties from this shameful business were 160 men and 250 horses. Wellington was furious. 'The Royals and the 3rd D.G.', he wrote, 'were the best regiments in the cavalry in the country, and it annoys me particularly that the misfortune has happened to them.'[7]

An officer of the Royals put it down to 'three months' previous bad education received from Slade'.[8]

*   *   *

Le Marchant, who led the immortal charge of the heavy brigade at Salamanca on 22 July 1812, was Slade's exact opposite. Unlike the great majority of British cavalry officers before and since, he was a serious student of his profession. When only a junior officer he had tried to put right what Dr Johnson as early as 1773 commented upon as the absurdity 'that our soldiers should have swords and not be taught to use them'.[9] In the Flanders campaign of 1793–4 Le Marchant noticed that the troopers knew so little about how to wield their weapon that instead of slashing the enemy, they often inflicted wounds on their own horses' heads and even on themselves. He therefore, after much research, especially as to the practice in the Austrian army, developed a system of defence and attack, which he taught to his regiment and submitted to the Commander-in-Chief, the Duke of York. The Duke, impressed, had it printed,[10] and in 1797 ordered every cavalry officer to buy a copy. At the same time Le Marchant designed a more efficient type of sword, with which every regiment was soon equipped. Later he became first Lieutenant-Governor of the Royal Military College, which had evolved from an idea that had occurred to him while he and Lord Paget were moulding the 7th Light Dragoons into one of the finest regiments in the army.

At the battle of Salamanca on 25 July 1812, he was in command of a brigade, consisting of the 3rd and 4th Dragoons and the 5th Dragoon Guards, between 750 and 1,000 sabres in all. Wellington, when he saw that Marmont by over-extending his left had given him his great chance, personally ordered Le Marchant, who was advancing between and behind two infantry divisions, to charge at the first favourable opportunity. He chose a moment of confusion when, though some of the French battalions were breaking, the leading British infantry brigade, confronted still by large numbers, thought itself lost. With a ghastly roar, never forgotten by the survivors of the onslaught, the 'heavies', the 4th and 5th leading and the 3rd in support, all in perfect order, emerged from the smoke, thundering past the astonished British infantry. The brigade broke into the flank of the first two battalions who vainly tried to form a square to meet it. Some were sabred, others left for the infantry to pick up.

Next, the second French line, three complete battalions, in better order than the first two, had to face the relentless sabre-work of the heavy horsemen. These, too, after firing a volley which emptied numerous saddles, were rent asunder, their component parts scattered. Almost without altering pace, hastily dressing their line and closing the gaps, the three regiments, by now intermingled but still under control, were led by Le Marchant against a further three battalions. These, much blown from doubling for over a mile to get into position, only had time to form imperfect squares before firing a volley at their assailants. They fired too late, for though many of the leading dragoons fell, the impetus of their horses could not be stopped. There followed a deadly fight of sabre against bayonet which ended for the French in total flight. Even Le Marchant now had difficulty in keeping his wildly exulting squadrons under control. He himself was killed outright; only exhaustion stopped his men. Cotton, as night was falling, sent in his three light brigades to continue the pursuit and complete the victory.

When Wellington saw Le Marchant's first onslaught he shouted to Cotton, who did not join the charge till its later stages, 'By God, Cotton, I never saw anything so beautiful in my life; the day is *yours*'. It was in fact of course Le Marchant's. Only he (and perhaps Lord Paget) of all the officers in the mounted arm, seemed capable of controlling more than a few squadrons in battle. In about half an hour he had destroyed three French divisions. The losses of his brigade were 105, an amazingly low figure which proves that shock action in the age of gunpowder when properly used without the slightest hesitation, could still be not only decisive but also economical. A British private later described what that assault meant to the French receiving it: 'Hundreds of beings, frightfully disfigured, . . . black with dust, worn down with fatigue, and covered with sabre-cuts and blood, threw themselves down among us for safety.'[11]

Next day, at Garcia Hernandez, the most astonishing cavalry feat of the whole war was accomplished. Part of Bock's German brigade, which numbered less than 450 sabres, actually broke a perfectly formed square, while another scattered a large column of infantry. In all, three battalions were virtually annihilated. Bock suffered from extreme near-sightedness. When ordered to charge at Garcia Hernandez he was obliged to ask a colonel of artillery to 'be good enough to show us the enemy'.[12] Other cavalry generals who suffered from poor eyesight in the Peninsula were Charles Stewart and Sir William Erskine. The same defect applied to Scarlett who led the heavy brigade charge at Balaclava forty-two years later.

* * *

These were the last of the important cavalry contributions to the Peninsular War. At Morales de Toro on 2 June 1813, General Colquhoun Grant with the 10th and 18th Hussars inflicted over 200 casualties on the French cavalry for only 21 of his own. In the pursuit after Orthez on 27 February 1814, the 7th Hussars cut off two battalions and took numerous prisoners, but the terrain of the Pyrenees and Southern France is unsuited to cavalry operations on any scale. Nevertheless, Wellington had been reinforced by two brigades in time for the 1813 campaign. One of these consisted of two squadrons from each of the Household Cavalry regiments. The Blues, which had seen service in Flanders eighteen years earlier, settled down quite quickly, but the Life Guards, who had last left the shores of Britain sixty years before, astonished everyone at Lisbon by their helplessness. They even discarded their curry-combs and brushes, believing them unwanted in the field, and had to be provided with new ones.

The cavalry's overall efficiency greatly improved in the last two years of the war. This was largely because the more feeble of the brigadiers such as Slade and Erskine were gradually replaced by capable men like Hussey Vivian and Grant.

* * *

Ever since he had left Portugal Wellington had been starved of cavalry. Time and again he had been unable to reap the full fruits of his victories for lack of fresh cavalry to throw into the pursuit. Seldom did he possess superiority in numbers over the French. One reason was the dearth of suitable horses after many years of war. There was even an occasion when the officers and men of four regiments were sent home because their horses were needed to make up deficiencies in other regiments. But industrial unrest at home was the chief limiting factor. The distress in the manufacturing districts, of which the Luddite riots were the most serious manifestations, called for mounted troops to maintain order. In Yorkshire, Lancashire and

Cheshire alone, five regular cavalry regiments were needed for this purpose.

<hr />

(iv)

The Waterloo Campaign, 1815

At Waterloo, in June 1815, the Allied cavalry, excluding the Prussians, numbered about 12,400, of which some 7,400 were British. This was a far larger quantity than had taken part in any Peninsular battle. Its efficiency was impaired by the distribution of units over a wide area of country during the weeks preceding the battle. This was necessary for administrative reasons, especially as regards forage supply. The intention of the cavalry commander, Lord Uxbridge (the Lord Paget of Corunna fame) had been to form his brigades into divisions. But the difficulties of doing so within the very short time available proved insuperable. This failure was 'the cause of the loss of many lives on the 18th June'.[1]

It meant, too, that during the battle of Quatre Bras, fought on 16 June, the cavalry, instead of assisting the infantry, was engaged in marching towards the battlefield.

On the 17th, the cavalry successfully covered the infantry's retirement to the position of Mont St Jean. In the course of the operation, the 7th Hussars, through no fault of their own, were repulsed by the French *lanciers* at Genappe, and the 1st Life Guards, as soon as the *lanciers* had debouched from the village, retrieved the situation by a successful charge.

Between 10 and 11 a.m. on 18 June, the cavalry took up their positions for the great battle. The two heavy brigades were placed centrally in the line, between the farm of Mont St Jean and the point where the famous so-called sunken road, the crest of the Allied position, crossed the Charleroi-Brussels *chaussée*. The Household Brigade in 'brigade mass', was to the right of the *chaussée*, the Union Brigade to its left. In front of them were Alten's and Picton's infantry divisions, concealed by the slope leading up to the sunken road. In front of Picton, mistakenly placed on the forward slope, were Rijlandt's Netherlanders. In the farm of La Haye Sainte, which stuck out like a breakwater, were Baring's King's German Legion infantrymen. The light brigades were on the flanks of the position.

Napoleon opened the battle just before midday with what was intended to be a diversion against the Allied right at Hougoumont. Here there raged all day what was virtually a separate battle, in which the cavalry played only a minor part. At about this time, Uxbridge, who had earlier been given *carte blanche* by the Duke, sent orders to his brigade commanders to act discretionally without awaiting orders.

Just before 1 p.m. Napoleon's great artillery barrage opened up on the centre. More than half an hour later Ney led D'Erlon's corps, perhaps 16,000 men, supported by cavalry and preceded by skirmishers, against Wellington's left centre. The western echelons of the close-packed mass of infantry drove Baring's men from the orchard of La Haye Sainte and swept into the garden behind the farm itself. Wellington at this moment sent in a battalion of Hanoverians to assist Baring, but a regiment of *cuirassiers* cut them to bits, and prepared to charge up to the crest. To the east of the *chaussée* at much the same moment, Rijlandt's Netherlanders fled from the field before the enemy reached them. Picton was quick to fill the breach thus made. Pouring a volley into the surging waves of men, Kempt's infantry charged with the bayonet, holding them back for a brief breathing-space.

It was now, somewhere near 2 p.m., at one of the most critical moments of the battle, that the great charge of the heavy brigades took place. Uxbridge, who had been assisting at Hougoumont, arrived near the cross-roads in time to see the Hanoverians being sabred below him, and the French columns advancing against Picton. Without a second's delay, he 'galloped up to the Heavy Cavalry', as he wrote later, 'and ordered the Household Brigade to prepare to form line, passed on to Sir William Ponsonby's, and having told him to wheel into line when the other Brigade did, instantly returned to the Household Brigade, and put the whole in motion.'[2] By the time he had made these arrangements and given the order to charge, the situation had become very dangerous. Picton had fallen, and his two brigades, only about 3,000 strong, and with no reserves behind them, were facing some 10,000 of the enemy infantry. These were on the point of pouring through the gap left by Rijlandt's desertion. Indeed, the leading Frenchmen had already gained the crest when, the redcoats making intervals for them, the 'heavies' charged over the ridge.

The seven leading squadrons of the Household Brigade collided with Dubois's *cuirassiers* like 'two walls'. They had the advantages of the descending slope, of being fresh and of riding much larger horses. The French turned and fled. This was probably the sole fair test of heavy cavalry versus heavy cavalry during the battle.

The Union Brigade, at the same moment, tore into the mass of infantry in front of it, the Scots Greys, who had been detailed for supports, charging with the first line consisting of the Royals and Inniskillings. Within a few minutes, as the two brigades, soon inter-mingled, swept the demoralized enemy into the valley, some 3,000 prisoners and two Eagles were taken. D'Erlon's men at this moment resembled nothing so much as a confused and unresisting mob. They were confused because the incline behind the sunken road, and the hedges which lined it, hid the British troops, except for the guns and skirmishers on the forward slope, until the very last moment. For instance, only the head-dress of the British cavalry, sitting on their horses, could be seen from any part of the French position.

On the right, the 1st Life Guards and two squadrons of the Royals now pursued the *cuirassiers* to the cutting south of La Haye Sainte, where many of them were overtaken. But numbers of the 1st Life Guards were shot down by Bachelu's infantry from either side of the cutting. As the two brigades crossed the valley they cut to pieces two field batteries, sabred the gunners, drivers and teams, and wrecked fifteen guns so completely that they were put out of action for the rest of the day. Some accounts declare that had supports been at hand it might have been possible to bring away some of these guns.

The Blues, like the Scots Greys, had been intended as supports, and indeed had started off as such, but when passing the orchard of La Haye Sainte they had drawn up to the front line. Unlike the rest of the brigade, they were kept well in hand.

Wildly excited by their success, scattered parties of all the regi-ments (except perhaps the 1st Life Guards and the Blues) now rode up to and into the enemy's great battery, some even penetrating as far as the artillery wagons behind. But retribution for rashness was at hand. The 2nd Life Guards and the Royals soon found themselves heavily fired on by infantry, and attacked by two regiments of *cuirassiers*, while the Scots Greys, well to the east, were badly cut up by a regiment of Jacquinot's *lanciers*.

Never, perhaps, have horsemen achieved a greater success over formed infantry and cavalry than did the heavy brigades at Waterloo. A mere eighteen squadrons, about 2,000 sabres strong, had so completely smashed an infantry corps, part of its artillery and a cavalry brigade, that these were virtually out of action until late in the day, and then so reduced in numbers and enthusiasm as to have no material effect on the battle. But the 'heavies' paid a high price. Many of their officers, including the colonels of the Greys and Royals, as soon as they saw that their men had got out of control, sacrificed their lives in vain efforts to rally them. Uxbridge, too, immediately after the overthrow of the *cuirassiers*, had sounded the rally, 'but neither voice nor trumpet availed'.[3]

One of the inherent flaws in the British cavalry of this date was their tendency to break up in pursuit, after a successful charge. It was aggravated at Waterloo by two factors: the initial failure, already noticed, to group brigades into divisions, and the lack of time available for concise, detailed instructions before the charge. If the first might have been avoided, certainly the second could not have been, for as an officer of the Royals said, 'had the charge been delayed two or three minutes . . . it would probably have failed, for the leading Frenchmen had already gained the crest of the position when the attack was ordered.'[4]

The fact that no divisional commanders had been appointed was chiefly responsible for Uxbridge's great mistake in leading the attack himself. Had he remained behind to direct operations, as he confessed that he ought to have done, and been able to leave the leadership of the charge to a divisional commander, he could have conserved at least a squadron or two of the Blues and Scots Greys. More important, when he saw that the 'heavies' had gone too far, he could have brought into action the nearest brigade of light cavalry. This was Vandeleur's to the left. Although two squadrons of the 12th Light Dragoons from that brigade did move forward off their own bat, Vandeleur, in spite of the discretionary order which he had received at the start of the battle, was tardy in bringing the rest of his troops to the rescue. This was almost certainly due in part to his fear of moving without direct orders from the Duke, under whom he had served in Spain, and also because he seemed, as did other of the brigadiers, unaware that Wellington had put the cavalry entirely in Uxbridge's hands. As it was, both Vandeleur and Vivian, who followed him, as well as one of the regiments of Dutch-Belgian cavalry, were able to give some protection to the exhausted 'heavies' on their return, but not before the cream of them had been lost for ever.

A comparative calm now spread over the battlefield. This was soon followed by a cannonade of unprecedented proportions, as Napoleon brought more guns into action in preparation for his next attack. Wellington could scarcely believe his eyes, but it was nevertheless true that Marshal Ney, to whom the Emperor had entrusted most of his cavalry, was about to launch a massed cavalry attack against unbroken infantry. This was duly launched at about 4 p.m. against the Allied right wing, which occupied the 900 yards between La Haye Sainte and Hougoumont. Ney undoubtedly thought that the slight, protective rearward movement which Wellington had ordered when the artillery fire first became really heavy implied that the British infantrymen were on the point of breaking. He was further deceived by what he could see, through the dense smoke, of groups of wounded, convoys of prisoners, empty ammunition wagons, and a number of (non-British) fugitives streaming towards the forest of Soignes.

To draw attention away from his main assault, Napoleon sent ten squadrons of *lanciers* and twelve guns to threaten the right near Hougoumont. Uxbridge at once detached Sir Colquhoun Grant's brigade to deal with them. As the brigadier was about to charge with the 13th Light Dragoons and the 15th Hussars, he heard the *lanciers* cheering the attack of the *cuirassiers* on their right. He at once, with great restraint, relinquished his prey and returned to his original position, ready to assist in the counter-attacks about to be launched. Ney's cavalry, meanwhile, closely packed, and a perfect target for the British guns, came on at their traditional trot. In twelve successive waves, they beat against and around the sides of the immovable 'squares' (or, more correctly, oblongs), arranged chequerwise, into which the redcoats had been formed.

As this valiant tide of horsemen expended itself (slowly, for they were riding uphill, and the rye crops reached to their horses' girths), Uxbridge made a determined counter-attack with the 7th Hussars, 23rd Light Dragoons, 1st and 3rd Hussars of the King's German Legion, two regiments of Brunswick cavalry, and (though they proved useless) three brigades of Dutch-Belgian cavalry. The *cuirassiers* were driven clean off the plateau into the dead ground under the southern slope of the ridge. They recovered wonderfully quickly, made a fresh assault, but met with an exactly similar fate.

As these twice-repulsed squadrons, perhaps forty in number,

streamed back, they met newly formed comrades ready to renew the attempt. Behind these they re-formed, and, preceded and protected by artillery fire, the fresh led the exhausted – perhaps 12,000 horsemen in all – in a third heroic charge; but their speed was now greatly hampered by the churned-up mud and the dead and dying men and horses which were the legacy of the two earlier attempts.

Still not sated with defeat, yet another wave of French cavalry threw itself against the rock-like squares of redcoats. As Uxbridge counter-attacked again, the enemy horsemen for the fourth time rallied near the bottom of the incline and renewed the attack. As they did so, the British artillerymen, who were getting used to the drill imposed upon them, retired into the squares (rolling one wheel of each gun before them), while the British cavalry re-formed behind the infantry, ready to counter-attack. This they did as soon as the exhausted Frenchmen once more, slowly and reluctantly, fell back. Yet again they were chased by Uxbridge's cavalry to the line between La Haye Sainte and Hougoumont whence they had started. Ney repeated these incredibly gallant but uniformly unsuccessful charges again and again. Some say that as many as twelve separate assaults were made.

Eventually, seeing that the squares were quite unbreakable by cavalry alone, the enemy launched a series of attacks using cavalry and infantry in conjunction. One of these was temporarily held by a timely charge of the remnants of the Household Brigade. This failed to make a lasting impression, for the Dutch-Belgian cavalry, whose support was vital, not only refused to follow, but in running away upset a part of the 3rd German Hussars, who were also in support. These, quickly recovering themselves, charged and broke the *cuirassiers* immediately in their front, but flank attacks forced them to retire almost at once.

The state of the British cavalry at the most critical moment of the day which was now at hand was not encouraging. The Dutch-Belgians were worthless. The strength of the 'heavies' was gravely impaired. Grant's, Dörnberg's and Arentschild's brigades were in little better plight. Vandeleur's (whose casualties also had not been small), and Vivian's (which had been the least engaged of all), were the only two still capable of sustained effort.

Now at long last, Ney captured La Haye Sainte, thus obtaining a base at the very centre of the Allied position. For one frightful moment the French had before them a completely unguarded section of the Allied line. The Marshal, however, let the fleeting moment pass, and the gap was closed in time. During this crisis, and, indeed, from 4 to 6 p.m., the heavy brigades fulfilled what an officer of the Royals called 'the most trying duty of the day.[5]' They were extended in single file to make a show, virtually stationary, under severe artillery fire, and suffering from incursions of skirmishers, their casualties mounting all the time. When Uxbridge recommended Somerset (commanding the Household Brigade) to withdraw from the heavy fire, he replied that if he should do so, the Dutch-Belgian cavalry behind would move off immediately. Towards the end of the day, the original eighteen squadrons of British heavy cavalry had been reduced to something like the equivalent of two. Before this happened, however, they were twice more called upon to attack.

Before long, the anxiously awaited Prussian cavalry appeared on the left. It at once took over Vandeleur's and Vivian's light brigades' positions. These then moved to the right of the *chaussée*.

Suddenly, and to the surprise of nearly everyone present except the Duke, the end was at hand. At about 8 p.m., Wellington ordered the whole line to advance. The two light brigades, followed by the cheering infantry, immediately charged the recoiling Imperial Guard. A panic now seized the French, and they were chased off the field.

(v)

The British cavalry in India up to 1815

The first cavalry regiment to be sent out to India had arrived in Madras as far back as October 1782. It was the 23rd Light Dragoons, which in the following year was renumbered the 19th. Specially raised to assist the Honourable East India Company, it supplemented certain infantry battalions which had been sent for the same purpose at intervals over the previous twenty-five years.

Founded in 1600 for the sole purpose of carrying on trade as lucratively as possible, the Company found itself, from the first half of the eighteenth century, forced to engage in military operations. Two factors were responsible for this. First, the decline of the strong, centralised Moslem dynasty of the Great Moguls, by which India had been more or less firmly ruled for two hundred years. This had led to unstable governments in the territories where the Company's trading establishments were situated. Second, the French, taking advantage of these conditions, sought to secure a controlling influence with the local rulers, and thereby to oust the British, their chief European rivals. Most reluctantly, in consequence, the Company was obliged to spend money on levies, locally raised, trained and paid. These were officered by Europeans, for the most part amateurs and adventurers.

Between 1741 and 1767, the French had been virtually expelled from India and the whole of Bengal acquired for the British. In Clive's astonishing victories, of which Plassey in 1757 is the most famous, the minute forces with which he beat the hordes opposed to him included a negligible quantity of horsemen.

At the period when the 19th arrived upon the scene, the Commander-in-Chief in India was Sir Eyre Coote, appointed like his immediate predecessors, by the Government, but paid by the Company. He was engaged at the time in fighting the French-backed Hyder Ali of Mysore in Southern India. In two recent battles, Coote had much felt the lack of cavalry with which to follow up his extremely able enemy. The Mysorean light horse had proved itself not only numerous, but also well adapted to partisan warfare. 'They veiled the movements of their own army', writes Fortescue, 'in a cloud of mystery; they hung about their enemy like rooks about a heron, hustling, threatening, swooping, always too far away to receive injury, always near enough to inflict it.'[1] Coote had therefore written to the Court of Directors, urging them to obtain the loan of a regular cavalry regiment from home.

Until the 19th arrived the only armed horsemen at the disposal of the Company had consisted of insignificant numbers of Europeans, recruited chiefly from its civilian employees, and varying numbers of irregular natives hired from local nawabs or paid directly from Company funds.

The death of Hyder Ali and an uneasy peace treaty soon put an end to the war. In the seven years that followed, the regiment's colonel, John Floyd (who as a mere boy, had charged with the 15th at Emsdorf), devoted his very considerable talents to founding the first regular native cavalry in India. Officers and men of the 19th were employed, not only in Madras, but also in Bengal and Bombay, to form local horsemen into disciplined, well-trained units, under

British officers. The success of his system laid the foundation of that native cavalry, upon which, to an important degree, rested the power of the British in India for the next century and a half.* Floyd was the father of the native cavalry. Between 1789 and 1799 (under Lords Cornwallis and Wellesley in the wars against Tipu Sultan, the son of Hyder Ali), Floyd proved himself the first of our great leaders of cavalry in India. As a major-general he led two brigades in the campaign of 1799. These were made up of the 19th, with two regiments of Madras native cavalry, and the 25th Light Dragoons,† which had come from England, via the Cape, three years before, and two further native regiments. His handling of this first considerable mounted force to be used in India was masterly. The charges he led were instrumental in winning the battle of Malavelli, and the confidence he instilled into his native regiments throughout the campaign was a lasting legacy.

That legacy was first drawn upon in the Second Maratha War‡ which opened in 1803, four years after Floyd himself had gone home. With the death of Tipu and the destruction of his power at Seringapatam in 1799, there remained only the loose confederacy of the fierce, predatory tribes of the Marathas to prevent the pacification of southern India. Napoleon, with an eye to expelling the British from India, supplied officers and arms for the Marathas, who numbered their horsemen in tens of thousands, and could bring large quantities of artillery into the field.

Against Sindhia, one of the most able Maratha leaders, Lord Wellesley, the Governor-General, pitted two armies. One was based in the south, commanded by his younger brother, Arthur Wellesley, the other in the north by General Lake, the Commander-in-Chief. The cavalry regiments employed, each with two horse artillery guns attached, numbered fourteen. Wellesley's army included five regiments of Madras native cavalry and the 19th, while Lake employed five of Bengal native cavalry, as well as the 8th Light Dragoons, which had arrived in India from Egypt in 1802, and the 27th and 29th Light Dragoons (renumbered the 24th and 25th that year), which had arrived in 1797.

---

* For details of the mounted troops, European and native, raised in India between 1672 and the beginning of the nineteenth century, see Appendix, p. 294.

† This regiment had been raised in 1794 as Gwyn's 25th, and was renumbered the 22nd Light Dragoons in January 1803. It was disbanded in 1820. (See p. 44.)

‡ The First Maratha War had been waged from 1778–81. The Third (see p. 194) started in 1817 and lasted two years.

Prologue

In Wellesley's first general action at Assaye in 1803, which was a victory narrowly snatched from the jaws of disaster, the 19th Light Dragoons and the 4th Madras Native Cavalry, led by Colonel Maxwell, saved a British infantry regiment from annihilation. A dashing charge routed the enemy's cavalry, then smashed the first line of infantry and fell upon the guns. No sooner had these two regiments returned exhausted from the pursuit than they were called upon to charge a fresh brigade. Maxwell was killed at the moment of contact. As he died he involunarily checked his charger. Interpreting this wrongly, the squadrons behind him swerved, crying 'Halt, halt!' Confusion followed, but they soon rallied and were able to get safely away. A lieutenant of the 19th, though his arm was smashed early in the battle, took part in the charge, his mangled limb hanging by his side. A sergeant of the regiment, though pierced through the lungs by a pike, remained in the saddle to the end of the action.

A month later, at the end of the action of Argaum, the same brigade pursued the beaten Marathas by moonlight, killing and capturing 3,000 of them, and taking elephants, camels and baggage in large quantities.

Lake's campaign, meanwhile, had gone ahead even more swiftly and decisively than Arthur Wellesley's. In September 1803, he delivered Delhi, the capital of the Mogul Emperor, from the Marathas. On 1 November, he won the battle of Laswari, the most hotly contested which had been fought in India to that date. After one of those remarkable forced marches which were to become so great a feature of subsequent military history in India, Lake marched all his cavalry a further twenty-five miles in six hours to overtake the enemy at first light.

Colonel Vandeleur's brigade (8th Light Dragoons, and 1st and 3rd Bengal Native Cavalry) first charged and broke through the Maratha front, but, though they temporarily captured some guns, failed to disrupt it. Next, the two regiments of Colonel Macan's brigade (25th Light Dragoons and 4th Bengal Native Cavalry), under very heavy fire, charged the Maratha gunners who were partially concealed in the long grass. They then galloped through the cannon, which were chained together, and formed up beyond them. The gunners immediately crept from beneath their guns and continued to serve them. Macan, nothing daunted, charged back, and then again forward, but all to little effect. Lake soon called off the cavalry to await the arrival of the infantry.

Later in the battle, the 25th, after waiting concealed in a hollow, exposed to ricochet shot, emerged to save an infantry battalion from disaster. The regiment then delivered a remarkable charge against the Maratha artillery. By a frontal attack under severe fire, they first scattered the gunners, then swept away two lines of infantry, and finally fell, once again, upon the cavalry, completely routing them. As they returned from the pursuit, they were called upon to attack yet another large body of infantry. This they did, cutting it to pieces.

The only remaining Maratha force refused to break and fly. Nevertheless the second cavalry brigade made up of the 24th Light Dragoons and the 6th Bengal Native Cavalry, cut off their retreat and sabred large numbers of them.

The 8th, 24th and 25th Light Dragoons lost in this lengthy battle, 164 of all ranks, killed and wounded. The five native regiments lost ninety-one between them. This indicates how much of the brunt of actual fighting was borne by the white regiments.

With the virtual destruction of his armies, the tussle with Sindhia came to an end. Holkar, the other considerable Maratha leader, still remained to be dealt with. Hostilities against him opened in May 1804. At the end of December the following year he had been subdued.

One cavalry incident in the campaign is specially worth recording. On 17 November, Lake, by a night march, completely surprised the enemy near Furruckabad. The 8th Light Dragoons were thereby given an opportunity to revenge Holkar's ghastly mutilation of British prisoners. For ten miles the flying Maratha horse were relentlessly chased. No quarter was given, and one estimate states that as many as 3,000 of them were actually killed, and many wounded. Others tried to hide in trees, but the troopers discovered them and shot them down with their pistols: one of the very rare cases in which these weapons proved truly useful to dragoons. Before the action was over the cavalry (which included the 1st Bengal Native Cavalry) had covered altogether more than seventy miles in twenty-four hours, a feat of endurance seldom equalled even in India.

* * *

It was the policy of the Government to keep those princes and their families whose lands had come under British suzerainty in impotent luxury. After Tipu's death in 1799, his relatives were thus detained in the fortress of Vellore, under no restraint except forced residence.

Around them were gathered numerous impoverished and idle adherents, mostly from Tipu's defeated armies.

Sir John Cradock, freshly arrived in India to command the Madras
Army, thought fit, in 1805, to issue regulations for the native troops.
These included a new pattern of turban, prohibition of caste marks
on the face, and the shaving off of beards: all offensive to the men's
religions. Cradock's object was merely to impose upon the men a
greater degree of uniformity. The native regiments in and around
Vellore not unnaturally concluded that forcible conversion to Christ-
ianity was imminent. Actively assisted by the Mysore princes and
their followers, a considerable revolt was planned. It was given
impetus when refusal to comply with the regulations was treated as
mere insubordination, and duly punished.

In July 1806, a peculiarly favourable opportunity offering itself,
a battalion of native infantry attacked the practically unarmed officers
and men of the 69th Foot, massacring many of them as they lay in
bed within the fort. A British officer who lived outside the walls,
understanding what was afoot, sent off to the depot of the 19th Light
Dragoons, fourteen miles away, a message to their commander,
Lieutenant-Colonel R. R. Gillespie. That officer, a man of dashing
and adventurous past, at once set out with one squadron of the 19th
and a troop of the 7th Madras Native Cavalry, leaving orders for the
rest to follow. He arrived to find the 69th making a final desperate
stand, with the last rounds of their ammunition about to be expended.
There were four gates for him to penetrate. The last proved intract-
ible. With the help of a rope, therefore, he hoisted himself up, all the
while under murderous fire, to join a dwindling party of the 69th
atop the gateway. He turned a few of the rampart guns inwards to
keep the mutineers temporarily at bay, but all seemed lost when at last
his two galloper guns came on the scene with the rest of the cavalry.
Gillespie ordered one of the guns to blow in the gate, which was
immediately done. He then led the remnants of the 69th in a
bayonet charge, so as to make way for the entrance of the dragoons.
Some of these then dashed through the narrow passage-way into
the inner court, and sabred three or four hundred of the mutineers.
Those that escaped through a sallyport were cut down by another
squadron of the 19th. Both inside and outside the fortress, the 7th
Madras Native Cavalry actively assisted their white comrades.

The Vellore Mutiny was taken very seriously in London. The
Governor and Cradock were recalled, 4,000 extra troops were sent
from England, and the obnoxious dress regulations totally rescinded.

The ring leaders were, of course, punished. Six were blown from guns, five shot, eight hanged and five transported. Gillespie was granted £2,500 by the Company, and all ranks of the cavalry present, both white and native, were given additions to their pay.

This was not the last time that thoughtless, pedantic regulations sparked off rebellion in the native ranks; but it is one of the few examples of really swift and courageous action nipping mutiny in the bud. There were very few Gillespies in Bengal fifty-one years later. Had there been more, the great Indian Mutiny would certainly have been more speedily contained.

* * *

The perfectly extraordinary mutiny of the Company's European officers in Madras, which took place in 1809, affected cavalry and infantry alike. It arose, in part, from friction between the relative situations of the King's officers and the Company's officers. The latter were often superior to the former in intelligence and education. Their knowledge of the native languages and their influence over the native troops were the chief factors upon which British rule depended, and they were well aware of this fact. Unlike the King's officers, who performed their military duties for their own sake, for honour and for promotion, the Company's officers' chief motive for serving was gain. Since they were the servants of a commercial concern, this was not unreasonable. Under Sir George Barlow, the Governor of Madras, stringent efforts were made to limit these officers' legal opportunities for personal enrichment. These they considered theirs by right, in compensation for cutting themselves off from home. It so happened that Sir George, who possessed a rigid and unpleasant character, had a pathological hatred of soldiers. With considerable energy, he persecuted and harried them at all points. Their legitimate complaints, which included resentment at King's officers receiving lucrative appointments hitherto assigned to them, he treated with contempt, refusing even to forward them to higher authority. He was not above setting the native troops to spy upon their officers' words and actions. He instituted what was virtually a reign of terror.

The result, in short, was an officers' mutiny which embraced the whole Madras army. It led, at one point, to a collision between native and King's regiments, in which 150 lives were lost. Large numbers of officers were cashiered, dismissed or suspended. There followed, however, a general amnesty, and within four years nearly every officer who had taken part in the mutiny had been reinstated. Further, all their important demands were speedily conceded. Fortescue rightly says that, in the last resort, a British officer had no legal title to justice, and that if that principle is pushed to its logical extreme, as it unquestionably was by Barlow, there can be only one result – a mutiny.[2]

1

*Post-war rôle of the army at home – reductions greater
in infantry than cavalry – alterations in regimental
establishments – eight regiments disbanded – constant
changes of station*

No period was more difficult for the British army at home than that
between Waterloo and the Crimea. During twenty-two years of
almost perpetual war against the French, it had grown in size and
organisation, skill and experience, until, by 1815, it had become in
many ways as efficient as any of the great continental armies. The
process had been painful and costly, but it had been worthwhile. It
had been a chief factor in establishing a triumphant and lasting peace.

The Great War, as it was called until an even greater one eclipsed
it, had cost Britain some £800,000,000 and many thousands of lives.
When it was over, there existed overseas an empire quite unlike, and
more diffuse than, anything that had been known a century before.
Increasing commitments all over the world had to be defended and
consolidated. In the thirty-nine years of peace in Europe the army
fought in India and Afghanistan, in Arabia and Burma, in South and
West Africa, in China and New Zealand. In what became known as
the 'Long Peace' it gained forty battle honours.

* * *

At home, the end of the war produced great distress in the manufacturing and agricultural districts, which led to deep and dangerous discontent. No such thing as a police force had yet been invented. The Metropolitan Police were not constituted until 1829. Counties were not empowered to establish permanent and salaried forces until ten years later. Indeed, an effective organisation for the whole country did not exist until after 1856, when county constabularies became obligatory. In the first trying years of peace, therefore, 'the only power which stood between the country and anarchy was the Army.'[2] In Ireland, too, agrarian crime and political unrest called for troops from England in large numbers. Peel, however, when Chief Secretary for Ireland, had established in that country a new principle, which Fortescue has rightly described as 'of the first importance to military history'.[3] In 1814 he set up the Peace Preservation Force. This was the nucleus of the Royal Irish Constabulary which soon 'acquired a reputation for vigour and aloofness from local partialities'.[4] Thus the army in Ireland was relieved of many of its more trying duties.

*   *   *

It was inevitable that reductions in the army should take place as soon as peace came. Except when actually at war, the British parliament and people have, until quite recently, treated their soldiers with distrust and contempt. 'When war is on and danger nigh', ran the toast of an old farrier-sergeant in the 14th Hussars, *'God and the soldier!* is all the cry: When war is over and all things righted, God's forgot and the soldier slighted.'[5] This habit had arisen in the past, partly from a freedom-loving nation's dread of tyranny, and, in part, from the fact that large military establishments cost money. In the first half of the nineteenth century, a new type of anti-militarism was growing up, based, as the French historian Halévy has put it,

'on economic – not, as formerly, on constitutional grounds . . . England was overburdened with taxation and the officers who sat in Parliament – whether retired or active mattered little – were landowners as well as soldiers. They desired the abolition of the income-tax and this involved a reduction of the army estimates. Attached more closely to their class than to their profession, they were thus rendered incapable of forming a distinct military party at Westminster. But without leaders the British Army could never become a Praetorian guard . . .'[6]

The usual result of a persistent policy of military retrenchment was the swelling of the ranks in inefficient and expensive haste at the threat of war or rebellion, and the spending of as little as possible on a bare minimum the moment the threat disappeared. Nothing illustrates this attitude better than the determination of the War Office to maintain, throughout the Victorian period, an insufficient establishment of horses, always choosing to buy them after, rather than before, the need arose. As late as 1878, for example, an official committee declared that it would be possible to mobilize one army corps in twenty-two days, provided 5,674 horses could be found. It was suggested that of these some 2,000 ought to be bought, while the rest should be obtained by dismounting troops not immediately required.[7]

*   *   *

In 1816 the rank and file of the regular army numbered 225,000, of which 35,000 were in India and 35,000 in the army of occupation in France. In the following year, Palmerston reckoned that there were only some 16,000 effective regular soldiers of all arms in England proper. When the occupation of France came to an end in 1818, there was a decrease of 26,000. The total establishment in 1819 was about 113,000. In 1827 it was said that there were not enough troops available in the country to allow of a fitting military funeral for the Commander-in-Chief, the Duke of York.[8] Ten years later, on the accession of Queen Victoria, the establishment was 111,000, of which 10,656 were cavalry; but, in fact, as was generally so in those days, the army was then short of some 9,600 men. The official United Kingdom figures (excluding Ireland) for the years 1838 to 1848 give an average of about 29,500.[9] It was estimated that just before the Crimean War the British cavalry numbered 7,500 at home, with 3,100 in India. At the time of Waterloo the figures were 16,400 and 5,500 respectively.[10]

*   *   *

The post-Waterloo reductions were not as great in the regular cavalry as in the infantry. It was upon mobile troops that governments chiefly depended when it came to the suppression of riots. 'It is much more desirable', said the Duke of Wellington, 'to employ

73

cavalry for the purposes of police than infantry; for this reason: cavalry inspires *more terror* at the same time that it *does much less mischief*. A body of 20 or 30 horse will disperse a mob with the utmost facility, whereas 400 or 500 infantry will not effect the same object without the use of their firearms, and a great deal of mischief may be done.'[11]

* * *

For the first seven years of the peace, cavalry regiments were much disturbed by continual alterations in their establishments. Between the end of 1815 and 1822, the cavalry of the line on the Home establishment was reduced five times. Roughly speaking (for there were minor regimental variations) the first post-Waterloo reductions laid down that each regiment should have eight troops with a strength of 720 of all ranks, with 581 horses. By November, 1818, when the occupation of France had ended, the strength of the eight troops had been brought down to 439 of all ranks, with 273 horses. By 1822, there were only six troops, 360 of all ranks and 250 horses.* The

---

* The same scale of reductions, more or less, applied to the Household Cavalry and to the 1st (King's) Dragoon Guards, which regiment was always treated differently from the rest of the cavalry of the line.

A typical establishment of a regiment of the line was as follows:
17th Light Dragoons (reduced to Home establishment on return from India), May 1823: –
6 troops.

Officers:	Other ranks:
1 colonel	1 regimental sergeant major
1 lieutenant-colonel	6 troop sergeant majors
2 majors	1 paymaster sergeant
6 captains	1 armourer sergeant
6 lieutenants	1 saddler sergeant
6 cornets	1 schoolmaster sergeant
1 regimental quartermaster	12 sergeants
1 paymaster	18 corporals
1 adjutant	1 trumpet major
1 surgeon	5 trumpeters
1 assistant surgeon	6 farriers
1 veterinary surgeon Total: 28.	282 privates† Total: 335.

Grand Total 363.
253 troop horses, including those for NCOs and trumpeters.
(P.R.O., W.O.4/720.)
† It is difficult to say at what date the term trooper replaced private in the

establishment of regiments stationed in Ireland sometimes varied from that in the rest of Britain. Regiments serving in India still had eight troops, with 745 officers and men, all mounted, and also maintained a small recruiting troop at home.

By 1822, eight cavalry regiments had been disbanded, leaving twenty-four in being. Ten of these saw no overseas service for nearly forty years. They were chiefly 'heavies' (Dragoon Guards and Dragoons). Light cavalry was obviously more suitable for Indian and colonial service, if only because the remount horses available in those parts were generally unsuitable for mounting heavy troopers. During these forty years attention to training for war was largely neglected. So much so that in 1820 the *Rules and Regulations for the Formation, Field Exercise and Movements of Cavalry* were out of print.[12] Troop stations were chosen rather as centres from which to aid the civil power than for their training facilities. More often than not there was neither drill ground nor riding school available. 'Brigade', and even sometimes 'divisional' field days were held at widely separated intervals, chiefly in the vicinity of London. On 25 May 1822, for instance, the 10th and 15th Hussars, and the 14th Light Dragoons held a field day on Hounslow Heath. Four days later they were joined by the Household Cavalry, when the equivalent of twenty-one squadrons exercised together. In July 1823, a heavy brigade, consisting of the three regiments of Household Cavalry, and a light brigade, composed of the 3rd Light Dragoons, and the 7th and 15th Hussars, formed a cavalry division for a few days of manoeuvres on the Heath. But only a few regiments ever enjoyed the benefit of this type of training.

It was extremely rare for a regiment to be assembled in one place. The 1st King's Dragoon Guards were not once brought together as a regiment between 1828 and 1843.[13] That was an exceptional case. More typical was the experience of the 15th Hussars whose troops did not come together between 1816 and 1821.[14] A regular cavalry regiment's component parts, especially in Ireland, were habitually spread over a large area, sometimes covering hundreds of square miles. It was common for troops to be split up into even smaller detachments, so that for weeks at a time a sergeant with a handful of men might not see his troop commander, let alone his commanding officer. In 1815, for example, the 4th Dragoons were dispersed all over southern Ireland in twenty-six detachments of troops and

cavalry. It was not general till the end of the nineteenth century. Sometimes there is confusion because troop horses were also known as troopers.

half-troops. They were but a small part of nearly 1,900 separate detachments of the army spread over the whole of Ireland, emanating from 441 stations.[15]

A further bar to efficient training was imposed by constant changes of station. The 5th Dragoon Guards, for instance, crossed to Ireland and back again eight times in thirty-three years. Between 1817 and 1854, their regimental headquarters were stationed in more than fifty different places.[16] Between 1819 and 1857, the 7th Hussars made seventeen major moves between England, Scotland, Ireland, Canada and India, altering quarters within each country innumerable times.[17] The experience of nearly all cavalry regiments of the line was much the same.

'The difficulty is, that where there are no soldiers, the magistrates must have yeomanry.'

SIR CHARLES NAPIER, 1839[1]

(ii)

The yeomanry: constitution and establishments – governments' usual preference for regulars in police work

To assist the regular regiments at home in the police work which was their chief occupation, but for which their numbers were far from adequate, was the Volunteer Cavalry, better known as the Yeomanry. Its existence dates from 1794, when twenty-seven 'Corps of Yeomanry Cavalry' were raised in various counties. In war their chief object was to assist in repelling invasion. In peace it became 'the suppression of Riots and Tumults within the County'.

Until 1802–3, yeomanry regiments were mainly dependent upon private subscriptions, and were commanded in effect as much by 'Committees of Subscribers' as by their titular commanding officers. At first, 'they were subject to no discipline except their own rules, which could only be enforced by public opinion.'[2] At no time did the commanding officer's powers extend beyond the imposition of fines and the threat of dismissal.

The yeomanry, like all volunteer and auxiliary forces, came under the Home Department until 1855, when the War Office took them over. The Home Department's control over the movements of the regular army was also considerable. As a good modern authority has put it:

> 'The real authority for altering the stations of troops on home service was the Home Office, not the Horse Guards: it was at the Home Secretary's behest that the Commander-in-Chief issued the necessary instructions to move a company of infantry or a troop of horse from one town to another, and though the Home Office usually consulted the general in charge of the District before ordering such a movement, it was not bound to do so.'[3]

The yeomanry consisted, for the most part, of 'the Yeomen of England, with Noblemen and Gentlemen as Officers',[4] which is to say 'tenant-farmers and their sons, acting under the command of their landlords and their landlords' sons'.[5] Captain J. Arthur Lloyd's Troop of the Shrewsbury Yeomanry Cavalry, for example, consisted of three officers and a quartermaster, three sergeants, three corporals, a trumpeter and forty-one privates. Nearly all these are known to have been tenants or servants on the Lloyd family's properties.[6] In some troops, such as those of the Edinburgh Light Horse in the 1820s, all ranks consisted 'entirely of gentlemen of the highest class'. 'I have seen these gentlemen,' wrote Lieutenant-General Sir Harry Smith, 'after a long, heavy, and wet night's march, every one dressing his own horse, feeding him, etc., like a German Hussar, ere they thought of anything for themselves.'[7]

In industrial districts the officers were often factory owners and their agents, with small manufacturers, innkeepers and tradesmen in the ranks. The basic requirement, of course, was that each officer and man should be able to provide a suitable horse and saddlery, either by ownership or on hire.* Any member could resign at any time, except when actually on service. Certain annual periods of training and 'permanent duty' were laid down from time to time,

---

* Until the beginning of the twentieth century, unlike the *silladar* cavalry in India (see p. 179), no allowance was made for a horse killed or injured on service. Nor did the yeoman himself receive compensation for injury. During the great agricultural depressions in the last quarter of the nineteenth century, there was a considerable falling off of volunteers for the yeomanry from their inability to afford the costs and bear the risks.

but these were not always enforced. Government provided arms and ammunition; all other equipment was provided by the yeoman himself, or by his commanding officer. In 1817 an annual capitation grant of 30s. was made for each 'efficient' yeoman. Out of it all charges for uniform were to be defrayed. For this it was always inadequate. The Earl of Plymouth, for instance, paid £6,200 into the regimental fund from his own pocket when new troops (known from the colour of their horses as the 'Grey Squadron'), were added to the Worcestershire Yeomanry in 1832. Between 1854 and 1871, the Earl of Dudley spent over £4,000 a year on the same corps. An average regiment cost about £10 per man per annum in the 1830s.[8]

For many years from 1817 onwards, when actually 'called out', officers received the pay and allowances of the regular cavalry, and other ranks five shillings a day. Every officer and man was exempt from paying the otherwise universal Horse Duty upon the animal he actually used on service. He was further exempted from liability to act as a parish or special constable. The adjutant of each regiment was generally a regular cavalry officer.*

Until 1869 when a certain degree of standardization was introduced, the number of troops in a regiment of yeomanry, and the number of men in each troop, varied considerably. The troop was generally named after the district or town from which it drew its members, and as often as not acted independently of the rest, sometimes being called upon when the remainder of the regiment was not. The service of troops of yeomanry was tendered voluntarily, upon their formation, to the Crown, through the Lords-Lieutenant of Counties, who had sole discretion in granting commissions. These were not, of course, unlike those in the army proper, purchasable. As in the case of the regular army, the yeomanry was summoned to the aid of the civil power by requisition of the Lords-Lieutenant or the magistrates. Its liability to be thus called out lasted until it became subject to the Territorial Force Act in 1908. On occasions the Home Secretary conferred the power of calling out the yeomanry upon the general commanding a military district. In 1839 such au-

* In 1830, Lieutenant Pettit, adjutant of the Wiltshire Yeomanry, at the age of 76, was quite incapable of performing his duties. The authorities, however, refused to retire him, or to appoint Lieutenant Peniston, who had been acting in his place for years past, on the grounds that Peniston had never served in the regular cavalry. Consequently, when Pettit died aged 82, he was still 'Lieutenant and Adjutant' of the Wiltshire Yeomanry! (Graham: *Wilts*, 91–2).

thority was given to Sir Charles Napier, commanding the Northern District. In 1842, all the yeomanry regiments from the Scottish border to Worcestershire were placed under General Sir Thomas Arbuthnot in Manchester.[9]

In 1817 the yeomanry consisted of nearly 18,000 effective rank and file. In 1826 there were sixty-two regiments of yeomanry in England, Scotland and Wales; in 1840, there were fifty-five.[10]* As the years went by, numbers varied according to the internal state of the country. As soon as a period of apparent quiet succeeded one of turbulence, reductions came about, sometimes from lack of interest on the part of the local property owners, but more often by order of government. Thus in 1828, feeling comparatively safe and in a fit of economy, government disbanded all yeomanry regiments which had not been called out in the past ten years. Twenty-four of these, after more than thirty years' service, were done away with.† Two years later, when the Reform Bill riots were causing fresh alarm, nearly all of them were resurrected, at great expense. These units lost their seniority.‡ Regiments raised in 1794, as a result of this two year hiatus, now found themselves junior to others raised as late as 1817. This was both unjust and short-sighted. When the Flintshire Yeomanry Cavalry was disbanded in 1838, its Commandant wrote to the Home Secretary pointing out that the effectiveness of the yeomanry was 'occasioned more by its passive existence than its active display'.[11] The 1838 reduction was of the order of 25 per cent, leaving the number of men about 14,000 on the eve of the Chartist troubles. After the riots of 1842, however, 'the conduct of the Yeomanry Cavalry in every district', according to Peel, the Prime Minister, 'having been admirable',[12] an increase in numbers was decreed. The 1850 figure, nevertheless, was about the same as that of 1839.

* In many parts of the country the numbers of volunteers in the third decade of the nineteenth century were not much less than the numbers of the Territorial Army a century later. The enrolled strength of the yeomanry in Devonshire in 1820, for example, was 2,623 while the Territorial strength in the county in 1923 was 2,835. (Benson Freeman, 33.)

† Some regiments, especially those with wealthy colonels, were willing to continue in existence without pay, or allowances, and government grudgingly accepted their services. Such were the North Devon and Royal 1st Devon regiments. (Benson Freeman, 35–6.) Officers and men from some disbanded regiments would in fact muster in an emergency as if their troop still existed. (Loftus, Charles, *My Youth by Sea and Land*, 1876, II.)

‡ This had its effect when mechanisation took place in the 1930s, for the senior regiments were the first to lose their horses.

Even in the most disturbed districts, at the worst periods of distress, the yeomanry was not called upon with very great frequency. The Cheshire Yeomanry, for instance, aided the civil power on only eighteen separate occasions between January 1817 and April 1848.[13] The Staffordshire Yeomanry was on duty, at the behest of the magistrates, for eighty days between 1814 and 1824, though in the summer of 1842 its duty averaged twenty-two days per troop. In 1822 the Himley troop was kept out dealing with rioting colliers and stone-getters for twenty-three consecutive days, and in 1842 for fifty days' continuous duty.[14] This was very exceptional.

* * *

There may have been some truth in Thomas Bewick's scathing reference to 'the pride and folly which took possession' of the yeomen's 'empty or fume-charged heads when they got dressed in scarlet',[15] yet it is astonishing how forbearing were the 'long-sworded and whiskered captains' of Cobbett's phrase,[16] and their non-commissioned officers and men. Time and again these amateur soldiers were called upon to receive showers of verbal insults, interspersed with stones, fragments of bricks, broken bottles and filth, yet bloodshed seldom occurred.

It was not surprising that the yeomanry were unpopular with the masses. They were, after all, upholders of an existing order from which the evil condition of the working classes seemed to stem. Nevertheless when it came to the question of parliamentary reform, there were those in the ranks of the yeomanry who were decidedly in favour of it, as indeed were many of the upper and middle classes generally. In 1831, for instance, a mutiny nearly took place in the Salisbury Troop of the Royal Wiltshire Yeomanry because its captain, Lord Arundell of Wardour, had voted against the Reform Bill. The sergeant-major and thirty privates signed a 'remonstrance' which was forwarded to him. Trouble was avoided by eight of the privates resigning at once and Lord Arundell following their example shortly afterwards.[17]

The yeomanry's geographical distribution was erratic. In 1839, for instance, the manufacturing districts of the Midlands were well supplied. Yet Lancashire had but 171 men in three troops, although the county's population was greater than that of Worcestershire, Warwickshire and Staffordshire combined. These three counties had 1,886 men in twenty-five troops. The counties of Nottingham,

Leicester and Derby had twenty troops with 1,450 men, yet Durham, with its large numbers of coal miners, possessed not a single troop.

* * *

It was to be expected that the Whigs would have special reasons for distrusting the yeomanry, which was likely to be, from its composition, Tory; but at any rate from the 1840s onwards, the Tories also discouraged its use when regulars were available. 'I much prefer the assistance of regular troops', wrote Sir James Graham, the Tory Home Secretary in 1842, 'to calling on a Yeomanry force'. [18] In this he was echoing the words of Lord John Russell, the Whig Home Secretary, who said in 1838 that he 'would rather that any force should be employed in case of local disturbance than the local corps of Yeomanry'. [19] Sir Charles Napier, commanding the Northern District, did not agree. 'I am sorry', he wrote, 'Lord John doubts the expediency of calling out the yeomanry. There are no doubts on my mind; it is the best way to meet either a local or general rising.' [20] To the Colonel of the York Hussars Sir Charles wrote: 'I am a strong advocate for calling out the yeomanry; it shews the disaffected that the loyal are both able and willing to put them down if they resort to physical force. The present apathy and total dependence on the regular troops is bad; it argues a want of self-reliance in society: force should be met by force on the spot.' [21] Sir Harry Smith thought that there was no system which could

> 'be adopted of such importance to our country as the yearly calling-out of the Yeomanry for a few days' exercise. It brings', he wrote in 1844, 'the educated aristocracy in contact with the less favoured in life, the cultivators of the soil – landlords with tenants. It shows the latter in their true character – honest, manly, and liberal fellows, and teaches them to look up to their superiors, while it also shows the former what a noble set of men their tenants are, obedient, but as proud as an English yeoman ought to be, and that, thus engaged in the defence of our country and in the maintenance of our rights as British subjects, they are to be treated with the respect due to every individual of the social compact.' [22]

Beside their relative efficiency, there were a number of reasons why governments usually preferred regular troops to yeomanry. The most obvious was the fact that fairly or unfairly, the local connections of the officers and men gave the yeomanry 'the character of parties to the dispute'.[23] Another was that, should disturbances occur at harvest time, large numbers of the officers and men were occupied in gathering in their crops. But the most potent reason was a financial one. Regular troops had to be paid whether employed or not, whereas every time the yeomanry was embodied, government had to incur additional expense.

In Ireland the use of the yeomanry was a much more tricky business, for almost to a man yeomen were Orangemen and Protestants, while the rioters were Catholics. In a well-known affray at Newtownbarry in 1832, the magistrate called out the yeomanry (which he himself commanded) in preference, it seems, to an easily available regular military force, for the constraint of a distress for tithes. A number of deaths resulted and in consequence the principal magistrate was censured and not reinstated.[24]

*   *   *

There were many types of police work, beside quelling mobs, for both yeomanry and regular cavalry to do. In London, for instance, the Household Cavalry was often employed in traffic control, especially at the Sovereign's levees. In coastal areas, large numbers of troops were tied up in assisting customs officers. This meant endless patrolling, but at times it could be both exciting and tiring. In August 1818, two horses of the 6th Inniskilling Dragoons died of exhaustion whilst following 'smuglers' into the hills above Forfar.[25]

On the coasts of Devon and Cornwall, where the wrecking of ships by the placing of false lights was a recognized means of livelihood, the protection of cargoes, known as 'wreck duty', was a frequent occupation for the yeomanry. When, for example, in December, 1833, the *Elizabeth* of Liverpool on her way to Calcutta became stranded on the bar of Bideford, detachments of the North Devon Yeomanry spent nine days and nights, watched by a frustrated crowd of nearly 2,000 people, escorting the cargo to a depôt by day and guarding it by night. For these services they received from government £194.[26]

On occasions troops were called upon to protect treasure trove. One such was the finding by workmen in the river Dove at Tutbury, in June 1831, of more than 100,000 coins. These formed the military chest of Thomas, Earl of Lancaster, abandoned in his flight from Edward II in 1320. Disturbances broke out among the hun-

dreds of people who came to scrabble for the coins. The Burton
Troop of the Staffordshire Yeomanry was called out to restore order
and to try to preserve the treasure for its rightful owner, the King.
After a couple of days, it was relieved by a troop of the 15th Hussars.[27]
Neither regulars nor yeomanry were strangers to the rôle of fire-
men. When, for instance, in 1839, the men of the Wiltshire Yeomanry saw flames issuing from the village of Steeple Ashton, near
Trowbridge, they thought the fire must be the work of Chartists.
On their arrival they found no rioters, and a large part of the village
alight from innocent causes. They managed, by their exertions, to
save what was left of the buildings.[28] In the same year the 9th Lancers put out a fire on a farm near Staines. The insurance company
offered 'to distribute a trifle among the men' for their 'able and
prompt assistance'. This was declined because no damage had been
done to clothing or regimental property. Two years later, after
dealing with a fire near Exeter, the same regiment accepted £20 for
the men whose uniforms had been spoilt by fire and water.[29] Similarly the Lunatic Asylum Protector Insurance Company awarded
£40 in 1832 to the non-commissioned officers and men of the 14th
Hussars for their part in putting out a great conflagration at the
Gloucester asylum.[30]

'On becoming soldiers we have not ceased to be
citizens.'
Unknown, *Humble Representation*, addressed
to Parliament by the soldiers of Cromwell's
army, 1647

(iii)

*Regulars and yeomanry in aid of the civil power – the
Jeremiah Brandreth riots – the 'Blanketeers' – skill
required to disperse large crowds – the 'massacre of Peterloo' – the Reform Bill riots in Bristol – Chartist riots –
billeting difficulties*

During the war the unrepresented masses of the manufacturing
districts had borne low wages and high prices with stoicism. A

miserable harvest in 1816, the harsh working of the Corn Laws, the deterioration of trade and the unemployment which came with peace, made conditions unbearable. The earliest attempts at anything resembling a concerted insurrection took place in the Nottingham and Derby area in 1817. These were known as the Jeremiah Brandreth riots, after a young framework knitter who led the starving operatives. In the worst of these disturbances, the mob, armed with homemade pikes and a few fire-arms, was put to flight with pathetic ease by the prompt appearance of a troop each of the 15th Hussars and the Derbyshire Yeomanry. Brandreth and others were arrested, tried and hanged.

In the same year the unemployed of Manchester attempted a march upon London to petition the Prince Regent. The King's Dragoon Guards, supported by the Cheshire and Staffordshire Yeomanry prevented the 'Blanketeers' (so called from the blankets they carried) from getting very far. One marcher was mortally wounded by a sabre cut on the head, and a private of the King's Dragoon Guards had a deep indent made in his helmet by a brickbat. It seems, by modern standards, unnecessary to have used force to halt this march of unarmed workers. The magistrates, however, could not see how the men were to maintain themselves *en route* without recourse to intimidation and plunder. They were probably right.

In London, the Household Cavalry, who carried printed orders to avoid giving offence to the citizens, had to deal with a number of riots. On one occasion in 1817 the Life Guards dispersed an armed mob in the City. They struck 'with the flat of their swords only, right and left, upon which the arms were thrown away, and taken up by the Troops'.[1] It seems that they consistently showed equal restraint in what was agreed by all soldiers to be the least satisfactory of military duties. This did not save them from becoming known as the 'Piccadilly butchers'.

The dispersal of large crowds was a matter of some skill. Mounted troops properly directed could break up and move immense bodies of people without injury to anyone. By feints, by backing, by rearing and by dexterous horse management, mobs of any size could be baffled and harmlessly scattered. Everything depended upon discipline and cool leadership.

*   *   *

The best known, if not the most catastrophic of the incidents of this period, occurred in St Peter's Fields, Manchester on 16 August 1819, at a monster meeting arranged by the 'Manchester Reformers', at which 'Orator' Hunt was to be the chief speaker. The 'massacre of Peterloo' might never have taken place if the local yeomanry and their mounts had been less raw and more amenable to discipline. The meeting which had launched the 'Blanketeers' two years before was held on the same site. The instigators on that occasion had spoken to a large crowd from improvised hustings (just as Hunt was to do in 1819), but by 'a judicious movement' of the King's Dragoon Guards, the speakers had been surrounded and arrested. The mob offered no opposition and dispersed quietly.

There is reason to suppose that the same thing would have happened at 'Peterloo' (though the crowd was much larger), had the Manchester and Salford Yeomanry been a disciplined body. But it was not. It had only been formed in 1817, as a result of the 'Blanketeer' affair. The officers were mostly 'wealthy master manufacturers',[2] and the men tradesmen, such as butchers, butter factors, calico-printers, cheesemongers, corn-merchants, innkeepers, ironmongers, tailors and watchmakers.[3] One was a commission-agent, another a dancing-master. Unlike the true yeomen of the countryside, they were far from being skilled horsemen. Many of them, too, were said to be men of political rancour obsessed with class hatred. These dis-advantages might have mattered less had the yeomanry been employed in concert with the other, more seasoned, troops which the magistrates had at call. These were six troops of the 15th Hussars, two horse artillery guns, six troops of the Cheshire Yeomanry and some infantry, all under command of an infantry officer, Colonel Guy L'Estrange.

Unhappily, and for some unknown reason, the troop of Manchester Yeomanry, not more than 50 strong, was kept under the immediate command of the magistrates. These gentlemen, soon after the meeting started, decided to use some part of the military to escort to the platform the Deputy Constable (a paid official of the Court Leet) so that he might arrest Hunt and his associates. For this purpose they had already lined a route through the crowd with special constables. The magistrates expected the arrests to be peaceably accomplished and the crowd to disperse as they had done in 1817. Indeed Hunt had let it be known before the meeting that no resistance was to be made should he and the other leaders be arrested.

The magistrates, having decided to arrest, sent off to Colonel

L'Estrange to place his troops in readiness. This he did with skill and discretion. At the same time they sent a second messenger for the yeomanry. Having less far to travel, this was the first body of troops to arrive on the scene. 'They halted in great disorder', says an impartial and well-placed witness, 'and so continued for the few minutes they remained. This disorder was attributed . . . to the un-disciplined state of their horses, little ascustomed to act together.'[4]

Hunt, on seeing this sorry display, shouted 'Stand firm my friends! You see they are in disorder already. This is a trick. Give them three cheers.'[5] The crowd of not less than 60,000 unarmed men, women and children, dressed in their Sunday best and carrying flags and banners, did as they were bid. The yeomanry and the special constables cheered loudly in reply. The troop commander then began to lead his men, still in much disarray, toward the platform. At first they tried to go slowly, five or six abreast, but soon they opened out and increased their speed. 'With a zeal and ardour which might naturally be expected from men acting with delegated power against a foe by whom it is understood they had long been insulted with taunts of cowardice, they continued their course, seeming individually to vie with each other which should be first.'[6]

As they rushed into the crowd, these amateur horsemen, their horses terrified by the noise of the shouting, swept even the special constables aside. It was not long before 'swords were up, and swords were down'.[7] Amidst great confusion the arrests were made. Until then few casualties had occurred, but it seems that at this moment the cry went up from the horsemen: 'Have at their flags', whereupon they dashed all over the place 'cutting most indiscriminately to the right and left'[8] in order to secure these trophies.*

To the magistrates, and indeed to the 15th Hussars and the Cheshire Yeomanry (who had just arrived at the edge of the crowd), it now seemed that the Manchester Yeomanry were clearly 'in the power of those whom they were designed to overawe . . . It required only a glance', wrote Lieutenant Jolliffe of the 15th Hussars, 'to discover their helpless position, and the necessity of our being brought to their rescue.'[9] It appears, nevertheless, that the most lethal weapons with which the crowd could either defend themselves or

---

* The behaviour of the Manchester Yeomanry gave yeomanry generally a bad reputation for many years to come. Sir Charles Napier in 1839 spoke of yeomen as 'over-zealous for cutting and slashing'. (Journal, 15 Aug. 1839, Napier, II, 73.) This, in fact, was not often the case after Peterloo.

assail the engulfed horsemen, were walking sticks and possibly a few stones.

Viewing the scene before him Colonel L'Estrange asked the chairman of the magistrates what he should do. 'Good God, sir!' replied that frightened man, 'don't you see they are attacking the Yeomanry? Disperse the meeting.'[10] In consequence, the 15th Hussars were given the commands 'Front!' and 'Forward!' The trumpet then sounded the charge.

'When fronted', says Jolliffe, 'our line extended quite across the ground, which, in all parts, was so filled with people that their hats seemed to touch.

'The charge . . . swept this mingled mass of human beings before it: people, yeomen, and constables, in their confused attempts to escape, ran one over the other; so that, by the time we had arrived at the end of the field, the fugitives were literally piled up to a considerable elevation above the level of the ground. . . . The hussars drove the people forward with the flats of their swords; but sometimes, as is almost inevitably the case when men are placed in such situations, the edge was used. . . . The greater amount of injuries arose from the pressure of the routed multitude.'[11]

A cotton-weaver saw 'ten or twelve of the Yeomanry Cavalry and two of the Hussars cutting at the people, who were wedged close together, when an officer of Hussars rode up to his own men, and knocking up their swords, said, "Damn you, what do you mean by this work?" He then called out to the Yeomanry, "For shame, gentlemen; what are you about? the people cannot get away." They desisted for a time, but no sooner had the officer rode to another part of the field, than they fell to work again.'[12]

The exact number of casualties is in doubt, but it seems unlikely that more than eleven people were killed.[13]

*　　*　　*

Less well known but infinitely more destructive than Peterloo were the Reform Bill riots in Bristol. These constituted the most disastrous outbreak of popular violence in Britain during the nineteenth century. They could have been contained, as were many others, had the military commander and the civic authorities acted with even a modicum of firmness.

The immediate cause was the violent anti-Reform speeches of the Recorder of Bristol, Sir Charles Wetherell. These had made him extremely unpopular in the city. Demonstrations were therefore expected when he came to open the assizes in October 1831. Available to deal with these were some three hundred special constables, one troop of the 3rd Dragoon Guards and two troops of the 14th Light Dragoons. By chance the senior officer in the city was a man quite unsuited to an emergency: the half-pay 'resident inspecting Field Officer of the Bristol recruiting district', Lieutenant-Colonel Brereton.

The riots started in earnest soon after Sir Charles had entered the Mansion House. The ground floor windows were broken, and the mayor read the Riot Act from the balcony. This had no effect and before long the building was broken into. Sir Charles decided to escape while he still could. This he managed to do, disguised as a postilion. After two hours of inaction, during which much damage was done, the mayor asked Brereton to clear the streets with the troop of the 3rd Dragoon Guards and one of the troops of the 14th. When these arrived, the mob cheered them and shouted 'God save the King'.

Brereton, advised by Major Mackworth, aide-de-camp to the Commander-in-Chief, who happened to be in the city, gave orders to the cavalry to ride through and 'walk away' the rioters, without drawing swords. After some hours of this fruitless operation, the crowd still had not dispersed, and three troopers of the 14th had been wounded by missiles. Eventually, after the mayor had read the 'Riot Act' for the second time, Brereton ordered the 14th to charge, using only the flat of their sabres. This was temporarily effective.

Soon the mob erupted again, this time at the Council House, some distance away. The 14th again charged, but as their patience was wearing thin some of the men discharged their firearms, while others employed the cutting edges of their swords. One person was killed and others were wounded, one mortally. The effect was immediate, and the rioters speedily dispersed. For some hours of the night all was more or less quiet.

Thinking the riot was over, the special constables whom Mackworth had organised for the protection of the Mansion House withdrew to their beds. So did the few troopers who were patrolling the square in front of the building. Consequently, when the mob reassembled at dawn, there was nothing to stop them sacking the

Mansion House, raiding the cellars, and conducting an orgy in the square.

In spite of the previous day's experience, Brereton refused for some considerable time to call upon the cavalry again. When, at the mayor's request, he eventually did so he noticed that the 3rd Dragoon Guards, who had taken a passive rôle the day before, were cheered by the mob. The 14th, on the other hand, were met with groans and threats and cries of 'bloody blues', after the colour of their uniforms.[14] Brereton thereupon shouted to the mob that no firing would be allowed and asked them: 'If I send the 14th away, will you return to your homes?' The answer was a resounding 'Yes'. He then rode up to Captain Gage, commanding the 14th, and said: 'It appears that the whole of this disturbance is due to the presence of the 14th; you will therefore take them to their quarters.' Gage had no option but to leave the city, fighting a small rearguard action all the way. His rear threes had several times to fire their pistols, and a few further casualties resulted. When the 14th arrived at Keynsham, they set about grinding their swords, fully expecting to be again called upon to use them.

Having thus fooled poor Brereton into sending away two thirds of the only force at hand to control it, the mob at once set about firing and looting the buildings in the vicinity with impunity. The 'city Bridewell' was stormed and its prisoners freed. The New Gaol suffered the same fate. Both were burnt to the ground. The toll houses, the Bishop's Palace, the Chapter House containing six thousand books and eventually the Mansion House were set alight. So were numerous private homes.

Throughout the afternoon and well into the night Brereton dithered. He refused to give Captain Warrington of the 3rd Dragoon Guards any sensible instructions. He turned down the proffered services of some 250 army pensioners living in the city. At 11 p.m. the Dodington Troop of the Gloucestershire Yeomanry, for which the mayor had sent during the morning, reported to Brereton. He declined to give them any orders whatsoever without the support of a magistrate. No magistrate could be found, all of them having slunk off to try to save their own houses. The yeomen therefore waited impotently for two hours before marching out of the city again. Earlier the Bedminster Troop of the North Somerset Yeomanry had reported and had received similar treatment. The Bath Troop of the same regiment was ordered to march for Bristol, but many of its members refused to do so, being 'Bristol sympathisers'. Most of these were afterwards dismissed. However by 5 a.m. on 31 October, the third day of the riots, the whole of the North Somerset Yeomanry, including some of the Bath Troop, was converging upon Bristol.

The rioters, never very numerous, were in complete control throughout the night, watched by thousands of by now terrified citizens. Originally most of the onlookers were sympathetic towards the demonstrations against Sir Charles. It was only gradually, as the looting and burning progressed that the spectators began to form themselves into squads to protect property. Many of the rioters were burned to death looting the upper stories of buildings which their comrades fired beneath them. Others were later found dead from excessive drinking. Almost unbelievably Brereton now retired to his lodgings and went to bed. Captain Warrington was left in charge. This officer, who was in a very poor state of health, eventually received at 3 a.m. a note from the mayor (who had taken refuge at some distance from the scene) requiring 'the officer in command of the troops to use the most vigorous measures to suppress the riot'.[15] Warrington refused to act except in company with a magistrate. Two hours later, when one was finally procured, Warrington still declined to call out the dragoons without consulting Brereton.

Brereton, when woken up, reluctantly gave his consent. The troop of the 3rd Dragoon Guards, therefore, was brought into Queen Square, most of one side of which was in flames. Major Mackworth now arrived, saw that the whole city must soon be ablaze, and called out: 'Colonel Brereton, we must instantly charge.' Without waiting for an answer, he gave the order: 'Charge men, and charge home!' Although they caused numerous casualties the dragoons were too few in number (not more than thirty-six in all) to be able to effect much. Seeing this, Mackworth, apparently on his own responsibility, galloped off to Keynsham to bring back the 14th Light Dragoons. These arrived (accompanied by some of the Bedminster Troop) at about the same time as another squadron of the regiment came into the city from Gloucester.

For several hours the 14th set about them in earnest. First they cleared Queen Square in a single charge and then ferreted out individual members of the mob from the narrow streets. The official figure of dead was twelve, while sixty-seven wounded were received into hospital. There were almost certainly more, who from fear of being charged with rioting did not go to hospital. Inevitably, a few innocent bystanders got hurt as well. From first-hand contemporary accounts, it appears that on two separate occasions men of the 14th completely decapitated rioters with a single sweep of the sabre, one with a back-hander. This was a feat very rarely accomplished. The grinding of the weapons of the 14th seems to have been worthwhile.

By mid-day, while regular troops and yeomanry from all over the south-west were converging on the city, the riots were over. 180 prisoners were later tried. Four were hanged, thirty-two transported and fifty-four imprisoned. Brereton and Warrington were court-martialled. Brereton committed suicide in the course of his trial. Warrington was allowed, in view of his illness, to retire from the service and sell his commission.[16]

The Bristol riots, in which the city was delivered over to fire and pillage for three days, are the supreme example of what could happen if initial firmness in the commander of the troops was lacking. That there were no comparable catastrophes in Britain throughout the century, and especially during the Chartist riots, is a remarkable testimony to the judgment of officers in command of troops. This is especially so when it is considered how great a risk they ran, when aiding the civil power, of being condemned for using what might later be stigmatized as unnecessary force.

As a direct result of the Bristol riots a clear legal ruling was made. It laid down that 'where the danger is pressing and immediate ... and from the circumstances of the case no opportunity is offered of obtaining a requisition from the proper authorities, the *military* subjects of the king, like his civil subjects, not only may, but are bound to do their utmost to prevent the perpetration of outrage.'[17] In spite of this, the military remained understandably reluctant to act without specific instructions from a magistrate.

*   *   *

Other notable Reform Bill riots occurred in Derby, Dudley, Exeter, Nottingham (where the Castle was burned down), Shrewsbury and Worcester. None of these was allowed to get entirely out of hand, and casualties were not numerous. There were serious riots at Merthyr Tydfil in 1831, not directly connected with the Reform Bill. These resulted in twenty-five deaths and the disbandment of the Glamorganshire Yeomanry for 'supposed misconduct'.

Few very serious individual disturbances occurred during the rest of the century, though the Chartist riots in the late 1830s and through the 1840s were numerous and kept regulars and yeomanry more fully engaged than ever before.

Ireland, too, continued to require troops. But when the Chartist unrest first became a serious threat, Ireland was comparatively quiet. Between December 1838 and August 1839, for instance, it was thought safe to bring three cavalry* and three infantry regiments across the Irish Sea to the Northern District of England. When, as from 1843 onwards, disturbances in Ireland again began to compete with those in England, the overall shortage of troops, which was always felt when trouble affected numbers of areas at the same time, became acute. This was partially overcome by the increasing use of railways. 1842 was the first year in which large numbers were moved by rail from the garrisons of southern England to the disturbed areas of the north. 'You send a battalion of 1,000 men from London to Manchester in nine hours;' said the Quartermaster General in 1844; 'that same battalion marching would take seventeen days.'[18] At the same time the growing use and efficiency of steamships made the transference of regiments from the Irish to the English commands a speedy affair. Even in the 1820s the crossing could be made in as little as fourteen hours.[19]

* * *

Sudden concentrations of large numbers of troops in a disturbed area, such as so effectively nipped in the bud any really disastrous riots during the Chartist agitations, created problems of accommodation. The military commanders, no less than the innkeepers, rightly resisted wherever possible the billeting of small detachments in inns. The danger of their being overpowered, or being 'got at', was clear. Yet suitable barracks were not always available. To overcome this the magistrates and richer residents of some manufacturing towns paid for the hire of buildings as temporary barracks. On occasions, nevertheless, perilous dispersal took place. In 1839, Sir Charles Napier complained to the magistrates of Halifax that the cavalry were 'quartered in the very worst and most dangerous manner. Forty-two troopers', he wrote, 'in twenty-one distinct billets. Fifty resolute Chartists might disarm and destroy the whole in ten minutes.'[20]

* * *

* 2nd Dragoon Guards, 1st Royal Dragoons and 8th Hussars.

The task of escorting and guarding men arrested in civil commotions was a major and often dangerous duty for the cavalry. For example, in 1842, a small detachment of the 11th Hussars escorted seventeen prisoners to Elland station for rail transport to Wakefield:

'The prisoners were placed in two horse-drawn omnibuses guarded by soldiers. An attempt was made to rescue them, but this was unsuccessful, and the charges were safely lodged in the train for Wakefield. Now it happened that, just after the two omnibuses arrived at Elland, a third omnibus left the station with a load of ordinary railway passengers who . . . had alighted from the train at Elland. This vehicle proceeded . . . along the road which had just been used by the military escort. When it arrived at Salter Hebble, where the road runs alongside a very steep hill, it was met by a mob of several thousand working men anxious to be avenged on the authorities for the arrest of their comrades. Having ascertained that the omnibus contained only railway passengers, and that none of the officials participating in the escort were inside, the mob was about to grant it a safe passage, when the party of soldiers returning from Elland came up behind it. Immediately the crowd began to hurl enormous stones – some of them weighing as much as 20 lbs – down on to the troops and omnibus. Arrayed on the heights the mob enjoyed a tremendous advantage. Under the impact of the volley of stones the omnibus horses shied, and became entangled with the cavalrymen, three of whom were felled from their steeds and left lying on the ground. A section of the mob rushed down upon the prostrate soldiers, who had been abandoned by their comrades, destroyed their [weapons] and kicked and beat their bodies in a brutal fashion. From this predicament they were rescued by the return of their companions, who loaded with ball and opened fire on the crowd. . . . The incident furnished a striking illustration of the danger of employing troops in small parties.'[21]

* * *

By the early 1850s the police rôle of cavalry had become comparatively unimportant. There were to be occasions in the last half of the nineteenth century, some of which will be described in succeeding volumes, on which both regulars and yeomanry were called to assist the civil power. Their employment then was generally limited, except sometimes in Ireland, to acting as auxiliaries to the local police forces. They were no longer the principal instrument of suppression.

2

(i)

'The Cavalry Spirit' – *the difference between heavy and
light cavalry* – *training: the charge, sabre positions* – *types
of swords*

To be able, with speed, to manoeuvre a number of horsemen into a
well-dressed line; to throw that line at a wavering enemy with shattering rapidity; thus, in an instant, to smash all opposition, imposing
irreversible disintegration, and, finally, to pursue with relentless
vigour: these, in the thinking of the majority of British cavalrymen,
whether heavy or light, were the chief objects of all training. Preparation for the great and glorious moment of truth was virtually
everything.

In most continental armies there was always a more or less pre-
cise division between the respective primary duties of the two
branches of the cavalry, the heavy being reserved in the main for
the charge, and the light for reconnaissance and out-post duties.
But in the British army

'the number of Cavalry', as was stated in the 1844 *Queen's
Regulations*, 'being small in reference to the Amount of Force

annually voted by Parliament, it is of the utmost importance . . . that both the *Heavy* and *Light* Cavalry should be equal to the *Charge in Line*, as well as to the *Duties on Out-Posts*.'[2]

*　　*　　*

It was the general practice for a morning's cavalry drill to end with a charge. In his biography of Captain Louis Nolan, Colonel Moyse-Bartlett describes what it was like:

'The regiment moved off, flanks steady, files dressing to the centre, knee to knee but never touching. [Regulation distance was six inches.] On the command "Trot!" the pace was applied gradually, the line remaining steady. Some 200 yards from the point of impact came the order "Gallop!" and at fifty yards the final command "Charge!" Down came the long line of lances or swords from the "carry" to the "engage". Slightly in advance, the centre of the line entered the opposing formation like a pivot.'[3]

Whether the charge should be delivered in one rank or two was a question which much engaged the minds of military men. The single rank or 'rank entire' school slowly won the day. It was held that the second rank, following closely on the heels of the first, was more likely to confuse it than to bring it useful succour. It became established practice, therefore, for the second line to be kept back some 400 yards as a support, or first reserve, at the disposal and discretion of the commander.

A vital part of training was to learn how to clear the front quickly after a charge so that the supports could have an unimpeded field over which to deliver a second charge as soon as possible after the first, or, alternatively, so that the reserve could advance with speed to the pursuit.

'In training, the charge therefore ended with a double flank retirement in column of troops and the reformation of the first line behind the reserve.'[4]

For offence and defence, once he had entered the mêlée, the trooper was taught some twenty or so sabre positions: 'right guard', 'left guard', seven other 'guards', '1st, 2nd and 3rd points' (or thrusts), the 'parry', and seven 'cuts'. As a general rule, when cutting, men

'A Military Seat on Horseback without Stirrups', 1817. The 'tongs across a wall' (*See p.* 102)

6. 'The Military Seat, as it ought to be', 1853. The 'short stirrup with leg bent' military seat. (*See p.* 102)

7. 'A Recruiting Party', 2nd Life Guards, *c.* 1840's or 1850's

8. The Scots Greys escorting the Lord-Lieutenant of Ireland, 1840

were told to aim at the top of the headstall of the bridle so as to cause the bit to fall from the horse's mouth, thus making it impossible for the enemy horseman to steer his mount. There was always much controversy about the relative merits of pointing and cutting, though of course there was a place for both.

Newly joined young officers had also, of course, to be initiated into the mysteries of cavalry drill. As always the non-commissioned officers were responsible for this. Cornet Anstruther Thomson gives an amusing glimpse of the 'principal drill-sergeant' of the 9th Lancers at work in 1836. He was

> 'a little ugly man, with his chin-strap behind his jaw, but very smart and a capital soldier. In teaching sword exercise he desired us to "thrust the pint (point) well home and *turrn* the *sworrd* to render the wound incurable".'[5]

There were two types of regulation sword for cavalry troopers: one for the heavy and the other for the light regiments. New patterns for both were introduced in 1796 to the specification of Le Marchant. The light cavalry sword, slightly curved and thirty-three inches long, was not unlike the Indian tulwar. It was very well designed for cutting and slashing, but it was bulky and the hilt gave poor protection to the hand. Another disadvantage was the blunting effect of the unlined steel scabbard, a defect which applied to the heavy cavalry pattern too. Captain Nolan advocated wooden scabbards instead of steel ones. These he had seen and admired in use by the Nizam of Hyderabad's irregular horse. They prevented blunting and also made no noise, doing away with 'the necessity of wrapping straw or hay round the scabbards, as now customary when engaged in any service in which an attempt is to be made to surprise an enemy'.[6] They were never adopted in the British service, largely because of looks and their supposed fragility.

The heavy cavalry pattern of sword, which had a broad, straight blade, thirty-five inches long, was a singularly inefficient weapon, being nearly useless for either cutting or thrusting.

In the early 1820s the light cavalry was issued with a new type, with a 'half basket' hilt. It was two and a half inches longer than its predecessor. At first it proved less effective, but in due course modifications brought it up to standard. A new heavy cavalry sword was not issued till the early 1830s. It was slightly curved and an inch longer than the earlier pattern. It proved more efficient than its forerunner, but neither the light nor the heavy type gave full satisfaction. Both were replaced by a superior universal pattern in 1853, just in time for the Crimean War.[7]

'In the charge, it is a matter of indifference what weapon a soldier carries. The chief thing is that he should be well mounted, and that he should bear in mind the unshakable resolution to ride the enemy down with his horse's breast.'

Seidlitz[1]

(ii)

The reintroduction of lancers – types of lance – its value questioned – the lance in India

The drill for lancers differed, of course, from that taught the swordsman. It included 'waves' and points, as well as the 'round parry' and other curiosities.

The siege of Bhurtpore in 1825–6 (see p. 209) was the first occasion for over two hundred years on which the lance was used in action by a British regiment: the 16th Lancers. By the time of the Model Army, the long lance of chivalry, called by Montecuculi 'La Reine des Armes Blanches', had become practically extinct in Europe, though there had been Scottish lancers at Dunbar in 1650 (see p. 34). At the opening of the nineteenth century only the Poles, the Cossacks and the Arabs made any considerable use of the weapon. In 1807, Napoleon introduced a single regiment of Polish 'Lancers of the Vistula' into his army. Impressed by their success, and by that of the Cossacks, he converted nine French dragoon regiments into lancers in 1811. In the same year interest in the arm began to revive amongst British cavalry officers. At Albuera, in May, Polish lancers were first encountered by Wellington's infantry. In September his cavalry fought them for the first time at El Bodon (see p. 52). Three weeks later the adjutant of the 15th Light Dragoons wrote in his journal: 'Cornet Baron Leon (1st Dragoons, King's German Legion) arrived at the regiment for the purpose of instructing us in the Lance Exercise. Ordered fifteen lances to be made with flags. Selected twelve men to practice the Lance Exercise.'[2] In December, 1811, Frederick Ponsonby, the colonel of the 12th Light Dragoons had some lances made in Portsmouth and took them out to Spain. He himself had become proficient with the weapon, and was anxious to show his regiment less how to use it than 'how to attack the [Polish] Lancers with their swords' and to accustom his horses to the flags.[3]

In the same year a Captain Drouville submitted a paper to the Commander-in-Chief which was later published as *On the Formation of British Lancers*.[4] At a levee in the Horse Guards in 1814, Major Reymond Hervey de Montmorency of the 9th Light Dragoons, who had spent three years as a prisoner on parole in Paris, studying amongst other things the training methods of the Polish lancers, presented his *Proposed . . . Exercise and Manoeuvres of the Lance . . . adapted to . . . The British Cavalry*[5] to the Duke of York. This remained the chief textbook upon the subject for many years.

It was probably the limited success of the French 1st *Lanciers* against the 7th Hussars at Genappe on the day before Waterloo (see p. 57), which finally decided the British Army to introduce lancers into the cavalry. The first idea was to attach a lance troop to each regiment in much the same way as riflemen were attached to infantry battalions. Fifty men of the 9th Light Dragoons were selected for training under de Montmorency and Sergeant-Major Robert Cooke, of that regiment, at Hampton Court. They were later reviewed at the first parade of lancers in Britain in modern times. This took place in the Queen's Riding House at Pimlico in April 1816 before an invited audience. It was followed in September by a General Order directing that the 9th, 12th, 16th and 23rd Light Dragoons should be armed with the lance, deprived of their carbines, and designated lancers. The 5th Dragoon Guards, and possibly other 'heavy' regiments, were given the lance in 1817 as an aid to horsemanship in the riding school. Riding drill with lances, wrote an inspecting officer, had 'the effect of making the men very active, and obliging them to be constantly attentive to have their horses in hand, giving them a graceful and active seat on horseback.'[6]

At first, the lance carried by the new lancer regiments was an unwieldy weapon of fifteen or sixteen feet in length, considerably longer, even, than the tilting lance of the sixteenth century; but it was almost immediately reduced by six or seven feet. To it was attached a pennon, in the corner of which was a small Union Jack. The butt was carried in a leather socket attached to the stirrup, and the stave, as in later models, had a loop for the arm. It so happened that at Waterloo, Captain Mercer of the Horse Artillery had acquired a French lance from the field of battle. Later he deposited it in the Rotunda at Woolwich.[7] In 1827, Major Vandeleur of the 12th Lancers, having extracted it from there, showed it to a board of cavalry officers. These considered it 'a weapon infinitely better than that now in use'.[8] It was 9 ft 1 in long and weighed 3 lbs 11 oz, and was finally approved in 1829. The shaft was made of ash, the point and butt of steel. The flag was 2 ft 3 in in length and 1 ft 4 in wide. All these measurements were altered from time to time in the next eighty years or so, but only marginally. Ash was generally super-seded by bamboo in 1877.*

For many years following its introduction, the value of the lance in conjunction with or instead of other weapons, especially the sword, was a matter of impassioned controversy. Numerous ex-periments were carried out. At the Maidstone cavalry depôt, for instance, in 1834, both heavy and light cavalry were equipped on trial with virtually all the possible weapons, each man being burdened with pistol, carbine, sword *and* lance.[9] A captain who was with the 16th Lancers at Bhurtpore condemned the use of the lance in the rear rank. Writing in the early 1850s he said, 'The front rank using the lance, and the rear rank supporting with the sword (the lance being slung on the bridle-arm), is a most formidable array and probably much more so than both ranks using the lance.' Twenty-six years later, Major S. Boulderson of the 17th Lancers, thought 'the best armament for British Cavalry' was 'lance and sword in the front rank, and sword and carbine in the rear rank'.[10] Captain Nolan believed that the only advantage of the lance lay

'in the moral effect produced (particularly on young soldiers), not only by its longer reach, but by the deadly effect of the home thrusts'.[11]

* By 1908, the lance used in British cavalry regiments averaged about 3 lbs 14 oz in weight.
In 1864 it was decreed that the lances in the Bengal Army were to be of bamboo, with a bayonet-shaped head, not less than ten feet long, not more than eleven and a half feet, and the weight not over four pounds. (G.O.C.C., 3 May, 1864, Cardew, 333.)
The selection of bamboos was a matter of great difficulty. They had to be of exactly the right size to fit the sockets of the point and butt, for once the bark is cut or scraped the interior is liable to perish. Further, the canes are affected by a number of diseases which are not easily detected. Hence, on average,

He thought it useless in the mêlée for 'the moment the lancer pulls up and the impulsive power is stopped, that instant the power of the weapon is gone'.[12]

*   *   *

In India the first known lancer regiment is that of the Frenchman, Allard, in the service of Ranjit Singh, early in the 1820s. Though, from their inception, Skinner's, Gardner's and the Rohilla Horse carried some sort of lance or spear, it was not until the 1840s that the lance proper was given to any British native regiments. The 1st Bombay Light Cavalry, for instance, was converted in 1842. None of the *silladar* regiments was officially armed with the lance until after the Mutiny. John Jacob, the great Commandant of the Scinde Irregular Horse, thought the lance useless for Indian light cavalry. 'It may be very showy,' he wrote in the 1840s, 'but out of 500 lancers not half a score will be found really masters of their weapons of war.'[13]

'Good riding and skill in the use of the sword are the fundamental points of all cavalry tactics.'
GENERAL DE BRACK, quoted by Nolan[1]

(iii)

The military seat – basic field movements

The basis of all cavalry training, which usually took the raw recruit not less than two years, was good horsemanship and horsemastership. The teaching of *military* riding was a first essential. It differed in many respects from civil riding. 'Left to his own free natural seat,' wrote Nolan, 'the Englishman beats the world in a ride after hounds and a run across country.' But in the cavalry what was thought of as a 'smarter' seat had long been adopted. 'Our officers look upon their military seat, with the bumping, as part of their equipments, put it

11/12ths of the bamboos sent for approval were discarded. (Sargeaunt, B. E. 'The Progress of the Lance', *Cavalry Journal*, III (1908), 79–80.)

on when they fall in on parade, but wisely discard it at all other times.'[2]
Fig. 5, facing p. 96, (upon which Lord Anglesey, the leading
equestrian arbiter of the day, wrote in 1817, 'Stiff, formal and insecure'), shows the classic 'long stirrup and straight leg' seat, sometimes stigmatised as 'tongs across a wall'. Based largely on Continental
models this 'balance-seat' originated in necessity.

> 'It was indispensable when combatants, sheathed in armour,
> ran a course with lance in rest. The upright seat enabled them
> to carry the weight of the armour with more ease, and the long
> stirrup supported the leg at that point to which the weight of
> the armour pressed it down.'[3]

The opposite to the 'balance-seat' was the 'short stirrup with leg
bent' (Fig. 6, facing p. 96). It was much closer to the natural
seat described by Nolan. From the 1850s onwards the protagonists
of this seat steadily gained ground, adding greatly to the comfort and
security of the military rider. A factor in bringing about this change
was the experience of the two Sikh wars. The irregular horsemen of
the Khalsa, using short stirrups, then proved themselves superior to
the British cavalry riding with the long stirrup, especially in the
mêlée.

Another peculiar skill required of the military rider was the
capacity to manage his mount with one hand, leaving the other free
for his weapons.

*　　*　　*

There were twenty-one basic field movements with which the
cavalryman was required to become conversant. The most important
of these was the ability to ride across country, keeping in line and
maintaining correct spacing. The operational unit was the squadron,
divided into a right and a left troop. Each troop, not including the
trumpeters and farriers, consisted in theory of twenty-four other
ranks. The space between the front and rear ranks into which these
were divided, varied depending on whether the squadron (of which
there were generally either two or three in a regiment), was in 'Order'
(twenty-four feet), 'Close Order' (eight feet), or marching in fours
(four feet). The normal interval between squadrons in line was
twelve yards.

There were numerous ways in which squadrons marched and
manoeuvred, all of them designed to make advancing, retiring and

changes of front speedily effective. Usually the squadron leader and the two troop leaders rode in front of the front rank, while the three junior officers – the serrefiles – rode (accompanied by the trumpeters and farriers) in rear of the rear rank. The squadron sergeant-major generally rode in the centre of the front rank, and the squadron marker behind and near the centre of the rear rank. When a regiment marched as a whole, it often did so in 'Close Column of Squadrons'. This entailed a massing of all the troopers, with their officers on the flanks, and all the trumpeters and farriers in the rear.

'Cavalry ought to be at once the feeler and the feeder of an army.'

Valentine Baker, quoting Nolan[1]

(iv)

Reconnaissance – skirmishing – picquets – vedettes

The emphasis upon the charge and its aftermath obscured what were in reality the more important rôles of cavalry in an age of improving artillery and small arms. These consisted chiefly in reconnaissance, patrolling, skirmishing, and escorting and protecting the rest of the army. The provision of 'eyes and ears' in the field was always a vital task of the mounted branch, but its unglamorous nature ensured that it received little detailed attention by the average cavalry officer. It was given low priority during training although it demanded intelligence and application of a high order.

The regulations provided that when a military column was on the march in war it should be preceded, flanked and closed by cavalry patrols. Riding far in advance of all, taken from the advance guard, was a 'point' consisting of two men. Further back (the distance depending upon the type of country and visibility), came a small patrol, which in turn preceded a larger one. If the advance guard was provided by a three squadron regiment, one of its six troops furnished these forward patrols. In bivouac or camp, picquets formed an encircling guard. Beyond these, just in sight, was a chain of vedettes, each generally consisting of two men. There was a code with which vedettes indicated the type and size of an approaching enemy: circling of both horsemen to the right meant cavalry, and to the left, infantry. When one man circled to the right and the other to the left, the enemy force was a mixed one. The more numerous the enemy, the more speedy was the circling.

In the first half of the nineteenth century the relative importance, from the battle-winning point of view, of the charge and of cavalry's other less glorious functions, was changing. Particularly was this so after the invention in 1823 of the cylindro-conoidal bullet, and the adoption of the percussion cap in 1839. It is notorious, but very understandable, that few cavalrymen relished the need to recognise this unpleasant aspect of modern warfare. Many of them indeed refused, well into the twentieth century, to face it at all.

'To burnish a sword-scabbard until one could see to shave in it was thought more of at Maidstone than dexterity in the use of the sword itself.'

SERGEANT HENDERSON, 15th Hussars[1]

(v)

The Cavalry Depôt – Riding Establishments

In 1773 there were only two regimental riding schools in the United Kingdom. One belonged to the Blues, the other to the Bays. As time went on more were built. The first Cavalry Riding Establishment, serving the arm as a whole, was at Pimlico. Its date and origins are obscure. It was probably founded in the early 1790s. In 1823 it was moved to St John's Wood,[2] and in 1832 to the Cavalry Depôt at Maidstone in Kent, where the accommodation was for many years notoriously inadequate, and conditions were singularly primitive. Here were housed the depôt troops of regiments serving abroad (in the 1840s, six in India and one in South Africa). The non-commissioned officers and men of these troops were engaged in training recruits for their regiments.

The Cavalry Riding Establishment

'Whether a man rode every day, or never crossed a horse until he joined his regiment, was in a great measure', wrote a sergeant of the 15th Hussars, 'dependent upon himself. . . . The paucity of horses [there were only forty or fifty for 400 recruits] rendered it impossible to instruct one-half the recruits in their stable duties.'[3]

The Riding Establishment, on the other hand, which now joined the Depôt, was 'a nursery for riding-masters and rough-riders'.[4]* *Queen's Regulations* laid down that

'In order to give full effect to the approved system of Equitation which has been established throughout the Cavalry Service, the Commanding officers of Regiments are called upon, from time to time, to select certain Non-commissioned Officers and Soldiers, and to send them to the Riding Establishment at Maidstone, for the purpose of being practised in the Equitation Exercises, and of being rendered competent, on returning to their Regiments, to afford instruction, and to maintain the system of uniformity in training both Men and Horses.'

The men were to be unmarried 'and able to read and write. . . . It is expected that every party shall consist of the most exceptional Men and Horses in the Regiment'.[5] There were generally at any given time two men from each regiment making a total of about fifty. A Commandant presided over a staff, of which the chief members were a riding master, usually a major, a rough-riding sergeant-major and six rough-riding sergeants. The Higher Equitation course was very laborious, and there were those, such as Private Pennington of the 11th Hussars,[6] who thought that it was far too formal and stiff, tried to cram too much into too short a time, and was dedicated far too much to the style at the moment in fashion.

* Rough-riders were non-commissioned officers who by virtue of their excellent horsemanship were assigned as assistants to the regimental riding master. The basic qualification was the capacity to ride unbroken (rough) horses.

'The rider must live only for his horse, which is
his legs, his safety, his honour and his reward.'
An old cavalry soldier, c. 1800[1]

(vi)

*Types of horses – remount problems – Government studs in
India – stallions, geldings or mares? – the veterinary
service – farriers – docking and nicking – shoeing – sore
backs – the saddle*

An overriding wish of cavalrymen through the ages has been that
their horses should be large and swift enough to sweep away all
opposition in one shattering rush. But other considerations have always tempered this prime desire. Chief among these is stamina,
particularly the ability to keep going on short rations.

It is generally agreed that the finest horses in the world for cavalry,
and much else, are the English Thoroughbreds. These were developed
from the Arab stallions and mares imported by James I and Charles I,
and upon which Charles II laid the foundations for the present breed.

The Kehilans, as they were called in Arabia, are believed to have
been bred in the desert for over 5,000 years. They had always been
kept pure, and their pedigrees meticulously recorded. In due course,
by careful selection and further importations (especially by William
III), the English Thoroughbreds, inheriting the Arab's staying
power, their noble looks and 'kindness of disposition',[2] became
speedier and larger than their progenitors – and the envy of the
world. 'No horse', wrote Captain Louis Nolan in 1853, 'can compare with the English, – no horse is more easily broken in to anything and everything, – and there is no quality in which the English
horse does not excel, no performance in which he cannot beat all
competition.'[3]

In the last three decades of the eighteenth century a new and increasingly popular method of fox hunting came into being in England. Hounds were then introduced that were bred to run at great
speed. To keep up with them a new type of hunter was required. It
had to be capable of carrying heavy men over difficult fences at very
nearly the pace of a racehorse.

Hunters of this type, possessing a large proportion of thorough-
bred blood, gradually became the chief mounts of the British cavalry
in the nineteenth century. Their average height in 1800 was about

fourteen hands, three inches. A century later it had risen to fifteen hands, two and a half inches.* The mean weight of such a cavalry horse was about 1,000 lbs, and it was meant to be able to carry one fifth of that weight.[4]

As a general rule, experience on campaign showed that the larger the horse, the less it could stand fatigue, exposure and privation. On the other hand when it came to delivering or receiving a charge, size was an important factor. Though obviously big, heavy men needed larger mounts than smaller men, there was no very clear distinction between the types of horse in the heavy and light regiments. Big horses were often to be found in light regiments, but the opposite was less often true. 'We have no real light cavalry in the British service', wrote Valentine Baker in 1858.[5]

The normal daily ration in barracks at home consisted of twelve lbs of hay, ten of corn and eight of straw. On the line of march it was adjusted to eighteen lbs of hay and only eight lbs of corn. In cool weather a horse drinks about five gallons of water a day. In hot weather its demands grow speedily.

The chief disadvantages of the hunter compared with lesser breeds were sensitivity to extreme changes of climate, and dependence upon regular and ample forage supply. Time and again, though, it proved itself superior in other respects to the types employed by the great continental armies. In a flying approach march followed by a charge, for instance, the hunter type had no equal.

*   *   *

The average length of life of a horse, in normal conditions, is little more than 20 years. Taking into account the years of infancy, training and senility, and discounting disease and war casualties, not much more than ten to twelve years of use could be got out of each animal. The provision of remounts, therefore, was a never-ending preoccupation of officers commanding cavalry regiments.

In the continental armies and in India, Government studs provided remounts. In Britain, typically, this form of state control was always

* Up to the beginning of the seventeenth century, the usual type of cavalry horse had been the 'Great' or 'Black' horse, which stood over sixteen hands.

William III imported large numbers of blacks, and for many years, except in the Bays and the Greys, black was considered the correct colour for the British cavalry.

One hand = four inches. The height of a horse is measured from the bottom of the hoof to the top of the withers.

disliked. In peacetime it was expensive. Further, as Major Tylden writes in his classic *Horses and Saddlery*, the finest book on the subject produced in the twentieth century,

'The remount market was always well liked by the large number of people who bred horses, especially in Ireland. Prices, if not high, were satisfactory, and men breeding for the better class markets always had a number of young horses who were just not good enough for the purpose, but would sell well enough as remounts. The result was that in peace we could mount the Army in the open market and always did so.'[6]

The normal practice was for an officer to be detailed to buy three-year-olds in the open market, generally at horse fairs. Since most dealers and private individuals, for various reasons, preferred to buy four-year-olds, army buyers, at any rate in peacetime, often had first choice. Nevertheless there was much competition at various times from the agents of the continental armies buying for their national studs at inflated prices. There was a particularly dangerous drain in this respect from the export of really good stallions and mares for breeding purposes. The worst aspect of the private enterprise system was the sudden and enormous increase in prices once speedy wartime expansion became necessary.

*   *   *

In India as early as 1794 the Honourable East India Company had established a Stud Department. Sixteen years later what became the Remount Department was opened, and became responsible for all purchasing. The chief difficulties in India were the small size and intractability of the thirteen or so local breeds, the little interest taken in horse breeding by most Indians, and the expense of running the studs. This last was largely due

'to so much of the science of crossing local mares with imported stallions being at first mainly guess-work. The first thing that a British officer had to do when posted to Indian Cavalry was to disabuse himself of nearly all he had learnt about remounts in the U.K.'[7]

In 1808, William Moorcroft, a distinguished civilian veterinary surgeon, gave up a lucrative practice in London to become Super-intendent of Studs in India. He trained a medical man to help him produce a good all-round mount. This he was on the point of achieving when he was murdered on a horse-buying expedition near Bokhara in 1825. Thereafter, for many years the studs reverted to

'the control of their original incompetent superintendents, inexperienced infantry and cavalry officers. . . . The product', says the historian of the Royal Army Veterinary Corps, 'was the laughing-stock of the Army and the despair of the East India Company. . . . From first to last the Studs cost millions; the mismanagement was staggering and unbelievable.'[8]

Pure Arabs were bought between 1810 and 1813 by Lieutenant St J. Blacker, 1st Madras Light Cavalry, to the number of 584, of which 402 were picked for the cavalry. These were described as '14.2 high, short limbed, boney, full chested, broad across the loins, round sided and deep barrelled.'[9] Later on, other types were imported: Persians, with the Arab's qualities, but lacking its pure breeding (according to Valentine Baker, 'valuable, hardy and temperate troopers'); Gulf Arabs, a cross between Persian and Arab; 'Turcomans'; 'Walers' from the Colony of New South Wales, said to be inferior to the English horse only in stamina, and the Cape Horse from the Cape of Good Hope. This last was not indigenous to South Africa. It was the result of crossing the eastern blood which had arrived there in the eighteenth century, with English Thoroughbreds imported in the early years of the nineteenth century. It was tall, (averaging some fifteen hands), and especially hardy and tough. 'You could not kill him with a hatchet', wrote General Rimington in 1904. He was the product of

'the survival of the fittest, for often a foal has to travel long distances when only a few days old. . . . Those who survive have to put up with great changes of temperature, and winter feed of any quality was often not available for the mares or stock.'[10]

Cape Horses were often long-lived, sometimes giving fourteen years' service before being cast.

Writing after the loss of horses which took place in the First Afghan War (see p. 217), Outram stated that it was a fact

'now fully proved and admitted by all parties that the Arab and Persian horses stand their work and privations infinitely better than stud and country-breds. The latter, although younger, stronger and in far better condition at starting, have invariably been the first to give in, while they seldom rallied afterwards. A few Cape horses lately imported to the Bombay Army have also proved themselves superior to our stud-breds.'[11]

When the 10th Hussars went to India in 1847, there was no regiment returning home, as was usual, whose horses they could take over. The first remounts given to them were 150 Arabs and Persians and 50 Cape horses. This shows what was probably the general proportion at that date. Most of the Arabs in this case were entires, that is ungelded males, which, as always, because of their tendency to fight, were a menace in stable and horse line.

For many decades the burning question as to whether stallions, geldings or mares were best for cavalry, formed an important part of military controversy. Up to the middle of the century entires were more generally used for military purposes. They were supposed to possess greater stamina than their castrated brethren, until, in the 1850s, more or less scientific tests 'proved' that there were no differences in this respect. They were certainly much better looking and probably more courageous. For such reasons their protagonists discounted their disadvantages. These included greater expense to feed, a higher accident rate, and the debarring of the employment of mares in their vicinity. It is no surprise to learn that with many of the officers and most of the men they were very unpopular.

*   *   *

The health of horses was in the hands of the Veterinary Surgeon who presided over the regimental Farrier Major (equivalent in rank to sergeant) and the Troop Farrier and Assistant Farriers. Not until the first decade of the century was much in the way of professionalism introduced into the veterinary arm. In 1796 a Board of General Officers had reported that the heavy loss of horses in the cavalry sprang from 'the total ignorance of those who have at present the medical care of them'.[12] It recommended that a qualified man taken from the civilian Royal Veterinary College at Camden Town* should be attached to each cavalry regiment. This recommendation was gradually put into effect, but the majority of veterinary surgeons re-

* This had been founded in 1791. 'The importance . . . to the mounted corps of the Army cannot be exaggerated. Prior to this according to Sir Walter Gilbey, "the English veterinary practitioners had followed principles which were hardly free from the taint of witchcraft and sorcery".' (Tylden, 16.)

mained for some years mere grooms and farriers from civil life, without any specialised training. Indeed the first Principal Veterinary Surgeon to the Cavalry, Edward Coleman (who held the post, as a civilian, for forty-three years) believed that men with medical training made the worst veterinary surgeons, and that the sons of farriers made the best!

This attitude towards the regimental veterinary officer endured for many years. His treatment was radically different from that accorded to medical officers. He was *classed* as a cornet for the first ten years of his service, and only after twenty years could he be classed as a captain. He was put on a par with these ranks 'for the purpose of allotting quarters and for no other purpose'.[13] By contrast, an Assistant Regimental Surgeon became a properly commissioned lieutenant on appointment. The writer of an article in *The Veterinarian* of 1830 had no hesitation in stating that 'the tag, rag and bob-tail set' of men in the regimental veterinary service were not worthy of rank.[14] If this view of army 'vets' was commonly held by civilians of the profession, it is little wonder that cavalry officers looked down on them. The veterinary surgeon of the 1st Life Guards, writing in 1828, says that 'even when the Veterinary Surgeon is a gentleman by extraction, education and bearing, he mingles with the officers of the regiment only under painful restrictions'.[15]

Sidney Herbert, when he became Secretary at War in 1845 made great efforts to improve the material if not the social lot of the veterinary surgeon, especially his pay. He is, wrote Herbert, 'a most valuable class of man, greatly improved in attainments of later years, but having had no increased advantage whatever. The number, however, is small, being limited to the small number of cavalry regiments.'[16] Herbert managed to get small increases in retired pay. Yet this remained much less than that of paymasters and regimental surgeons. After thirty years' service, the veterinary surgeon received 12s. a day, whereas his fellow regimental staff officers received 15s. For many years this sort of invidious distinction persisted. In 1846, for example, the widow of Mr Bird, the veterinary surgeon of the 4th Light Dragoons, 'with the relative rank of Captain after more than thirty years' meritorious service' received £30 a year, 'or £6 less than is awarded the widow of a Cornet or Quatermaster'.[17]

The troop farrier's dress (unlike that of the trumpeters whose uniform was elaborate and gay) was very plain, even sombre. His saddlecloth bore upon it a cross hammer and pincers. In a wallet, known as a 'churn', were kept spare horseshoes and nails, as well as, up to 1852, 'a case of phlemes [lancets], a bleeding stick, drenching horn, clyster pipe [an injection syringe] and two bandages'.[18] He bore no arms except an axe, which was used for destroying wounded horses. Amongst his many duties was the correct numbering of the horses. Early in the century the numbers were cut in the hair. Later on they were branded on the hoof. The docking of tails (which deprived the horse of its natural fly-whisk), as well as the even crueller practice of nicking, both of which were abandoned after 1840, were operations habitually performed by the farriers. Nicking involved the making of an incision at the root of the tail so as to make the horse carry it higher.

Shoeing was perhaps the farrier's most vital task. *Queen's Regulations* laid down, in exceptionally bad English, that he was

'carefully to examine each foot of every horse at least twice a week; when broken nails are to be replaced, the clenches of the nails fresh turned when necessary, and the hoof between them and the shoe lightly rasped and made smooth. . . . The Farriers are held responsible for every deficiency in regard to shoeing reported to them is promptly attended to'.[19]

The life of a horseshoe was reckoned to be about a month in ordinary conditions. On average good hind leg shoes would last for between 175 and 250 miles of travelling on the roads of the day. The supply of sufficient horseshoes and nails was a major problem for the mounted branches of the army at all times. A few spare shoes were generally carried on each man's saddle, and the forge carts carried reserves, but the weights involved were a serious consideration

'and though horseshoes', as Tylden has pointed out, 'might be captured from a retreating enemy, or either shoes or suitable iron requisitioned in the country where operations were taking place, the main dependence was on supplies carried with the force itself'.[20]

Another of the farriers' duties for many years was the bleeding of their charges. This practice was regularly performed in health as well as in illness, it being believed that the drawing off of blood contributed to the maintenance of general robustness.

From 1818 onwards the regimental veterinary surgeon was re-

quired to make a daily report of sick and lame horses to the commanding officer, based on information supplied by the troop farriers.

The earliest exact statistics about the health of cavalry horses were
published in 1838. They showed that in one heavy cavalry regiment
on the Home establishment (probably the Inniskillings), 2.8 per cent
of the horses died over an eight-year period (1830–7) and that
8.3 per cent were cast. Pulmonary trouble was the chief cause of
death. There were only six cases of glanders and three of farcy.*
22 of the 158 horses cast had gone blind.[21]

The commonest of all the minor complaints, indeed the chief
bogey of the cavalryman, was the sore back. This was caused, of
course, by the rubbing of the saddle. The military saddle differed
from the civilian one in the need to keep the heavy weight of a fully-
accoutred cavalryman and all his incidental equipment clear of the
animal's spine. To this end it was built upon a frame or 'tree',

> 'which consisted of two arches or forks, one to fit over the
> withers and the other over the back, joined by pieces of wood
> called sideboards, shaped to fit the horse'.[22]

So as to minimise sore backs, pads were provided beneath these side-
boards. The whole construction was set upon a blanket folded a
number of times over the back. Numerous and diverse were the
patterns of saddle tried from time to time, but the basic principles
always remained much the same.

*   *   *

In India the veterinary service of the army was far behind that at
home. In 1832, for example, not a single veterinary surgeon had
been seen inside any of the Company's studs for six years. The medical care of cavalry horses was almost entirely in the hands of native
practitioners. In 1821 the experiment of training half-caste 'Assistant
Apothecaries' as 'Sub-Assistant Veterinary Surgeons' was tried in the
Bengal army. It failed. Five years later the first veterinary officer
from home joined the Company's service. Not until 1827 were
veterinary surgeons sent out regularly from England. In 1832 there
were thirty-one of them. The first Principal Veterinary Officer was
not appointed till the 1860s.

* Glanders is a contagious disease of horses, asses, mules, etc., caused by
Bacillus Mallei. Symptoms include inflammation of the mucous membranes,
especially of the nose, with a discharge of sticky matter, and hardening of the
glands of the lower jaw. Farcy is a similar disease, associated with ulcerating
enlargements upon the head and legs.

3

'The worse the man, the better the soldier.'
'There are no bad soldiers but only bad officers.'
Attributed to Napoleon

(i)

Types and classes of the rank and file – illiteracy

During the first half of the nineteenth century, at a rough estimate, two out of every three men who joined the ranks of the army were illiterate. The first serious analysis of literacy was made in 1858. It showed that one-fifth of the troops could neither read nor write, and that another fifth could read but not write. Only five per cent were credited with 'a superior degree of education'.[1] As late as 1863, a cavalry recruit found himself in a barrack-room of fifteen men, 'not one of whom could write, and only one could read'.[2]* There are therefore few first-hand accounts of what life was like in the ranks. These few, being written by men of comparatively high attainments, are seldom truly representative.

* In the 1840s, 41 out of every 100 men and women in England, according to the Registrar-General's returns, were unable to fix their signature to the marriage registers.
      Until 1928, it was still considered necessary to teach the soldier the penal sections of the Army Act by reading them aloud, in full, four times a year. This may, of course, have been due more to the innate conservatism of the authorities than to the number of illiterate men. (Whyte, 16.)

A further difficulty in arriving at the truth is that some historians tend to overcolour the disagreeable side of life in the ranks, while others generalise, treating the army as a whole. In fact, conditions in the various branches of the service varied considerably. For instance, the quality and the standard of living of the men in the cavalry were considerably higher than those in the infantry. Moreover, the traditions of individual regiments, and the characters and riches of their commanding officers, produced further variations.

An infantry staff-sergeant, writing in 1846, compiled a list of reasons for which men entered the army at that date:

'1. Indigent. – Embracing labourers and mechanics
   out of employ, who merely seek for support   80 in 120
2. Indigent. – Respectable persons induced by misfortune or imprudence   2 in 120
3. Idle. – Who consider a soldier's life an easy one   16 in 120
4. Bad characters. – Who fall back upon the army as
   a last resource   8 in 120
5. Criminals. – Who seek to escape from the consequences of their offences   1 in 120
6. Perverse sons. – Who seek to grieve their parents   2 in 120
7. Discontented and restless   8 in 120
8. Ambitious   1 in 120
9. Others   2 in 120.'[3]

Wellington is recorded as saying that men enlisted 'from having got bastard children, some for minor offences, many more for drink'.[4]* Some doubtless did, but the chief inducement, as the first category of the staff-sergeant's list shows, was some sort of security. In 1843, for example, a man of superior stamp, son of a turner, enlisted in the 7th Dragoon Guards mainly, it appears, because his father's business was declining, and on account of his own consequent inability to find a job. Amongst those who joined with him were a tramp 'enlisted in a police-court by special authority'; a prisoner recently discharged after a year's sentence, and 'two young gentlemen who had held good positions in a city firm, but the said firm being rather too slow for the fast notions of the gentlemen in question, they made up their minds to have a spree and together enlist'. There were also 'two clerks, both of whom had lost their

* Adding, which is often forgotten: 'It really is wonderful that we should have made them the fine fellows they are.'

character', and a young son of 'the reputed owner of several steamboats . . . Everyone seemed to pity him, he seemed so very simple. In short, in voice and manner he was more like a young girl, which caused him to be named by one of the party, "Susan".'[5]

* * *

Life for the lowest classes in the Britain of the first half of the nineteenth century, especially those slaving in the sub-human conditions of the industrial districts, was often so hard that the security offered by the army must have seemed comparatively attractive. Food, shelter and regular wages, received in whatever harsh circumstances, were preferable to unemployment and starvation. This was particularly true immediately after Waterloo, for the distress following twenty-two years of expensive war was widespread alike in town and country.

Generally speaking, there can be little doubt that much of the scum of urban Britain found its way into the ranks, especially of the infantry. The fact that all debts under £30 were remitted on enlistment certainly encouraged dishonest men to join the army so as to defraud their creditors.[6]* Nevertheless surprisingly large numbers of recruits, especially for the cavalry, were respectable, quiet country lads. In 1831, for instance, two young Scottish labourers found work in an Edinburgh market garden, intending to stay a year or two

> 'for the chance of getting situations as journey men in some nobleman's establishment, but seeing the melancholy prospect before them,' to use the words of a comrade, 'they went out at the dinner hour of their first day there, went direct to the High-street . . ., found a recruiting party of the Scots Greys, and enlisted as soldiers. The sight of the bothy suggested that they might be better lodged, paid, and fed in a barrack-room, while it was hardly possible for them to be worse lodged than there.'

Another labourer, one who had had some schooling, saw six of his friends leave agricultural employment to join the same regiment, because the wages were so low and the seasonal nature of their jobs made them liable to unemployment at any time. He himself, who had been 'harbour building at 11s. a week', left that work because most of his fellow workers

* The Mutiny Act clause providing exemption from arrest for debt to a limit of £30 was not repealed until the Army Act of 1955.

'were the very *débris* of civilized mankind . . . some of whom were literally without a shirt, and without tools, when they came; who borrowed tools, borrowed shirts, earned 18s. a week, and drank it all in whisky, week after week, for months together. . . . We had quarry men and labourers . . . with whom it was impossible to work without wasting some part of our wages in whisky.'

This led his comrades 'to leave the works to be soldiers; other employment could not be obtained, and any change seemed better than killing toil at the shore, the payment of which was but the means of getting more drink'.[7]

'British soldiers . . . are, generally, I think, a happy and joyous band.'

SIR CHARLES NAPIER in 1851[1]

(ii)

Rank and file: bounty – free issue

The private soldier was enticed into the army by an initial bribe. This was known euphemistically as 'bounty'. It varied in amount depending upon the exigencies of the period. At the beginning of the Revolutionary War with France, for instance, when orders went out that the ranks of regiments were to be filled up urgently, the bounty given a cavalry recruit was £14 14s. od. Robert Long, who became a general of note in the Peninsular War, was the subaltern in charge of a recruiting party of the 1st Dragoon Guards in 1793. He received £5 for each man recruited, out of which sum the recruit received £2 18s. od. immediately.[2] It is never easy to assess exactly what sums were paid to whom. In 1814, for example, the 'levy money' was £19 12s. od. for the cavalry and £23 for the infantry: an indication of the difficulty in filling the ranks after so many years of war. Levy money included as well as the bounty 'the contingent expenses and encouragement to the Bringers etc. etc.'. As soon as peace came the bounty was reduced to £5 4s. od. for the cavalry (£6 6s. od. for the infantry).[3]

From his bounty, the newly enlisted man soon discovered that he was compelled to buy his kit. It seldom, in fact, covered the cost. In the early 1830s for example, a recruit in the Scots Greys received £2 12s. 6d. as bounty. Of this he was given in actual cash only 10s. The outfit which he was obliged to buy cost him altogether over £5. His free issue consisted of one pair of cloth overalls (though he required two), one stable jacket and a dress coat annually. He was also allowed 6s. a year for boots, 3s. for gloves, and a new cloak every six years. Among the items for which he had to pay were:

'a forage cap, a leather stock, four linen shirts, two flannel waistcoats, two pairs of flannel drawers, four pairs of worsted socks, two pairs of gloves, a pair of gauntlets (gloves reaching to the elbows), a curry comb and brushes, a horse's mane comb, sponges, soap, bath brick, save-all, with knife, fork, spoon, razor, comb, shaving tackle, two towels, turn-screw, picker (for horses' feet), button stick, button brush, rot-stone to clean buttons, boot brushes, blacking, clothes brush, brush bag, horse's nose bag, corn sack, horse cloth (the cover for the stable); account book with printed regulations, saddle bags, and two pairs of straps for overalls (trousers)'.[4]

In 1819, the necessaries which a trooper of the 18th Light Dragoons was required to buy fell into twenty-eight categories. They cost him £5 16s. 9d.

	£	s.	d.		£	s.	d.
'Flannel drawers		5	11¼	Curry comb and brush		4	0
Flannel waistcoat		7	5¼	Mane comb and sponge			8½
Shirts		7	5	Water sponge, per oz.		2	2¼
Worsted stockings		2	6	Horse picker			1½
Stable trousers		7	9	Turnscrew and worm		1	0
Forage cap		2	6	Corn bag		1	6
Stock and clasp		2	0	Oil tin		1	0
Shoes		8	0	Scissors		1	6
Boots		18	0	Black ball			10
Gloves		1	8	Valise		12	6
Hair comb			6	Saddle blanket		18	11¼
Razor		1	3	Braces		2	6
Shaving box and brush		1	3	Night cap		1	8
Shoe brush			11				
Cloth brush		1	2		[5	16	9]'[5]

In the 1840s a trooper's bounty came to £6 17s. 6d. while what he had to buy with it cost £8 3s. 7½d.[6] The difference he had to borrow, probably from his officer. Out of his basic pay he then repaid his debt by instalments.

'For a soldier I listed, to grow great in fame, and be shot at for sixpence a day.'
CHARLES DIBDIN (1745–1814), *Charity*[1]

(iii)

Rank and file: pay – stoppages – 'clearings' – desertion – enlistment for life – limited service – wilful maiming – 'bringers' – taking the shilling

For seventy years from 1797, the soldier's basic pay remained at 1s. a day for infantrymen and 1s. 2d. for cavalrymen. In 1800, 1d. a day 'beer-money' had been granted, though recruits did not receive it until after a certain period. This replaced an earlier free issue of 'small beer'. Theoretically, a minimum of 4s. pay a week was guaranteed by the State, but it was not until 1847 that it was laid down that no soldier was to receive, whatever the circumstances, less than 1d. a day in actual cash. The numerous stoppages from pay included the real price, up to 6d., of his bread and meat ration.

Other deductions included a variable sum, known as 'clearings', for maintenance of necessaries and for washing, something for barrack damages, and at one time 1d. a week each for the regimental surgeon and agent. A cavalryman had also to find ½d. a week for the riding master, while the horses were at grass. There were further stoppages exacted when men went overseas, such as the cost of whatever small amount of tropical kit was thought necessary.*

* Since 1825 Bibles and Prayer Books were given at the public expense to any soldiers who could read, and who expressed a wish to have them. These were provided by the Naval and Military Bible Society which had been founded

All this left the British soldier with very little indeed. Nevertheless, for some years after 1815, his pay was roughly double that of a French or Prussian soldier. In 1836, the Poor Law Commission had declared the soldier to be ill-paid compared with any other class. This was probably so. In 1832, for instance, the average weekly wage of an agricultural labourer was about 12s. and that of an artisan 33s., while the cavalryman received only 8s. 9d.[2] Trooper Henderson of the 15th Hussars found in the 1840s that in India he was

'better off as regards pay, by reason of the extreme cheapness of everything in that country. . . . I am quite sure that no skilled mechanic in England earning two pounds per week at his craft, having a wife and three children to support, is near so well off as a private soldier of a Queen's regiment quartered in Bangalore barracks was in my time – I mean the married men; the great advantage of the matter being that family affairs as to expense were in India in directly an inverse ratio to what they are in England. The larger the family in India, the more money there was in proportion to support it, which is not quite the case at home.'[3]

*   *   *

Since the recruit was seldom given any indication of the true pay situation when he attested, it is little wonder that men constantly deserted soon after joining the colours. 'I am sorry', wrote the Duke of Cumberland, as Honorary Colonel of the 15th Hussars, to the lieutenant-colonel, in 1826,

'you are not as successful as you could wish as to the Recruiting and Remounting of the Regiment, but actually it is better to be *slow* and *sure* than take bad men or horses, especially the *latter*,

in 1780. The Horse Guards Circular letter authorizing this free issue went on to say:

'Each Man who is found, upon the usual periodical examination of his Necessaries to have lost or disposed of his Books, shall be again provided from the Depot of Bibles, Testaments, &c., at his own expense; and Commanding Officers of Corps will address to the Chaplain-General a Return every Six Months of such deficiencies.' (*Addenda to the General Regulations and Orders for the Army.... Jan 1822 to Jan 1830*, 1830, 472–4.)

In 1844 an order was published which allowed the soldier to keep his Bible and Prayer Book when he left the army. Perry, Capt. A. L. 'Gunners and the Bible', *The Gunner*, May, 1961, 104.

as they remain, while the others you are sure of getting rid of by *Desertion!*'[4]

It was not uncommon for a man to desert as soon as he had received his bounty, and then to re-enlist in another regiment so as to obtain a fresh bounty. One man was known to have rejoined eighteen times before he was tried and hanged. To put a stop to this practice a soldier who deserted was sometimes sentenced by court-martial to be indelibly marked with the letter 'D'. If an incorrigibly 'bad character' was sentenced to be discharged (which was a very rare occurrence) he might be marked with the letters 'B.C.'. This humiliating branding was not abolished until the Cardwell Reforms of 1870.

Further, though for long periods of the nineteenth century men could choose between limited service and enlistment for life, most of them failed to resist the temptation of an increased bounty which committed the taker to unlimited service. The bounty rates for limited service recruits were generally two-thirds of those for unlimited service. The reforms brought in by William Windham when he became Secretary at War in 1806 included the introduction of three periods of limited service: in the cavalry, ten years, seven years and seven years, making a total of twenty-four.

Two years later a clause was added to the Mutiny Act to permit men to enlist, once again, for life. For limited service the bounty was, at that date, £11 11s. 0d., while for unlimited service it was £16 16s. 0d. The vast majority of recruits opted for unlimited service. For instance, between 1817 and 1828, only eighteen out of every thousand recruits in the London district engaged for limited service. In Ireland the figure was lower, in Scotland higher. In 1829 limited enlistments were abolished. In 1847 the tables were turned and enlistment for life was abolished once and for all. For twenty years from that date the maximum length of engagement in the first instance was limited to twelve years for the cavalry (ten for the infantry). Re-enlistment was permitted for a further twelve years (eleven for the infantry).[5]

Some indication of how unattractive conditions in the army could be, at any rate before the reforms of the 1870s, is given by the numerous instances of self-maiming and crime committed as a means to a discharge. Such offences were treated with great harshness.

'When men maim themselves,' said Lord Hardinge in 1836, 'or commit crimes . . . to obtain their discharge, and even to become convicts, as was the case in New South Wales a few years ago, the men were ordered to remain to perform the duties of scavengers to the rest of the Regiment, according to the old custom of the Service. . . . A Commanding Officer lately complained that he had six or seven of these maimed men, who were a dead weight and disgrace; but the example is so important, that the Commander-in-Chief has, I understand, not given way, but has directed the Commanding Officer to keep them as long as they live in the sight of the Regiment as a warning to others to avoid the same fate.'

Cases of wilful maiming and 'of tampering with the eyes' so as to procure a discharge were still known as late as 1863.[6]

*   *   *

For each man a recruiter or 'bringer' could inveigle into 'taking the shilling' he received a certain sum known as 'bringing money'. If the recruit deserted within three months of enlisting, the recruiter's fee was not paid.[7] Physical fitness was virtually the only qualification called for. Whether a man was a criminal or a lunatic mattered nothing to the recruiter. Robert Long's party was told to avoid any man with 'fits, rupture, broken bones, sore legs, scalded head, blear eyes or running sores'. He was instructed that only Protestants and natives of Great Britain could be considered as recruits.*Apprentices, seamen, marines, 'colliers, stragglers or vagrants' were disallowed. Within these limits 'any fine boy' over sixteen (but no man over thirty), was eligible, so long as he was 'perfectly straight, well-featured, in every way well-made, and not heavy limbed'.[8]

A detailed account of an enlistment in a cavalry regiment has been left by Trooper William Lucas. His father, who had been discharged from the Grenadier Guards on account of a rupture with a pension of 6d. a day, tried to discourage him from joining up, saying that it would break his mother's heart. Undeterred, William, who in 1845 aged fifteen had been 'a footman or page', soon tired of that occupation, got a job on the railway which he found equally uncongenial and determined to enlist at the first opportunity. This came the following year. 'My mate that I used to work with,' he wrote in an un-

---

* Until an Act of 1837, it was assumed that the Crown had no power to enlist foreigners. By that Act such power was given, so long as the number serving together did not exceed one in every fifty native-born soldiers. No foreigner was permitted to hold a commission.

published memoir many years later, 'happening to see one of the Inniskilling Dragoons . . . told him about me wanting to enlist and made an appointment for us to meet the next night . . . which we did at the Lord Nelson Public House, St. Pancras Church New Road. . . . I was very well satisfied with myself as I found that the Regiment was in Ireland, and I intended enlisting and getting away before my parents knew anything about it.'

Next day he was taken to Charles Street, Westminster,

'where a recruiting party belonging to the Regiment was billeted at the Public House called the Ship. On our arrival there, I was at once introduced to the Sergeant and Corporal, who formed the party, as a young man who aspired to Military fame. The Sergeant was a jolly looking old Soldier standing over six feet high and I daresay about 14 stone weight. The Corporal was a very fine smart looking soldier but very slight and tall. As it was a wet morning, the room was full of soldiers of different Corps, most of them drinking and smoking away with all their might. As soon as I sat down Gin was called for, but it being early in the morning I did not care about having any of it then. I was then taken up stairs to be measured by the Corporal, but I was a quarter of an inch too short, he said, being only 5 feet seven inches and a quarter, the standard being 5 feet 7 and a half.* But the Sergeant said he would make that alright if I was determined to enlist; but I will say that for him, he gave me every chance, as he gave me a very good description of a Soldier's life, but when he found I was fully bent on going, he enlisted me to serve Her Majesty in the 6th or Inniskilling Dragoons until I was legally discharged. Of course the Enlisting shilling was to be spent, which was soon done by me calling for a half pint of Gin at once. . . .†

'Next morning after Breakfast I paraded myself at the

* Lucas's younger brother, however, who followed him into the army a few years later, was not accepted for the Inniskillings because he was too tall. He therefore joined the Royal Horse Guards.

† Between 'taking the shilling' and being attested, the recruit could procure his release by payment of what was known as 'smart-money' to the recruiter. In the 1840s this amounted to £1. At that time about four per cent of recruits who enlisted into the East India Company's service in London paid 'smart-money'. Marshall was informed 'that from about fifteen to twenty per cent in Scotland obtain relief from enlistment in this way, 'from which it may be inferred that in that part of the Kingdom, recruits do not generally belong to a very destitute class'. (Marshall, 109.)

Sergeant's quarters, and received my day's pay, viz. 1 shilling, after which I saw the recruiting Parties on Parade in full dress and was very well pleased. That night I had to remain at the Sergeant's quarters to sleep as I was to be sworn in on the following morning, and had to remain in bed till about 10 o'clock to grow the quarter of an inch that I was short. I got up washed and dressed myself and was taken to the officer and was measured again and found to be the exact height. I was then sworn in by a Magistrate, having been previously inspected by the Doctor, and received 7s. 6d. cash as part of my bounty.'

After a few days' leave, during which his father offered to buy him out, and his 'dear Mother and Sister were in a great way about me at home, but no more than my Brother George who sobbed and cried like a young girl', he embarked on a steamer at London Bridge for the voyage to Dublin. 'On arriving on board I was given over to a staff sergeant, who served me out with an old great coat, and told me to make myself at home on deck, as that was where we had to stop until we arrived in Dublin.' Also on board were some thirty recruits for various regiments serving in Ireland, 'most of them being very nearly naked and half starved by the looks of them. . . . They appeared very rough characters.' In the Beggar's Bush recruiting dêpot near Dublin,* the recruits 'were some 10 times as bad, the most of them without a shirt to their backs, some with a Mariners old coat on, and some with an Artilleryman's. . . . I began to wish myself back again, if such were to be my companions always.' However, the men for his own regiment, who all came from the town of Enniskillen, he found 'very respectable'. He was glad to leave the depôt 'as there was nothing but fighting and quarrelling all the day long'.

On reaching the regimental barracks after some days' marching,

'the old staff sergeant contrived to ease our pockets of a little

---

* One of the first operations performed upon recruits upon entering a depôt was the close cropping of their heads. This system 'has been adopted', wrote an infantry recruit, 'in order that recruits may, like barbers' shops, be known by their *bare poles*, should they desert, or attempt to quit the barracks before being clothed in uniform.' (MacMullen, 14.)

Until 1804, the very reverse had been the case. Long hair drawn back to form a queue was obligatory. The time consumed in greasing and powdering was immense, and the uncleanliness engendered revolting. Sir Walter Scott described the soldier's hair of those days as 'a Hottentot head-dress of tallow and flour'. ('Character of the Duke of York', *Annual Register*, 1827, 462.)

spare cash, as he said it was always the rule to make [him] a
present on reaching the Regiment. . . . In about a fortnight I
got my Regimentals, and was sent to Riding School to learn
the Art of Equitation, and many were the falls I received before
I could manage it. . . . We got very bad rations, and only that
I had some money by me that no one knew of, I should have
come very poorly off, as the old Soldier who had me in charge
always used to take my daily pay, and I was very lucky if I obtained a drink of porter out of it, as he always drank Whiskey,
which I could not bear to taste or smell, however he learned
me the way to Soldier and assisted to clean my things, which I
found very useful when I became a first class recruit, coming in
from Riding School at half past eleven or twelve o'clock, with
my things dirty and for drill again at half past two in the afternoon'.[9]

'Of what use are plumes, bandoliers, sheep-skins,
shabraques, &c.'

CAPTAIN NOLAN[1]

(iv)

Rank and file: uniform – unsuitability of clothing

From the point of view of efficiency in the field the uniform of the
British cavalryman was about as ill-designed as it was possible to
conceive. Everything was sacrificed to good looks on the parade
ground. The clothing was notoriously close fitting, possessing, indeed, some of the disadvantages of knights in armour. In 1852
during an action against the Basutos (compared at the time to cossacks), some of the 12th Lancers' horses fell and refused to stand to
be remounted with the enemy closing in behind. Except where comrades came back to hold their horses for them, all the dismounted
men were killed, entirely because they were unable to mount without
help, their overalls being too tight.

Writing in 1853, the year before his dramatic death at Balaklava, Captain Nolan could

'never believe that our hussar uniform . . . is the proper dress in which to do hussar's duty in war – to scramble through thickets, to clear woods, to open the way through forests, to ford or swim rivers, to bivouac, to be nearly always on outpost work, to "rough it" in every possible manner.'[2]

In India neither for the European nor for the native was there any concession to the climate.

'There is scarcely a more pitiable spectacle in the world', wrote Nolan, 'than a native trooper mounted on an English saddle, tightened by his dress to the stiffness of a mummy, half suffocated with a leather collar.'[3]

In the 1820s an officer of the 16th Lancers wrote in his diary of the regiment on the march:

'We halted for four hours: but the syces [grooms] had not come up, so dependent is a soldier in India, the utmost confusion prevailed, and some men could not dismount from their horses.'[4]

This ridiculous state of affairs may not have been entirely due to the tightness of the uniform and the cumbrous nature of the equipment, but these certainly played their part.

'La Soupe fait le soldat.'
Old French Proverb

(v)

Rank and file: diet – 'tommy' – 'skilly' – cooking utensils – obligatory third meal – the 'who shall'

As to the soldier's diet, it was meagre indeed. The daily ration, fixed in 1813, was three-quarters of a pound of beef and one pound of bread. The bread was usually 'black' or brown, and sometimes so badly baked that it would stick to a wall like paste. It was known as 'Tommy'.[1] Even paupers and convicted felons received white wheaten bread. They were known to sneer at the redcoats for faring worse than themselves. To pay for these rations, sixpence a day was stopped from the soldier's shilling. In 1854 this was reduced to 4½d. No cook was provided, the men themselves taking it in turn to produce boiled beef, beef-broth, potatoes and a thin gruel, known as 'skilly'. There were never any means of roasting or baking. A wealthy commanding officer, however, would sometimes supplement his men's diet. The sole utensils provided as barrack-issues were two coppers for every eight cavalrymen (or twelve infantrymen), one for the meat and the other for the potatoes; one beer-can and two tin mugs. To each man were issued a bowl, trencher (or platter), and a spoon. As a general rule there were only two meals a day, one at 7.30 or 8.00 in the morning and the other at 12.30 or 1.00. If the trooper required anything further to eat during the remaining nineteen hours of the day he had to buy it either in the local town or from travelling salesmen. In 1840 a third meal was made obligatory. At the same date the men were empowered to appoint one of their number as caterer and to make their own choice of tradesmen.

In 1843 Private 'Buck' Adams, of the 7th Dragoon Guards, when he first entered his barrack-room after enlisting, found the troop

'just sitting down to dinner. I was at once taken possession of by a huge Irishman who stood 6 ft 3½ ins. high, not a particle of the upper part of whose face was discernible for the amount of hair which covered it. He placed me at a table and before me a plate of boiled meat, a basin of soup and a piece of bread. Potatoes with their jackets on came rolling towards my plate from both ends of the table, each man contributing one or two from his allowance. By the time they had finished their contributions I had a pile of potatoes in front of my plate, I should think about forty in number. Then I was questioned.

'"Where do you come from, youngster? Who 'listed' you?"

'Then I heard my tall friend with the hairy face say: "Be jabers, he's not the size of a midge. Never want a horse to mount him so long as yez can get a buck goat."

'"Now, my lad, don't be shy; take the jacket off yer taters," said another. "Paddy, chuck down that lump of salt. Here's some pepper" – handing me some black-looking stuff in a piece of dirty paper.'

Adams was then shown the way to the canteen, where 'as they were kind enough to give me part of their dinner, I could not well do less than give them some beer and tobacco in return. The quantity of beer and tobacco consumed in less than 10 minutes amounted to two shillings and six pence.'[2]

In some barracks at meal times a curious custom existed, which was known as the 'who shall'. When the appointed carver had cut a portion, he called out to a man stationed with his back to him: 'Who shall have this?' The plates were then meant to be 'bobbed out' in strict rotation. What too often happened in fact was that the intonation of the carver ensured that the least attractive portions went to the least liked men. When the 'shall' was strongly stressed, it generally meant that some unfortunate recruit would receive a plate containing the largest amount of 'timber'.

Altogether, more than half the soldier's pay went on food. Nevertheless, he was probably better fed than a large section of his civilian counterparts.

'Marriage is to be discouraged as much as possible. Officers must explain to the men the many miseries that women are exposed to, and by every sort of persuasion they must prevent their marrying if possible.'

Rules and Regulations for Cavalry, 1795

'The scenes I witnessed and the language I heard . . . I have never forgotten.'

PRIVATE ADAMS, after enlisting in 1843[1]

(vi)

Rank and file: billeting – barracks: shortage of space, beds and bed clothes, water, lighting, ventilation – wives and children – hospitals

Up to the end of the eighteenth century troops on the Home establishment had almost invariably been billeted in private lodgings,

usually ale-houses. 'This', as the French historian Halévy has judiciously put it, 'was one of those peculiar usages which distinguished
England from the rest of Europe and satisfied the nation that it was
really free.'[2] Innkeepers were required by law to provide straw,
candles, food and drink, and they much objected to the impost. The
men were consistently fleeced. This gave birth to the epigram: 'The
Angel treats us like devils, and the Rising Sun refuses us light to go
to bed by.'[3] In 1792 the post of barrackmaster-general was created.
During the Napoleonic wars, large numbers of barracks were put up
all over the country, chiefly so as to have concentrations of troops
ready to repel invasion. By 1805, 203 permanent or hired buildings
were in use, designed to hold 17,000 cavalry and 146,000 infantry.
Those specifically for the cavalry were often sited in unlikely places,
such as Barnstable and Modbury in Devon, and Bridport in Dorset.
The reason for these was to provide centres from which to combat
smuggling (see p. 82). Other permanent stations came into being
in areas where serious rioting had taken place.

In Ireland, the situation was entirely different. 'There the Irish
Parliament readily trusted the Crown with compulsory powers for
the acquisition of land for barrack purposes' from an early date.[4]

Most barracks were designed in the shape of a square, as much, it
was said, to keep the men in as to keep the enemy out. To start with,
almost nothing was provided in these prison-like blocks, except
dormitories. Into these, which had small windows placed high up
in the walls, an unbelievable number of men could be packed. Two
years after the Crimean War it was stated that the average allowance
of air for a soldier in barracks was only 400 cubic feet, while for a
convict it was 1,000. In some barracks and 'in five military hospitals'
there were less than 300 cubic feet per man.[5] Some of the rooms were
less than seven feet in height. In the Cavalry Barracks at Maidstone,
which in the 1840s and for many years and after, served as depôts for
the cavalry regiments in India (see p. 104), the men, according to a
trooper of the 15th Hussars, were

'packed . . . so closely that I have seen them sleeping on the
tables used for dining, under the tables, and in the coal-boxes!
This in the middle of summer.'[6]

In 1816, there were still few beds as such. In some barrack-rooms,
palliasses were still laid on the floor; in others, there were wooden
cribs filled with straw. In each of these there was just room to cram
four men. The official issue of bed clothes varied from time to time,

but generally included a palliasse, two blankets and a bolster. By the 1820s, on the insistence of the Duke of Wellington, individual beds had become common. In some cases as little as five inches separated them from each other, while between them and the communal eating table, which ran down the centre of the room, there were often no more than nine inches. One room, only thirty-two feet by twenty, was used to accommodate as many as twenty persons. In 1842, during the Chartist riots, forty-eight men were accommodated in a room seventy-two feet by thirty-six feet and twelve feet high. An officer who visited them could not see the occupants for smoke.[7]

In such a room there lived not only soldiers, but also a number of their wives. William Lucas, when he arrived at the Inniskillings' barracks in Ireland, was 'rather surprised to see in the room I was sent to, 18 men, two married men and their wives and about 6 or 7 children'. At night these were separated from the single men by a blanket or sheet thrown across a rope.[8]

Until late in the century, most sergeants and seven per cent of the rank and file were permitted to marry. At a conservative guess, a further seven per cent were married without leave. Over eighty per cent of the men were therefore forced to lead bachelor lives in barracks.[9] There was never any legal bar to marriage, but only those wives officially sanctioned, whose names appeared on the Married Roll, were made any provision for by the State. The existence of all other wives was totally unrecognised. The general rule was that for every 100 men six or seven were allowed to live in. In the 1870s the proportion was one wife for every eight cavalrymen, and one for every twelve infantrymen.[10] These women, who made a pittance by doing the soldiers' washing, sometimes cooked their extra food for them and were useful as nurses when men went sick. They knew no home but the barracks. It was the Household Brigade which pioneered the idea of married quarters. In 1852 a group of officers raised £9,000 to build a hostel for fifty-six families. When, eight years later, the first official married quarters were erected, the hostel was bought by the War Department for only £8,000!

When a regiment was ordered for foreign service, no more than a limited number of women was allowed to accompany it. The wives of all non-commissioned officers and men who had married with leave had to draw lots to determine which should go and which stay. These were very harrowing occasions, for more often than not the workhouse was the sole refuge for those left behind, especially the 'illegal' wives and children. The State paid for the 'legal' ones to proceed to any part of the United Kingdom they chose. After that they were abandoned. Often a subscription was set afoot among the men to assist them, but the sums collected cannot have been very great. One trooper, in 1843, described the scenes at parting – husbands from wives and fathers from children – as 'a disgrace to the name of England'.[11] In 1814, the young wife of a Scottish soldier walked from Edinburgh to Folkestone only to draw the 'to be left' ticket. She and her new-born child died before her husband embarked. He had no time even to bury them.[12] 'It was no uncommon thing', wrote Lord Wolseley, 'to see women rushing madly into the water after the boats which carried away their husbands from them.'[13] Other wives were sometimes nippier. In 1845 Trooper Pearman, who formed part of a draft for India, reported in a letter home: '4 Married women of the 3rd Light Dragoons were smuggled on Board [at Gravesend] and taken out with us without leave.'[14]

The situation of wives who became widows in a campaign abroad was a peculiarly distressing one. After the First Sikh War the 3rd Light Dragoons had '14 or 15 widows. . . . Most of them', wrote Trooper Pearman, 'were married in a month after our return to quarters. Soon forgot the one dead. Some of them had had 3 or 4 husbands.'[15] The dilemma in which these women found themselves was that if they were not re-married within six months, they lost their allowance and became destitute. In the middle of a campaign, however, no chaplain could in fact marry them 'without a License and without the usual delay of publication of Banns', neither of which was practicable.[16] A trooper of the 15th Hussars thought that the emigration of young women to India should be encouraged, so that

'the men may have greater facilities for marrying; because, as any Indian officer knows, a married man in India is always best off, and, in most cases, the most efficient soldier – the direct reverse of this being the case with a soldier at home'.

Marriage between European soldiers and native women was not officially forbidden or frowned upon. Pearman writes about a Trooper Walker of the 3rd Light Dragoons who, when the regiment was about to return from India, received £100 from another man 'to change regiments, which they got done. Walker', says Pearman, 'had a black wife and wanted to stay in the country.'[17]

In the barrack-room, whether at home or abroad, the soldiers' wives shared the conjugal bed. There they gave birth to their children. There they brought them up.* There, too, they shared, with the men, the large wooden 'urine-tubs' which served both for the natural functions, and when emptied, for washing. Sir John Fortescue's father once heard a sergeant speak of a promising recruit as 'a smart, active boy, always first in the urine-tub in the morning'.[18]

For every eight troopers, one roller-towel was provided each week. By the 1840s, however, individual towels were being supplied – but at a price. One recruit had to pay 1s. 0½d. for a coarse rag towel, 16 in. × 12 in., the actual value of which, he calculated at 1½d.[19] More often than not the sole supply of fresh water was a single outdoor pump, or conduit, which served hundreds of men, perhaps a whole regiment. The supply of water was often defective. In 1824, the lieutenant-colonel of the 15th Hussars reported that the water in the cavalry barracks at Cork was 'so injurious, being impregnated with copper, that the men are obliged to buy for their drinking, and the horses have to go for it upwards of half a mile twice a day'.[20]

After dark, the artificial lighting in barracks must have been minimal, for the weekly allowance of candles was fixed at 2½ lbs for every eight cavalrymen. For every *twelve* infantrymen, the issue was only 1¼ *lbs* a point which well illustrates the superior treatment accorded the cavalry.

The ventilation of barrack-rooms, at no time good, was made worse by the universal habit of the lowest classes in those days, of excluding, whenever possible, the entrance of fresh air. This came, of course, from lack of fuel in the poverty-stricken homes from which most of the rank and file came. The atmosphere was consequently close and foetid. This, combined with the most elementary drainage, created conditions in which disease was rampant. In India, however, as Trooper Henderson of the 15th Hussars discovered, European soldiers were often 'infinitely better off than in England, as regards ventilation, water, and other sanitary matters'.[21]

There was little incentive to report illness. Soldiers' wives would go to great lengths to conceal infectious diseases in their children, for if it were discovered, they were liable to be turned out of barracks, without a roof over their heads. The hospitals to which soldiers who had exhausted the curative capacities of the regimental doctors were

* In the 1850s there was a floating population of about 10,000 women and children in the army, other than enlisted boys.

sent differed but little from their barracks. Overcrowding, lack of drainage, boiled beef, primitive washing facilities existed equally in both.

'Where soldiers are to be ruled, there is more logic in nine tails of a cat than in the mouths of a hundred orators.'
KINCAID, J. *Random Shots from a Rifleman*, 1835[1]

(vii)

Rank and file: major punishments: death, imprisonment, flogging – barrack-room courts-martial – 'booting' – minor punishments: 'taps', gagging, the black hole

Much has been written about the appalling severity of military punishment in the eighteenth and nineteenth centuries. Certainly by the standards of the twentieth it was brutal. The ultimate deterrent was, of course, the death sentence. At the time of Waterloo there were over two hundred capital offences in civil law alone. 'A man might hang for chipping the balustrade of Westminster Bridge or impersonating a Chelsea pensioner.'[2] In the army, amongst the crimes for which death was the penalty as late as the 1840s were mutiny, desertion, striking superior officers, plundering, burglary with violence, 'giving false alarms', sodomy, 'carnally abusing children', 'ravishing women', and strangest of all, 'riotously *beginning* to demolish a house'.[3]

One of the most convincing descriptions of the execution of a soldier comes from the pen of a private in the 32nd Foot, who, in 1847, witnessed the shooting of Trooper Palmer of the 9th Lancers in Meerut. Palmer had been sentenced for striking his commanding officer in the face with his cap.

'It was early in the morning, before daylight, that we paraded for the execution, and formed in three sides of a square, the open side being left for the balls to pass through when the soldiers fired. The unhappy man was then brought from his cell under an escort of a section of men, commanded by an officer, his arms being tied behind him by a cord a little above the elbow. . . . He was taken to the left of the square, next to his own regiment. . . . Everything was so still that a pin might be heard to fall. I stood trembling all over, until I could not keep a limb still – my teeth chattered in my mouth. . . . Several fainted, and others had to fall out. . . . After the first dawn I could see the party stand with the prisoner, when they were ordered to proceed in the following manner: first the provost with his arms reversed; then the band and drummers, playing the "Dead March", the drums being muffled in black; next the firing party, with arms reversed; then the coffin, borne by four men; next to this the prisoner, in company of the minister praying, and his comrade on the left of him, flanked by a man on either side with swords, the escort following. . . . As he passed his own regiment he bade his officers and the men farewell, and told them he hoped it would be a warning to all to keep from drink; for it was that and bad company that had brought him to this. . . . When they got up to my regiment I looked at him. He was pale, though he appeared to be prepared for his fate, which I suppose he was. The minister had hold of his arm, but he walked with a firm step, keeping the step to the drum, and with the party. He was dressed in a clean white shirt, a black handkerchief, his stable jacket (with the collar turned back), white trousers, and stable cap. As soon as he got to us, he began to weep, and was going to say something; but the minister spoke to him, and I suppose told him to continue in prayer. Poor man! I thought my heart would melt in me. . . . On getting to the end of the square, they turned across to the open side, about the middle, and the coffin was put on the ground. The escort fell back; the firing party took up their distance; the man knelt upon the coffin; the provost blufted him, then drew back; the minister read the funeral service; the man prayed; as the minister finished, he said, "Lord, have mercy upon my soul!" and the minister, putting up his hand as a signal that all was finished, the report of the muskets was heard as they poured out a volume of smoke, and the man fell dead. Two balls had passed through the heart, one through the breast, another through the head, and another through the thigh. After the whole of us had marched by the body, it was put in the coffin as it fell, and buried.'[4]

The commanding officer of the 9th Lancers at this time was James Hope Grant, a remarkable and humane man, much loved by his men. The description which he gives of this case in his diary is a most moving one. Palmer, aged twenty-seven at the time of his execution, was an orphan, who had been brought up by an uncle, a distiller in London. Palmer

'turned out wild and extravagant, and this uncle had, as a last resource, sent him out as a settler to New South Wales. After he had been there for some time, he became acquainted with a handsome young convict girl who had been transported for stealing, and fell in love with her. He obtained the sanction of the authorities to marry her, and they lived together in harmony until he suddenly had suspicions that she was untrue to him. Maddened with jealousy, he could, he said, almost have murdered her; and at last, fearing lest he should commit some desperate act, he secretly fled from the country and returned to England. Shortly after landing, he enlisted in the 9th Lancers, then on the point of embarking for India, but on arriving at Calcutta he deserted and took passage in a homeward-bound ship. Ere reaching the Cape his identity was discovered by some person on board, and he was sent back to India.'

Before long he received proof from Australia that his wife was innocent. This made him quite desperate to rejoin her. He was egged on to strike his colonel by 'one M'Shee, a precious blackguard'. He believed that his punishment (as till then had been the case for similar offences) would be transportation back to New South Wales, and to his wife. He was the second of three men who were shot for the same crime at Meerut, within an eight-day period. The example of these three executions had the effect of putting a speedy end to the striking of officers, which had become dangerously prevalent. 'The bad characters', wrote Hope Grant, 'arrived at the conclusion that there was little satisfaction in running the risk of being shot for the satisfaction of being transported.'[5]

*   *   *

In 1833 no less than one in every five of the men on the Home establishment was confined in *public* jails. Statistics for 1839 show that the commonest offence for which men were sent to prison in that year was desertion: 1,180. Next came absence without leave: 930, followed by 'making away with necessaries': 636, habitual drunkenness: 414, drunkenness on duty: 289, violence to superiors and insubordination: 159. At the bottom of the list were 'quitting or sleeping on post': 73 and plain 'disobedience': 67.[6]

*   *   *

Generally speaking, from the middle of the eighteenth century till its virtual abolition in the 1870s, flogging (or being 'touched over' as it was called in barrack-room slang), was the foundation upon which discipline rested. It was, after all, as Lord Wolseley put it some time after abolition, cheap and simple, and it 'withdrew the soldier from his duty for the shortest length of time'.[7] The alternatives were all unsatisfactory. Penal companies proved, when tried in West Africa, to be equivalent to a death sentence. Dismissal, while there was no short-term service, and while criminals were sometimes pardoned on condition that they enlisted, was out of the question. At a time when a man of good conduct was allowed (though not always) to buy himself out, to give bad characters a free discharge would have placed a premium on bad behaviour, and acted as the opposite to a punishment.

It is often forgotten that the civil courts also depended to a large degree upon the lash. Nor is it well known that even more drastic than punishments meted out by courts-martial were those which were commonly carried into effect by the men themselves. 'Barrack-room courts-martial' were often held upon some particularly bad character. Especially was this so in the case of a thief. The oldest soldier was normally the 'president' of the 'court', its other members being the next two oldest soldiers and the two youngest. In the cavalry the commonest sentence was a flogging with a double-buckle strap, an instrument infinitely more painful than the lash. The culprit was not stripped, the biting power of the buckle making this unnecessary. 'Booting' was another form of barrack-room punishment sometimes inflicted in the cavalry. It consisted in flogging the soles of the feet with a belt.* On occasions, too, habitual drunkards had boiling oil or water poured over their backs, while still drunk. Punishments such as these became less common from 1815 onwards.

* In the infantry 'scabbarding' on the bare posterior was the equivalent; 'booting' would have rendered an infantryman unfit to march.

*   *   *

Flogging

The history of flogging as an official punishment in the army does not start till 1713. Though the lash was in use in the seventeenth century, chiefly in time of war, it was in that year that general power was first given to courts-martial to inflict corporal punishment in time of peace. Until 1811 no other form of punishment could be given for 'immorality, misbehaviour or neglect of duty'. In 1807 it became illegal to award more than a thousand lashes under any circumstances. After 1812, if a man was unable to bear the whole of his sentence at one session, the remainder was remitted. In the same year, no regimental court-martial was empowered to award more than 300 lashes and this was further reduced to 200 in 1832. District or garrison courts-martial (to which the duty of trying the principal offences was transferred in 1829), could award up to 300 lashes. In 1833 the number of crimes punishable by flogging was reduced and they were more clearly defined. In 1859 and 1867 they were further reduced. In 1868, money fines were substituted for flogging as the normal punishment for ordinary drunkenness.

As a result of the Royal Commission on Military Punishments of 1836, the number of lashes was limited as follows: general court-martial, 200; district or garrison court-martial, 150, and regimental court-martial, 100. In 1847 no more than fifty lashes were allowed under any circumstances.

That corporal punishment speedily declined as the chief form of punishment in the army after the report of the Royal Commission in 1836 is shown by the fact that in that year only 163 floggings took place while in 1835 the number was 246.

In the native army in India flogging was totally abolished as early as 1835, but the great increase in crime which followed necessitated its re-introduction in 1845. Sir Hugh Gough, Commander-in-Chief in India at the time, believed that it was 'rather a boon than an act of coercion, as it will, from fear of its infliction, deter the evil-disposed and bad characters from entering the Service'.[8]

*   *   *

There are in existence many first-hand descriptions of floggings, most of them embroidered. One of the more convincing is Sergeant-Major Mole's. In all his twenty-five years' service in the 14th Hussars, he witnessed only two floggings, which shows how seldom they took place, at any rate in good cavalry regiments, from the 1860s onwards. Though the one he describes occurred in 1866, and is therefore outside the period covered by this volume, there is no reason to suppose that it differed from earlier, similarly harrowing experiences:

'Amongst those who entered the regiment at the same time as myself', he wrote, 'was one who acquired a character for being very light-fingered, and was known as the "Lifter". Within a few months he was twice up in front of the colonel for offences which were really theft, but which, as he was a young soldier, were so altered as to give him another chance.

'It happened one Sunday morning that a visitor, in the course of strolling around the barrack-rooms, expressed a desire to obtain an army razor. . . . The Lifter happened to hear this, and offered to get one for a quart of beer; and this being promised him, watched his opportunity and stole one from the kit of a recruit. . . .

'Colonel T[hompson], much against his will, was obliged to send the prisoner up for court-martial. In due time the Lifter was tried, found guilty, and sentenced to fifty lashes, and to be dismissed the service with ignominy. . . . One day the whole regiment turned out for foot-parade in full dress, with arms, the officers in front of their troops, the same as for a general's inspection.

'The Lifter was marched on to parade under charge of guard, and with him all the other prisoners in confinement at the time, that they might experience the benefit of his example. When he reached the centre of the front of the regiment he was halted, and the adjutant, stepping up to the colonel and saluting him, received some papers, which he began to read. They detailed the finding of the court-martial, and the sentence awarded. As the Lifter's name and number were read out, he snatched off his cap and threw it on the ground in a devil-may-care way, and then took three paces forward in a jaunty, off-hand manner, and grinned out of insolent bravado.

'The reading over, the regiment received the order, "Fours right", whilst the band moved up a little . . . and we proceeded to the riding-school to the strains of a merry tune.

'Filing in, we packed ourselves four and five deep against either side. At the further end opposite the door stood a triangle, the farrier-major and two brawny farrier-sergeants, with their jackets off, their sleeves rolled up, and each holding a dreaded cat-o'-nine-tails. Up to them the prisoner was marched by the guard, and the doors were then shut. The floor being covered with tan not a sound was heard, and the silence was almost deathly. . . . The gloomy dead walls of the riding-school added an indescribable terror to the scene. By the triangle stood the colonel, the adjutant, the doctor, and the chaplain. Colonel T. . . . now called the regiment to attention, and then, turning to the farrier-major, gave the order in a husky voice – "Proceed".

'. . . the two farrier-sergeants seized the Lifter and began tying him up to the triangle. His jauntiness was all gone now, and he screamed at the top of his voice for mercy. . . . The farrier-sergeants hastened to perform their task, and in a minute the prisoner was triced up, and his shirt stripped from his back, which was exposed to view.

'At this moment the chaplain stepped up to the colonel, and after saluting him, begged mercy for the poor devil, who was screaming and wriggling in anticipation. But Colonel T. . . ., in a stern voice, pointing to the doctor, said, "the prisoner is now in his hands". Then looking at the farrier-major, he raised his hand as a sign to begin, and turned his head away.

'"*One*," cried the farrier-major in a loud, clear voice, for he was hardened to these scenes. Round swung the lash and fell with a sickening thud on the quivering flesh, whilst the Lifter writhed with the most ghastly contortions I have ever seen. Although my stomach turned at it, and I felt sick as a dog, my eyes were fascinated by the spectacle. Slowly and methodically the farrier-major continued to count, the strokes falling as regularly, until twenty-five was reached, by which time the man's screams had dwindled into a low, prolonged moaning.

'The doctor now stepped up and felt his pulse; and then signed for the punishment to proceed.

'The second farrier-sergeant now relieved his comrade, and took up his position on the left, whilst the farrier-major resumed his count. At the fortieth lash the prisoner suddenly gave a convulsive jerk, and then hung limp. The doctor raised his hands, the counting ceased, and the falling blow was diverted. And a sigh of relief went up from the officers and men alike, when the doctor stepped up to Colonel T. . . . and said –

'"Sir; he can bear no more."

'The insensible form was then untriced and made over to the hospital orderlies, who were ready at hand with restoratives. . . .

Directly he had crawled out of the building, the band struck up a lively march.'

A fortnight later the Lifter was formally expelled from the barracks. As the gates closed behind him he spat contemptuously 'and then putting his extended fingers to his nose, shouted out, "A soldier's farewell to you." But . . . at this moment two policemen suddenly appeared, and amidst the suppressed laughter of the regiment, seized him. We heard afterwards that he had been wanted some time, and only got out of the clink to walk into the jug.'[9]

In some regiments it was the duty of the farriers to inflict corporal punishment. In others it was shared between the farriers and the trumpeters. Responsibility for training in the art rested with the Trumpet Major. Until well into the nineteenth century, the victim was required to pay the Trumpet Major for the pleasure of being flogged.

*　　*　　*

There was a wide range of minor punishments available to the commanding officers of regiments. For small offences such as a knapsack out of place, or a wrong fold in the bedding, a man might be required to answer his name every hour to the sergeant of the guard, from reveille to sundown. This was known as 'taps'. Other small punishments included 'gagging, wearing the jacket inside out, drinking salt water, bread and water diet, stopping a man's ration of grog, or diluting it . . ., trotting round in a circle, standing fully equipped in heavy marching order with the face to the wall . . ., the stocks, the black-hole'.[10] Extra drills, heavy marching drills, additional parades, extra guards and confinement to barracks are, of course, still with us.

The punishments which were sometimes awarded by regimental officers, without any sort of trial, could be severe. William Lucas, who became officers' mess waiter in the Inniskillings in the 1850s, came under a new mess president, whose predecessor had allowed the mess to be locked up when no officers were dining in. On one such occasion, therefore, Lucas went off duty at 6 p.m. as had been the accepted practice. The new mess president, however, wanted a bottle of soda water at 10 p.m., and could not, of course, get it. For Lucas, who had a clean sheet hitherto, he ordered the following punishments: forty-eight hours' solitary confinement, his hair to be cut short, five days' marching order drills, fourteen days' confined to barracks, forfeiture of two days' pay, and return to troop duty.[11]

Contrasted with this petty severity is Cornet Anstruther Thomson's account of tolerance in the 9th Lancers. When he joined in 1836

'the men were a wildish lot, and very often late for watch-setting, but as long as the duty was well done not much notice was taken. When the orderly sergeant reported men absent at watch-setting, "Give them half an hour" was the usual answer.'[12]

*   *   *

In general the severity of punishments, and the indignity of many of them, were steadily reduced in the years following Waterloo. This was due less to agitation in Parliament than to the common sense humanity of such Commanders-in-Chief as Hill and Hardinge, and not a few commanding officers.

'The man who enlists into the British Army is, in general, the most drunken, and probably the worst man of the trade or profession to which he belongs, or of the village or town in which he lives.'
THE DUKE OF WELLINGTON, 1829[1]

(viii)

Rank and file: leisure – daily routine – drunkenness: grog shops, staggered pay days, in India – coffee and reading rooms – venereal disease – recreations – health – education: regimental schools – good conduct pay and badges – savings banks – pensions – discharge

In peacetime the soldier once trained seldom went short of leisure. The cavalrymen always had less of it, because there were the care of his horse and the maintenance of often elaborate equipment to attend to. The infantryman, without these occupations, was usually left to his own devices from four in the afternoon till 9.15 p.m., when he was required to be in quarters. In the cavalry there were 'evening stables', sometimes as late as 7 p.m. For recruits the day was usually a full one. During the cold season in India a typical day for a young soldier of the 14th Light Dragoons in 1847 was:

> 'riding school at 6 o'clock till ½ past 8, stables at 9, carbine drill from 12 till 1, and sword drill in the evening from ½ past 4 till ½ past 5, and this with the time taken up to clean our accoutrements takes up the whole of our time'.[2]

Until half-way through the century, to fill in his hours of leisure, the soldier once past the recruit stage had little resort except to alcohol. Since 1802, malt had been so heavily taxed that beer was beyond the pockets of the poorer classes. Spirits, therefore, took its place. Drunkenness in those days was universal. In the civilian it was no more than a vice, but in the soldier it was a crime, for he, in theory, must be ready for duty at all times. The State, nevertheless, encouraged excessive drinking, for in each barracks there were official canteens for the exclusive sale of spirits. It is supposed that these originated from the difficulty in preventing the smuggling of spirits into barracks. The Board of Ordnance soon took over this lucrative business, letting the canteens to the highest bidders on three-year contracts. By 1847, the Ordnance estimates showed an annual profit from this source alone of nearly £54,000.[3]

The commanding officers of regiments were supposed to be able to exercise control over these grog-shops, but it was impossible, in practice, to stop large-scale extortion or to ensure good quality. As the contractor not only paid a high rent for the canteen building, but had also to pay monthly 'privilege money', the prices were often exorbitant, and the quality infamous. When later on other goods were allowed to be sold, such as vegetables, they too were generally below standard. There is evidence to show that the spirits were coarse and fierce beyond what was normally sold in public houses. No wonder, then, that crimes of violence and insubordination, including the frequent striking of officers, resulted. So as to limit the drinking bouts which followed the receipt of pay, and the consequent fighting which broke out in barracks, pay days were often 'staggered', ensuring that only a small number of men was able to get drunk on any one day.

In India the consequences of too much drink were more dangerous, while the temptation, especially during the hot season in the plains, was greater than at home. Trooper Tookey of the 14th Light Dragoons found the three hot months of 1848

'unbearable with the prickly heat, mosquitoes, sand flies and other insects. Unless a man gets lushy every night with arrack or Company grog, which is strongly impregnated with opium, he cannot sleep a wink. With the officers it is different, as they have a native to fan them during the night.'[4]

Two years earlier, at the end of the First Sikh War, each man in the 3rd Light Dragoons received a lump sum of £7 12s. 6d. *batta* money. On top of this considerable sum, as Trooper Pearman wrote in his diary, 'most of us had money we had made on the campaign (lute [*sic*]). . . . There was a great deal of drinking, and men dying every day from the effects.' A bottle of Bass's Stout or Burton Ale cost the equivalent of 3s. 6d., but strong rum cost only 2s. for three pints. Of this 'you could have as much as you like to drink', though it was forbidden to consume it outside the canteen. To overcome this regulation there were

'plenty of men who made Bishops, a sort of bladder to fit into their shirt inside their trowsers, . . . to hold about 8 drams, and smuggle it out of the canteen. This way these men sold it to the other men, mostly at Gun Fire in the morning, 5 a.m. This they called Gun Fire Tots. We got it as we turned out to drill. These men would save a lot of money and drink nothing for some time. This was called "to put the bag on". But when they did break out, they would drink to such an extent that they had mostly to go to Hospital from the effects.'

Also in barracks, Trooper Pearman recorded, was

'a woman named Paddy Burns, called "the old tin kettle". She had a Tin Baby made with a wax face. This she would take into the Canteen at evening and mimick a cry, and then give it a little grog. The child's body held more than a gallon. She would get the men to get many rupees worth for her, and she used to then fill the child. When full, she would mimick the cry, and say, "Ah, I must take the young devil to its mother, I suppose", and out she would go by the sentry. This she would sell at 4 annas per dram in the night – when it only cost her one anna . . .'[5]

In 1847 the proposal was first made in Parliament that coffee-rooms should replace spirit canteens and that all profits should be ploughed back so as to maintain reading-rooms for soldiers. This important reform, first suggested by Sir Henry Hardinge some years earlier, was soon affected and proved beneficial from the start.

Reading, since so many men were illiterate, was only a partial answer to the recreation problem. The fear of seditious literature coming into soldiers' hands, especially after the French Revolution, caused the reading of books to be frowned upon. Certain enlightened commanding officers, however, had instituted regimental libraries from their own resources, even as early as the 1790s. In 1831, the inhabitants of Nottingham raised a subscription for the 15th Hussars who had just dealt with a Reform riot in that town. They particularly asked that a part of the monies should 'be employed in purchasing books with a view to establishing a permanent library for the use of the men'.[6] The first Government-sponsored reading-rooms in barracks date from 1838. By 1851, about 100,000 volumes existed in army barracks and some 16,000 NCOs and men subscribed to regimental libraries. These were especially welcome in India. In the hot season, when the day began with reveille at half-past four in the morning, and was followed by an hour's riding school at five, the men had 'nothing to do', as Trooper Tookey of the 14th Light Dragoons recorded in 1847, 'except clean our accoutrements till 6 o'clock in the evening, when we go to stables for ½ an hour. . . . We have', he added, 'an excellent library with which we pass away many an hour that would otherwise hang heavy on our hands.'[7]

Another of the soldier's recreations can be deduced from the high incidence of venereal disease. Certain infantry units, in the 1850s, are known to have had a quarter of their men affected, and in the 1880s the proportion was about the same.[8]

In India, depending upon the station, the officer commanding it and the time of year, the soldier's life and recreation could be both cheaper and often more rewarding than at home. In Ambala, for instance, in 1848, Trooper Tookey,

'had a very merry Xmas, lots of balls and races. . . . You will no doubt laugh at a Ball being given by private soldiers, but I can assure you they are very splendid affairs, the only thing we are short of is ladies.

'We had [a ball] in our troop about a fortnight ago, most of the officers attended and we had the pleasure of putting them about 3 sheets in the wind. The adjutant and riding master were led home by two men each and the Orderly Officer put to bed in the Barrack Room. Such a one could not have been got up in England under £150; it cost us about £30, but we found our own labour for nothing. . . .

'We have also had lots of pony races and though I cannot say much for the speed, they made lots of fun.'[9]

Lahore, too, between the First and Second Sikh Wars, Trooper Tookey found

'a very gay station with everything as accommodating to the health and happiness of a private soldier as it is possible to be, thanks to Col. [Henry] Lawrence, the late Resident. There are gardens at about 10 minutes walk from the barracks fitted up on purpose for us, with a beautiful reading room well supplied with books and papers, ball and skittle alleys, a racquet court and all gymnastics. In it are growing oranges, limes, pomegranates, melons, peaches and grapes for our own eating.'[10]

Until the middle of the century, organised games and sports were rare, though there is a record of the Grenadiers playing football in Belgium in 1815, a thing unknown in most regiments at that time.[11] The 1836 Royal Commission on Military Punishments recommended that soldiers should be urged to play 'manly games'. Racquets, fives, football and cricket were specially mentioned. In 1841 cricket grounds had begun to be made in all the large barrack stations.[12] 'Daddy' Hill, when Commander-in-Chief, even suggested that fives courts should be built in every barracks. It was not until after the Crimean War that any form of compulsory physical training was introduced into the army.

* * *

As a result of monotonous diet, unsanitary living quarters and alcoholism, the standard of health of the troops was frequently deplorable. The death-rate within the army was consistently and dramatically higher than outside it. From 1819 to 1828 the annual mortality per thousand men was fifteen at home and fifty-seven on foreign service. In the middle of the century, the average mortality rate for the *civilian* population of military age was seven-and-a-half to nine per thousand. In cavalry regiments it was eleven per thousand. In the Foot Guards it was nearly twenty-and-a-half and in the line infantry, eighteen per thousand. The death-rate from tuberculosis among soldiers was five times as great as among civilians.[13] Suicides, too, were more common in the army. One authority states that during some unspecified seven-year period between 1815 and 1845, 35 out of 686 deaths which took place in the Dragoon Guards and Dragoons serving in the United Kingdom, 'were occasioned by self-destruction'. This works out at about one in twenty of the total deaths, and compares with 1 in 340 for the whole of England and Wales for the year 1835.[14]

* * *

Colonel Le Marchant, whose plan for a military college for officers resulted in the foundation of Sandhurst (see p. 156), had also recommended a Legion for the education of non-commissioned officers and soldiers. This had been turned down on the grounds that 'it was inconsistent with the habits of the country to raise private soldiers to so close an equality with their officers, as well as from the apprehension that the measure might prove injurious to the service at large by leading to frequent promotions from the ranks'. Nevertheless in 1801 there was opened the Duke of York's School, Chelsea, which gave an education to the sons of soldiers and non-commissioned officers, especially of those killed in action.[15] The numbers thus provided for were not great.

The oldest of the military *boarding* schools was founded in Ireland as a philanthropic institution for the destitute children of soldiers serving in that country and for those of Irish soldiers overseas. In 1769 it was established as the Royal Hibernian Military School, and lasted in varying forms, producing Army Schoolmasters and Bandmasters, amongst others, until 1922 when the army left Ireland.

For many years there had been schools of an unofficial nature within regiments. Soon after 1662, the officers of Fort St George, Madras obtained the services of a schoolmaster from the East India Company. The garrison at Tangier possessed, in 1685, three schoolmasters. From the 1760s onwards references to regimental schools in Britain become quite frequent. These were usually started on the initiative of commanding officers and often financed by the officers as a whole. They were designed to provide some sort of rudimentary education for the soldiers' children as well as for their illiterate fathers; but they varied enormously both in type and scope.

The enlistment of boys, particularly as trumpeters, buglers and drummers, had been common at least since Marlborough's days. In

146

1813 an official quota was laid down for each unit: up to fifty boys a year. These could be sent to India or to any colonial station, and compulsory daily school was their lot. In the cavalry, at this time, numbers of them were trained as apprentice farriers, saddlers and armourers.

In 1809 a sergeant of the Bedford Militia refused to attend the regimental school when ordered to do so by his commanding officer. 'I will soldier with anybody,' he said, 'but I won't be made a boy of.' He was gaoled. There followed a celebrated legal case, *Warden v. Bailey*, which established, incidentally, that no soldier might resist an order on the grounds that he doubted its legality. On appeal, the judge gave a ruling which cast a shadow over army education for years to come. 'It is no part', he declared, 'of the military duty to attend a school and to learn to read and write.' This would have pleased the officer who pointed out that a fellow that can write can draw petitions.

Despite the outcome of this case, all commanding officers were directed in 1811 to establish schools in their regiments 'for the instruction of young soldiers and the children of soldiers'. Adult pupils were charged 6d. to 1s. a week. A return of 1842 shows that, on average, the surprisingly large figure of eighty men per unit were prepared to pay this sum for a voluntary elementary education. In 1840, there were some 16,000 young girls accompanying the army in all parts of the world, and for these a schoolmistress per regiment was added to the establishment.

In 1812, regimental schools were for the first time included in the Army Estimates. It was not until 1846, when that remarkable man, the Rev. G. R. Gleig, already holding the post of Chaplain-General, was appointed the first Inspector-General of Schools, that army education was placed on a centralised basis. In that year the Corps of Army Schoolmasters, open only to qualified teachers, was founded and for the widely varying regimental schools were substituted the Army Schools.[16]

*   *   *

In 1815 there was still in force a seventeenth-century regulation which forbade soldiers to enter public parks and gardens in London. There were notice boards at the gates proclaiming: 'No Soldiers, Servants in Livery or Dogs Admitted.'[17] This was not surprising, for as late as 1779 an Act had been passed for the purpose of impressing all the thieves, pick-pockets and vagabonds of London into the army. For some years after that it was common practice for magistrates to hand over vagrants to the nearest recruiting officer.

Hopes of advancement in the profession were limited. It was difficult for an illiterate man to rise above the lowest ranks. As early as 1806, pay had been graduated according to length of service; but the increases were granted whether the soldier's conduct had been exemplary, indifferent or bad. In 1836, however, Viscount Howick, the Secretary at War, instituted for the first time good-conduct pay and badges. Every man who had a clean record of seven years' service received an extra 1d. a day and a badge. After fourteen years' unblemished service, he was given another 1d. a day and a second badge and after twenty-one years a third badge and a third penny. At first, the Government, unbelievably, made the soldier pay 3s. for each good-conduct badge he earned. On promotion to the rank of sergeant a man's good-conduct pay was withdrawn.[18]

* * *

Until 1842, when an Act of Parliament sanctioned the establishment of Military Savings Banks, the soldier had little spur towards thrift, for there was nowhere safe for him to keep anything he was able to save. This Act, which was introduced by Macaulay, the historian, when he was Secretary at War, guaranteed a yearly rate of interest not exceeding £3 16s. per cent to the non-commissioned officers and men who deposited.

* * *

Until 1829, the pension a soldier received on release, whatever his behaviour had been, remained at an uniform 6d. a day. By Royal Warrant in that year, the principle of length of service and good character was first established. 1s. a day for twenty-one years' service, with an additional ½d. a day for every extra year became the norm. In 1833, however, Parliament, in a fit of economy, again cut the pension by half; but the Secretary at War, Viscount Howick, three years later, partially compensated for the damage done by increasing the pension in proportion to the increase in good-conduct pay.

In the 1820s it was reckoned that for every man who received a normal pension for twenty-one years' service, there were three who claimed it for physical disability. As much of this ill-health was thought to be discreditable, arising from avoidable disease and excess, it was decreed from 1829 onwards that no disability pension should be awarded except for wounds or hardship on active service.

* * *

In 1829 the cost of buying a discharge, which from 1817 had remained at £20 whatever the length of service, was graduated according to the years spent with the colours. Henceforth, a free discharge could be obtained after fifteen years' service; after sixteen years' service a bonus of six months' pay was given, and so on, on an ascending scale. A man with more than sixteen years in the army was thereby enabled to retire with a small capital sum. Nevertheless the return to civil life in a *laissez faire* society was a considerable problem.

* * *

As has been shown, the problems of leisure in the cavalry were always less than in the infantry. The private had only himself, his musket and his kit to look after. The trooper had his horse and saddlery to maintain as well. Further, a certain degree of equestrian skill and capacity for horse-management was required of him. (See p. 102.) These extra occupations not only took up more of his time and added interest to his life, but also engaged him in a sense of responsibility not called for in the foot soldier. Another advantage was that the experience of dealing with horses which his military training gave a cavalryman assured him better prospects of civil employment. Usually, therefore, the cream of available recruits (after the Artillery and Engineers had taken their share) was to be found in the mounted arm.

Moreover, the cavalryman was brought into daily touch with his officers at stable-duty which tended to ameliorate rigidity of class-distinction in a mutual love of horses. Trooper Mole, when he joined the 14th Hussars in the 1860s, found that a chief characteristic of his comrades was 'their fondness for the horses, and the care they took of them.'[19] All these things were instrumental in ensuring a self-respect and sense of vocation too often lacking in the infantry-man. They also led the horse-soldier to look down upon his comrades in the infantry. The man who rides a horse usually feels superior to the man who walks. The horse was as much a status symbol in the past as the motor car is today. It was a token of prestige compounded of spirit and speed.

'I remember when the men had only one regular meal a day, and when the only breakfast they took before morning stables was a large glass of rum.'

An old general, speaking in the 1880s[1]

(ix)

Rank and file: the beginnings of reform in living conditions

From the end of Marlborough's wars until Waterloo living conditions in the army had remained substantially unchanged. Nor, as has been seen, was there much alteration in pay rates, though the purchasing value of money had halved between 1792 and 1815. The determined parsimony of the State was the cause. Wellington, realising this, consistently opposed pay increases foreseeing that if they were granted Parliament would insist on cutting down the armed forces below a safe level. Others, like William Windham, a distinguished Secretary at War, were against them on the grounds that more money in the pocket would lead to more licentiousness, followed by an intensification of the severity of punishments. Further, and more basic, the old concept that the soldier belonged to and should therefore be provided for by his commanding officer died hard. In many cases, indeed, the regimental officer was the forerunner of the revolution which by the end of the nineteenth century had effected major reforms in army conditions. Fortescue, in his definitive *Canteens in the British Army*, has well summarised the position:

'Regimental officers worked busily to counteract the mischief of the State. In many regiments, regimental badges and medals were given to men of steady good character, thus encouraging the well-conducted by reward instead of only deterring the ill-conducted by punishment . . .

'It occurred to them that men drank from sheer exhaustion in the evenings, and they provided for them the means of obtaining cheap suppers and innocent coffee . . . . One colonel of Highlanders at the Cape formed a theatrical company from among the men, who took to the new recreation with enthusiasm and played their parts remarkably well. In fact the soldiers welcomed anything that offered any variation from the usual monotony; and the success which attended every effort of the officers showed that the men, or at any rate most of them, preferred to be sober and to lead quiet lives. . . .

'The evil dealing of the State and the counter-measures of the officers were all brought to light by a Commission [*A Commission on Military Punishments 1836*]; and at last in 1836 the State began from very shame to learn from the officers.'[2]

4

'See, now comes the captain all dawb'd with
gold Lace.'

JONATHAN SWIFT, 1732[1]

(i)

*Types and classes of officers – examinations for commis-
sions and promotion – uniforms: premium on wealth –
moustaches*

No one has better expressed the outlook of the officers of the
British army at the beginning of the 'Long Peace' than the French
historian, Halévy.

> 'The English officer', he wrote, 'made it his first point of honour
> to be a gentleman. The code of his class obliged him to keep
> his distance from the non-commissioned officers and privates.
> He had joined the army to fight, not to perform the wearisome
> duties of an accountant or jailor. There was therefore nobody
> in the British Army, either in the infantry or in the cavalry,
> whose specific duty it was to do the work which in Continental
> armies fell to the subalterns. The charge of everything that makes
> up the daily life of an army – marching formations, pitching
> the camp – was left to the non-commissioned officers.'[2]

Wellington had striven intermittently to alter this outlook but had largely failed. When he became Commander-in-Chief he succeeded no better; nor, in truth, did he really try. It was to take the best part of a century, the lessons of the Crimean War and the combination of Wolseley and Cardwell to transform the British officer into something approaching a professional.

*   *   *

From 1815 to 1850, and for some years later, there were not many officers in the cavalry and infantry who were not products of the public schools. These institutions, with a few exceptions, provided almost no military or 'modern' subjects in their curricula. It was not until the late 1840s that any form of test was introduced for a man wishing to buy a commission. The examination's chief purpose, at first, was to establish that he had received the education of a gentleman. It included papers on 'military drawing' and on one European language. In the early 1860s a lieutenant, before being promoted to captain, was for the first time required to pass a professional examination. The Duke of Cambridge, when Commander-in-Chief, held as late as 1870 that it was impossible to 'force the officers of the British army to go into classes, or to be instructed, by order of the authorities'.[3]

Under the stress of the Napoleonic wars, commissions in the army had been obtained by all sorts and conditions of men. After Waterloo, officers tended once again to be drawn from the class which had usually supplied them, namely the younger sons of the gentry, many of them possessed of no more than a modest competence. In the cavalry, however, there was also an influx of officers from the really wealthy classes. At that time, as a result of the industrial revolution and the manufacture of war supplies, there were many 'new rich', and what in a later age were called 'profiteers'. It was a great temptation for such men to see their sons dressed in showy uniforms, astride high-bred chargers, accoutred in glittering, burnished horse-furniture, 'outshining the sons of great county families and the owners of proud and ancient names'.[4]

*   *   *

The designing and altering of uniforms, always an absorbing hobby of Hanoverian monarchs, became in the case of George IV, both as

Regent and King, an obsession. Many cavalry colonels, being rich men, followed in the royal footsteps, vying with each other in producing gorgeous uniforms for their officers and men, the cost and impracticability of which stagger the sartorial imagination. It took many years for this state of affairs to return to even a semblance of normality. The premium which it placed upon wealth, very often to the exclusion of other qualifications, was a root cause of much that was wrong with the mounted arm in the Victorian era.

Fortescue was told by an officer of the 7th Hussars who commanded a royal escort early in Queen Victoria's reign, that he had lost £700 as a result of that one duty. He had ridden seven miles on a dusty road and then been overtaken by a thunderstorm. His jacket, pelisse and shabracque were ruined and his first charger, worth £350, died of a chill.[5] It was quite common for cavalry officers to find themselves compelled to re-equip as often as four times a year.[6] In 1839, it was calculated that an officer's uniform invariably cost well over a year's pay. A tailor's book of about 1830 shows the cost of the basic uniform of an officer of the 15th Light Dragoons:

Full-dress pelisse	£35	5s.	od.
Undress	19	os.	od.
Full-dress jacket	27	os.	od.
Undress	16	os.	od.
Dress pantaloons	8	18s.	6d.
Dress vest	13	os.	od.
Undress	3	18s.	od.
Greatcoat	12	12s.	od.
	134	13s.	6d.[7]

This represented a very considerable expenditure when compared with his pay (see p. 168).

*   *   *

As regards facial hair, there were numerous instructions over the years applying equally to officers and men. From 1812, hussars were required to wear moustaches, while dragoons and 'heavies' had to shave the upper lip. After 1841, moustaches became general for all cavalrymen.

'There is not a young man in the army that cares
one farthing whether his commanding officer,
his Brigadier or the Commander-in-Chief himself approves his conduct or not. His promotion
depends not on their smiles or frowns – his
friends can give him a thousand pounds with
which he goes to the auction room in Charles
Street and in a fortnight he becomes a captain.'
MAJOR-GENERAL CRAIG, 'Adjutant-General'
the in Low Countries campaign of 1794[1]

(ii)

*Officers: purchase system, first commissions – free com-
missions – 'gentlemen volunteers' – Royal Military
College, Sandhurst – Military Seminary, Addiscombe*

From the creation of a standing army until the Cardwell reforms of
the 1870s, the normal method of obtaining the King's Commission
as an officer in the cavalry and infantry (but not in the Artillery or
Engineers) was by purchase. More often than not demand exceeded
supply. In 1847, for instance, there were more applicants for commissions than could be supplied in twenty years.

The purchase system originated, in part, from the desire of commanding officers, charged with raising regiments, to reclaim some of
the expense they were put to, by requiring officers to pay for their
commissions. These, which became in effect their private property,
they in due course sold to their successors, and so the process went
on down the ages. By law, nevertheless, the State could and sometimes did use its veto against the purchase of commissions by undesirable persons. When augmentations in the establishment took
place, either within existing regiments or by the formation of new
ones, all the new officers were found either from the half-pay list
(see p. 167), by transfer from other units or by commissions without
purchase (see below).

The system applied to all ranks from cornet to lieutenant-colonel.
There were, however, exceptions. Up to 1858, commissions were
often granted free to gentlemen who raised regiments at their own
expense. There are numbers of instances of great magnates or their
sons, especially at the opening of wars, becoming lieutenant-colonels
in command of the regiments they had created. There were cases,

too, even as late as the 1850s, of gentlemen who raised 100 rank and file being made ensigns without purchase. First commissions were also sometimes granted free to non-commissioned officers, as a result of a recommendation of the Commander-in-Chief for gallantry in the field. It was very unusual for such officers to rise, until late in the nineteenth century, beyond the rank of cornet or ensign.

Between 1834 and 1838, out of 227 first commissions in the cavalry only six were granted without purchase. The proportion in the infantry was higher. 'Gentlemen volunteers' were also sometimes given free commissions. The practice of impecunious gentlemen accompanying armies on active service arose in part from their hopes of thus gaining a free cornetcy. Finally, cadets who had successfully passed through the Military College at Sandhurst received their commissions free. Of these, however, for some years there were not great numbers. In 1829 there were 212 cadets, in 1832, 180 and in 1846 only 145.

Until 1858, Sandhurst was in effect a military public school. Cadets generally paid fees, though for a time there were small numbers of 'charity' admissions. The course lasted for three or four years, from thirteen or fourteen to eighteen years of age (until 1858, when the entrance age was raised to between sixteen and eighteen). Before passing out the boys had to satisfy the examiners in the 'six steps essential to obtain a commission', namely mathematics, fortification, military surveying, and three of the following subjects: French, German, siege operations, landscape drawing, military drawing, Latin, general history and geography.[2] That the course was not devoid of difficulty is shown by the fact that out of 650 boys entered between 1838 and 1848, as many as 200 failed to pass out. Most of these then bought their commissions in the normal way.

Founded in 1801, on the initiative of Colonel Le Marchant (see p. 54), and General Jarry, a French *emigré*, the College had produced by 1848 some 360 generals and field officers. During its first forty-six years it was calculated to have supplied 180 officers on the Adjutant-General's and Quartermaster-General's Staffs. Of its first 3,000 cadets, 100 were killed and 270 wounded in action.

Even by the public school standards of the day life at Sandhurst was exceedingly hard. Fagging was onerous and bullying flourished. From contemporary accounts the advice which Dickens put into Major Bagstock's mouth, when advising Mr Dombey upon a school for his son, is hardly exaggerated.

'None but the tough fellows could live through it, sir, at Sandhurst. We put each other to the torture here, sir. We roasted the
new fellows at a slow fire, and hung 'em out of a three pair of
stairs window, with their heads downwards. . . . We were iron,
sir, and it forged us.'³

Meals were meagre. Breakfast, for instance, consisted of a bowl of
milk with bread and a little butter. In the 1830s there was no canteen,
no ante-room, no billiard room, no library even of books on military
subjects and there was nowhere for cadets to go in their spare time
except to their own cell-like studies.*

Riding was a compulsory subject and from all accounts it was well
and rigorously taught. In the 1860s there came to Sandhurst as
riding master a remarkable character called Captain Brooke. In the
early 1840s he had purchased a cornetcy of horse, but was soon compelled to sell out to pay his debts which were considerable. He then
enlisted in the Turkish irregular cavalry and served with them in the
early days of the Crimean War. After the war he somehow managed
to obtain the Sandhurst post. 'With his violent oaths, his incessantly
waving whip and even a brandished pistol' he for many years terror-
ised the cadets. Off duty, though, he was a gentle, kind man, much
interested in amateur theatricals. He later founded the Sandhurst
Dramatic Society.⁴

*   *   *

Between 1809 and 1861, the Honourable East India Company maintained a Military Seminary at Addiscombe, near Croydon. It trained
cadets for the Indian artillery and engineers and from 1816 for the
infantry. A few of these last later transferred to the cavalry. Chief
amongst them were John Jacob (see p. 229), and Sir George Lawrence (see p. 218). Addiscombe's most famous products were Lords
Napier of Magdala and Roberts of Kandahar. Conditions were, if
anything, even tougher than at Sandhurst. The standard of work
required seems to have been higher, though the entrance examination, according to John Jacob, was not difficult. 'All we had to do',

* The 'serviceable linen' which a cadet's parents were obliged to provide in
1830 consisted of 'Day Shirts 8; 4 Night. Pairs of Short Worsted Stockings 6.
Pairs of Short Cotton ditto 8. Pairs of Stocking Web Drawers 4. Pocket Hand-
kerchiefs 8. Towels 5. Night Caps 4. Flannel Waistcoats 4.' (21 June 1830,
papers concerning Cadet H. W. Paget, son of Sir E. Paget, Governor of the
R. M. College, *Plas Newydd Papers*.)

he wrote in 1826, 'was an easy sum in vulgar and decimal fractions and to construe a few lines of Caesar.'[5]

'To the young officers of the British Army. Stick to your trade, young gentlemen. The wheel of fortune is always going round, and every spoke comes uppermost in its turn. I was SIXTEEN years a SUB.'

Dedication by MAJOR GENERAL GEORGE BELL in his *Rough Notes by an Old Soldier*, 1867

(iii)

Officers: purchase system, promotions – brevet rank – official tariff – 'over-regulation' prices – the evils and supposed advantages of the system – condemned by Royal Commission of 1857 – abolition in 1871

All promotion was gained by purchase, except when establishments were augmented, or the demise of an immediately senior officer yielded a free 'death-vacancy' (always provided that no objection came from the commanding officer or the Commander-in-Chief).* Sir James Hope Grant of the 9th Lancers, one of the finest cavalry officers of the mid-nineteenth century, who had paid £5,000 for his commissions up to Captain's rank and who possessed little money beyond that obtained both his majority and lieutenant-colonelcy without purchase from these two causes. An officer was free in fact, if not officially, to retire whenever he wished even in war time without reference to any period of service, and to recover the value of his investment.

* Between 1834 and 1838, promotions took place as follows:

	By purchase	Without purchase
To lieut-colonelcies	39	28
To majorities	108	41
To captaincies	485	131
To lieutenancies	784	247

When it was desired to accelerate the military progress of officers on grounds of special merit or bravery and vacancies for regimental promotion did not exist, they were granted brevet rank without extra pay. Such promotion was not recognised regimentally. It applied only 'in the army as a whole', and often led to undesirable anomalies. A brevet lieutenant-colonel, for example, might be a junior major in his regiment. Nevertheless by virtue of his brevet rank he might well be senior 'in the army as a whole' to his own commanding officer. Indeed he might even be the senior lieutenant-colonel in the brigade of which his regiment formed a part, so that the proper brigade commander being absent, he would automatically find himself acting as brigadier over the head of his own commanding officer.

*   *   *

Both William III and George I had tried, the first to abolish the purchase system, and the second to curb its worst effects. Neither succeeded, for the basis of the system, like so much else which was bad in the service, came from the determination of parliament not to bear, where it could possibly avoid it, the proper financial cost of the army. Until provision was made for officers to receive retirement pensions (which did not happen until 1877), and until a compulsory retirement age was laid down (as first happened in 1858), the necessity for the buying and selling of commissions overrode whatever warrants and regulations the sovereign might make. George I issued a warrant which fixed the prices of the various commissions; but like a number of later ones it did nothing to check the payment of 'over-regulation' prices. These unlawful additions to the official price, stigmatised by Gladstone as this 'gross, widespread and mischievous illegality', were punishable by severe penalties. These, which included cashiering and civil law imprisonment, were never exacted. Over-regulation prices tended to diminish or disappear in time of war, for by death the price of the commission was, until 1856, totally forfeited, the immediately junior officer usually stepping free into the dead officer's rank, thereby gaining a considerable windfall. From this arose the oft-quoted toast given by younger officers: 'A bloody war on a sickly season.'

Equally, on promotion to major-general a lieutenant-colonel lost the value of his commission once and for all.* This, of course, ensured that beyond the rank of lieutenant-colonel wealth was no

* The rank of full colonel was given by brevet only.

longer the criterion. When Sir James Scarlett, who led the Heavy Brigade at Balaklava, was made major-general a fellow officer commented that he lost thereby 'all his money. He has however married a rich wife, and will not feel this.' For others becoming a major-general was a real hardship. In 1856 Colonel Parlby of the 10th Hussars was, according to Colonel Hodge of the 4th Dragoon Guards, 'in a great state of mind about' the prospect of promotion. 'He like myself cannot afford to be promoted, and he does not like to lose his occupation.'[1]

In 1838, there were 123 major-generals. Of these, only ten had not paid any money on their way up the ladder. The rest had invested in their commissions at one time or another sums varying from £6,200 to £100. Nine of these, each with more than forty years' service, at the time of his promotion, had paid £20,364 between them.

*   *   *

An officer who wished to stay in the army but did not like to risk losing the value of his commission by death or promotion to major-general was able to exchange with an officer on half-pay who wanted to sell out. In theory this was not allowed unless the selling officer, if a captain, had completed eighteen years' full pay service, or if a subaltern, fifteen. The exchanging officer received the official difference between the full pay and the half-pay commissions.* The seniors of each junior rank who benefited by obtaining a step in rank would then club together to give the full-pay officer the remaining money which he would have received had he sold out.

More common was the case of the officer (being the senior of his rank) who let it be known that he would sell out immediately if his juniors, who stood to gain a step by his doing so, offered him a good over-regulation price. Since all purchase monies had to be lodged with the army agents it was customary to evade the law by the payment of the extra money as a debt of honour after the commission had been gazetted or even by the payment of an exorbitant sum for a sword or a horse. Nevertheless, from 1783 to 1824, certificates,

---

* The rates of difference between a full pay and a half-pay commission were fixed by a Board in 1821. For the cavalry of the line, they were as follows:

Lieut.-Col.	£1,533
Major	£1,352
Captain	£1,034 3s. 4d.
Lieutenant	£632 13s. 4d.

counter-signed by the commanding officer, were required from every officer buying or selling a commission stating that regulation price was all that was promised, given and accepted!

The State had the power, not often used, to hold back part of the regulation price in every transaction. In some cases this was used to form a reserve fund from which to improve half-pay, or to provide special relief for widows and orphans of other ranks as well as officers.

How bad for discipline the system could be is illustrated by a well-known case in which a deputation of regimental officers waited on an unpopular commanding officer enquiring the figure at which he would sell out. To his horror the sum of £17,000 which he named was immediately accepted. When he protested that he had meant guineas and not pounds his juniors held him to the lesser figure.

Until its abolition in 1871, the official tariff list of commissions remained as laid down in 1783 and amended in 1824. In the cavalry of the line, for instance, the regulation price of a lieutenant-colonelcy was £6,175;* but by 1856, the average *over-regulation* price was £7,825, making a total of £14,000.† In fact, even higher sums are known to have been paid – £18,000 in one case.[2] Lord Cardigan's expenditure is a classic example. By laying out £28,000 he rose from cornet in 1824 to lieutenant-colonel in 1830. When he became major-general in 1847, he lost every penny of this investment. It was rumoured that he bought command of the 15th Hussars for between £35,000 and £40,000, and later spent over £40,000 in buying command of the 11th. It was also said that Lord Lucan bought command of the 17th Lancers for £25,000, going over the head of the senior major, who sold out in despair and entered the Portuguese service. Rumours, probably well-founded, of regiments changing hands for as much as £57,000, were rife in the 1850s.[3]

The bad points of the purchase system are obvious. An old officer was unlikely to show deference to a young man promoted over his head not for merit but merely because he possessed a sum of money which he himself lacked. Further, when a commanding officer wished

	Lieut-Col.	Major.	Captain.	Lieut.	Cornet/ Ensign
*					
Life Guards	£7,250	£5,350	£3,500	£1,785	£1,260
Royal Horse Guards	£7,250	£5,350	£3,500	£1,600	£1,200
Cavalry of the line	£6,175	£4,575	£3,225	£1,190	£840

† In the infantry the prices were: regulation, £4,500; average over-regulation, £2,500; total: £7,000 (exactly half that in the cavalry of the line).

to retire the scope for selection of his successor was severely limited. The next senior major in the regiment who had the price of a lieutenant-colonelcy generally succeeded to the command, whether fit for it or not, even though the Commander-in-Chief had the power of veto. If there were no major in the regiment rich enough, a major was brought in from another regiment or from half-pay to be lieutenant-colonel in command.

Officers without money inevitably became 'bent and bald under that cruel game of golden leap-frog of which they are the eternal victims'.[4] Another evil was the virtual restriction of officers to one class – the upper. This excluded many suitable candidates. Sir Charles Trevelyan told the Purchase Commission in 1857 that his object in advocating abolition was 'to hold out such an inducement to the soldier of promotion and distinction as will draw to the army the middle class. They would be especially suited for employment as administrators because of their training in business habits.'[5]

*   *   *

A number of supposed advantages of the system were advanced by its supporters from time to time. The most telling of these was the fact that there were, as has been shown, exceptions to the rule. It was further pleaded, rather speciously, that a better class of officer in point of education entered the commissioned ranks of the army than would otherwise be the case. All that can be said for this argument is that education was to a great extent the prerogative of the rich. It was also claimed that no officer could buy promotion who would not have been equally eligible without purchase (which was highly questionable), and that no step in rank could be bought without the qualifications of a certain number of years' service (which was only true in theory).* But stronger than these arguments was that which asserted that the system facilitated retirement, thereby

---

* By a regulation of 1711 the right to sell a commission, whether it had been purchased or not, was limited to those who had served twenty years or more. This rule was certainly not scrupulously observed, and had, in fact, been modified so that an officer of less than twenty years' service was allowed to receive a part of the regulation value of his commission. This was reckoned at £50 for each year of service at home, and £100 for each year of foreign service. Up to 1862 the allowance was £100 for each year's service, whether at home or abroad. After twenty years' service he might receive the full regulation value.

accelerating promotion which otherwise tended to stagnate in peacetime.

'If officers ... knew', declared *The Economist* in 1855, 'that they
would receive the value of their commissions at any time and
without any hazard, they would never sell out at all until actually
laid aside by decrepitude; and the service would be crowded with
old valetudinarians and promotion be entirely stopped. At
present these men are induced to retire in time from the fear of
losing all if they delay too long.'

In the Artillery, Engineers and Marines, where promotion was exclusively by seniority, it was painfully slow.*

Other firmly held beliefs were that purchase offered security
against favouritism; that a system of selection was more open to
abuse in this respect than one based on money; that it might cause
'ill-feeling in the Army and encourage officers to hate each other',
and, above all, that a professional army would make England like
Prussia, 'neither more nor less than a military despotism'. This was
no doubt what Sir Walter Scott had in mind when he wrote in 1827
that though the system was 'an evil in a military point of view, it was
indispensable to the freedom of the country'.[6]

Lord Salisbury believed that 'seniority tempered by selection'
would soon degenerate into 'stagnation tempered by jobbery'. Lord
Panmure recalled the dictum of the French War Minister during the
Revolutionary period, who suggested that 'the effect of giving
promotion solely for merit would not in reality be favourable to
political liberty, because a Staff composed of soldiers of fortune
would be much more likely to support a Dictator than would a body
of officers who were already bound to the ancient institutions of
their country'.[7] Wellington had been insistent that the purchase system brought into the service 'men who have some connection with
the interests and fortunes of the country besides the commissions
which they hold from His Majesty. It is this circumstance', he argued,
'which exempts the British Army from the character of being a
"mercenary army", and has rendered its employment for nearly a
century and a half not only not inconsistent with the constitutional
privileges of the country, but safe and beneficial.'[8]

* In evidence before the Commission of Enquiry into the System of Promotion
and Retirement, 1838–40, Sir Alexander Dickson, Royal Artillery, said: 'After
a man had served 30 or 40 years you might as well turn him into the street as
expect him to retire on half-pay.' In the 1850s there were not many captains in
the two scientific corps under sixty.

It was further suggested that the *esprit de corps* of regiments would be damaged by the end of purchase. In fact, the reverse was probably more true, for the system offered special inducements to officers to exchange into regiments other than their own. A rich officer, if at all ambitious, naturally wished to go into a regiment in which many of the officers were unable to purchase so as to secure for himself more speedy promotion.* Furthermore, so long as it remained possible in practice but not in law to sell out or to exchange at any time, a regiment posted to an unhealthy climate was apt to lose many of its less conscientious officers before sailing, and find itself well below establishment. The cavalry, however, unlike the infantry, was rarely posted abroad in peacetime, except in the case of the light regiments to India. This made the mounted service specially attractive to the rich *flâneur*, the 'swell' and the 'plunger'. A typical example of how rich young officers faced the threat of Indian service is given by Captain Anstruther Thomson. When he discovered, in 1841, that his regiment, the 9th Lancers, was under orders for India, he told his best friend that he had 'been to London to see about an exchange. I mean', he said, 'to go into the Carabineers.'

"'Oh, d—n it, no. Don't be a heavy and wear a brass hat." I said: "The only other regiment in which there are vacancies is the 13th. There is a Captain and Lieutenant who wish to exchange." "Let's go together wherever we go," said he. "All right," I said, and we wrote at once and effected the exchange. I exchanged with Captain Reid and paid £1,500 for the exchange, making my Troop cost £6,500.'[9]

* The Royal Commission of 1856 examined the services of fifty-two generals, with the following result:

12 had served in 1 regiment
4 „ „ „ 2 regiments
8 „ „ „ 3 „
9 „ „ „ 4 „
11 „ „ „ 5 „
4 „ „ „ 6 „
3 „ „ „ 7 „
1 „ „ „ 9 „

Colonels of regiments seem to have been able to veto exchanges of which they disapproved. In 1820, the Duke of Cumberland, Honorary Colonel of the 15th Hussars, refused consent to an exchange between a subaltern of the regiment and another of the 38th Foot. His object, he said, being 'to bring young men into the Regiment who will rise progressively, and by being thereby thoroughly grounded in the system of the corps will, I hope, become good cavalry officers'. (Wylly, 262.)

Officers more adventurous than Captain Thomson were often prepared to go out to India, but once there were apt to exchange or sell
out if ordered up-country without the prospect of action. The oft-
quoted case of Beau Brummell who sold out of the 10th Hussars
when ordered to the remote, unfashionable station of Manchester,
was not the only one of its kind.

* * *

The whole system of purchase, as Fortescue has written, 'being
utterly illogical, iniquitous and indefensible, commended itself
heartily to the British public. . . . It was in its essence such a game of
chance as should, long before its abolition, have brought it under
the purview of the Gaming Acts.'[10] One aspect of the element of
chance was the fact that a non-purchase officer who obtained a step
through the death or promotion to major-general of a senior officer,
suddenly became possessed of a valuable asset which he could then
sell, even though he had never bought a commission in his life.* This
sale of unbought commissions had in fact been forbidden as early as
1711, but the rule had never been enforced.

* * *

Looking back from a century ahead, it is astonishing that the system
should not have been abolished earlier, especially as the purchase of
all civil offices had long since disappeared. It was unknown abroad;
nor did it operate in the Royal Navy. It had been condemned by responsible authorities, including the Royal Commission of 1857, yet
it survived until 1871. Why? There were two main reasons. The
majority of officers (Sir Garnet Wolseley thought as many as 99 out
of 100), were in favour of its retention, even those without means.
One such officer told the 1857 Commission that he had been 'bought
over' eighteen times, yet, after eighteen years he held the rank of
captain. 'I consider', he added, 'I should have been many years longer
in getting it if there had been no purchase.' Many a young cornet

* Supporters of the system urged that since a lieutenant-colonel who had purchased could sell-out, it was possible to argue that a rich officer on occasions
actually paid for the retirement of a poor one. This, however, was chiefly a
financial advantage to the public.

liked the system, for, as Sir George Trevelyan explained to the Commons in 1868:

> 'The commissions of a young officer are frequently bought with money which he would not get under any other conditions. . . . A young officer who at present can lay his hands upon £2,000 whenever he thinks fit to sell out knows that if it were not for the purchase system one of those thousands would be in his father's pocket and the other in his maiden aunt's reticule.'[11]

The other chief reason for the delay in abolition was undoubtedly the cost. Parliament felt disinclined to end a practice which saved the taxpayer money. 'The economists', wrote Cardwell, the Liberal Secretary of State for War, to Gladstone, 'will rise against us if we make any change to the disadvantage of the taxpayer.'[12] Had it not been for the startling successes of the Prussian army in the Franco-Prussian war, which alarmed Parliament and people alike, Cardwell might well have failed in this, one of the greatest of his army reforms. 'It began at last to dawn upon the mind of even the taxpayer', wrote Wolseley, a rabid abolitionist, 'that our Army was as far behind that of France as that army had lately proved itself to be behind the army of Germany.'

Another factor which made abolition a matter of urgency in the 1870s was the need in a modern army to be able to effect exchanges between all arms. Until abolition it was impossible to transfer officers of the non-purchase corps (Royal Artillery, Royal Engineers, Royal Marines, and certain Indian regiments raised in 1862) to the rest of the army and *vice versa*. Further, officers in these corps were ineligible for appointment on the General Staff. Nor could the militia be combined with the regular forces while regular officers were distinguished by purchase.

As it was, the Bill, which contained a number of other provisions beside abolition of purchase, was passed through the Commons with difficulty and virtually thrown out by the Lords. Compelled to drop the Bill unless some other method could be found, the Government fell back upon the fact that an Act of Parliament was not needed to abolish purchase. An Act of 1809, it was discovered, prohibited the practice except so far as 'fixed by regulation made or to be made by the Crown'. The Cabinet therefore advised the Queen to cancel the existing Royal Warrant by issuing another. Once this had been done, since an Act was still essential to provide the necessary finance, Parliament's hand was forced. The Regulation of the Forces Act,

1871, much altered, finally passed both Houses and received the Royal Assent. The provisions of the Act, and how they affected the officers of the army, will be considered in a later volume.

'Your profession must be like your mistress, see as many faults and imperfections as you please, before you adopt it, but that once done, you must believe her infallible.'
A father's advice to his son on entering the army, 1833[1]

(iv)

Officers: half-pay – full pay – messing costs – charges – allowances – generals' emoluments – pensions

After Waterloo, as has been seen, a large reduction took place in the size of the army. Numerous regimental officers, therefore, found themselves without employment. For these, if they did not wish to sell out, and if they were unable or unwilling to rise to general's rank, there was only one course of action. They must retire on half-pay, a sort of retaining fee for future service.* So long as half-pay officers made periodical 'offers of service' (whatever their state of health) they still remained in line for promotion. No officer with less than three years' full pay service was entitled to half-pay. The scale

* Half-pay was also a means of rewarding meritorious service; indeed a sort of pension.
    An officer transferred from a regiment to the half-pay list had to accept a commission much inferior in value to that which he had purchased. He would also lose 'over-regulation' price. Provision was made by a warrant of 1830 for a small number of officers to retire on full pay; twelve lieutenant-colonels, twenty-four majors, ninety captains, sixty lieutenants and thirty ensigns/cornets. This cost the State about £55,000 per annum. No vacancies, however, could be filled until the annual expenditure fell below £40,000. The prospects for regimental officers of retirement on full pay, until they were very old, were therefore limited.
    From 1819 until 1829 officers filling civil offices were allowed to retain their half-pay. The Act of 1829 was, however, reversed in 1833.

of half-pay was the same in 1815 as it had been a hundred years before. It was always much less than half the full pay rate. After thirty years' service, for example, an officer whose full pay had been £600 a year, received only £146 a year on half-pay. There were numbers of officers granted brevet lieutenant-colonelcies for distinguished conduct in the Peninsular War, who for more than twenty years after Waterloo remained on half-pay of £127 a year in the rank of captain. In 1838 there were more lieutenant-colonels and majors on half-pay than there were on full pay. In that year, out of 8,834 officers in the army, 3,968 were retired on half-pay.

* * *

The full pay of officers, until the abolition of purchase, was looked upon as little more than an honorarium. In 1833, Wellington declared that most officers received 'but little for their service beside the honour of serving the King'. He estimated that the total remuneration of a lieutenant-colonel of cavalry was £1,400 a year. This included the profit which he made on the supply of uniforms to his regiment. As late as 1869, Charles Clode, in his authoritative *Military Forces of the Crown*, stated that 'offering pay as an inducement to a lower class of officers to join the Army would be a doubtful expedient'.[2] Though the rates had been increased on at least four occasions since 1797, their real value seventy years later was considerably less than at that date.

A cornet in the cavalry received 8s. a day and a lieutenant-colonel 23s.* There were also Field Allowances designed to cover the cost of transport of baggage and equipment on service. These ranged from 1s. a day for a subaltern in peacetime, to 4s. 6d. for a lieutenant-colonel in wartime. Cavalry officers were also entitled to certain forage allowances for their horses and baggage animals. In the infantry it was possible for a subaltern to live on his pay if he exercised self-restraint, but even in the less swanky cavalry regiments it was virtually essential for a cornet to possess an independent in-

---

* Pay of cavalry officers in 1815:
Lieutenant-Colonel 23s.   per diem.
Major   19/3d.   „
Captain   14/7d.   „
Lieutenant   9s.   „
Cornet   8s.   „

come. In 1815, the Colonel of the Greys stipulated that a gentleman, in order to be eligible for a cornetcy in that regiment, must have
at least £200 per annum besides his pay.[3] Cornet Anstruther
Thomson is an example of the average officer of his day. When he
joined the 9th Lancers in 1836 he brought with him an allowance of
£300 and a private servant. The regiment provided him with a bat-
man as well and he paid him 'two shillings and sixpence a week. His
wife did my room, washed and mended, for two shillings a week.'[4]
Other junior officers were less well endowed. A subaltern's breakfast,
it was said, often consisted of no more than 'a drink of water and a
pull at the belt'. In 1846, the weekly charge for messing each officer
of the 8th Hussars in Ireland, was 'about £2 8s. 1d.'[5] There is ample
evidence that in many cavalry regiments the cost of his messing was
greater than a subaltern's pay.

In 1857 the cost of dinner in the mess was officially limited to
2s. 6d. for the cavalry. By the end of the century the cost of food
alone was not allowed to exceed 4s. a day; but it is certain that in
many regiments more than this was demanded in defiance of *Queen's
Regulations*.

If an officer lived in barracks he received an allowance for coals
and candles. If he were married and lived in lodgings no such per-
quisites came his way. It is difficult to understand why this should
have been. Fortescue puts it down to 'the usual source of absurd and
iniquitous regulations – the natural craving of clerks to save themselves trouble'.[6]

*   *   *

Among other charges imposed on officers were three guineas on
joining his regiment to be paid to the riding master for 'Instruction
in Riding', two guineas for 'Breaking Horses' and one guinea for
'each Horse subsequently broken'.[7]

Until 1842, when passage-allowances were first introduced, each
officer on being posted overseas had to find the price of his own passage. When he reached India he found living conditions reasonable
and often luxurious but the Government in London credited the
rupee to him at 2s., while paying it to him in India as worth 2s. 6d.
thereby mulcting him of 4s. in the pound. In 1842 a captain of the
3rd Light Dragoons wrote home from India that a troop was 'little
worth having now, as I can save nothing out of my pay, so it is time
for me to come home. . . . I would sooner serve for love at home

than 2,000 rupees per month in this country.'[8] This was a widely held view at that time.

* * *

The financial position of general officers was no better. As we have seen, an officer on promotion to major-general lost the value of his commission. Further than this, until 1814, a general received no pay as such. If he were in command in the field or on special duty or on the Staff, he was paid accordingly. Otherwise, the only ways in which he could draw any emolument were by obtaining the colonelcy of a regiment, or the governorship of a fortress or colony, or by continuing on the strength of his regiment as a nominal major or captain. When 'unattached pay' for generals* was introduced in the year before Waterloo, there were twenty-nine drawing half-pay as majors, and sixty-nine as captains. Four years later the unattached list was limited to 120, at a time when 320 were receiving unattached pay and sixteen nothing but regimental pay. In 1834, however, the limit was removed.

* * *

Some sort of pensions for widows and dependents of dead officers had been granted from the early eighteenth century. Pensions for wounds or loss of limbs date from 1812. By the 1850s a cornet's wound pension was £50 a year, a captain's £100, and a lieutenant-colonel's £300. A lieutenant's widow received £60 if her husband had been killed in action, and £40 if he had died otherwise; a major's widow £120 and £70 respectively, and a colonel's widow £200 and £90 respectively.[9] If an officer left no widow his mother or sisters received the pension in her place. There was also a compassionate fund from which a dead officer's children were granted small pensions. From 1833, pensions as 'rewards for distinguished services' were instituted. These replaced sinecure garrison appointments.

* General   £693 10s. od. per annum.
  Lieutenant-general £593 3s. 4d.   „
  Major-general   £456 5s. od.   „

'There are no officers in the world like English
gentlemen.'

SIR CHARLES NAPIER, 1839[1]

(v)

*Officers: all socially equal – confidential reports – medical
certificates – leisure – drunkenness – crime and punishment – army chaplains – paymasters – quartermasters –
riding masters – medical officers*

One of the more significant differences between the British and the
continental armies was (and perhaps still is) that, off duty, all British
officers were, in theory, socially equal. Senior officers did not take
advantage of their rank in the mess, and so long as the ordinary code
of gentlemanly conduct was observed, there were few definite rules.
Great scandal was caused, for instance, when the Duke of Cumberland (who was said to prefer Prussian officers because they were more
deferential) struck with his cane an officer of the 15th Hussars of
which he was colonel-in-chief.

The introduction, in the early years of the century, of confidential
reports on officers was considered to have turned the army, 'whose
constitution is based on the most scrupulous adherence to the highest
and nicest principles of honour, into a gradual corps of spies from
the ensign up to the general. . . . The fawning and servile' wrote a
Peninsular veteran, 'are sure to escape and not infrequently with
rewards.'[2] Equally the idea that medical certificates should be required by officers absent from duty was held to be a gross assault upon
the sanctity of an officer's word of honour. Discipline in these circumstances was by modern standards loose.

As for cavalry officers' leisure pursuits, they centred chiefly around
the horse. Hunting, racing and steeplechasing, by the 1840s at least,
were highly organised within regiments. Lord Anglesey, however,
who was considered the great arbiter in matters of military and civil
equitation, condemned 'the practice of Steeple Chases' as 'highly
objectionable'.[3] The 1842 Regimental Standing Orders of the 5th
Dragoon Guards stated that 'during the hunting season officers may
reckon on such arrangements being made as will enable them to
pursue this diversion'.[4]

The habit of heavy drinking was universal. An amusing and

typical example is related by a Norfolk Yeomanry officer at the height of the machine-breaking riots in East Anglia in 1831. He and his fellow officers were entertained in Norwich by the officers of the Royal Dragoons. After a 'sumptuous repast' he and a few others were asked to stay behind

> 'and to favour them with some songs. We readily agreed, not guessing at their intention, which was, according to their expression, "to sew us up"; but our adjutant, who was an old campaigner, declared to me in a whisper what their intention was, and I passed the hint to . . . the others. I sang several songs, and they kept it up with great spirits till it was very late, but we were very cautious in taking wine. Not so our hosts, who indulged so freely that they were all left under the table; they had locked us in, but we hunted for the key, and finding it in one of their pockets, we "turned the tables" on them by locking them up in their own mess-room for the night, and leaving the key in the door, walked home safe and cool.'[5]

* * *

More than in most social clubs, it was important, especially in the cavalry where so many officers were rich, that men should be of the same class, habits and financial standing if harmony in the mess was to be assured. There are numerous stories of informal subalterns' courts martial, as often as not arising from some unfortunate officer being unable to compete socially or financially. Such a one was Cornet Thomas Ames of the 4th Hussars, who, in 1854, was forcibly fed upon pap, whilst being slapped 'to stimulate the powers of deglutition' by three fellow officers. They then mutilated part of his moustaches. *The Times* heard of the incident and thundered: 'Why allow wealthy and titled libertines to bully a young man of different disposition out of a regiment . . .?' In reply, Lord Ernest Vane-Tempest, one of Ames's persecutors, wrote that 'nothing that could be constructed into an insult was addressed by me to him, although his peculiar English and mispronunciation of the letter "h" produced some remarks in joke which caused a great deal of laughter. . . . I remarked that his whisker wanted trimming, and a pair of scissors being brought I cut off some of one whisker.'[6]

There was an astonishing difference between officer and man when it came to crime. This is well illustrated by the case of Lieutenant-

Colonel French in command of the 6th Dragoon Guards (The Carabiniers) who was court-martialled in 1820. He was found guilty of 'keeping a woman in barracks' and admonished. He was also found guilty of 'inflicting a greater punishment on three sergeants than was awarded by court-martial' and reprimanded. On the counts of 'publicly dealing in horses; fraudulent conduct in the sale of a horse to Mr Hall, previous to his obtaining a cornetcy in the regiment; selling a remount horse for 30 guineas, and of causing the troop registers of horses to be cut and defaced', he was acquitted. The King, in confirming the findings, regretted that the Colonel of the Regiment had 'withdrawn his confidence' from Lieutenant-Colonel French, who did not even resign his command.[7]*

The exclusive nature of the majority of cavalry regiments was, on the whole, well maintained during the nineteenth century. The number of men commissioned from the ranks was very small indeed. On this point the Duke of Wellington was unequivocal:

'In truth', he said, 'they do not make good officers; it does not answer. They are brought into society and manners to which they are not accustomed; they cannot bear being at all heated with wine or liquor. . . . I think in general they are quarrelsome . . . and they are not persons who can be borne in the society of the officers of the army; they are men of different manners altogether.'[8]

Sergeant James Anton of the 42nd Highlanders went so far as to call it

'no less than a robbery of the country, seeing that commissions are sold to gentlemen, educated and qualified to hold them, to give one to an individual of no influence and whose only merit may be that of being thought well of by his commanding officer, and daily in his presence, but still one who perhaps would sell his country as Esau did his birthright for a morsel of pottage.'[9]

'Poor men', declared *The Times* in 1855, a little too sarcastically, 'are all very well in their own place. . . . To make a man an ensign for merit is only to teach him in the most forcible manner possible that he has entered a profession in which merit is not considered.'[10]

Among distinguished exceptions to the rule was General Sir James Craig, who entered the army as a trooper in the Household

* For another example of leniency to an officer, see p. 269.

Cavalry, and died in 1812 as Colonel of the 78th Foot. Another was Sir John Elley, who was a full colonel at Waterloo, and died a lieutenant-general in 1839. He, too, had enlisted as a trooper in the Blues.

*   *   *

In 1796, an Army Chaplain's department, with a Chaplain-General at its head, was set up. Up till then regiments had appointed their own chaplains. The new dispensation did not at once lead to an increase either in numbers or quality. Bad pay was one reason, and it was not until some years after Waterloo that suitable men in sufficient numbers were attracted to become military chaplains. In 1844, the Rev. G. R. Gleig, already mentioned, was appointed Principal Chaplain, and it was he, almost single-handed, who brought to the department the high reputation which it enjoyed towards the end of his thirty-one years' tenure of the office, and has done ever since.

On his appointment, he received instructions from Hardinge, the Secretary at War. He was told to exercise great caution and discretion in the appointment of army chaplains:

> 'In the greater part of the regiments the majority consists', wrote Hardinge, 'of Episcopalians. In the 14 Scottish regiments the majority are Presbyterians, and in many other of the regiments recruited in Ireland, the majority are composed of Roman Catholics; and the case may not infrequently arise in which in the same hospital the clergymen of the three different religious persuasions may be attending the sick on the same day.'[11]

Presbyterian chaplains were officially recognised in the army in 1827 and the position of Roman Catholic ones was regularised in 1836.

*   *   *

Of the other 'professional' officers who formed part of the regimental staff, the paymaster, the quartermaster, the riding master and sometimes the adjutant were generally promoted from the ranks.* When

---

* Cornet Anstruther Thomson says of the adjutant of the 9th Lancers in 1836: 'Cooke was an Irishman who had risen from the ranks and was a fine specimen of an old soldier. He had been promoted over the head of the Regimental Sergeant-Major.' Upon which the R.S.M. 'broke his sword in two and placed it on the fire saying his soldiering days were over.' (Thomson, I, 43.)

For the status and duties of the veterinary surgeon see p. 111.

this was the case they were considered as of a different, inferior class of officer and so treated in the mess. The regimental medical officers, on the other hand, were generally looked upon with more tolerance. Many of them were products of the universities. Most of them bought their commissions in the usual way. Some even bought combatant commissions as well as their specialist ones, thus increasing their pay. Under them was the regimental hospital staff, headed by a sergeant, and including a varying number of orderlies. Professionally they came under a medical board which dealt with all appointments, especially those of extra-regimental surgeons and physicians in garrison and general hospitals.

'A soldier's honour is as sacred as a woman's virtue.'

GEORGE SIMMONS[1]

(vi)

Officers: duelling – notable duels

An essential part of the gentlemanly code was the practice of duelling. For those who resorted to it the very severest penalties were laid down both by civil and military law. But since men like the Dukes of York and Wellington, to protect their personal honour, found it necessary to break the law in this way it was not easy to stamp out. Nevertheless by the mid-1840s, the weight of public opinion, led by Prince Albert, had put a virtual end to it. In the British army it died out long before it did so in the armies of Europe.

Two of the most notable duels of this final period were fought by cavalry officers. In 1840 Captain Tuckett, formerly of the 11th Hussars, after selling his commission, had written to the *Morning Chronicle* alleging that the Earl of Cardigan, in command of that regiment, had regularly insulted his officers in the mess, while avoiding a duel by virtue of his position as commanding officer. Since Tuckett was now a civilian Cardigan deemed it no breach of military law to challenge him. In the resulting duel, Tuckett fell wounded. Cardigan then faced trial by his peers in the House of Lords and was acquitted due to a technical quibble. The indignation of the press was boundless and undoubtedly did much to rouse public opinion against duelling.

The duel, however, which did even more to put an end to it took place three years later. Lieutenant Monro, of the Royal Horse Guards, called out his brother-in-law, Lieutenant-Colonel Fawcett, of the 55th Regiment. After a personal row, Fawcett had lost his temper and, in the presence of a servant, ordered Monro out of the house. Fawcett was shot dead and Monro fled the country. The Government view, when the case was debated in the Commons, was that Fawcett ought to have swallowed his pride, and said: 'I acted hastily in turning you downstairs, and for the language at which you justly took offence I tender an apology.' Public indignation, in this case, was levelled more against the Government which refused to grant Fawcett's widow a pension, than against Monro and the seconds. It was chiefly as a result of this duel that the Articles of War were amended; but the new provisions were, in fact, very little different from those which had existed for over a century. It was more 'the influence of civilization', as Sir Robert Peel put it, which produced 'the necessary effect'.

'A military gent I see – and while his face I scan,
I think you'll all agree with me – He came from
Hindostan.'
THACKERAY, W. M. *The Newcomes*, Bk.I, Ch.I.

(vii)

*Officers: in the East India Company's armies – difference
of status – extra-regimental employment –* batta

The position of officers in the armies of the Honourable East India Company was entirely different. Until the amalgamation with the Royal army after the great Mutiny of 1857, the European officers in native regiments, as well as in the small number of completely

white corps, were servants of the Company, not of the Crown. Originally they had been recruited from its civil ranks. Clive, for instance,
had been a Company's 'writer'. Other officers had been found from
foreign sources and sometimes from Royal regiments. There was,
of course, no purchase system. The officers of the Royal army enjoyed precedence over Company's officers of the same rank. This,
beside being a source of jealousy, clearly indicated the difference
in social status between the two. In the early days there was some
justification for this, for both in morale and technique the Royal
officers were generally superior; but as the Company's army developed, that superiority became progressively less marked. Company's officers could only serve within the Company's domains.
However excellent senior officers might be they were barred from
employment in, say, a European theatre of war.

In the early nineteenth century when a subaltern arrived in India
to serve in one of the Company's regiments he discovered that unless
exceptionally lethal campaigns or decimating epidemics came to
carry off his seniors and contemporaries, he had little hope of rising
to the command of his regiment in less than forty years. Even so
exceptional an officer as John Jacob (see p. 157) did not reach the
rank of captain (in the Bombay foot artillery) until he had seen
nineteen years' service. The more enterprising officers, therefore,
looked for extra-regimental employment. Such posts as Collector
of Land Revenue were increasingly filled by seconded officers; but
the spheres in which the well-educated officer was becoming more
and more engaged were the political and semi-diplomatic. In 1825
the Duke of Wellington noticed that 'by far the majority of the
officers of the regiments [of the native army], and, of course, the
best officers, those who best understand the language, manners, and
customs of the natives . . . are employed in civil and diplomatic
situations. . . . '[1] The 'soldier-civilians' and 'soldier-politicals' were
well paid, and often found themselves wielding power and shoulder-
ing responsibilities well beyond any their rank or length of service
warranted. By the civilians they were apt to be considered interlopers
and by their fellows deserters in pursuit of fame and riches. The system contained valuable elements of liaison and flexibility; but it was
apt to draw away from regiments their best officers.

Once the ambitious subaltern had mastered a native language or
two, such as Marathi or Persian, he was ready to don a 'black coat'
and to set forth, as a distinguished historian of the period has put it,
'to plumb the depths of Durbar intrigue, to spy out lands forgotten

since the days of Alexander, or to spend long strenuous months with theodolite, staff and chain, in hills and jungles where the face of a white man had never been seen'.[2] Another favourite outlet for the enterprising officer, as will be seen in later chapters, was the raising and officering of provisional, local and, particularly, irregular corps of cavalry and infantry.

In 1828, the Company's officers were dealt a blow which further lessened the attraction of straightforward regimental service. One of the earliest economies which that liberal governor-general, Lord William Bentinck, imposed after his arrival in India was the reduction by half of the officers' *batta*. This was an extra allowance granted primarily during service in the field, but also wherever quarters were not provided by the Company. The cutting of what had come to be regarded as part of pay caused immense resentment. In Calcutta the governor-general was subjected, even by commanding officers, to a social boycott. In Bombay the retiring governor was allowed to depart for home without the customary expressions of regret.

The native soldiers, especially in Bengal, when they realised that only their officers were to suffer from the economy axe, 'formed an overweening estimate of their own importance.'[3] This was aggravated when, in 1835, Bentinck abolished flogging as a punishment for native soldiers throughout India, while retaining it for the European troops! (see p. 137.) Though ten years later Sir Henry Hardinge repealed it, Bentinck's flogging order, coupled with his 'half-batta' measure, worsened relations between officers and men in native regiments, and played its part in bringing about the catastrophe of 1857.

5

'The Irregular Cavalry is of peculiar importance in India'

LORD WILLIAM BENTINCK, 1835[1]

(i)

India: regular and irregular (silladar) *native cavalry regiments*

In India, by the second decade of the nineteenth century, there were three types of cavalry available to the Company. Beside the Royal regiments from England, which were of course entirely European, there were native regiments with white officers. These, except in Madras, where all regiments were regular, were of two sorts, irregular and regular, or *silladar* and *non-silladar*. The word is a Maratha corruption from the Hindustani *Silahdar* meaning a soldier wearing armour or bearing arms. The basic difference between the two was that the irregular cavalryman, like the yeoman of England (see p. 76), supplied, in principle, his own horse. He also provided his own accoutrements, stabling, attendants, forage, camp equipment, clothing and weapons (except, in some instances, fire-arms), but not his ammunition or medical stores. In return he received a small amount of pay: twenty or thirty rupees a month throughout most of the nineteenth century.* For the regular cavalryman, on the other hand, the Government found everything.

The *silladar* and *non-silladar* systems evolved from those which had existed in the mercenary horse of the Marathas and Mysoreans in the distant feudal past. Each prince who could afford it maintained a sort of household cavalry, known as the *paga* horse,† which was

---

* Irregular regiments were still selecting their own patterns of clothing and equipment well into the nineteenth century. As late as 1914, complete uniformity had not been achieved.

The total cost of equipment for a trooper in the Poona Auxiliary Horse was estimated in 1839 to be:

Horse equipment	Rupees	Annas
Bridle	1	3
Saddle	7	6
Cloth Bridle ⎫		
Crupper ⎬	3	4
Breast plate ⎭		
Martingale	0	12
Saddle cloth	4	8
Surcingle	0	6
Gram-bag	0	8
Common coir brush	0	4
Halter	0	4
Head and heel ropes	1	0
Jool	3	0
	22	7

Personal equipment	Rupees	Annas
Cloth coat	10	0
Boots	2	10
Spurs	0	8
Pouch and belt	2	0
Pair of pistols	25	0
Priming horn	1	4
Holsters	2	8
Spear	2	4
	46	2
	68	9

(Equivalent to about £6 19s. at that time.)

(Lambrick, *S.I.H.*, 30.)

† *Paga* was a Maratha word meaning a body of horse under one commander, in which the horses belonged to the state; or the stable or building where the horses were kept.

paid and equipped entirely at his expense. The *pagas* were more than mere hirelings, for they were actual adherents of their master. If his cause was lost, they were adrift on the world. It was upon them that the princes chiefly relied in a conflict. Minor chieftains had to rely upon *barghirs* (literally, 'rein-holders'), men unable to bring their own horses who were paid in the form of a contract which ceased the instant the horse provided was killed. *Barghirs* were the lowest order of horsemen. Considerably higher were the *khudaspas*, the true predecessors of the *silladar* troopers. These provided their own horses and served under a leader commissioned by his prince. They were paid by him according to the value and size of their horses.

The earlier *silladar* regiments were specifically divided into *khudaspas* and *barghirs*, and later there were often some of each within regiments. 'The Khooduspas are men who ride on their own horses, and receive their pay complete; the Bargeers are men who ride on horses supplied by other men, receiving *one third* of the pay – the other two-thirds belonging to the owner of the horse.'² The bona fide *khudaspa* came to be known as a *silladar*. His and his horse's place or 'berth' in the regiment (known as an *asami*) was looked upon as property. It could be sold at any time or 'bequeathed from father to son or for the subsistence of the widow or family of the *silladar*'.³ It could be sold to the highest bidder 'provided the substitute be considered fit for the service by the Commandant' of the regiment.⁴ In 1841, about twenty *asamis* in the Scinde Irregular Horse were owned by persons not actually serving in the regiment. The regimental clerk owned four, and, more surprising, three were owned by one of the *bhistis* (water-carriers).⁵ On his death the *silladar*'s family retained the *asami*, and (at any rate until the 1840s) a *barghir* was enlisted to ride his horse. Native commissioned officers were allowed to own from two to five extra horses, according to their rank. These were often ridden by *barghirs* enlisted for the purpose. In the 1840s the average value of an *asami* was 250 rupees. In Gardner's Horse it was between 350 and 400 rupees. From 1861 onwards the substitute system was abolished.

Since native princes were notoriously unstable financially, both *barghirs* and *khudaspas*, more often than not, received their pay so fitfully that it became accepted practice for them to recoup themselves by plunder and the levying of contributions. As licensed marauders, left on the death of their horses with no financial resort, neither class of horseman had much incentive to energetic or disciplined action in the battlefield. To overcome this and other disadvantages, the British, in their own *silladar* regiments, instituted in due course certain reforms. A recruit, instead of bringing a horse and kit, brought their value in money. On discharge he returned the horse and kit with which he had been issued to the regiment and received back their market value in cash. The replacement of horses and equipment was covered by a 'horse fund' in every troop, to which each man subscribed from his pay and horse allowance. In the course of the years, and in the different regiments, many variations of these two 'provident funds' grew up, but in whatever shape they operated they were designed to ensure that troopers were not left destitute or in debt at the end of their service. Equally important was the proprietary pride in the regiment which his share in its economy gave each man.

Crime in *silladar* regiments was very much less than in regular regiments. At the regimental durbar, often held as frequently as once a week, such disciplinary measures as were necessary were taken. Its chairman was the commandant, and he acted as judge and arbitrator. 'Anyone could come forward and speak, down to the lowest regimental sweeper. The regiment followed the proceedings with wrapt interest and never seemed to find them too long.'[6] Claimants for leave, loans and compassionate allowances were interviewed at these durbars; new recruits came before them, and every conceivable subject, from debts to details of equipment was discussed. Leave in time of peace was generous. In Gardner's Horse, for instance, before 1914, two periods of furlough were given annually, each for three-and-a-half months. Until as late as 1905, in some *silladar* regiments, troopers fed their horses by buying fodder from the 'troop-bunnias', merchants attached to each troop. The regiment was, in a way, a business concern as well as a fighting unit. For instance, it bought, bred, trained and sold horses and baggage animals, and it farmed on a considerable scale, chiefly for grass. But above all it was very much a 'family', and from that aspect of its being it drew great strength.

Silladar regiments were cheaper to maintain than *non-silladar* regiments. In 1911, a Captain of the 20th Deccan Horse, pointed out that all that Government did for the irregular trooper was

'to supply bandolier, rifle, ammunition, and the cost of the feed of his horse and half-share of a transport animal; and the tremendous business of maintaining, equipping and mounting regiments of four squadrons of six hundred and twenty-five sabres or lances, as the case may be, then devolves upon the man and his British and native officers'.[7]

In 1835, Lord William Bentinck, then Governor-General and Commander-in-Chief, wrote:

'The Irregular Cavalry . . . is the favourite arm of the native. It attaches him to our Service by the strong ties of interest and affection. It prevents their being engaged against us, and if the system were sufficiently extended it would, at a trifling expense, afford us all the advantages, moral and military, which the Russians have derived from the Cossacks. . . . The Rohillas and all the highest caste and bravest men of India, who will not enter our ranks from dislike to our rigid discipline . . . have no repugnance to serve in the Irregular Cavalry.'

Nine years later Sir Henry Rawlinson, the great Assyriologist, who distinguished himself in the First Afghan War, stated that 'the Irregular Cavalry forms an outlet for the gentry, who do not otherwise enlist'.[8]

Recruits for the *silladar* cavalry were drawn in the main from the *zamindar*, or landowner and farmer classes, and from among the sons of the native officers and men who were allowed, within a certain percentage, to keep their families inside the lines of each regiment. The native officers were usually men of good birth and standing. In Bengal there was an increasing tendency to select them from the ranks on the sole ground of seniority. In Bombay seniority was only one of a number of recognised qualifications. In irregular regiments, at least until after the Mutiny, there were no European commanders of squadrons and troops, most regiments having only three or four white officers in all. This gave the irregular native officers a far higher status than was enjoyed by their equivalents in the regular cavalry, the most senior of whom ranked below the most junior European cornet, and who could never aspire to substantive command even of a troop.

Before the Mutiny, the proportion of the various religions and castes in regiments of the Indian army was more a matter of chance than intention.* After that great upheaval, care was taken, for

* In 1848, for instance, the Scinde Irregular Horse consisted of 140 Brahmins and Rajputs, and 34 Marathas, while 85 per cent of the men were Muslims. (Return of 21 Sep. 1848 of Indian officers and men in the regiment, quoted in Lambrick, 179.)

obvious reasons, to achieve a balance between at least the two great religions. In the Bengal army there was generally a greater spirit of caste exclusiveness, both in *silladar* and *non-silladar* regiments, than in the Bombay army. Yet something like half the rank and file of the Bombay regulars came from some parts of the Bengal Presidency. Even high caste men in the Bombay army ridiculed class exclusiveness. The Brahmin and the 'untouchable' often shared the same tent, each aware that he stood primarily upon his merits as a soldier.[9]

* * *

Before 1861, the irregulars were apt to be employed much as were the yeomanry in England. They were consistently spread over the countryside in small detachments, at the beck and call of the district collectors and magistrates. In the field they were often allotted the chores, such as guarding lines of communication, and rearguard, foraging and camp protection.*

* * *

The regular, or *non-silladar* native cavalry regiments, beside being more expensive to maintain, naturally attracted a lower class of man. He needed stricter discipline and had less incentive to be a good and loyal soldier. Nevertheless, admission into the ranks of the Indian army, even the regular portion of it, was, nearly always, 'an object of competition, and dismissal one of severe punishment'. By comparison with England where pay was sometimes below that of common labourers, native regular soldiers received two to three times the wages of an Indian agricultural worker.[10] As for dress, equipment and horse-management, these, in the Company's regular regiments, were slavishly copied from those prevailing in the Royal cavalry. The tight jacket and strapped 'over-alls', the sabretaches, the shabraques, the shakos and the helmets, all these the Indian regular trooper was forced to adopt in spite of their patent unsuitability to the Indian climate.

In 1857, when the moment of truth arrived for the Bengal Army, all ten of the regular cavalry regiments had to be disbanded for varying degrees of disloyalty, while eight of the eighteen irregular regiments remained steadfast. In 1861, after the Mutiny, when the native

* For a note upon the establishment of irregular regiments see Appendix 3, p. 296.

army was reorganised and amalgamated with the Royal army the regular or *non-silladar* system was virtually abolished,* except in the Madras Presidency where the *silladar* system had never been introduced. In 1914, under the stress of modern war, the system broke down, never to be revived.[11]

> 'Then we have the nigger regular cavalry, who are, I hear, worth nothing, and the irregular horse, who are very good fellows and fit for service in every way.'
> LIEUTENANT F. ELLIS, 9th Lancers, 1848[1]

(ii)

India: the founders of the silladar *cavalry, James Skinner and William Gardner – Gardner's Horse – Skinner's Horse – other irregular regiments*

The founders of the *silladar* or irregular cavalry in British India were James Skinner and William Linnaeus Gardner. Each in his way was a classic example of the man of action taking advantage of the wide field of adventure which India provided in the eighteenth and early nineteenth centuries. Both were peculiarly bold and skilful leaders of horse. In almost all other respects they were totally dissimilar. Gardner, aged forty-four in 1815, was the well-educated son of an Irish infantry major and an American lady. Skinner, seven years younger, was the half-caste son of an impoverished Scottish subaltern in the Company's service, and a Rajputni girl. Gardner's 'tall, commanding figure, soldier-like countenance and military air'[2] were in marked contrast to Skinner's stocky stature, dusky complexion and almost homely appearance.

In 1783, at the age of 12, Gardner had been bought an infantry ensigncy in England. Eleven years later (five of which were spent in India) he resigned from the army and raised and commanded a

* In 1912, there were thirty-eight irregular and only three regular regiments of native cavalry in the Indian army.

brigade of infantry for Holkar (see p. 67). He distinguished himself in a number of battles against Sindhia, experienced the most amazing adventures, and married a thirteen-year-old native princess. Just before the Second Maratha War (see p. 65), he was sent to Lord Lake to find out what terms would be offered if Holkar refused to join the other Maratha leaders against the British. Gardner's mission was abortive. Holkar was angry, suspected him of treachery, and publicly stated that had he stayed one day longer in Lake's camp, 'the walls of his tents would have been cut down'. Unable to brook this insult, Gardner drew his sword and 'attempted to cut Holkar down, but was prevented by those about him. Ere they had recovered from their amazement' Gardner sprang upon his horse and got clean away. His wife and her attendants were allowed to join him later, which speaks well of Holkar.

Gardner next entered the service of Amrit Rao, the Peshwa's brother (see p. 195). Soon afterwards, when the war was about to begin, he was ordered, as were all officers of British descent in the service of the princes, to resign his employment. Amrit Rao, however, was determined to keep him going so far, it is said, as to have him tied to the mouth of a gun and threatening to blow him from it if he did not agree to serve against the British. He remained adamant but was kept under the strictest guard, while Amrit Rao thought how best to effect his purpose. Gardner, however, escaped his escort. Shouting 'Bismillah' ('in the name of God'), he jumped off a forty-foot precipice, swam a river, hid with a trustworthy native, and eventually joined Lake's camp disguised as a grass-cutter.

Lake at once gave him command of a body of Jaipur irregulars, with whom he saw some service against Holkar in 1804. Five years later he was ordered to raise a regiment which was known as 'Lieutenant Colonel Gardner's Corps of Irregular Horse', soon abbreviated to 'Gardner's Horse'. (See Appendix, p. 297.) Its initial purpose was the policing of the newly-ceded provinces between the Ganges and Jumna. Headquarters were established on the commanding officer's own estate. This he had originally held by 'firman' from the Emperor of Delhi, who had adopted Gardner's high-born wife as his 'daughter'. The British continued it in his possession, for the maintenance of his irregulars.

The regiment, which consisted chiefly of Hindustani Mahomedans, soon became famous throughout Hindustan. It attracted many of the best swordsmen and riders from the scattered armies of the native states. The men were dressed in an emerald green coat with silver lace, and red *pyjamas*. Their arms were lances, shields, tulwars and long matchlocks. The regiment's first establishment consisted of two European officers beside the commanding officer, and 600 troopers in six *risalas* [troops] commanded by native officers. It is said that a particularly efficient swordsman could earn as much as 150 rupees a month, which was half Gardner's own pay.

*　　*　　*

Skinner's life, meanwhile, had taken a very different course from Gardner's. He had been apprenticed at the age of sixteen to a Calcutta printer, from whom he had at once run away. Already he wanted to be a soldier, but by a new decree of the Company 'no person, the son of a native Indian' could be appointed to any civil or military position. An influential godfather then providentially launched him on his free-lance career by introducing him to Sindhia's famous French general, de Boigne, who gave him a commission. For ten years Skinner fought under de Boigne and his successor, Perron, making a considerable name for himself.

In 1803, like Gardner, he was compelled, much against his will, for he felt no particular loyalty towards the British, to quit the Maratha service. Lake's charm, his excellence as a soldier and his first-class army soon won Skinner over. After the battle before Delhi in 1803, some 880 men of Perron's regular cavalry, all Mahomedans and mostly Skinner's old comrades, declared their willingness to serve the British. These men, when asked to choose a commander, unanimously shouted: 'Sikander Sahib!' *Sikander* is the Hindustani for Alexander the Great, whose fame as a soldier was still alive fifteen hundred years after his Indian invasion. With this great name, for his exceptional powers of leadership, was Skinner punningly dubbed by his irregulars.

The regiment which thus came into being (six years before Gardner's Horse), was the first of all the properly constituted British *silladar* regiments and later became the senior cavalry regiment in the Indian Army. It was known as 'Captain Skinner's Corps of Irregular Horse', or 'Skinner's Horse' for short. Its fame throughout Hindustan was even greater than that of Gardner's Horse. Skinner infused into his men a corporate spirit and regimental pride seldom equalled anywhere. Benevolent and just, he was nevertheless a strict disciplinarian. He is known to have had defaulters flogged with a martingale which must have been even more painful than the cat.

'Hindoostanees', he wrote to a fellow officer, 'are best ruled by a rod of iron – grant them too much indulgence, and they go to the Devil.'[3] He dressed his officers in the light dragoon uniform of the British Army as discontinued in 1812, and was still doing so at least as late as the 1830s. It comprised a dragoon helmet adorned with a white cockade, a dark blue coat with silver facings, a red and gold cummerbund, white buckskin breeches and black Wellingtons. The men were given red turbans, cummerbunds of the same colour, edged with silver, white *pyjamas* and long yellow jackets. From these they soon came to be known as 'The Yellow Boys'.

At the start, Skinner and his brother, Robert, were the only European officers. Their services during the rest of the Second Maratha War were spectacular. The regiment, which was increased successively to 1,200 and 1,700 men, was publicly thanked by the Commander-in-Chief nine times. It shared in Lake's famous pursuit of Holkar from Delhi to Fategarh, in which the cavalry and horse artillery averaged twenty-five miles a day for the last fourteen marches. After Holkar's surprise at Fategarh, Skinner hunted him for an epic seven days, during which 'the Yellow Boys' marched forty to fifty miles each day. He received from Lake, in recognition, a horse with silver trappings. On two other occasions he received swords of honour and on another a pair of Lake's personal pistols. In 1815, he was directed to increase his strength to 3,000 men, divided into three corps of 1,000 each. Thus came into being the 2nd and 3rd Regiments of Skinner's Horse. (See Appendix p. 297.)

*　　*　　*

Also in 1815 there were formed three irregular regiments composed chiefly of Rohillas, a race descended from the Afghans who, after conquering Rohilkand, had settled there many years before. These corps were placed on the same establishment as Skinner's Horse, except that they had no galloper guns attached. Only the 1st Regiment, raised by Lieutenant H. Roberts, long survived the Third Maratha War. Towards its end a few further bodies of irregular horse were raised in the Bengal Presidency, only to be disbanded as soon as peace came. (See Appendix, p. 295 for details of these regiments.)

*　　*　　*

The earliest of the *silladar* regiments to be raised in the Bombay Presidency was the famous Poona Horse. (See Appendix, p. 297.) This was the mounted element of the Poona Auxiliary Force which had come into being as a result of the treaty concluded with the Peshwa at Poona in 1818, under which it was to be recruited, commanded and controlled by the British, but maintained by the Peshwa (see p. 195). Only the cavalry survived the Third Maratha War, for which the force had been specifically raised. The artillery and infantry were disbanded soon after its conclusion. The first establishment was 5,000 sowars in ten *risalas*. The instruction for the corps' formation ordered that the men were to be 'Sunis, Shaikhs, Moguls, Pathans, Scindians, Beloochis, Shiahs, Hindustanis, Brahmins, Rajputs, and Mahratta spearsmen – men of low caste not to be admitted – Mussalmans especially Synds, Sikhs [*sic*], and Hindustanis, to be preferred'.[4] Arms, dress and discipline were truly irregular at the start. In the year of the corps' formation a Bombay Engineer officer wrote: 'Every day gave us fresh cause to curse these rascally irregular horse who only embarrassed us in action, and ruined our character among the inhabitants.'[5] Much employed though it was in the Third Maratha War, the Poona Horse did not cover itself with glory. In the epic defence of Corygaum on 1 January 1818, for instance, numbers of a dismounted detachment deserted.

No further regiments of irregular horse were raised in Bombay until the First Afghan War in 1839, when the Gujarat Irregular Horse (see Appendix, p. 298) and the Scinde Irregular Horse came into being (see p. 299). In 1850, the Southern Mahratta Horse was raised. It was largely composed of descendants of the old Maratha cavalry (see Appendix, p. 298).

6

'The Gurkha war, the first and possibly the most
arduous of all our hill-campaigns.'
FORTESCUE, *History of the British Army*[1]

(i)

India: the Nepal War, 1814–1816

With Napoleon finally defeated, peace settled on Europe. In India
the case was very different. The tough and masterful policy of Lord
Wellesley had subdued the chief enemies of British dominion, but
his intention of creating a new, strong and peaceful empire upon
the ruins of the old Mogul one by means of British political supremacy was frustrated by the Company and by Ministers. His successors,
Cornwallis, Barlow and Minto were instructed to eschew further
responsibilities and ensure maximum economy. Relations with and
protection for those native states which bounded the territory
actually ruled by the British were mostly discontinued. The false hope
was now entertained that British India could live peacefully in a
vacuum, with commerce reigning undisturbed within her own con-
fines, while anarchy reigned upon her frontiers.

   With the advent of Lord Moira as governor-general, however,
the need to resume the policy so cogently summed up by Fortescue:
'India having been taken by the sword, must be held by the sword',[2]
was once again made clear. Thus, even before the Great War in

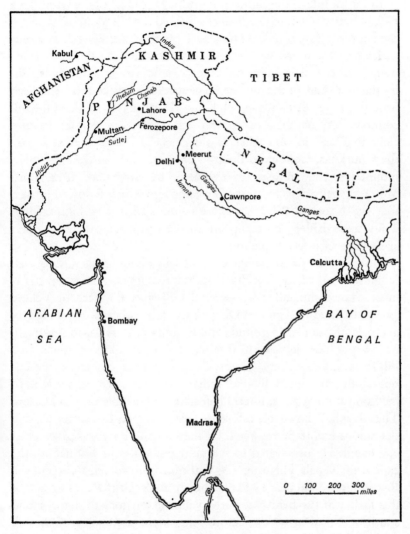

Map 1

Europe had drawn to a close, the British in India had become engaged in the first of many expeditions into the highlands on her northern frontiers.

In the middle of the eighteenth century the chief of the Gurkhas, a race of hardy hill-warriors, had established the kingdom of Nepal on the southern slopes of the Himalayas overlooking Bengal. For centuries past there had been chronic conflict between the great land-owners in the plains and the minor chieftains of the foothills. But by the first years of the nineteenth century the low country had been brought under British rule, while the Ghurkas had subdued the hill country. Between these two powers a long series of frontier disputes came to a head in 1814 when two districts of Bengal were seized by the Ghurkhas. Convinced that the British could not penetrate their mountains, they refused to evacuate. In November 1814, Lord Moira formally declared war. The campaign which followed proved that the Nepalese tribesmen were soldiers of a very high calibre. They were drilled and equipped on the European model but their arms were of inferior quality.

Moira's plan of campaign consisted in dividing his 34,000 men (against about 12,000 Gurkhas) into four columns. The two western-most were commanded by General Gillespie, the hero of Vellore (see p. 68) and by Colonel Ochterlony. The other two were led by generals of peculiar ineptitude and timidity who failed to make any headway. Gillespie was killed while leading an abortive attack on a hill fort but Ochterlony, 'almost the only general of really conspicu-ous ability produced by the Indian Army',[3] after six months of methodical operations, utterly defeated the Gurkha army at Malaon. The Gurkhas, however, refused to agree to the British terms, and operations had to be resumed. Of these Ochterlony was given chief command. He penetrated to within a few miles of Katmandu, the capital of Nepal. This time the Gurkhas were forced to accept the British terms, and peace was concluded in March 1816. As a result of this little war the British acquired valuable territory to the west and south of Nepal in which, before long, were sited some of the hill stations of government and army.

From the hilly nature of the country, mounted troops were of little use in the Nepal War, yet, in its first phase two regiments of Bengal native cavalry, and detachments from two others* were used, chiefly

* The Kandahar Horse; 7th Bengal Native Cavalry; one troop, 6th Bengal Native Cavalry; two *risalas* (troops or half-squadrons), Gardner's Irregular Horse, two *risalas*, 1st (Skinner's) Local Horse.

dismounted, both to maintain communications between scattered posts in a roadless country and to supplement the infantry. Also engaged was a squadron of the 8th Light Dragoons, a regiment which had been in India for twelve years, distinguishing itself at Laswari in 1803 and dramatically revenging Holkar's atrocities after Farruckabad the following year (see p. 67).

At the unsuccessful storm of the hill fort of Kalanga on 31 October 1814 in which Gillespie lost his life, part of this squadron, numbering about 100 men, volunteered to take part in the attack on foot, behaving, according to the governor-general, 'with extraordinary firmness'.[4] But the sowars' sabre proved no match for the Nepalis' *khukuri*. John Pemble, the historian of the war, describes what happened:

'The dragoons were put at the front of the combined column of attack. . . . They had splendid *brio* as they . . . surged up the eastern glacis of the fort . . .; but it was a pace which the infantry, encumbered with knapsacks and muskets . . . could not equal . . . . [Consequently] they found themselves much too far in advance and entirely unsupported. Nepali soldiers were swarming over the walls of the fort. . . . *Khukuris* unsheathed, they engaged the oncoming dragoons in a fierce hand-to-hand struggle, thrusting within the point of the sabres and parrying every swipe before it could be completed with shields borne on the left arm. These they wielded with dazzling dexterity. "There was no end to the damn pot lid", recalled one dragoon later, "no getting over, nor under, nor round about it. It was like bad luck – everywhere!"'[5]

Casualties amounted to four killed and fifty-eight wounded. This seems to have been the sole instance, at least in the nineteenth century, of regular British cavalry attacking a hill fort. It is interesting to learn that the squadron sergeant-major of the 8th, John Mawdsley, was recommended for a commission in consequence of his gallantry in the assault.[6]

In the second phase of the war the only cavalry employed in Ochterlony's highly successful operations were five troops of the 1st Rohilla Cavalry.* These were raw levies specially raised for the campaign by Colonel Gardner (see p. 186) at Moira's behest.

From the cavalry point of view the war is of minor interest. In

* In 1823, this regiment became the 3rd Local Horse and in 1840 the 3rd Irregular Cavalry.

the history of British India it is notable, chiefly, for the conversion from enemies into the staunchest of friends and allies of some of the finest foot-soldiers who ever served the Raj.

'Security and comfort established where nothing but terror and misery before existed ... We have bestowed blessings upon millions.'
THE MARQUESS OF HASTINGS after the Third Maratha War[1]

(ii)

India: the Third Maratha and the Pindari Wars, 1817–1819

For his successful conduct of the Nepal War, Lord Moira was created Marquess of Hastings. The next task which confronted him was nothing less than the restoration of political and social order throughout central India.

'The well-ordered administration of Mughul times had disappeared. . . . The state of the country was in nothing more clearly revealed than in the spread of social diseases whose germs always lurk within civilized societies ready to multiply and break forth should favourable conditions arise. The most obvious of these was dacoity, of which the Pindaris were the supreme example.'[2]

To the eradication of these marauding bands Hastings now turned. The Pindaris had originally been no more than the army scavengers of the Marathas, 'a race which was long the terror of every native power and which, after many desperate and doubtful struggles, yielded only', in Macaulay's words, 'to the fortune and genius of England'.[3] Drawn from all creeds and classes, their sole object seems to have been the pursuit of plunder. By 1814 their numbers were believed to exceed 25,000. They were well mounted and thought nothing of marches of astonishing length. It was said that they sustained their horses by spices and liquid stimulants. They formed (which is saying little) what was probably at the time the best cavalry commanded by natives in India. Armed with spears, which they used with great accuracy, and a few matchlocks, they were unencumbered with baggage or tents.

By 1816 their raids, carried out in total secrecy and at lightning speed, had become intolerable. These were launched chiefly from those Maratha states which occupied the vast areas of central India not under British rule. In some sort of control of these states were five Maratha princes, including Daulat Rao Sindhia at Gwalior and Holkar at Indore who, though humbled in the Second Maratha War (see p. 65), were still at large.* The most dangerous of the chiefs was the Peshwa, Baji Rao (known by the British soldiers as 'Budgerow'†) at Poona, who dreamed of the expulsion of the British and of himself at the head of a revived Maratha confederacy.

At first Hastings may have had some vague hopes of enlisting the help of these princes in extirpating the Pindaris from their lands but it soon became clear that they were actively encouraging them. For many years they had found them useful in their quarrels with each other and now they could be useful in harassing the British. Hence what might have been a comparatively simple Pindari war developed into the Third Maratha War, employing a British army larger than any seen before in India and lasting from 1817 to 1819. 'In our original plan', wrote Hastings, 'there was not the expectation or the wish of adding a rood to the dominion of the Honourable Company.'[4] In the event, the whole of central India was pacified and vast territories were taken under British rule.

The war produced no great battles. This was chiefly because the quality and cohesion of the enemies' armies were never of a high order. Whenever a considerable British force made its presence known, the enemy was careful to melt away. This led to innumerable forced marches and as many petty actions. In these respects, and others, the war resembled those of the campaigns which followed the Great Mutiny forty years later and was fought over much of the same inhospitable ground. As in 1858–60, severe physical hardships were imposed on all arms but especially on the cavalry. Unending tracts of swamp, jungle and mountain, some of which had never

* The Sindhia was the same man who had been defeated in the Second Maratha War, but the Holkar who was subdued by Lake in 1804 had been succeeded by an eleven-year-old boy, whose mother acted as regent.

† The name for a large keelless river boat, much used by Europeans on the Ganges.

before been visited by white men, had to be crossed and recrossed while temperatures could vary in the course of a single march from 29 to 110 degrees Fahrenheit. Neither food nor drink nor clothing made the slightest concession in those days to a tropical climate. Medical arrangements were of the most primitive and the scourges of cholera and heat stroke caused more casualties than did the enemy.

From the commanders' point of view the prime difficulties were administration, supply and, above all, communication. For instance, as the crow flies, the distance between northern and southern head-quarters was seldom less than 700 miles, while the chain of defensive posts in the south extended some 850 miles. When the governor-general moved from Calcutta to take command of the Grand Army at Cawnpore he occupied over two months in making the journey down the Ganges. It generally took weeks, and often months, for orders and reports to pass between the various headquarters and outlying columns. All these problems were overcome, by the standards of the day, with energy and economy.

The Grand Army and the Army of the Deccan which, by a strenuous feat of organisation, Hastings assembled to the north and south of the Maratha states during nine months of 1817, numbered between them, about 111,000 men. The cavalry consisted of 2,200 British regulars, 7,800 native regulars and, it is said, 22,700 native irregulars. The Royal regiments consisted of the 8th, 17th, 22nd and 24th Light Dragoons, of which only the 17th and 22nd took any considerable part in the war. There were eight regiments of Bengal and six of Madras Native Cavalry. The irregulars included parts of Skinner's Horse, Gardner's Horse, the 1st and 3rd Rohilla Horse, about 4,000 Mysore Horse and three regiments of the Poona Auxiliary Horse.

Working in conjunction with these were eighty-four horse artillery guns. As had been the practice in India since 1799, two of these six-pounder 'galloper guns', or 'flying artillery', were usually attached to each of the regular regiments, while the rest were formed in native batteries. In one division of the Army of the Deccan, however, a light artillery brigade was formed which consisted of one troop of Madras Horse Artillery as well as all the 'galloper guns' of the cavalry regiments.[5]*

Early on in the campaign the need for compact, swift-moving, 'flying columns' was realised, and it was in these that the cavalry in

* In India galloper guns ceased to be component parts of cavalry regiments in 1819. (Govr.-Gen.'s Order in Council, 18 May 1819.)

large numbers played a vital rôle. Since the enemy so seldom closed with such mobile detachments, it was generally necessary for the horse artillery to be well forward on the march. The co-operation between cavalry and horse artillery throughout the campaign seems to have been admirable.

There can be no certainty as to the numbers of the enemy. Estimates vary from 200,000 (of which 130,000 were horse) to almost half that number. It seems certain that less than 40,000 horse were ever actually brought into the field.

An example of the type of cavalry action which was to become common in the war occurred even before it had started. On Christmas Day 1816, Major J. L. Lushington, with 350 of the 4th Madras Light Cavalry, chanced while on police duty to learn of the presence of a band of 2,500 Pindari horse near Poona. Next day he covered fifty-two miles between 1 a.m. and 6 p.m. before coming upon them. He at once charged and then pursued for ten miles, killing or wounding, it is said, 700. He suffered only one casualty.[6]

Four months later, again near Poona, there occurred an instance of what could happen when two bodies of equally raw irregular horse came into conflict. Two thousand of the Peshwa's new levies were promptly charged and dispersed by 800 of the Nizam of Hyderabad's Reformed Horse under two British officers of the Bombay army, Captains Davies and Pedlar, both of whom were wounded. These two officers rode well ahead of their men and engaged the enemy single-handed, cutting down man after man. By their example they turned the Nizam's 'wild horsemen into heroes'. Without it, the action would certainly have been inconclusive. Their casualties were 74, but the Peshwa lost 400 killed and wounded.[7] In the following six months there occurred a number of minor affairs, and one more considerable action. This was the defeat of the Peshwa at Khadki, largely accomplished by the infantry and artillery.

*   *   *

The first engagement of any size in which the cavalry played an important part was the battle of Sitabaldi which took place outside Nagpur. It was fought against the Bhonsla, one of the five principal Maratha chiefs. On 25 November 1817, he massed his troops against the British Residency. This was separated from the city by the two small hills of Sitabaldi. The Resident at once occupied these with most of the infantry and artillery of Lieutenant-Colonel H. S.

Scott's 'Nagpur brigade'. This numbered in all no more than 1,500 effective native troops, of which the cavalry element was three troops of the 6th Bengal Native Cavalry, under Captain Charles Fitzgerald, with a few men of the Madras Bodyguard.

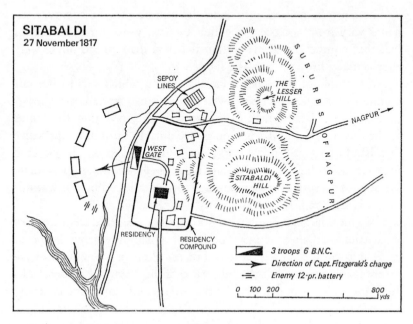

SITABALDI
27 November 1817

SEPOY LINES

THE LESSER HILL

SUBURBS

NAGPUR

OF NAGPUR

WEST GATE

SITABALDI HILL

RESIDENCY

RESIDENCY COMPOUND

3 troops 6 B.N.C.

Direction of Capt. Fitzgerald's charge

Enemy 12-pr. battery

0   100 200   800
                                                    yds

Map 2

At 6 p.m. on 26 November, the 3,500 Arabs in the Bhonsla's army led an attack upon the lesser hill. Nearly all the armies of the native princes contained Arab troops. Hardy, brave and fierce, they were excellent marksmen with the musket but chronically impatient of discipline. After fifteen hours of heavy fighting, accompanied by a bombardment from, it is said, thirty-five guns, the hill was taken. Before this happened the plain to the west of the Residency had filled with numbers of Maratha horsemen. At the same time a body of infantry, a number of camels with swivel-guns on saddles and a battery of twelve-pounders were threatening to enfilade Fitzgerald's 300 troopers. These were drawn up in line opposite the west gateway of the Residency compound, wherein the wives and families of officers and men were sheltering. Fitzgerald at once sent his Adjutant, Lieutenant John Hearsey, rightly classed as one of the 'fathers of the Indian Cavalry', to ask Scott for orders. These were that Fitzgerald was 'to take the first favourable opportunity that might occur to charge the enemy'.

Hearsey's account of the battle relates that

'Fitzgerald, on receiving the order, said that to charge such an innumerable body of all arms with three troops of cavalry, with any chance of success, would not be feasible. . . . He would therefore cross the dry watercourse in front of our position . . . so as to avoid being enfiladed, and should an opportunity occur, a charge could be delivered without that obstruction in front of us. . . . I told Captain Fitzgerald that I would not agree to desert the infantry, that we must do or die. . . . The native officers near, hearing us converse together, and partly understanding that a charge upon the battery and enemy was intended, gave a cheer, the Mohammedans calling out "Deen! Deen!" meaning "Our faith! Our faith!" and the Hindoos getting dust and throwing it on their heads, thus expressing that they were ready to be sacrificed. . . . The head of our column of threes [was] soon among the enemy, who turned and fled. . . . The flying horsemen could not be stopped; they dashed into their own battalion of infantry, putting them into great confusion.'[8]

While Fitzgerald pursued the cavalry and infantry, completely routing them, Hearsey wheeled to his left to capture two twelve-pounders. These he turned with effect upon the fleeing enemy, afterwards bringing them back in triumph to the Residency.

'It was beautiful', said Colonel Scott, 'to see the small speck of French grey open a way for itself amongst the thousands of the enemy's horse surrounding it, putting to flight a battalion of regular infantry and capturing the two twelve-pounders attached to it, and, furthermore, slowly retiring with their prize and using the guns effectually against the enemy, although orders had been sent to spike and abandon them.'[9]

The success of this startling and sudden charge against overwhelming numbers so demoralised the Bhonsla's troops that before long, aided by the explosion of an ammunition tumbril on the lesser hill, Scott was able to retake it. The Arabs, however, reformed at its foot and were about to retrieve their loss when Cornet Smith, with a single troop of the 6th, unexpectedly charged them in flank, killing large numbers.

The action, which had lasted sixteen hours, was virtually over.

The total British losses (376 killed and wounded, including 15 European officers) were more than a quarter of those engaged. Of the 6th Bengal Native Cavalry, Hearsey and Smith were both severely wounded, while forty-seven men and forty-five horses were killed or wounded. The regiment received 'Seetabuldee' as a battle honour, and Subadar-Major Bhagwan Singh, a Brahmin, who, just in time, had shouted out to Hearsey, 'Adjutant Sahib, there is a battery of twelve pounder guns on our left!', received 'for conspicuous gallantry', a gold medal, 300 *bighas* of land, and a pension of 100 rupees a month.

The action is important because it shows how determinedly native troops, both cavalry and infantry, could fight when well led even though no white troops were present. It is further interesting because most narratives categorically state that Fitzgerald made his charge 'in opposition to the most express injunctions' from Scott.[10] There seems, in fact, to be no basis for this, as the first-hand account of Hearsey, who was the bearer of Scott's personal order, makes plain.

It took a further action, on 16 December, finally to dispose of the Bhonsla. In this, which is known as the battle of Nagpur, the British force, which had been much reinforced, included all six troops of the 6th Bengal Native Cavalry, as well as the 6th Madras Native Cavalry, with six horse artillery guns. Two successful charges were made against artillery and horsemen, but at one point the horses could not be induced to face a body of sixty elephants. These had matchlockmen in their howdahs and caused a temporary check. The action was over and the enemy routed in an hour and a half. There followed a siege of the indomitable Arabs in Nagpur itself, but by the end of the year the Bhonsla had been finally subdued.

Two further small cavalry actions took place before this phase of the war was over. In a minor engagement near Jubbulpore, 150 miles north of Nagpur, on 19 December, Lieutenant Alexander Pope of the 8th Bengal Native Cavalry, charged with the reserve squadron of his regiment, under heavy fire, and captured the enemy's guns. Though severely wounded by a Pindari spear, he continued the pursuit with vigour.[11] Pope's successful action has particular interest, for thirty-two years later he was to be responsible for the catastrophe at Chilianwala (see p. 280). Two days later the 1st Rohilla Cavalry, which had been raised two years previously, destroyed a body of 400 Pindaris at Rajgarh, after a forced march of fifty miles.[12]

*   *   *

On 21 December 1817, at Mehidpur, it took only three hours for General Sir Thomas Hislop, commanding the Army of the Deccan, to inflict a decisive defeat on Holkar. In this, the only action of the war sufficient in scale to be styled a battle, the regular cavalry were formed into two brigades. These consisted of one squadron, 100 strong, of the 22nd Light Dragoons, and about 1,000 sabres of the 3rd, 4th, 6th and 8th Madras Native Cavalry. In support was a considerable number, perhaps 3,000, of the Mysore Silladar Horse (see Appendix, p. 298), under Capt. James Grant, of the 5th Madras Native Cavalry.

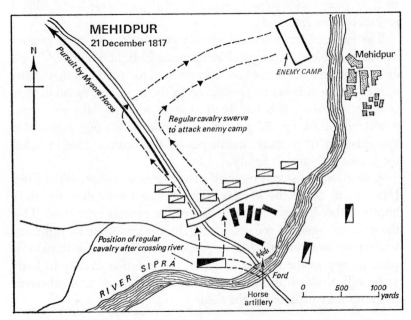

Map 3

Some 5,000 of Holkar's trained infantry were skilfully drawn up 800 yards from the steep banks of the River Sipra, with fifty to sixty guns, mostly heavy, in their front. Around and behind these milled a mass of perhaps 20,000 horse. To attack this strong position Hislop had to pass his troops over the river by a single easily negotiated ford. This he achieved, the light infantry being followed by the cavalry.

Parts of the Madras Horse Artillery (with the galloper guns of the 3rd and 8th Madras Native Cavalry) were then incautiously sent forward, unsupported, to deal with the overwhelming weight of

Holkar's heavy pieces. This they naturally failed to do, being themselves almost silenced. As a consequence the cavalry, while awaiting the infantry who took some time to prepare for the attack, received the full brunt of the enemy's artillery fire. Their trial was all the more severe as they were at the same time exposed to sniping from sharpshooters who had crept down a ravine on their left.

Before long Hislop's infantry attacked with the bayonet, and the cavalry brigades were at last able to charge through the guns and into the infantry. Holkar's horse fled without standing for a moment. His infantry soon followed suit. His gunners, though, stuck to their pieces with great intrepidity until they were struck down and their guns captured.

The two cavalry brigades had only gone a short distance in pursuit of the broken infantry before they caught sight of Holkar's main camp. Unable to resist the booty they hoped to find there, they abandoned their legitimate task, swerved to the right and found to their chagrin that the camp had been abandoned. The Mysore Horse, meanwhile, took up the pursuit and ironically enough captured a vast quantity of treasure, worth nearly £1,000,000. This included the jewels of Holkar's family.

A year later Hislop, on behalf of the regular troops, asked Lord Hastings to cause the Mysore Silladar Cavalry to disgorge their booty so that it might be made part of the general prize fund. This the governor-general refused to do. He was undoubtedly right, for while they were excluded from participation in the distribution of prize money to the regular army, all the irregular cavalry in India were still allowed at this date to retain possession of whatever property they captured in the field.

'This was done', wrote Hastings, 'on the plea that from the nature of their services, the irregular cavalry must get much booty which they never could be influenced to bring to general account.

'They were, therefore, to be satisfied with such gains as they could collect in their desultory operations. . . . [Nevertheless] the arrangement was not advantageous for the auxiliary horse, because they were shut out from participation in the more important treasures taken where fortresses surrendered; or in the donations issued to the regular troops in return for military stores made over to the Government. That upon a particular occasion the plunder acquired by the auxiliary horse went to an extraordinary amount, as is surmised to have been the case at Mahidpoor, cannot alter the terms of an established rule. . . .

'What the Silladar Horse effected was, as we apprehend, the duty distinctly committed to them. Is it pretended to have been held out to them, that if they brought their expected capture to the common stock, they should participate in the general distribution? No such thing is intimated; and it is obvious that they were supposed to be acting on the known established terms, till the suspicion of their having gotten an enormous prey excited the question whether their right could not be impugned.'[13]

In the battle of Mehidpur, the cavalry casualties were light. In the regular units only nine men were killed and twenty-four wounded, though 127 horses were either killed, wounded or missing. The Mysore Silladar Horse lost nineteen men killed and forty-seven wounded, yet they lost only thirty-nine horses. This may have been partially due to the fact that they did not come under the artillery fire before the main attack. On the other hand it must be remembered that, at this date, each man in the silladar cavalry owned his own horse, and was therefore more careful of it than was the regular sowar. The horse artillery lost five men killed and fifteen wounded, and fifty-six horses killed, wounded and missing.[14] The enemy's losses were about 2,500 men, which included virtually none of the cavalry, who did not stand to fight.

*   *   *

After Mehidpur, the war resolved itself into 'the weary task of tramping out the embers'.[15] This, in the first instance, entailed the hunting of the Peshwa, whose defeat at Khadki had not completely subdued him. Numerous small actions had to be undertaken before he was finally overthrown. In one of these, near Nipani on 17 January 1818, about 2,000 Maratha horsemen were attacked by Major Doveton with a squadron of the 22nd Light Dragoons and two of his own regiment, the 7th Madras Native Cavalry. These made three separate charges before the enemy were broken and put to flight. For the loss of only three men, Doveton claimed to have inflicted some 100 casualties.

For the mopping up phase of the operations a part of the Army of the Deccan was divided into two columns. Most of the infantry, the heavy artillery and the siege train were formed into a slow-moving corps for the express purpose of reducing the strong points and taking actual possession of the country. Most of the cavalry (two squadrons of the 22nd Light Dragoons, the 2nd and 7th Madras Native Cavalry and 1,200 of the Poona Auxiliary Horse), the horse artillery and 2,500 light infantrymen, were formed into a fast-moving corps under the command of Brigadier-General Lionel Smith.

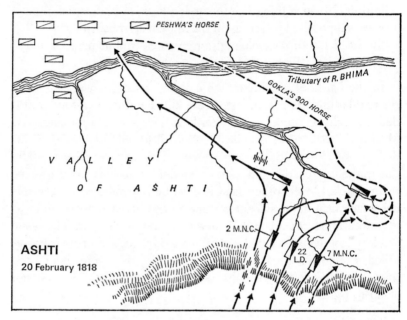

Map 4

On 20 February 1818, after many days of exhausting marches, the cavalry and galloper guns of this flying column eventually came upon the Maratha horse near Ashti. The Peshwa himself at once made good his escape, leaving Gokla, the most able of all the Maratha generals, to dispute the passage of a tributary of the Bhima river which lay between the opposing horsemen, and to give time for the retreat of the baggage. Smith, who was not a cavalryman, led his regiments in parallel columns of threes, with galloper guns on either flank, down a hillside towards a ravine which ran at right-angles to the stream. He seems to have intended to manoeuvre so as to be able to turn the enemy's left flank. In so doing he exposed his own left flank to the enemy. Even on a flat plain this would have been a dangerous manoeuvre. To 'form line in front' from such a formation the rearmost threes would need to gallop very fast, while to 'form

line to the left flank' would require considerable time for realign-
ment, during which the squadrons would be quite unable to receive
an attack.

The 7th, being on the right, were the first to cross the steep banks
of the ravine. Only three of their troops had succeeded in forming,
when Gokla, seeing his opportunity, swept across their front with
some 300 horsemen. As they passed they fired their matchlocks,
and then, circling round, charged into the right flank and rear
of the 1st squadron of the 7th, which had not yet completed its formation. Smith, who was present at this point, was wounded and the
squadron thrown into great confusion.

Indeed, had Gokla been supported at this moment by the rest of
his 4,000 or so horsemen, as he had ordered, Smith's force might
well have been annihilated. As it was, Major Dawes, commanding the
22nd, was given time to wheel back the right troop of his right
squadron and charge along the rear of the 7th. With his two squadrons and a troop of the 2nd, he completely routed the enemy. Gokla
himself was killed and about 100 of his men were killed and wounded.
One sowar of the 7th was killed, while only nineteen of Smith's
force were wounded, of which fifteen were from the 22nd, showing
once again how the European troops bore the brunt of the fight. In
all, forty-eight horses were killed, wounded or missing, of which
more than half were from the 22nd.

This minor cavalry affair is of interest because it illustrates the
folly of placing a commander wholly innocent of cavalry tactics,
unless he was particularly outstanding, in charge of a flying column.

*　　*　　*

Combats on the scale of Ashti were being fought at this time by
flying columns such as Smith's in many parts of the vast area of
operations of the Grand Army and the Army of the Deccan. Yet
these final months of the war in 1818 and 1819 were characterised
less by fighting than by seemingly endless marches and counter-
marches, with all the supply problems, wear and tear and hardship
which these entailed. In the south the need for cavalry became so
pressing that even the Governor's and Commander-in-Chief's
Bodyguards were brought into the field. At the very end, in 1819,
however, the situation was reversed. By then most of the Maratha
and Pindari soldiers had deserted their leaders, while the rest had
shut themselves up in numerous forts. The need now was for more

gunners and at one point some of the European light dragoons were converted into artillerymen to assist in this siege work.

In the north the army had been stripped of most of its cavalry and flying artillery to form a mobile detachment. To this was added a dromedary corps specially created for the campaign as an experiment. In one small engagement, there is record of two infantry companies being carried into action mounted behind the dromedary riders.[16]

There are few first-hand accounts of the last stages of the war. Of these Lieutenant Hearsey's is the most vivid. His description of the capture of the fortress of Chanda, and the Peshwa's final defeat in the combat of Seoni, on 17 April 1818, well illustrates the sort of work in which the cavalry was engaged:

> 'We made forced marches after Gunput Rao, the Nagpoor Mahratta Chief of Horse. I was sent with a light field force . . . to prevent Bajee Rao Peshwa from taking possession of the large and important fortified town of Chanda. It was an affair of horse and horse artillery. We attacked the advanced body of the Peshwa's force at Warora and drove them back. The garrison of Chanda opposed our force. My regiment (6th Bengal Native Cavalry) volunteered to act dismounted, and escalade the walls. Ladders had been prepared when orders were received from General Adams, commanding the troops on the Nerbudda, to join his force. . . . We did so, and moved the next evening, and marching all night, met the advanced guard of the Peshwa's army on the hilly ground near the village of Seoni. The force engaged consisted of a troop of Madras European Artillery, two galloper guns Native Horse Artillery, the 5th and 6th Bengal Light Cavalry and a squadron of the 8th ditto, and a regiment of Bengal Light Infantry, – the whole commanded by Lieutenant-Colonel Doveton. . . .
>
> 'Our artillery opened on the advancing enemy, the cavalry charged and drove the horse from one small hill to another, until the whole of the Peshwa's army was in complete *déroute*. His six guns and *matériel* were captured. We were on horseback from the afternoon of one day until 4 p.m. on the next day, the hot wind blowing like a fiery furnace blast in the middle of April. . . .'

What Hearsey fails to state is that in this minor action, his own regiment, the 6th Bengal Native Cavalry, which had so distinguished itself at Sitabaldi, failed to come forward to take part in it. It has been suggested that Colonel Gahan, its commanding officer, was either suffering from some unexplained pique[17] or was merely incompetent. The other point of interest is that General Adams, it seems, adopted the risky and unusual course of leading his column, as it made for the enemy, himself. Probably on account of the rough nature of the country, he rode well ahead of the light infantry, which surprisingly enough were *followed* by the cavalry and horse artillery.

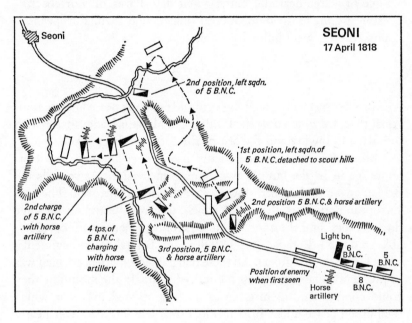

SEONI

17 April 1818

Seoni

2nd position, left sqdn.
of 5 B.N.C.

1st position, left sqdn.of
5 B.N.C.detached to scour hills

2nd position 5 B.N.C.& horse artillery

2nd charge
of 5 B.N.C.
.with horse
artillery

4 tps.of
5 B.N.C.
charging
with horse
artillery

3rd position, 5 B.N.C.
& horse artillery

Light bn.

6
B.N.C.

5
B.N.C.

Position of enemy
when first seen

Horse
artillery

8
B.N.C.

Map 5

When he came upon the Peshwa's advanced parties, he galloped back to form the infantry in square, and sent for the cavalry. With these and the guns, he drove the Maratha horse back upon their main body. While the guns opened up with shrapnel upon this large mass of the enemy, Adams put himself at the head of the 5th (the only regiment which had come up) and swept the valley clear. Quite unsupported (for the rest of the force was now some miles in the rear), he pursued with two squadrons, detaching a third to threaten the left and rear of whatever enemy might be beyond the next valley. Here he found an even larger number of Marathas. Immediately repeating the process, the cavalry charging wherever the ground allowed, he completed the rout of a force which one authority had calculated at 20,000 men.[18] Though his casualties were only two men wounded, Adams's achievement, with only one cavalry regiment and the horse artillery, was remarkable.

Hearsey's narrative concludes:

'The force then moved to the fortified town of Chanda and laid siege to it. A breach was made and was carried by storm in the month of May. The thermometer stood at 140°, attached to the bole of a tree near the battery that day. I was on horseback from 4 a.m. to 10 p.m. Several officers and men, Europeans and natives, were killed by strokes of the sun.'[19]

*   *   *

The process of finally pacifying central India was not complete until April 1819, by which time the Pindari and Maratha leaders had ceased to have a following and the last of the forts had been taken.

Throughout the war, the enemy had proved more or less contemptible in battle, but always cunning in evasion. As regards the British cavalry, they had played an exhausting part well. The two European regiments, the 17th,* which, towards the end, made some fine marches, and the 22nd Light Dragoons, emerge with considerable credit. So do most of the Madras and Bengal native regiments, and a few of the irregulars. All these had gained experience which was to prove invaluable in the next hundred years. In the meantime they could congratulate themselves on having assisted in a war which established peace under British rule, direct and indirect, over nearly two-thirds of the Indian sub-continent.[20]

---

* The 17th Light Dragoons had also taken part in numerous small engagements earlier in the campaign. In one of these, against a body of Bhils, a race of professional robbers, Sergeant-Major Hampson received an arrow in the mouth. Calmly plucking it out, he drew his pistol and shot the archer, before falling dead. (Fortescue: *17L.*, 118.)

Bhurtpore, 1825–1826

'The cavalry . . . had the pleasing excitement of constant
petty combats, invariably victorious.'
FORTESCUE, *History of the British Army*[1]

(iii)

India: the Siege of Bhurtpore, 1825–1826

For the five years which followed the Third Maratha War virtual
peace reigned in India. It was interrupted early in 1824 by the need
to conquer Burma, whose king had demanded the cession of Eastern
Bengal. The first Burmese War which followed was fought chiefly
by the infantry and ended two years later in the conquest of most
of the country. In its earlier stages the British suffered numerous
reverses. Under the impact of these and the consequent need for
reinforcements, some of the more factious rulers in central India
thought they saw a chance of resurrecting the misrule which
Hastings had lately overthrown.

Unfortunately at this time Hastings had been succeeded by Lord
Amherst, a new and weaker governor-general. His first big test came
when a case of disputed succession arose at Bhurtpore. An ambitious
cousin of the new infant chief of the Jats murdered his guardian and
assumed the regentship in defiance of the British. The remonstrances
of Sir David Ochterlony, the Resident at Delhi, and the hero of the
Nepal War (see p. 192), having failed, he collected a force to reduce
the great fortified city of Bhurtpore. Amherst repudiated this action
and Ochterlony died of a broken heart. The usurper, in face of this
British weakness, immediately claimed possession of Bhurtpore as
legal heir and to it flocked many of the discontented Maratha chiefs
and their followers. Its defences were strengthened and it soon became the centre and symbol of defiance to the British. Amherst was
forced to change his view. The fortress had clearly to be taken or
British influence would speedily disappear. Especially was this so,
since Lake, in the Second Maratha War, twenty years before, had
four times tried and failed to take it, due solely to the inadequacy of
his means. The myth of impregnability had now to be shattered.
Consequently a large force of infantry, cavalry and particularly siege
artillery was assembled under the new commander-in-chief, Viscount Combermere, Wellington's veteran cavalry commander in
the Peninsula.

A captain of the 11th Light Dragoons has left a vivid account of the march to Bhurtpore, in which he describes the vast hordes of native followers which were the invariable adjunct and often the curse of Indian expeditions:

'Each fighting man with us has more than one follower, and a large bazaar accompanies the camp besides. We carry the men's tents on elephants, and each elephant has two men; four water carriers to each troop; a cook to every 16 men; every horse has a man to cut grass for him; the men have six camels and two men per troop to carry their beds. Then come the grain grinders, tailors, bakers, butchers, calasseys, or men for pitching tents, and many others. Each hospital has six men, and of these there are 40, making 240, and there are 50 dhoolies for a regiment. I should say that for 560 officers and men we must have 5,600 followers, or 10 for each fighting man, this counting in the bazaar and officers' servants. I have in my own service 40 men, 10 camels, and a hackery, five horses and two ponies, this for a mere captain of Dragoons. I must, however, say that 25 men, five camels, and a pony would be another man's allowance if moderate, but I allow two camels to my troop, and choose to have things comfortable and abundant.'[2]

By 25 November 1825, the concentration was complete. In the second week of December a mixed force, mostly cavalry, including 600 sowars of Skinner's Horse, prevented the enemy from filling the moat. On 18 January 1826, the great fortress, eight miles in circumference with defences hard to match anywhere in the world, was finally captured. During much of the siege, the Jat horse, though always repulsed, and generally with ease, made numerous sorties. The eight regiments of the two cavalry brigades* employed in investing the greater part of the perimeter therefore enjoyed the not very dangerous excitement of almost daily action while living in comfortable quarters. At the end they had the pleasure of chasing and cutting down or making prisoner many of the 7,000 or so fugitives who managed to escape from the fortress.

* Brigadier-General J. W. Sleigh (11th Light Dragoons) commanded the two brigades. The first consisted of 16th Lancers, 6th, 8th and 9th Bengal Light Cavalry, and two troops of horse artillery. The second: 11th Light Dragoons, 3rd, 4th and 10th Bengal Light Cavalry and two troops of horse artillery. The silladar cavalry, as was often the case, seems to have been unbrigaded.

The prize money gained at Bhurtpore amounted to about £480,000. Of this Combermere received some £60,000. The share of a lieutenant was £250, a sergeant £8, a trooper £4, and a sepoy £2 14s. od.[3]

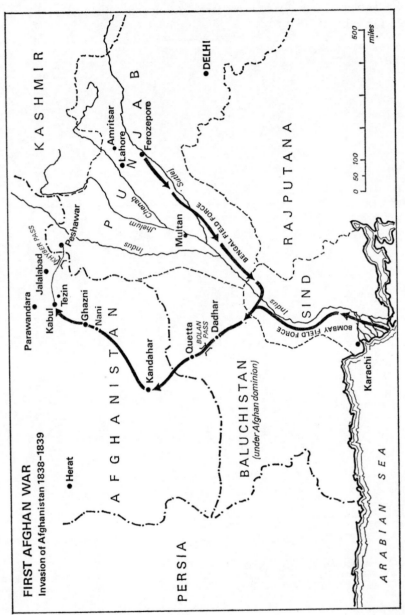

FIRST AFGHAN WAR
Invasion of Afghanistan 1838–1839

KASHMIR

DELHI

Amritsar
Lahore
Ferozepore

P U N J A B

RAJPUTANA

Sutlej

BENGAL FIELD FORCE

Jhelum
Chenab
Indus

Multan

Peshawar
KHYBER PASS
Jalalabad
Tezin
Parawandara
Kabul
Ghazni
Nani

A F G H A N I S T A N

Kandahar

Quetta
BOLAN PASS
Dadhar

S I N D

Indus

BOMBAY FIELD FORCE

Karachi

BALUCHISTAN
(under Afghan dominion)

Herat

PERSIA

A R A B I A N   S E A

0 50 100
0   500
miles

Map 6

7

'Not a soul was to be seen . . . on the line of march,
except when levelling a matchlock from some
almost inaccessible crag.'

LIEUTENANT D. H. MACKINNON, 16th Lancers[1]

(i)

India: the First Afghan War, I: 1838–1840

For twenty years from the end of the Third Maratha War, with the
exception of minor affairs such as Bhurtpore, India was virtually at
peace. Repose, retrenchment and reform were the keynotes of the
period. It was succeeded during the next eleven years by a series of
wars. The earliest of these, the First Afghan War, which opened in
1838, was (like the second, forty years later) a part of the general
Eastern Question which obsessed the rulers of Britain throughout
so much of the century. Since the 1820s 'the Russian threat to India
had begun to overhang the minds of Englishmen. It was in fact', as
Winston Churchill has put it, 'a gross exaggeration to suppose that
Russian armies could have crossed the ranges of the Hindu Kush in
force and arrived in the Indus valley. But the menace seemed real at
the time.'[2]

By ill fortune there had arrived in 1836, as governor-general,
Lord Auckland, who, though conscientious, possessed a vein of
moral weakness. On his appointment he had been told to consider

how best 'to counteract the progress of Russian influence'[3] in Afghanistan. This did not become an urgent problem until, in November 1837, the Persians under Russian influence besieged Herat in western Afghanistan. Three courses were now open to Auckland. He could concentrate upon defending the east bank of the Indus and leave Afghanistan to its fate. He could aid Dost Muhammad, its ruler, against the supposed Perso-Russian menace; or, should Dost Muhammad make difficulties about accepting British help, he could try to depose him by force and place another ruler in his stead. This last course was the one he chose.

In fact Dost Muhammad was desirous of an alliance, but only if the British would help him to win back Peshawar, which the Sikhs had recently taken from him. To this Auckland could not agree for, since the Treaty of Amritsar in 1809, the Sikhs under Ranjit Singh had been in strong and friendly alliance with the British. In fact the Sikh kingdom, 'one of the few really successful buffer states in history',[4] had been for many years a steady bulwark for British India amidst the dissolution of authority in the north-west, which had been going on since the latter half of the eighteenth century.

Dost Muhammad had come to power in 1826. Eight years later he had easily frustrated an attempt by Shah Shuja, representative of the old Durrani empire, to recover his family's ancient throne. It was this gentleman, a pensioner of the British, whom Auckland now proposed to restore to rule in Kabul, the chief city of Afghanistan. The governor-general hoped to achieve this under the Tripartite Treaty of June 1838, by which Ranjit Singh agreed to assist Shah Shuja with troops if Shah Shuja did the same for him. Since Shah Shuja was virtually a resourceless exile, the treaty meant, in practice, that the British, if the enterprises were not to collapse, would have to provide troops for him. Auckland had been outwitted by the Sikh ruler. On 13 August 1838, the decision was made to commit British troops to what was, in effect, an invasion of Afghanistan.

At this moment the only tenable reason for such a war was effectively removed. Under pressure from London (and with the aid of a small British landing from the Persian Gulf), the Persians were prevailed upon to raise the siege of Herat. Nevertheless, in spite of some doubts in London, and egged on by Sir William Macnaghten, his chief political adviser, Auckland decided to persevere with his plan. Thus of all the wars mentioned in this book the most pointless, and in some ways the most disastrous, was launched.

So as to maintain the fiction that Shah Shuja re-entered his country accompanied by his own troops, six thousand men were recruited from the Bengal army. They were paid by the Indian Government and commanded by British officers. (See Appendix, p. 298.)

* * *

The invasion was surprisingly successful. 'The Army of the Indus', formed in the summer of 1838, met little formal resistance. Kandahar was taken in April 1839. Ghazni, the only place to be defended, was stormed by the infantry in July and Kabul entered in August. Dost Muhammad became a fugitive and Shah Shuja was installed in his place. While the main invasion was being carried out by the British from the south, the Sikh force of 6,000, accompanied by a secondary force of 4,000 under Shah Shuja's heir, advanced into Afghanistan through the Khyber Pass. These, having helped to keep Afghan troops occupied in the north, entered Kabul some time after the Army of the Indus.

The army for the main invasion, excluding Shah Shuja's force of 6,000, numbered roughly 15,000 fighting men. It was composed of two field forces, one from Bengal and the other from Bombay. The Bengal force was about 9,500 strong. Its camp followers numbered 38,000 and its transport camels some 30,000. The cavalry brigade from Bengal consisted of the 16th Lancers, 535 strong (accompanied, it is said, by a pack of foxhounds!),[5] the 2nd and 3rd Bengal Light Cavalry and the 4th Local Horse. The 1st (Skinner's) Local Horse formed part of a reserve force at Ferozepore. It later entered Afghanistan in two parts. One detachment accompanied Sir William Macnaghten and Shah Shuja, the other was employed against the Baluchis in Sind.

With the Bombay force were two squadrons of the 4th Light Dragoons, 316 strong, the 1st Bombay Light Cavalry and a newly raised detachment of 300 men of the Poona Auxiliary Horse. Of these last, known as 'Ward's Horse', an infantry officer wrote at the time:

'that splendid band of auxiliary horse from Cutch, the finest looking fellows I ever saw. . . . They are dressed in green garments edged with gold, and red turbans tied under the chin like the old Mahratta soldiers; their arms are matchlock, lance, scimitar and pistols, and they appear to be excellent and practical riders. . . . They take good care to be excellently mounted.'[6]

Before Afghanistan proper was entered, the whole of the cavalry was brought together into a single division, commanded by Major-General Sir Joseph Thackwell, a veteran of the Peninsula and of Waterloo where he had lost an arm.

The expedition was attended by very considerable hardships. The Amirs of Sind objected to the British passing through their territories. The tribesmen of Sind, of Baluchistan (which was more or less under Afghan dominion) and of Afghanistan itself were often murderous and always hostile. Immense distances had to be covered. The Bengal troops, for instance, marched 1,005 miles from Ferozepore to Kandahar. It took them nearly 140 days. The reason for the roundabout route which they took was, it seems, the need to bring the Bengal force into Sind so as to assist the smaller Bombay force in cowing the Amirs into subjection to Shah Shuja. It has also been said that Ranjit Singh was reluctant to allow the British troops to pass through his territories.

Much of the terrain was waterless desert and desolate mountain. In a single April day the temperature could shoot up from 54°F. at sunrise to 100°F. at noon. Day after day the difference between the 5 a.m. and 3 p.m. temperatures, even in mid-winter, could be as much as 50°F.[7]

The commissariat arrangements were bad, especially those of the Bombay force. This last, which had been transported to the mouth of the Indus by sea from Bombay, was held up, immovable, for long periods, from lack of camels and other transport animals. Too much dependence had been placed upon local assistance. It was not forthcoming. The force took two months to march eighty miles up the river bank. Rations were severely cut. Those for the vast numbers of camp followers were reduced even below those of the native troops. These last were placed on half-rations, and even the quantity of the white soldier's loaf was reduced. There were moments when water was so scarce that there was insufficient for mixing the medicines for the sick.[8] Numbers of camp followers began to melt away as the expedition proceeded. Hundreds died of starvation and others were murdered as they tried to make their way home.

The crossing of the Bolan Pass, a narrow corridor over sixty miles in length, was a nightmare. Throughout its length hardly a vestige of forage or of fuel was to be found, while snipers and robbers relentlessly harassed the remaining camp followers at the rear of the columns. No effective limit to the quantity of officers' servants and baggage had been imposed. An officer of the 16th Lancers still had forty servants when he entered the Pass. His baggage, like that of many others, had been plundered, and his cook killed, before he emerged at the other end.[9] There is no evidence as to what had become of the pack of foxhounds by this time! Though often tainted, water was plentiful, for the River Bolan roared in full spate through the ravine. It had to be crossed no less than twenty-seven times. The torrent swept men and animals off their feet. On many occasions the water was up to the flaps of the saddles.[10]

Throughout the invasion the sufferings of the cavalry horses were great. In one blazing April day '70 horses died from want of food or mere exhaustion – 10 of the Lancers, 58 of the 2nd Native Cavalry and 2 of the 3rd.' Even as early as March, General Thackwell was writing in his diary that the lack of forage had 'completely ruined this fine cavalry, and will reduce us to a state of starvation'.[11]

The classic concern of the British soldier for fellow sufferers, especially helpless children, is instanced at this time by an officer of the 2nd Bengal Light Cavalry. He 'saw a trooper of the 16th Lancers, who had a soda-water bottle half full of water, pour the whole contents down the throat of a poor native woman's child, who was just dying of thirst.'[12] By the time the cavalry brigade left Kandahar, it had lost 464 of its mounts.* The 16th Lancers alone lost 193.[13] Thirty of these disappeared in a quicksand during a river crossing.[14]

At Quetta the daily ration of grain per horse was down to two pounds. When green fodder again became available, the horses suffered greatly from too rich a diet after too poor a one. There was a time when the cavalry horses had no grain or pulse (beans or lentils) for twenty-six consecutive days. They lived on such green forage as could be found, and often on very bad quality grass. When possible, dried clover mixed with grass was used. Barley sometimes became procurable, but in its whole state. Recourse was had to frying or boiling the barley but for large numbers this was obviously impracticable.[15] As the columns left Quetta, the headquarter's staff were alarmed to hear repeated firing. On investigation it turned out to be the shooting of sixty cavalry horses condemned as too weak to continue the march.[16]

On 20 April, Thackwell reported that all the troop horses had been without corn for five days. Within forty-eight hours, nevertheless, the cavalry performed a single march of twenty-three miles. It

* In the year ending 31 December 1839, 46 per cent of the cavalry horses of the Bengal, and nearly 28 per cent of the Bombay field forces became casualties from one cause or another. (Hough, Appx., 43.)

caused 'the death of several followers and of near 60 horses. . . The sun', wrote Thackwell, 'was at times absolutely roasting us.'[17]During this terrible day, the men of the 16th marched on foot, goading their miserable mounts with their lances. Captain George Lawrence of the 2nd Bengal Light Cavalry doubted whether 'a hundred effective men could have been mustered' in the three regiments of his brigade to oppose an enemy.[18] Under so great a strain discipline collapsed. After being virtually without water for forty-eight hours, the horses, when at last the precious liquid was sighted, made 'a sudden rush into the river as if mad'. Unavoidably the men, too, broke ranks in a mad scramble to quench their thirst.[19] At Kandahar more than eighty men of the 16th went into hospital with malarial fever, dysentery, jaundice and heat stroke.

At no moment could the army feel safe from marauders. At every halt guards had to be posted. The cavalry outposts often found themselves skirmishing with robber bands. One such was disposed of near Quetta by a detachment of the 2nd Bengal Light Cavalry. Cornet Toone of that regiment cut down its leader and decapitated him.[20] Even at Kandahar, where all seemed comparatively secure, murder lurked off the beaten track. One evening Lieutenants Inverarity and Wilmer of the 16th Lancers went fishing outside the city walls. Set upon by a gang, they were slashed with long Afghan knives and left to die.[21]

On the last lap of the march, from Kandahar to Kabul, fresh provisions were more plentiful. The heat, though, was intense and caused a number of deaths. To complete the misery there descended upon the land a plague of locusts.[22]

The sole occasion during the invasion on which cavalry was engaged against anything resembling a formal enemy was on the day before the storm of Ghazni. Shah Shuja's camp was attacked by swarms of mounted Ghazis, the most fanatical of the Afghan warriors. They were repelled by some spirited charges of the 1st and 2nd Shah's Cavalry supported by the 16th Lancers and the 3rd Bengal Light Cavalry. It appears that none of the regiments suffered casualties.

The first man to enter Kabul was Major Cureton of the 16th with a squadron each of the 4th and the 16th. He took possession of the citadel of Bala Hissar without opposition. Outside the city 400 Afghans had surrendered to him and he had found twenty-six guns abandoned. His detachment had marched sixty miles in less than twenty-four hours. The first phase of the First Afghan War was over.

Altogether it was very fortunate that Dost Muhammad had offered no organised resistance for the Army of the Indus was in no condition to meet it had it come.

*   *   *

The object of the invasion, it was now fondly believed, had been achieved. The army could return to India. Mountstuart Elphinstone, an ex-Governor of Bombay and a great authority on Indian affairs, had never doubted that Shah Shuja could be set up, 'but', he declared, 'for maintaining him in a poor, cold, strong and remote country, among turbulent people like the Afghans, I own it seems to me to be hopeless.'[23] He was right.

Though Dost Muhammad surrendered in November 1840 (see p. 222) his country remained in a state of continual unrest and sporadic rebellion. It was soon obvious, even to Macnaghten, the ever-optimistic chief political officer or 'Envoy', that only with the help of British troops could the new sovereign keep his throne. The presence of such foreign and infidel support naturally 'rendered an already unpopular régime an odious one.'[24]

Nevertheless a large part of the army had made for India in the autumn of 1839. The 4th Light Dragoons and the 1st Bombay Light Cavalry were among those troops which returned to Bombay. Their going, not surprisingly, was less impeded by the inhabitants than had been their coming. The extreme cold, however, caused great hardships. Their losses of men chiefly from cholera and of horses from wear and tear were considerable.

The Bengal troops which made their way home, via the direct route by courtesy of the Sikhs, suffered less. They included the 16th Lancers and the 3rd Bengal Light Cavalry. By the time they reached Ferozepore, they had marched 2,070 miles between 8 November 1838 and 31 December 1839, probably the longest distance ever marched by an Indian army in a similar period.[25]

The 16th suffered a minor disaster whilst crossing the river Jhelum by a 400 yard wide ford. The advance-guard crossed safely, but the main body, marching in column of threes, began to lose direction when three-quarters of the way across.

'In a moment more than 50 men and horses were swept rapidly down the river, and a terrible scene of confusion ensued, which was made worse by a number of baggage camels that had been trying to cross higher up, and which had also been swept away into the current, being now carried down through the 2nd and 3rd squadrons. These animals, however, were in the end the means of saving many of the men, who managed to cling on to them till they were landed.

'After a great deal of trouble most of the men and horses were got ashore lower down the river, but on the roll being called Captain Hilton and 10 men with 12 horses were reported missing.'

This tragedy was quite unnecessary. Thirty flat-bottomed boats had been collected and could have been used to ferry the regiment over in a few hours. Captain Hilton, however, had reported, on testing the ford, that he had crossed it easily, 'the water being just up to his knees on a moderate-sized horse'.[26]

The garrison left in Afghanistan consisted mostly of infantry and artillery. The only mounted troops were the 2nd Bengal Light Cavalry at Jalalabad and two troops of the 1st (Skinner's) Local Horse, one at Ghazni and the other at Jalalabad. Beside these there were the regiments in Shah Shuja's force, and certain highly unreliable Afghan levies officered by Europeans.

*   *   *

Within the next two years of increasingly uneasy occupation, there was formed the Scinde Irregular Horse. The nucleus of this famous corps was a squadron of the Poona Auxiliary Horse (see p. 189). Various other regiments arrived as reinforcements or replacements from time to time. These included the 5th Bengal Native Cavalry. All these regiments saw exacting service between the autumn of 1839 and the final catastrophe in the winter of 1841–2. Numerous small so-called punitive expeditions were set on foot by the 'politicals'. Of the minor actions which characterized these, the most interesting from the cavalry point of view are the combats at Dadhur on 29 October and at Parwandara on 2 November 1840.

At Dadhur 120 of the 1st (Skinner's) Local Horse charged right through and scattered a superior body of Baluchi tribesmen. They were led by an officer of native infantry. He, two native officers and fifteen troopers were wounded. One *risaldar* and two troopers were killed. 'A fine feat of arms' is Fortescue's verdict.[27]

At Parwandara two squadrons of the 2nd Bengal Light Cavalry

(about 220 troopers) composed part of Brigadier Sir Robert Sale's force which was attempting to catch Dost Muhammad. They formed one arm of a pincer which was about to ensnare some ill-mounted Afghan horsemen* led, as it happened, by the Dost himself who was seen to be urging them on with his turban in his hand. Captain Fraser, commanding the two squadrons, formed up his men ready to charge the trapped enemy. At this moment orders arrived recalling the cavalry. Indeed the recall was actually sounded by trumpet. In consequence the squadrons had 'already gone "threes about"' when Fraser, 'seeing the enemy coming down upon them, instantly gave the word, "Front; draw swords!" and, advancing well in front, ordered the charge.' As the troopers were attempting to obey this order the enemy foot-soldiers, carried as was the Afghan custom one behind each horseman, dismounted and began firing. It seems likely that the opportunity for an effective charge had passed before the troopers' swords were 'well out of their scabbards, or their officers had time to close up their ranks and to cheer their men by a few inspiriting words'.

Captain Lawrence, an officer of the regiment, though not present at the action, goes on to describe what happened next:

> 'Fraser with the other European officers dashed into the mass of the enemy before them, never dreaming that their men were not following close behind them. Alas! It was not so; both squadrons followed their officers, but scarcely at a trot, which soon subsided into a walk. . . . Our men, after feebly crossing swords with the enemy, who cut several of them down, turned and fled, leaving their officers to their fate.'

Fraser and another officer were severely wounded, and three other Europeans killed. Lawrence suggests that

> 'the officers did not give themselves time, although the Afghans were not advancing at speed, to see that they were followed closely by the men, and the troopers, just as they were about to advance, saw themselves cut off from their officers, some of whom were immediately slain, others severely wounded, and all this in so short a space of time that the

---

* Lawrence says that there were 400 of them. Another source says 'about 80'. Major Broadfoot of the Engineers found the Afghan mounted troops 'an ill-mounted mob, not to be compared to the Mahrattas'. (Lawrence, G., 45; Cardew, 175; Broadfoot, 128.)

men, scarcely knowing what they were about, hesistated and wavered. Hesitation with cavalry verges on, and soon produces, fear, and then all is lost, for the charge to be effective, requires the energy of body and soul of each individual trooper, to be conveyed again, by some occult influence, to his charger, so as to animate and inspire the animal with confidence while rushing into the battle. At such a moment, to be checked by even trivial causes is often disastrous, producing hesitation, ending in panic, among men who were the instant before full of high courage, ready and eager "to do or die" in discharge of their duty.'[28]

The men of the two offending squadrons were at once sent back to India where they were dismissed the service. The following year the regiment was disbanded with ignominy,* and the men of the remaining squadrons were drafted into other regiments.

This minor action has been discussed in some detail because of the light which it throws upon a rare case of native troopers belonging to a highly respected regiment turning tail. The generally accepted version of what happened[29] does not suggest, as Lawrence does, that it may have been the fault of the officers that their men did not follow them. Lawrence (later Lieutenant-General Sir George) might have been expected to show prejudice in favour of his fellow officers. The fact that he does not do so makes his account the more acceptable. Sir John Hearsey, writing in 1845, confirms Lawrence's view:

'One moment the three troops were put in motion to retire; the next they were halted and fronted to meet the foe, for the Dost, seeing them about to retire, charged them. A panic was the consequence, and such might have happened, and no doubt has happened, with the best European troops. . . . This must serve as a warning. It is not a time to shilly-shally with cavalry when the moment of attacking has arrived: in so doing the troops are jeopardised.'[30]

Dost Muhammad gave himself up almost immediately after the combat of Parwandara. It is thought that he realised that it was of no use to continue resistance against the power of British India, and

* In 1842 another regiment, the 11th Bengal Light Cavalry, was raised to replace the disgraced 2nd. It so distinguished itself at Multan that in 1850 it was renumbered the 2nd Bengal Light Cavalry. It mutinied at Cawnpore in 1857 and was, of course, again disbanded.

that his success in this action would lead the British to redouble their exertions. He had only been waiting for a victory before surrendering with honour.

'We shall never settle Afghanistan at the point of the bayonet.'

SIR ALEXANDER BURNES[1]

(ii)

India: the First Afghan War, II: 1841–1842

In November 1841, a concerted revolt broke out in Kabul. Sir Alexander Burnes, 'Bokhara Burnes', political officer with the army, was murdered. So, later, was Macnaghten. The newly appointed commanding general, Elphinstone, was infirm and almost imbecile. The troops became demoralised. With this sorry story of ineptitude leading to disaster this book is not concerned. Nor need it dwell on the ghastly retreat from Kabul in January from which only one man arrived at Jalalabad to tell the tale of horror. 'The repute of European arms', as Churchill has put it, 'was deeply smitten and the massacre resounded throughout the peninsula.'[2] The cavalry in this greatest disaster which ever befell the Indian army was two squadrons of the 5th Bengal Light Cavalry and some 700 assorted irregulars. These were virtually annihilated.

*　　*　　*

All was not, however, lost. At Jalalabad, Sale held out, and Kandahar and Ghazni were still in British hands. It was clear, nevertheless, that the country would have to be evacuated. The futility and vast expense of Auckland's Afghanistan policy were now accepted by nearly everyone. Lord Ellenborough, who, at this moment, replaced Auckland as governor-general, had to decide how best to get out of the scrape with least injury to Britain's reputation. He at first wished to deal the Afghans 'some signal and decisive blow' before quitting. Then, when Ghazni fell in March 1842, he was panicked into ordering immediate evacuation. By good fortune, however, Major-General Nott at Kandahar and Major-General Pollock, who had relieved Sale's 'illustrious garrison' at Jalalabad on 5 April, stalled, pleading lack of transport. Ellenborough, therefore, wisely allowed the two generals, both men of sterling qualities, such wide latitude that it was easy for them, before leaving the country, to retake Kabul. This they did in a combined operation on 16 September. The Europeans who had been made prisoner by Dost Muhammad's son and held as hostages were released. On 12 October Kabul was evacuated. The sole reprehensible act of the 'avenging army' was the blowing up of the chief ornament of the city, the beautiful Chitar Chata bazaar. The army then finally left Afghanistan by way of the Khyber Pass. Dost Muhammad was allowed to return to his country almost at once. He died twenty-one years later, aged eighty, still wielding absolute power.

*   *   *

Pollock's advance, which was a model of what mountain warfare should be, had been far from uncontested. It was not, however, until he was within twenty-five miles of Kabul that his cavalry was seriously engaged. He had with him at the action of Tezin on 13 September 1842, the 3rd Light Dragoons, 576 strong, the 1st Bengal Light Cavalry and about 600 troopers of the 3rd Irregular Cavalry, known as Tait's Horse. Opposed to him were some 16,000 of the cream of the Afghan troops under Dost Muhammad's son. It was in effect the enemy's last, valiant stand. As the infantry were storming their way into the Kurd-Kabul pass, the rearguard with the baggage* remained in the valley. It was guarded by the 3rd, part of the 1st, Tait's Horse and some horse artillery. The baggage acted as bait to the enemy. A large force, accompanied by some 2,000 horsemen, took up position 500 yards in front of the cavalry, and opened fire with two field pieces. As the horse artillery guns replied, the 1st

---

* As usual the 'tail' of Pollock's army was immense. Some idea of its size can be gauged by the fact that the 3rd Light Dragoons alone had with them 'upwards of 1000 camels laden with treasure, arms, ammunition, clothing . . .', and that it took the regiment two whole days to cross the Sutlej by a bridge of boats, in single file. (Unett, Captain Walter, Sep. 1842, quoted in Bolitho, 137–8.)

and Tait's Horse supported by Captain Unett's squadron of the 3rd, charged. Unett describes what happened next:

'Away we went. . . . In our front was the bed of a river, about 15 or 20 yards broad with steep banks. Fisher and Bowles were my troop leaders. On the opposite bank were two of the enemy's Horse, with numbers in rear of them. When close to the bank, one of the men on the opposite side presented his matchlock to me. I could see along the barrel. It flashed in the pan. I turned to Fisher, and said "Missed fire, by Jove!"

'I never took my eyes off the rascal. I pressed my horse over the bank, charged across, and the only thing I did not recollect is how I got up the opposite bank, as my grey Arab cannot jump at all. On seeing me charge, the enemy went about, and had got about 20 yards start of me. In an instant, however, I was beside the fellow, and at the pace I was going – about 20 miles an hour – without the slightest exertion passed my sword through his body.

'I then made a thrust at his friend. The place where I overtook them was a steep slippery bank with a ditch full of water; and when pressing my horse to thrust at the fellow, his hind legs sunk in the ditch and he fell backwards upon me. The dead man lay upon my right and his horse in the ditch. The other man and his horse were scrambling up the bank, with his sword flashing in my face. I could touch his horse, and had he tumbled back he would have fallen on the point of my sword. He was killed within a few yards. I saw him rolling on the ground, while one of my men was cutting at him.

'Having had much the start of my squadron, I was now in danger of being ridden over by my own men, as they were rushing on; but my horse was active and strong and with little to carry, and after a few struggles he got upon his legs again. I never loosed the reins, and was on his back again in an instant, and in about 200 yards regained my place again in front and found my men cutting up the enemy in small parties. A retreat was soon sounded, and we retired to our old position, and drew up in a line with a couple of guns, which now opened on the enemy. . . .

'All the officers and men of our regiment distinguished themselves. Fisher and Bowles killed several men with their own hands, and Yerbury had a narrow escape of being killed. His clothes were cut and his horse received a deep sabre wound in the neck. We captured a few of their horses. One of our men sold one on the spot to our Colonel for £30. My Sgt Major caught one, and I could have taken another, but I had something else to do just then.'[3]

Some fifty of the Afghan horse were cut down in this dashing charge. An infantry officer who was present at the engagement describes the gallant action of a *risaldar* of Tait's Horse:

'He had gone with a number of his men round a narrow track, in order to take a large body of Afghan horse in flank. But, on arriving close to them, a broad and deep ravine, which had not before been perceived, was found to intervene between the belligerents. The horses of the *sowars* could not get over such a place; but the gallant *Resaldar*, being mounted on a splendid Arab, made a dash over the yawning gulf, and cut his way right and left through the enemy and back again, before they had recovered from their astonishment. The heroic Mussulman took the leap back and rejoined his men in safety, having killed five Afghans in his desperate charge in less time than I have taken to tell the story. For this achievement he was afterwards very properly rewarded with the decoration of British India.'[4]

Three Afghan standards were captured in the course of this spirited action, one of them by Captain Goad of the 1st Bengal Light Cavalry.[5]

* * *

Nott's force was also opposed in its advance from Kandahar to Kabul. An example of its numerous engagements is the sharp cavalry skirmish which took place near Nani on 28 August 1842. It seems that Captain C. H. Delamaine,* commanding the 3rd Bombay Light Cavalry, while guarding the army's grass-cutters at work, through an excess of offensive spirit and in direct defiance of Nott's orders to retire, found himself cut off from the main army. With one squadron he charged uphill against some 150 Afghan horse. As he did so, his flanks were heavily fired upon by foot soldiers, of whose presence he had been unaware until that moment. The enemy horse then poured down the hill killing two of the 3rd's officers and wounding

* See p. 235 for this officer's actions in the battle of Hyderabad in the Sind War of 1843.

three more. The troopers, seeing their officers fall, turned and fled down the hill. They at once communicated their panic to the other squadrons below. Soon the whole regiment and some irregulars who were with it dissolved in flight. Altogether fifty-six men were killed and wounded.[6]*

A squadron of the 3rd retrieved the regiment's reputation to some degree on the army's return to India. Near Jalalabad on 29 October, its commander, Lieutenant Graves, laid an ambush for a large body of Afghan horse which was seeking an opening so as to attack the rearguard. At the right moment the squadron charged. It is said to have cut down as many as 300 of the enemy.[7]

The army was harassed all the way from Kabul to the Sikh frontier. Captain Unett reported that it lost twice as many men and horses on its return from Kabul as it had in the advance.[8] This was partly due to the extreme cold.

Thus, in typical fashion, ended what Greville called 'the most painful and disgraceful chapter in our history for many a long day'.[9]

* The truth of this account cannot be vouched for. I have been unable to find any account of the action other than Kaye's, though the high casualties are confirmed elsewhere. There is clearly some mystery. Lieutenant Trower of the 33rd Bengal Native Infantry, wrote in his diary,

'October 13th . . . I do not think our regular cavalry, who compose the forage escort, are doing their duty very well, for altho' the grass cutters have been often attacked, they have never once tried to come to close quarters with the enemy. I am sorry for this, for I would gladly see this arm of the service recover from the stain that has been thrown upon it by many circumstances during this campaign. It is rather curious regarding this subject, that in the despatch of General Nott, the 3rd Bombay Cavalry, who suffered a very severe loss, far exceeding that of any other corps engaged at Nanee, are not thanked, or even mentioned. I hope there is no good cause for this silence.' ('Diary of Lieut. C. F. Trower, 33 B.N.I., during the Afghan War of 1842', *J.U.S.I.*, Nov. 1915, 456.)

8

'My cavalry is sufficient to make the result of a
fight decisive.'
SIR CHARLES NAPIER to LORD
ELLENBOROUGH, 20 December, 1842[1]

(i)

India: the Conquest of Sind, 1843

Hard on the heels of the First Afghan War came the conquest of Sind.
'We have no right to seize Scinde, yet we shall do so, and a very
advantageous, useful, humane piece of rascality it will be.'[2] Thus
wrote that complicated but fascinating man, Major-General Sir
Charles Napier, who conducted the campaign. In September 1842,
Lord Ellenborough, the governor-general, gave Napier, at the age
of sixty, after only two years in India, supreme political and military
control in Sind and Baluchistan. These two men between them, at
a time when the authorities at home were virtually unanimous in opposing further acquisitions of territory, were responsible for the
annexation of a country the size of England in five months. The para-
dox is partially explained by the fact that in the 1840s it sometimes
took a year and never less than a dozen weeks to receive a reply from
London to a letter from India. Thus London's orders to Ellenborough

to avoid hostilities in Sind at all costs were received by him three months after the battle of Miani which virtually decided the contest.

Ellenborough was determined, partly for largely illusory commercial reasons, to impose on the Sindian Amirs a new and penal treaty to replace earlier ones which they had broken. The entire negotiation he left to Napier whose experience of such matters was limited. That general's desire to liberate the peasants of Sind from the tyrannous exactions of their rulers, combined with an inclination towards military glory, led inevitably to war.

Whatever the morals of the conflict the campaign itself was a model of its sort. Though the enemy was never very formidable Napier deserved, from the military point of view, the fame which it brought him.

It also brought to prominence John Jacob, called by Napier 'the Seidlitz of the Scinde Army',[3] one of the most remarkable soldiers and administrators in the history of British India. Jacob, whose name is commemorated in the city of Jacobabad, came of clerical, squirearchical and scholarly stock. Numbers of his family, before and since, have risen to high position, in India and elsewhere. As a boy he was nicknamed 'the warrior' from his bellicose propensities. All through his life he displayed a constitutional contempt for danger. To nerves of steel he added a first-class, enquiring mind, and a physical toughness which enabled him to withstand extremes of climate and pain alike. He was five foot ten inches tall and wiry in build. His love of romantic poetry – he placed Byron second only to Homer – was matched by a deep hatred of all forms of tyranny.

Born in 1812, Jacob was sent at the age of 14 to the Honourable East India Company's College at Addiscombe (see p. 157), under the auspices of a cousin in the Bombay Artillery. In that corps, after an above average school career, he was enrolled on his sixteenth birthday as a second-lieutenant. He departed for India without delay, never again to return home in the thirty years of life which remained to him. His voyage out, as was common in those days, took six months.

The artillery was his first love. Everything to do with guns and fire-arms fascinated him. The skill which he acquired as a mechanic led him to undertake practical work on the improvement of weapons. His lathe and his books were his constant companions even in the field. His other great joy was riding. He soon became famous for his fearless exploits in the saddle. In the hog-hunting field he was triumphant. He is known, too, to have run an antelope to death: an almost unheard of feat.

Except for one short spell in civil employ, this first ten years in India were spent with his regiment. He saw little active service until the First Afghan War, during which he was for a time attached to the newly formed Scinde Irregular Horse. It was then that he came under the notice of James Outram. With this most noble of India's soldier-administrators, Jacob formed a close and lasting friendship. Outram, on whose tomb in Westminster Abbey occur the words 'The Bayard of India', first given to him by Napier (who later fell out with him) and compared with whom, it was said in the Bombay army, a fox was a fool and a lion a coward, was at this time in charge of the Political Agency of Baluchistan and Sind. In November 1841, he recommended Jacob, now aged twenty-nine, for the command of the Scinde Irregular Horse, with which he made his reputation. For the next seventeen years he was commandant of this silladar regiment, which grew from a nucleus of the Poona Auxiliary Horse (see p. 189) into one of the finest of all Indian cavalry regiments. (See Appendix, p. 299). Its organisation and distinctive equipment were used as the model upon which the cavalry of the Indian army was reconstituted after the Great Mutiny of 1857.

When Napier took over from Outram, Jacob and his regiment joined the force which marched southwards from Rohri to 'thrash into sense', as Napier put it, the Amirs of Sind. He was present when Napier destroyed the desert fortress of Imamgarh (so as to show the Amirs that 'no retreat was secure'), and he took part in the three actions which decided the campaign.

The first of these took place on 17 February 1843, near Miani within sight of the towers of Hyderabad, the chief city of Sind. Napier here faced some 22,000 assorted tribesmen under a number of chieftains, with no more than 3,000 of his own troops. Of these, less than 2,000 actually took part in the battle.* His cavalry numbered about 800 and his sole European regiment (the 22nd Foot) about 500. There were, besides, three regiments of Bombay native infantry and twelve guns, drawn by camels, mules and horses.

The mass of the enemy's foot soldiers was hidden along some 700 yards of the dry bed of the River Fuleli. To their front was a walled wood protecting their left flank. Jacob, with the Scinde Horse, led

* A detail of 250 of the Poona Horse and four companies of infantry were employed as the baggage guard.

the advance guard. Going forward alone to reconnoitre the enemy's position, he failed, even at 200 yards, to see their well concealed main body. Nor, of course, could Napier, when he came on the scene.

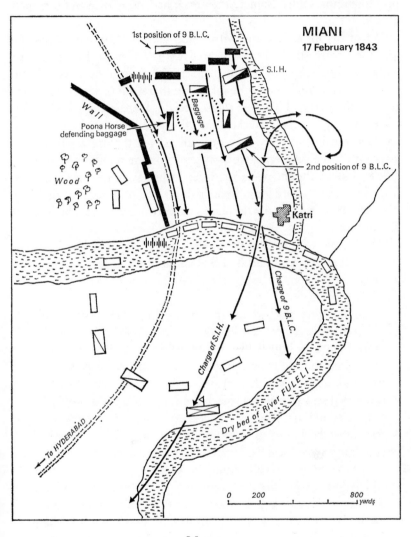

Map 7

What both men thought was the sole force against them was merely the reserve on the far side of the river bed.

For the best part of two hours, while waiting for the infantry and guns to form into line of battle, the Scinde Horse was under fire from matchlock and cannon. A detached squadron of the regiment, meanwhile, was searching the wooded environs of a village to the enemy's right front. It could find no way round, the ground proving impassable. Napier, therefore, had no choice but a frontal attack.

When his infantry came within 300 yards of the river bank, he and they were suddenly confronted with 'a row of dark faces just showing above the level of the plain',[4] with thousands more behind. But it was too late to alter his plan. He therefore ordered the infantrymen to charge. This they refused to do. Instead they fired volley after volley from their muskets into the seething mass before them. In thus refusing to obey they probably saved themselves from disaster. With their superior weapons and inferior numbers, they were able to destroy the enemy's front ranks, while avoiding the matchlock fire of the rest. Before long the British pushed forward into the river bed, and there followed a desperate hand-to-hand fight which lasted for an hour.

As this fierce struggle proceeded, with Napier himself riding between the two lines within a few yards of each, Jacob in his own words:

'went left and pushed my horsemen into the most awfully difficult ground you can imagine. We had so many falls that more than fifty horses were on their heads at once, and at the same time the fire from the village not sixty yards distant was tremendous, every nullah also was lined with matchlock men concealed in and firing through the thorns. A great number of our men and horses were shot here. My horse, a first-rate hunter, was mortally wounded through the belly and lungs, other balls struck my sword scabbard, etc. To my disgust the ground to the left of the village was absolutely impassable . . .! While we were still halted under fire endeavouring to form in ground that would admit of *no* order or arrangement a staff officer came to me saying we were wanted in front, and that the 9th [Bengal] Cavalry had refused to charge or would not charge. (These were his words. With the truth I have nothing to do.) I immediately pushed on at the trot, passed close under the right of the village, and charged shortly after crossing the river; we passed the [9th] Bengal Cavalry halted, one squadron in line on the left and the remainder dispersed about the village firing pistols into it. We charged right through the enemy's camp, slew more than a hundred of them and took Nusseer Khan's standard (a very old green flag with a lion and a sword and Nusseer's name on it). The Beloochees did not run; to a man they smote sternly to the last, as my fellows closed with them. . . Their cavalry seeing our charge and us in full possession of their camp fled altogether and never came into action at all; there were at least 5000 of them! Our charge decided the battle (the General told me so on the ground).'[5]

There had been, in fact, no question of the 9th Bengal Cavalry refusing to charge. It seems that Napier's order that they should do so had been misunderstood by Lieutenant-Colonel William Pattle, who as his second-in-command was responsible for all the cavalry. The delay was immaterial, for when the 9th did charge, it did so with effect.

The Baluchi foot soldiers fighting in the river bed, when they saw the British cavalry sweeping in to their rear and destroying their reserves, began to waver. The British infantry, perceiving this, charged and drove them back. But it still took the sustained fire of Napier's twelve guns to break them. Even then their dispersal never became a rout.

The British losses at Miani were 62 killed and 194 wounded, of which five killed and fifty-one wounded were in the cavalry. The Baluchis' casualties were very severe. Perhaps as many as 3,000 were killed and wounded. Napier's despatch after the battle was the first in the history of the British army to specify by name those other ranks who distinguished themselves. Hitherto, with very rare exceptions, only officers had been mentioned. The following extract from the roll of native officers and men of the 9th Bengal Light Cavalry who distinguished themselves in the battle is an example of a commanding officer's submission of names in obedience to Napier's wishes:

'Subadar Shaik Emam Bux	Engaged with two troopers in taking a standard planted near some guns, and which was most bravely defended by the enemy.
Havildar Shaik Emam Bux	Saved the life of his officer, Shaik Emam (Subadar), and his conduct was conspicuous during the day.
Trooper Mootee Sing	Saved the life of his officer, Captain Garrett [who was killed on 24 March at the battle of Hyderabad].

| Trooper Gungah Sing | Killed after a long and severe personal conflict with one of the enemy, when no assistance was at hand. |
| Trooper Nasser Ally | Behaved with great gallantry during the charge, and was severely wounded.'[6] |

*   *   *

Great victory against enormous odds though Miani was, there still remained in the field one Amir, Sher Muhammad Khan Talpur, who had taken no part in the battle. Thirty-five days after it, Napier, now master of Hyderabad, defeated some 16,000 of the Amir's Baluchi warriors at Nareja, a village on the River Fuleli a few miles from Miani. In the battle of Hyderabad, as it was called, some 5,000 British troops were engaged. These included much needed reinforcements which arrived three days before the action. As at Miani, Jacob and the Scinde Horse went forward to establish the enemy's whereabouts. This time they had a slightly less protracted cannonade to endure while the rest of the army came up.

Sher Muhammad's position ran from the river at Nareja for more than 1,300 yards along a steeply-banked double irrigation canal, in two lines, one behind the other. Its left petered out behind a single trench which ran at an oblique angle for another 500 yards. The British formation consisted of two cavalry regiments on either flank, and eleven guns dispersed in three groups among five infantry regiments (of which the 22nd was, again, the only European regiment), in the centre.

The engagement started with an inconclusive artillery duel. There followed an infantry and horse artillery assault upon the village to the left which Napier mistakenly supposed to be weakly defended. The third phase of the three hour contest was the charge of the 3rd Bombay Light Cavalry and the Scinde Horse on the right; and the final phase was the pursuit by the Poona Horse and the 9th Bengal Light Cavalry on the left.

The chief interest from the cavalry point of view lies in the third act of the drama. While Napier was directing the indomitable 22nd Foot supported by the horse artillery in a bloody hand-to-hand struggle on the left, he received news that the cavalry on the right had charged. He immediately rode over to see for himself. What he saw, in his brother William's inimitable words, was

'the whole body of cavalry at full speed . . . the spurs deep in the horses' sides, the riders pealing their different war cries, and whirling their swords in gleaming circles – there . . . the gorgeous troopers of the 3rd Cavalry, there . . . the wild Scindian horsemen, their red turbans streaming amid the smoke and dust of the splendid turmoil. For a moment the General gazed, at first with anger, then with admiration.'[7]

What had happened was that Jacob and Captain Charles Delamaine (see p. 226) of the 3rd Bombay Cavalry had noticed 'no signs of turbans or flourishing swords'[8] from that part of the embankment

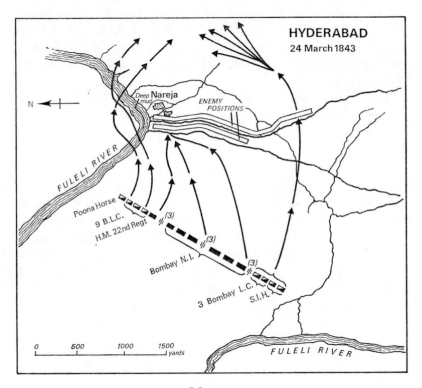

HYDERABAD
24 March 1843

Map 8

immediately in their front. They therefore assumed, and rightly, that it was not held. It seems that they persuaded Major Maurice Stack, the ineffective officer commanding their cavalry brigade, to order, without reference to Napier, an immediate charge. This he did. With Delamaine leading well ahead, the two regiments, some 850 strong, galloped across the two unoccupied canal embankments (the first eight feet, and the second seventeen feet high),[9] until they came upon the enemy's real left wing, lining a single embanked channel. They at once brought up their right shoulders and charged straight at it. In a few moments the Baluchi left was completely overrun. Speedily reforming, Jacob and Delamaine next fell upon the massed cavalry of the enemy, which, as at Miani, was in reserve. This fled at once and was pursued for several miles, many men being cut down or shot. Sher Muhammad himself was on the point of capture, when Pattle, the second-in-command, checked the pursuit to prevent the cavalry becoming too widely dispersed.

Meanwhile the main infantry and artillery struggle continued to the left and centre. When eventually the enemy began to break, Napier put himself at the head of the Poona Horse and the 9th Bengal Light Cavalry and drove the fleeing Baluchi foot soldiers back upon the sabres of Jacob and Delamaine as they returned from their pursuit.

The British casualties at Hyderabad were 39 killed and 231 wounded. Five of the killed and forty-eight of the wounded came from the cavalry. The enemy is supposed to have lost about 2,000.

*　　*　　*

Though Sher Muhammad was never captured, his brother was, and some seventy of his men were cut down by a charge of a troop of the 3rd Bombay Light Cavalry at Pir Ali on 8 June. Sher Muhammad's remaining followers were smashed by Jacob in an action at Shahdadpur on 14 June. The conquest of Sind was then complete. *Punch* represented Napier as reporting it in a telegram (an impossibility in Sind at that date!): *Peccavi* ('I have sinned').[10]

'We calculate alone on the bulldog courage of
Her Majesty's soldiers, and our loss becomes
what we lately witnessed.'
  SIR HARRY SMITH after the Gwalior campaign[1]

(ii)

India: the Gwalior campaign, 1843

While Napier and Jacob were beginning the difficult task of settling
Sind, trouble broke out in the state of Gwalior. This led to what is
variously known as 'the last Maratha War', 'the Gwalior Campaign',
and 'the Forty-Eight Hour War'.

Daulat Rao Sindhia, the ruler of Gwalior, one of the five Maratha
chiefs who had been brought to heel in the Third Maratha War
(see p. 195) died in 1827. He was succeeded by Jankoji Rao Sindhia,
a weak man, not unfriendly to the British. On Jankoji's death early
in 1843, a dispute concerning the succession of a boy ruler led to a
series of court intrigues, followed by disturbances and fighting. The
pro-British Regent was forced to leave Gwalior. So were the British
Resident and all the British officers of the Gwalior forces. An hostile
army in Gwalior of some 22,000 men with 300 guns was a menace
which no governor-general could ignore. Ellenborough, therefore,
established a 'camp of exercise and observation' near the frontier.

Up to the very last moment, even after some of the British troops
had crossed the frontier, Ellenborough was confident that the threat
of force would be enough to effect a peaceful issue. Indeed, the army's
position was chosen chiefly 'for the pomp and ceremony of a visit
from the widow [of Janokoji Rao Sindhia], the Maharaja and the
Court, which was expected in the then state of the negotiations'.[2]
When Ellenborough learned that the reduction of the Gwalior army
which he had demanded was not to be effected, and that a large force
had left the city of Gwalior to oppose him, he had no alternative but
to fight.* His despatch states that the operations were 'against the

* Virtually the first sight of the British army which the Marathas had was of
Lady Gough and Sir Harry Smith's Spanish wife, Juana, atop their elephants.
These ladies, with others, came under a heavy fire from the enemy's guns before
Maharajpur. Sir Charles Napier asked Smith: 'How came all the ladies to be in
the fight? I suppose you all wanted to be gloriously rid of your wives? . . . Poor
things! I dare say they too had their hopes. They talk of our immoral conduct in
Scinde! I am sure there never was any so bad as this.' (*Napier*, III, 45.)

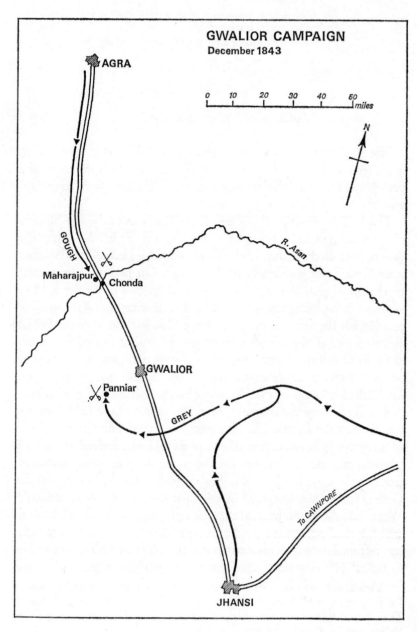

GWALIOR CAMPAIGN
December 1843

0   10   20   30   40   50 miles

N

AGRA

GOUGH

Maharajpur Chonda

R. Asan

GWALIOR

Panniar

GREY

To CAWNPORE

JHANSI

Map 9

mutinous troops which overawed and controled [*sic*] the Government of H.H. the Maharajah Jyajee Rao Scindiah, and attacked the British forces, on their advance to Gwalior to H.H.'s support'.[3]

There had arrived in Calcutta, early in August, fresh from a successful campaign in China (in which no cavalry took part), a new commander-in-chief. This was the Peninsular veteran and hero of Barossa (1811) General Sir Hugh Gough, aged sixty-four, a forceful soldier, famed for his bravery and determination if not for his brilliance as a general.

Gough divided his force of some 20,000 men into two wings, either of which he believed to be 'amply sufficient not only to repel, but to overthrow the whole Mahratta force in the field'.[4] In this he was proved right, though he later admitted that the 'politicals' had deceived him about the enemy. 'I thought', he wrote, 'I should have a mob without leaders. . . . I found a well-disciplined, well-organised army, well led and truly gallant.'[5] Gough, himself, commanded the right wing. Major-General Sir John Grey commanded the left wing.

On 29 December 1843, Gough fought the battle of Maharajpur and Grey the action of Panniar. In both, the Gwalior army was soundly defeated but at high cost to the British forces. Maharajpur was chiefly a contest of infantry and artillery. Gough first advanced frontally against a large Maratha battery defended by some 3,000 infantry in the village of Maharajpur; then against 2,300 infantry in the village of Shirkapur and finally against some 5,000 in the enemy's main position between Chonda and Dompura. The Maratha gunners were bayonetted to a man serving their pieces, which they regarded 'as objects of worship',[6] devotedly to the end. Fifty-six guns were captured.

Gough brought into the field about 4,800 infantry (of which two regiments were European, and eight native). He disposed of thirty field pieces, and some 1,340 cavalry. This last was divided into two brigades, one on either flank.* Evidence is scanty and conflicting as to exactly what part these played. They seem to have charged in support of the infantry as occasion offered. At one moment the 4th Bengal

---

* *3rd Cavalry Brigade* (Lieutenant-Colonel C. R. Cureton): 16th Lancers; Governor-General's Bodyguard; 1st Bengal Light Cavalry; 4th Bengal Irregular Cavalry (part of Skinner's Horse); detachment, 5th Bengal Light Cavalry.

4th Cavalry Brigade (Lieutenant-Colonel J. Scott): 4th Bengal Light Cavalry (Lancers); 10th Bengal Light Cavalry; detachment, 8th Bengal Light Cavalry.

The 3rd Brigade was supported by two troops of horse artillery, and the 4th Brigade by one troop.

Irregular Cavalry was ordered by Gough himself (who always wore a white coat in battle so as to be easily distinguished by his troops) to charge a 'considerable body of the enemy's infantry'[7] and a two-gun battery. This they did with great spirit but, being unsupported, they were unable to keep the guns, though they captured two standards. On the extreme left Lieutenant-Colonel Scott, according to Gough's despatch, 'was opposed by a body of the enemy's cavalry . . . and made some well executed charges with the 10th Light Cavalry, most ably supported by Captain Grant's troop of horse artillery and 4th [Bengal Light Cavalry] lancers, capturing some guns and taking two standards: thus threatening the right flank of the enemy.'[8]

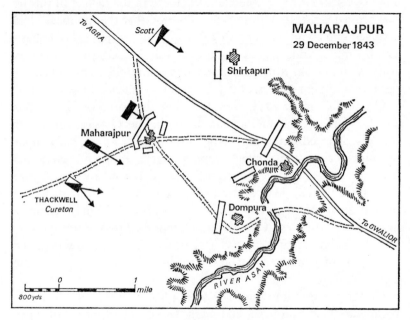

Map 10

The cavalry seem to have failed completely to follow up the victory. Gough's despatch says that they 'manoeuvred most judiciously on the right and would have got in rear of the position and cut off the retreat of the whole, had they not been prevented by an impassable ravine.'[9] In a letter to his son, however, he writes that Sir Joseph Thackwell, who commanded all the mounted troops, and was on the right flank, should have formed up close to the right-hand infantry brigade as he had been ordered. He would then have 'been one mile clear of any ravine, with a level country in front of him.'[10]

Thackwell himself blames the adjutant-general, Sir Harry Smith, another Peninsular veteran. Smith, he claims, 'highly disapproved of the position' in which Churchill, the quartermaster-general, wanted to place the 3rd Cavalry Brigade. Smith 'would not allow the cavalry to turn the ravines, or cross the ford to fall on the enemy's rear, therefore as my superior officer I was bound to obey.'[11]

The only known account by an 'other rank' of the cavalry occurs in a letter from a corporal of the 16th Lancers, the sole European mounted regiment present:

'Our squadron formed the advance-guard of our Division, consequently our troop led into the field.

'As soon as we arrived at good ground we formed line to the front under a heavy fire from the enemy's battery, and galloped under it about three miles to the right, but fortunately for us their guns were aimed for our lances, or half the regiment must have fallen. However, we managed to escape their shot very well, although we could hear them whistling like so much hail over our heads. Queer work, I can assure you.

'Well, we caught sight of the enemy's guns and charged them, and just as we got within 50 yards of them we discovered a tremendous ravine between us and the guns, so that all we could do was to retreat out of range of their fire. In this charge we lost two men and 21 horses killed; three horses and one man just in front of me fell. When we found we could not get at their guns we wanted to have a charge at their cavalry, but directly we advanced against them they turned tail and fled. . . .

'It was a tremendous hot day, the sun pouring down on us the whole of the time.'[12]

Lieutenant (later Field-Marshal Sir) Neville Chamberlain, attached to the Bodyguard which charged with the 16th, wrote in his journal: 'Our cavalry was badly placed, and we were the most unsuccessful troops in the field.'[13]

106 officers and men were killed at Maharajpur, 684 wounded and 7 missing. Of these the cavalry share was twelve killed, fifty-four wounded and four missing. The 10th Bengal Light Cavalry suffered the highest casualties: four men killed; three officers and twenty-six native officers and men wounded.

The action at Panniar which took place some twenty-three miles from Maharajpur on the same day and at about the same hour was chiefly an infantry affair. It was costly in men: 35 British killed and

182 wounded. Neither battle was anything but unimaginative tactically; both were prodigal of British lives. The campaign, nevertheless, was over in two days. Gwalior was entered and the State's forces were drastically reduced. Ellenborough's fear that the Gwalior army would menace his rear in the increasingly likely event of a war with the Sikhs had been effectively removed.

9

'One of the few sensible justifications of the
cavalry in its traditional *arme blanche* rôle of the
charge . . . was, that although of very dubious
value in European warfare, it was still potentially
of decisive importance against natives.'
      BRIAN BOND, *Victorian Military Campaigns*[1]

(i)

India: the First Sikh War, 1845–1846

What made war in the Punjab virtually inevitable was the death in
1839 of Ranjit Singh. From the age of ten this greatest of all nineteenth century Indian leaders had been ruler of the Sikhs. These
redoubtable warriors were members of a reformed Hindu sect.
Originally a purely religious community, founded in the fifteenth
century, the Sikhs had gradually adopted a military organisation in
addition to their religious discipline. The foundations of their military
power had been laid by Govind Rao (1675–1708), who was the first
to adopt the appellative Singh, meaning 'lion'. From his time dates
the Khalsa, the Praetorian Guard of the Punjab. It was Ranjit, however, who first made the Khalsa, with its so-called 'democratic'
organisation, into a really disciplined army. At his death he was 'un-
disputed master of a compact and well-knit kingdom possessing the

243

only army in India capable of meeting the Company's forces on equal terms'.[2] It was Ranjit who welded together the various Sikh confederacies. It was Ranjit who, using his European-trained army, extended the Sikh domains to the west, to the north and to the south. Only to the east did he make no conquests. His policy was expansion within the limits of the possible. He recognised that the great British power which reached to the River Sutlej, the eastern boundary of the Sikh domains, was too formidable to be successfully challenged. In 1809, as we have seen (see p. 214), he signed the Treaty of Amritsar with the British. This agremeent he had steadfastly observed.

With the removal of Ranjit's strong hand, the Sikh state speedily fell into a condition of political chaos. This was accompanied by the rise of factional military leadership. Assassinations and riots followed each other in quick succesion. The Khalsa, inevitably, took over. Sir Henry Lawrence, of all Englishmen the most likely to come by the truth, wrote that the Lahore government decided that it could not 'stand another month against the army . . . and that the vengeance of a foreign army would be a lesser evil than the fury of its own'. It was decided therefore 'to fling the soldiery upon British India, supplying them with every possible means of success, taking, if unsuccessful, the chance of clemency and forgiveness, and, if victorious, the merit and profit of repelling the English from Hindoostan'.[3] Fortunately for the British, it was this negative approach which accounted for the sometimes hesitant way in which the Sikhs waged what became known as the First Sikh War.

Over the years since Ranjit's death, as the crisis mounted, British reinforcements had been moved, bit by bit, nearer the frontier. By the start of the war, some 40,000 men and over 90 guns were assembled between Meerut and the Sutlej. Since the minimum estimate of the disciplined regular army of the Sikhs was 50,000 with 200 guns, nothing provocative could be read into these inadequate preparations.

In July 1844, Lieutenant-General Sir Henry Hardinge, another Peninsular veteran and a protegé of Wellington's, succeeded Ellenborough (his brother-in-law) as governor-general. He was particularly anxious, as a soldier, to prove 'that military men, in the conduct of affairs usually transacted by civil officers, on which peace or war hangs by a thread, can be trusted for their prudence as safely as those who, in the event of war would have no military reputation to gratify'.[4] He has been accused of being, in consequence, insufficiently prepared when the Sikh aggression occurred. A show of superior strength at the outset, it was argued, might have averted hostilities. However that may have been, the Sikhs with an army of some 50,000 men and 100 guns crossed the Sutlej on 11 December 1845, and war was inevitable. One part of the army advanced to a position near Ferozeshah, while another threatened but did not attack the isolated garrison at Ferozepore.* This numbered no more than 7,000 men. It was commanded by Major-General Sir John Littler, who at once entrenched and showed a bold front. His nearest supports were 5,000 men eighty miles away at Ludhiana. At Ambala, 160 miles away, were 10,000 more who had been ordered to move towards the Sutlej three days before the invasion. At Meerut, 115 miles beyond Ambala, were a further 9,000.

All these troops, now formed into 'the Army of the Sutlej', were at once set in motion for the frontier. As always, very little preparation for carriage had been made. 'We were quite unprepared,' wrote an officer of the 3rd Light Dragoons, the sole European mounted regiment within 250 miles of Ferozepore, 'for in this country one is obliged to have camels and carts, and numerous Niggers to carry tents and baggage.'[5] Nevertheless, by forced marches of a most harassing nature, a large part of the troops from Ambala and Ludhiana arrived at the village of Mudki on 18 December. So did the governor-general and the commander-in-chief.

Hardinge's 'Camp Clerk' relates that 'about 12 o'clock we reached Moodkee. . . . The first thing we did was to ride into a shallow tank which was there, and to allow the horses to drink to their hearts' content. Shortly after, the Cavalry arrived, and pouring by squadrons into the pool, made it a puddle.'[6] Among the first of the mounted

---

* The Sikhs could probably have done so with ease. They would then have been able to march to Bassian, the main depôt in the area, and capture that, before any considerable British force could have been brought against them. Had they achieved this the native troops would almost certainly 'have joined the enemy', as Hardinge realised, 'and we should have had a grand rising of the population in our rear as far as Karnal'. (*Governor-General's Minute*, 11 Nov., 1846.) There is evidence that treachery on the part of the Sikh leaders was responsible for this missed opportunity. (Bajwa, 325; Suri, V.S. (ed.) *Some Original Sources of Panjab History*, 1961, 68–70; Cunningham, J. D. *History of the Sikhs*, 1897, 263; but compare Broadfoot, 420–421.) Soon after the Sikh army had marched, Lal Singh, one of its two commanders, sent a messenger to Captain Nicholson, the agent at Ferozepore, giving him details of the Sikh intentions and expressing the hope that they would remain good friends. (Extracts from John Nicholson's journal, L2/Bk 169, Punjab Government Records; cited in Mahajan, J. *The Annexation of the Punjab*, 1949, 30.)

troops on the scene was Lieutenant Denham-Cookes's troop of the 3rd.

'We watered and picketed our Horses', he wrote, 'and our Mess-man having by some luck laid hold of a little grub, which we stood much in need of, having had scarcely anything to eat for the previous 6 days, we got under a Tree and commenced operations. We had made a little progress when a Native Trooper came up to us as hard as he could lick, and just managed to stammer out "Seik, Seik". At the same time the infantry bugles and drums sounded a beat to arms. We luckily had not un-saddled, and were formed in close column in 5 minutes. . . .
'By this time the Enemy's guns had opened.'[7]

This was at about 3 p.m. The Sikhs, probably at the most 4,000 infantry, 10,000 horsemen and 22 guns in strength,* were some two miles distant from Mudki when their artillery opened on the cavalry patrols. Their guns lined the edge of a belt of dense jungle and stunted trees. Between them and Mudki was open ground. Instead of waiting to be attacked across this, Gough, fearful that the Sikhs might have second thoughts and retire and in spite of the exhausted state of his men, advanced. 'I immediately pushed forward the horse artillery and cavalry,' he wrote in his despatch, 'directing the infantry, accompanied by the field batteries, to move forward in support.'[8]

There followed the sort of simple but costly battle which Gough found so congenial. For about half an hour his artillery (much inferior in calibre to the Sikhs') tried to silence the enemy's guns. Meanwhile he ordered his three cavalry brigades to sweep round both ends of the Sikh line, which overlapped his own on both flanks. Their orders were to outflank the enemy by charging as opportunity offered. To the right, where the jungle was at its thickest and the trees quite tall, went Brigadiers White (in command of the cavalry division) and Gough (the commander-in-chief's nephew). Both brigadiers, incidentally, belonged to the 3rd Light Dragoons. Their brigades consisted of part of the 4th Bengal Native Cavalry (Lancers), the 5th Bengal Native Cavalry, the Governor-General's Bodyguard, one troop of horse artillery, and the 3rd Light Dragoons in the

---

* It is probable that the Sikhs thought that they would be opposed by the British force from Ludhiana alone, and that they were unaware that much of the Ambala force was also present. This might be the reason for the smallness of the Sikh army at Mudki.

lead. Lieutenant Denham-Cookes, of that regiment, describes what happened:

'We advanced in open column of troops, the Comdr. in Chief and his staff taking off their cocked hats and cheering us. This was a fine inspiring sight, but it did a great deal of mischief, as it maddened our men and prevented the officers from keeping them back. . . .

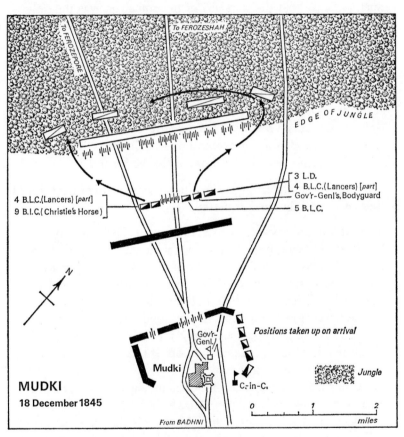

Map 11

'We kept advancing at a gallop – the dust was so thick that I could not see my horse's head, but every now and then I felt him bound into the air and found that he had jumped a bush.

'The enemy had now discovered us and the round shot came tearing thro' our ranks. The first shot took off a Trumpeter's head just behind me. . . .

'Our pace now increased, and the leading Troops (the only ones who could see their way as they had no dust) came upon the Enemy.'⁹

To the left of the 3rd was the Bodyguard.

'Conceive', wrote a young officer of that regiment, who was severely wounded in the charge, 'a brigade or column of troops galloping through a thick thorn jungle enveloped in clouds of dust so dense that the standard of my squadron was the only landmark I could recognise, approaching nearer and nearer to the thundering batteries of the enemy and the yelling crowd protecting them.

'Above all the din I heard the word passed to wheel into line; it was merely a left turn for each individual; and on we rushed at the same pace. Loud shouts of friend and foe arose on our right as our gallant dragoons [of the 3rd] dashed in, clearing all before them, and in another second we were in a mass of bloody-minded Sikh horse and foot, but chiefly the former.'¹⁰

The 3rd, meanwhile, 'owing to thick dust and the quantities of bushes and trees', became dispersed.

'I went on by myself,' wrote Lieutenant Denham-Cookes, 'my Troop having gone I know not whither, and the first object I saw was an Akali* who let fly and missed me. I then came on two more rascals, who did the same, one of whom tasted my sabre, which I found would not cut through him, as he was enveloped in cotton clothes. . . . I soon found a couple of my own men, and at the same time an Elephant came by us, with 4 Seik Chiefs making the best of their way off. If I had had a few more men I could have taken them.

'At this time I was in rear of the Enemy, and having gone far enough I turned back and met Hale, Fisher, Swinton (who was wounded) and a few Dragoons. About this time we met two Seiks under a tree, and Martin of the Native Cavalry attacked one of them, but in so stupid a way that the Seik sent his spear clean through Martin's breast and out at his back. . . . I saw it was no use attacking these rascals with a sword, so I bethought

---

* 'Akali. . . . A class of armed devotees among the Sikhs, worshippers of "Him who is without time, eternal". In practice they were "devoted to misrule and plunder".' (Wilson, H. H. *Glossary . . . of terms . . . in British India*, 1855, 15; see also Broadfoot, 352.)

me of my pistol; the right barrel missed fire, but the left did its duty well, and doubled the rascal up. Hale shot the other fellow.

'We continued on our return, when we came on a body of about 3,000 Seik Cavalry behind a village, directly on our road home. We saw there was nothing for it but to cut our way through. The Native Cavalry with us would not come on; but we went at them, as hard as we could go. Then the Seiks opened right and left, and gave us a most infernal volley – wounded Fisher and killed three Dragoons. . . .

'After we had dispersed the rascals in the charge, those that were not cut down took to the Trees and Bushes, where we could not reach them, and from this secure position they shot a number of our men. . . . After a short time we got our Carbines out and brought down 7 rascals out of one Tree, so they did not have it all their own way. . . .'[11]

Captain Tritton of the 3rd, acting as assistant adjutant-general to the cavalry, 'captured one of the enemy's Standards with his own hands.' Lance-Sergeant Hinds, with six or seven troopers of the regiment, 'succeeded in capturing two of the enemy's guns, after cutting down the whole of the armed party who were with them'.[12]

The Sikhs nicknamed the 3rd 'the Devil's Children' since they came upon them 'like a flash of lightning'. Their famous charge, however, was robbed of any truly decisive effect because of the jungle. By the time it was over, twilight was falling upon the field of battle.

While the 3rd thus turned the left of the Sikh army, the 9th Bengal Irregular Cavalry (Christie's Horse) and the rest of the 4th Bengal Native Cavalry, accompanied by three troops of horse artillery, threatened the enemy's right.

With the Sikh infantry 'almost invisible amongst the wood',[13] Gough now ordered his own infantry forward. Whenever the enemy made a stand, the British used the bayonet, and so, with his four European and nine native battalions, Gough drove the Sikhs from position to position, capturing fifteen guns.

His casualties were many: 215 of all ranks were killed and 657 wounded. Some of the losses were caused, as Gough admitted, 'by corps firing into one another',[14] as was inevitable in a night battle, particularly with troops that had not acted together before. Further, the Sikhs expected no mercy and gave none. Some of the 3rd's troopers who were wounded in the charge were found after the battle cruelly murdered. In consequence, whenever the regiment met the Sikhs again, its battle cry was 'Remember Moodkee', and many who would otherwise have been spared were ruthlessly killed.[15] It has often been suggested that most of the native infantry, and some of the native cavalry, failed to take their fair share of the fighting in the battle of Mudki. Whether this was so or not, it is a fact that two-thirds of all the casualties were among the Europeans who numbered less than a fifth of the troops present. Some say that the Sikhs invariably concentrated their fire upon the white regiments, confident that once these could be stopped, the native troops would give way.[16]

The 5th Bengal Native Cavalry had the greatest casualties of the native cavalry regiments: forty-nine killed and wounded, including two European and one native officer. The cavalry as a whole lost eighty-one of all ranks killed. Of these sixty-one were of the 3rd Light Dragoons which had gone into action 497 strong. Thirty-five of the eighty-seven wounded also came from that regiment. Its loss in horses, too, was very severe: 105 killed and 23 wounded. Such casualties as these could be expected from cavalry charging against batteries, especially where the guns were placed at the edge of a jungle. Whether, in view of its results, this celebrated charge was justified, is difficult to tell. That it was splendid and dashing there can be no doubt, though it seems possible that the troopers' enthusiasm rather ran away with them. For many years to come the men of the 3rd proudly bore their nickname of *Moodkeewallahs* bestowed upon them by the Sikhs. 'Oh! How I wished', wrote an infantry officer, 'for a 1000 more good British horse to join that whirlwind charge!'[17]

The battle of Mudki, which came to be nicknamed 'Midnight Moodkhee', was summed up by a Sikh who was present. Writing to his son, he said: 'The Ghorchurras [Sikh irregular cavalry] would not come on; the British charged; the Sikhs ran; lots killed and all or nearly all the guns lost.'[18] What chiefly struck young Lieutenant Taylor of the Bodyguard, was 'the hopelessness of a cavalry affair ever coming up to one's poetical ideas of it, as formed from the parade-ground or from written descriptions'. Commenting on Gough's tactical methods, he found that 'the Tipperary rush, though effective, is rather expensive in good material'.[19]

*   *   *

The badly mauled Sikhs now retired to a strong entrenched position around the village of Ferozeshah, about eight miles to the north-west of Mudki. Gough spent 19 and 20 December burying the dead and tending the wounded. Orders, meanwhile, were sent off to Littler. He was to bring away the majority of his 7,000 men from Ferozepore, without, if possible, the Sikhs who surrounded that town being aware of his withdrawal. He was to meet Gough in front of Feroze-shah early on 21 December.

Long before dawn on that day Gough's ponderous army, re-inforced on the 19th by two European infantry regiments and two eight-inch howitzers (the last reinforcements which could arrive for many days to come), struck camp and marched to a position from which an attack could be made against Ferozeshah from the south and west. When it was learned that Littler had not left Ferozepore till 8 a.m., having successfully deceived the investing force by leaving his picquets standing, Gough wished to start the battle without him. Though it was clear that Littler could not effect a junction till well after noon on what was the shortest day of the year, Hardinge opposed the commander-in-chief's plan most decidedly. The governor-general, curiously enough, had proposed that he should act as second-in-command to Gough. This arrangement had been accepted. When, however, Gough said to him 'Sir Henry, if we attack at once I promise you a splendid victory!' Hardinge, after prolonged discussion, was constrained to say: 'Then, Sir Hugh, I must exercise my civil power as Governor-General, and forbid the attack until Littler's force has come up.'[20]

Hardinge's intervention may or may not have been justified. What is certain is that, though Littler's troops* seem to have arrived by 1.30 p.m., the final arrangements for the forward movement of the whole army, now perhaps 18,000 strong, were not made for some unknown reason until between 3 and 4 p.m. This left, at the most, two hours of daylight.

After an opening artillery duel, in which once again the numbers, calibre and weight of metal of the Sikh artillery proved superior to the British, Littler, prematurely it seems, emerged from the dense brushwood on to the open space before the enemy's entrenchments, and commenced the assault. The Sikh batteries, which had ample opportunity for accurate gun-laying, drove his infantry back with

---

* Two native cavalry regiments; 62nd Foot; five native infantry battalions; two troops, horse artillery; 1½ Light Field Battery.

great loss. The cavalry which he had brought from Ferozepore consisted of the 8th Bengal Native Cavalry and the 3rd Bengal Irregular Cavalry, about 300 sabres each. Parts of these, acting as escorts to the two troops of horse artillery, retired (perhaps expediently, if not honourably) with the repulsed infantry, leaving their charges stranded. A sudden cessation of the Sikh fire, however, allowed the two gun troops to limber up and retire safely.[21]

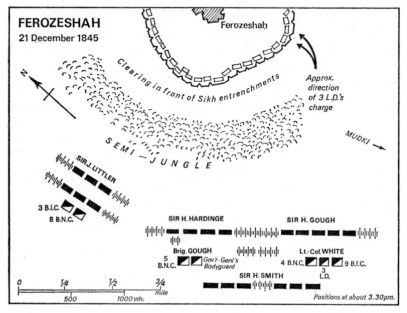

Map 12

All along the line the infantry now poured through the artillery to assault the entrenchments. Everywhere there was deadly conflict, but in time a precarious foothold was established and some of the Sikh batteries were carried. The devoted gunners were bayonetted at their guns.

At the height of the perilous 'see-saw' tussle which followed, just as it was getting dark, Gough gave two orders. In the centre he threw in Sir Harry Smith's reserve infantry division. This eventually succeeded in entering the village of Ferozeshah. At the same time he sent the right-hand cavalry brigade* to attack the south-eastern face of the entrenchments.

* 3rd Light Dragoons; 4th Bengal Native Cavalry (Lancers), and 9th Bengal Irregular Cavalry. The composition of the two brigades had been altered after Mudki.

With the remaining officers and men of the 3rd Light Dragoons to the fore (probably not many more than 350 sabres), Brigadier White led his three regiments to the attack, all the while under 'a most galling fire of grape'.[22] The 3rd, it was noticed, 'advanced with as correct a line as if at a review parade, the troop leaders of the second squadron giving the base in the usual manner, until in actual contact with the enemy.'[23] First they had to negotiate, in places, stumps and branches of trees lining a dry ditch and then a sloped bank. On top of this was a battery of Sikh guns and behind these their infantry entrenched in front of their camp.* Through all these the 3rd tore irresistibly. Lieutenant Denham-Cookes described the charge as 'the happiest moment' of his life. From one of the French officers in the enemy's pay he afterwards learned 'that the Seiks thought they had *beaten us*, until we charged and cut to pieces and dispersed 3 Battalions of their best infantry, which enabled our Infantry to rush in and secure the guns'.[24]

In the course of the charge, some of the bridles of the 3rd were cut by the enemy's swords, 'by which the riders became powerless, having lost command over their horses'. In consequence, several of the officers of the 9th Lancers, when they heard about it, 'had *chain reins* made for their regimental bridles.'[25]†

The British casualties were again high. This was partly due to the tents, tent-ropes and tent-pegs of the Sikh camp. These formidable obstacles to the keeping of a close-knit, well-dressed line, so essential to the success of cavalry shock action, wreaked havoc in the ranks of the 3rd. It seems that many of the men penetrated right through to the far side of the enemy's position, before returning 'by fours and fives',[26] covered, as was said at the time, 'with imperishable glory'.[27]

At both Mudki and Ferozeshah, casualties were caused when 'the enemy's matchlock men', as Captain Taylor of the Bodyguard remarked, '*ducked* in among the bushes, and let the cavalry pass over them, then jumped up and shot and sabred stragglers. Hence to lose your horse was to lose your life, and in the most disgusting way.'[28]

* * *

* One, but only one, eye-witness, writing seven months after the battle, states that the 3rd 'dashed . . . against a mass of *Seikh Cavalry* . . . and put the whole to flight' before reaching 'some works of great strength, which they also endeavoured to take, but were repulsed'. (Cumming, 278.)

† See p. 288 for the steel chains along the snaffle-reins of the Scinde Irregular Horse.

Throughout the heat of the day, the British army had been without water. Now through the long, bitterly cold night thirsts still could not be slaked.

'What a fearful night that was!' wrote Captain Cumming of the 80th Foot. 'The Seikhs kept firing incessantly: the glare of their burning camp, the explosion of mines and ammunition wagons, the wild cries of the enemy, the huzzahs of our own men, the groans of the wounded, who with the dead were strewn thickly everywhere, the trampling of men and horses, and the continual plunging of the shot amongst us formed a scene of terror which it is impossible to describe.'[29]

For the two commanders the anxiety was great. Hardinge remarked to one of the staff in the course of the evening: 'Another such action will shake the empire.'[30] What uncertain footholds had been gained had to be abandoned. Sir Harry Smith, finding himself unsupported, was forced to make the best of his way out of the village of Ferozeshah. The enemy reoccupied the entrenchments. Major Havelock, a member of Gough's staff, was not alone in believing that another half hour of daylight would have seen the enemy routed.[31] As it was the battle had to be re-started on the following morning.

'At the first faint whitening of the eastern sky', wrote Captain Cumming, 'our bugles sang out under the pelting of an iron shower. As they changed into the "advance", with a true British cheer the whole line moved forward. . . . Trench after trench was taken, sometimes retaken, for three long hours. . . . By one o'clock we had swept the whole entrenched camp and driven the enemy clear out of it.'[32]*

The line then thankfully halted, with the Sikhs in full retreat. The victorious army 'received its two leaders', in the commander-in-chief's words, 'as they rode along the front, with a gratifying cheer, displaying the captured standards of the Khalsa Army'.[33]

* There is evidence from a French officer who was present that one of the Sikh commanders fled from Ferozeshah in the course of the night, taking with him 'all his irregular cavalry and the gunners of 60 pieces of artillery'. (Bajwa, 280, quoting Mouton, Col. *Rapport sur les derniers évenements du Panjab*, 1846, 6.) If this were even partly true, it would help to account for the comparative ease with which the Sikh position was taken on 22 December. Another authority states that during the night 'the Akalis plundered the tents of . . . the Sikh Commander-in-Chief; a general riot ensued, and the remnants of discipline were lost'. (Broadfoot, 394.)

The exhausted men and horses had hardly time to satisfy their raging thirst at the wells of Ferozeshah, many contaminated by Sikh corpses, before the worst crisis of the two-day battle was upon them. A large new Sikh force – that which had been deceived by Littler's withdrawal from Ferozepore – now drove in the cavalry picquets, and approached Ferozeshah from the north-west. 'The only time I felt a doubt', wrote Gough to his son, 'was . . . when the fresh enemy advanced, with heavy columns of Cavalry, Infantry and guns, when we had not a shot with our guns, and our Cavalry Horses were done up.'[34] For an unbearably long time the Sikh guns pounded Gough's infantry. Too weary to attack with the bayonet, and with their cartridge supply dangerously low, there was little they could do in reply. Gough himself, when he saw some of the native regiments and even some of the Europeans wavering, restored their morale by galloping out alone in his famous white coat with one aide-de-camp to draw the fire upon himself.

At about 3 p.m. an astonishing thing occurred. The assistant adjutant-general, Captain J. R. Lumley, suffering perhaps from what later came to be known as 'shell-shock' but what was at the time diagnosed as sun stroke,* gave orders, as if from the commander-in-chief, to whatever units of the cavalry and horse artillery he could get hold of, to proceed at once to Ferozepore, out of the battle.

'Old (Brigadier) White', wrote Lieutenant Denham-Cookes, 'sent me to see where the Cavalry were going to. . . .

'On reaching the Cavalry, I gave old White's message, and they said, "We have orders to go to Ferozepore, and have a man to shew us the way; you had better come also."

'I replied, "I will see you —— first!"

'I regret to say that some of our men shirked off, and also 2 or 3 officers, whom I have cut in consequence. It was indeed a fearful time.

'On my return I gave my answer to old White, and at the same moment an A.D.C. came down and said that the Enemy's Cavalry were about to attack.'

* When, on the following day, Hardinge demanded an explanation Lumley was wearing nothing on his legs but 'paijamas'. He excused this unseemly dress on the grounds of his overalls being so riddled with balls that they had dropped off! He was shortly afterwards retired, escaping court-martial, it was said, on the grounds of insanity. (Hardinge, 99.)

This certainly seemed to be true, for large masses of Sikh horsemen were seen to be bearing down upon the infantry squares on the British right. They approached to within 150 yards and then wavered and came to a standstill. At once, as an infantry brigadier witnessed, 'the small surviving remnant of H.M.'s 3rd Dragoons, warily supported by native cavalry, dispersed the enemy, and, as it were by miracle, left us masters of the field.'[35] The native cavalry here referred to were, apparently, part of the 4th Bengal Native Cavalry (Lancers). Lieutenant-Colonel Bunbury of the 80th Foot states that the 4th 'formed a second line, but instead of following the example of the 3rd Light Dragoons, they wheeled round to the right, and formed in rear of the 80th! The commander of the regiment seemed greatly disgusted at this public exhibition.'[36] Lieutenant Denham-Cookes's account of this final charge shows to what straits the 3rd had been reduced:

'I regret to say that some of our men fell out, I hope because their horses could not move. We had not more than 74 men left. Old White disappeared and so did Sullivan [adjutant of the 3rd] (a regular cur). Old Hale and I cheered on our men, and I never was more relieved than when an A.D.C. came and told us that the enemy were in *full retreat*!! and that we were only to press them. We did so: it is lucky that we had no more to do – it seemed like an interposition of Providence, the Enemy's retreating at this time, when they had only to advance to win the battle. . . .'[37]

An officer of the 1st Bengal European Regiment (later the Royal Munster Fusiliers), describing this final phase of the battle, says that the Sikh cavalry 'made a struggle to maintain [their] ground, but gradually gave way' after a hand-to-hand fight; 'when the strange spectacle presented itself of hundreds of dismounted men fighting single combats on the ground, whilst their riderless horses were manoeuvring in front of our squares'.[38]

At least two reasons for the enemy's withdrawal at this moment have been advanced. One was that the Sikh commander, judging 'that if the British could capture such a position' as Ferozeshah 'after such carnage, any attack upon them while defending that position was hopeless'.[39] Another was that the Sikhs, seeing the majority of the British cavalry and horse artillery making for Ferozepore, suspected some clever outflanking movement.[40] It would be ironical, indeed, if it was Lumley's order which in fact saved the day!

Thus ended what a good authority has called one of the most momentous 'and certainly the hardest fought-out' of the battles engaged in by the British in India.[41] Neither the Sikh strength, nor their casualties can be more than guessed at. They lost seventy-three guns. The number of their killed alone has been put at between 2,000 and 3,000, but these figures are almost certainly too high. The British casualties were 2,877, of which 720 were killed, including thirty-nine European and seventeen native officers. An interesting feature of the official casualty list is the numbers of men returned as 'missing': 379.[42]

The 3rd lost fifty-five killed, including two officers, and ninety-three wounded. Their loss in horses was 197. In the two battles of Mudki and Ferozeshah they had lost 244 men: only nine short of half the number with which they had arrived at Mudki. As the historian of the British army put it, 'few regiments of horse in the world can show a finer record of hardihood and endurance'.[43]

The shortage of European cavalry at both Mudki and Ferozeshah was greatly felt. Hardinge wrote that the 'native cavalry did not behave well' at Ferozeshah,[44] and is supposed at one stage of the battle to have said that he would 'give half a lakh of rupees that H.M.'s 16th Lancers should arrive.'[45]

Of the three arms of the Khalsa the regular cavalry regiments were the least efficient. Excepting one or two, particularly the *cuirassiers* trained by the French General Allard, they were 'very inferior in every respect to the infantry. . . . While the latter are carefully picked up from large bodies of candidates for service, the former are composed of men of all sorts and sizes and ages, who get appointed solely through the interest of the different Sardars.' The men were on the whole 'miserably mounted and armed', and their horses 'under-sized and wanting weight'.[46] Some men of the 3rd told the governor-general's chaplain that at Mudki the enemy cavalrymen, 'though some of them fought bravely, could only fight by dismounting from their horses, and lifting their swords with both hands at once'.[47]

The irregulars (*ghorchurras*), on the other hand, were considered by John Lawrence 'both better mounted and finer men than the British *silladars*'.[48] These were, of course, only fit for the rôle of light cavalry.

Captain Cumming of the 80th, the day after Ferozeshah, visited

'the place where the 3rd had made one of their desperate charges.

At one spot there was a sort of circle of Seikh corpses, and in the middle two of our dragoons. One was a sergeant, dead from a deep sabre-cut in the back of his neck, dealt by some coward who had come behind him. The other was a sergeant-major: his right arm had been lopped off, and there was a deep sabre-cut across his face: he was drenched in blood. I thought him dead, but while I was looking on him sorrowfully he began to work in convulsions. I took my flask and moistened his face and temples with the cold water. He looked up, and with a great effort said "Thanks! Put it to my mouth." He swallowed some water greedily, but it worked up again from his throat with blood and froth. I was afraid he could not speak again, but asked him what his name was. "Bruce." "And where is Sergeant White?" [Cumming had met them both some weeks earlier]. He tried to turn his head, and with quite a strong voice said, "There – but I avenged him". He then vomited a large quantity of blood and immediately expired.'[49]

At a cabinet meeting after the news of Ferozeshah had reached London, Peel is supposed to have referred to it as a Pyrrhic victory. Wellington, however, retorted: 'Make it a victory; fire a salute, and ring the bells. Gough has lost a good many men; but what of that? You must lose officers and men if you have to fight a great battle. At Assaye I lost a third of my force.'[50]

*　　*　　*

Defeated but not demoralised, the Sikhs recrossed the Sutlej at Sobraon. There they awaited reinforcements. So did the British. Some 10,000 men who had been on the march from Meerut since mid-December began to arrive on 6 January 1846. Among them were the 9th and 16th Lancers, the 3rd Bengal Native Cavalry and the 4th Bengal Irregular Cavalry, three native infantry regiments and some artillery. The Sikhs now once again crossed the Sutlej. Their main army took up a strong position opposite Sobraon with its back to the river. At the same time, sixty miles to the east, a smaller force crossed near Ludhiana. Its object was either to intercept Gough's siege-train which was lumbering laboriously towards Bassian, or more likely merely to plunder Ludhiana and its environs. To deal with this threat Gough detached Sir Harry Smith with half of his infantry division, some cavalry and artillery.

On 21 January, Smith's baggage train was attacked on the march near Budowal. He lost some 200 men, including many sick and wounded. All the personal baggage of the officers of the 16th Lancers was taken. So was the whole of the regimental plate which it was still the custom to carry into the field.

'My orders to the baggage guard', wrote Sir Harry, '(composed of 400 Irregular Horse, to which I afterwards added one squadron of Regular Native Cavalry) were only half obeyed, or our loss of baggage would have been next to nothing; but young soldiers are excited under a heavy cannonade and apprehend more of its deadly effect than I have ever seen the heaviest cannonade (not grape and canister) merit.'[51]

That evening Sir Harry entered Ludhiana. After wading through deep dust for many hours, 'some of our poor infantry', wrote a corporal of the 16th, 'were so exhausted that we were obliged to carry them . . . on our horses'.[52] The 31st and 53rd Regiments of Foot remembered this with gratitude for many years.

Trooper Pearman, one of a draft for the 3rd Light Dragoons which was caught up by Sir Harry's force, certainly could never

'forget that day: Marching from one a.m.', he wrote, 'until 5 in the evening over thirty miles and under an Indian sun, with Brown Bess, 120 rounds of Ball Cartridge, and coat at our backs.* We had nothing to drink on the road. Some of the men's tongues were protruding from their mouths. At last the men could go no further, the enemy cavalry following close on our rear to cut up the stragglers. Sergt-Major Baker became beat and lay down. I said: "For God's sake, George, think of your wife and children." He had two children. He looked at me and said, "I can't". . . . When the Cavalry was about to charge us, we were ordered to form square, but were unable to do so. We made one corner, but got confused. . . . I had not suffered so much from thirst as some men. Roberts made water in his cap and drank it. Just as we became so confused, the 16th Lancers

* This draft of fifty-four men for the 3rd Light Dragoons was christened 'the Draft of the Bayonet Battery', on account, as Trooper Pearman said, 'of our marching with guns and bayonet with the 53rd, and being engaged with that weapon at Budowal. . . . If any of the draft got into trouble for years after, our Adjutant would say: "Colonel, this is one of the Bayonet Battery." The Colonel would then say: "Ah, poor boy!", and let them off, saying "Don't you come here again, or else I shall punish you very severely, mind."' (Anglesey: *Pearman*, 49.)

came down at a trot in open column of Troops and wheeled into line between us and the enemy, and saved us. If they hadn't none of our detachment would be here to tell the tale. They trotted towards the enemy Cavalry but they would not stand for the Lancers. They retired. . . .

'At last we got in sight of Ludhiana, 3 or 4 miles off, when Sir Harry Smith came to us, and looked at us with tears in his eyes. He said: "Poor boys, lay down now and rest for a time."

'Where we lay down there was a large shallow pond and into this we all went to drink. There were horses, camels, elephants, men, bullocks, all at once. The water was nearly like treacle, but down it went. While this was going on many of the 16th Lancers were fetching in men of the 53[rd Foot] and our detachment, on their horses in front of them.'[53]

Four days later, reinforced by the garrison of Ludhiana, which now included the 1st Bengal Native Cavalry, and by the rest of his Division sent up by Gough, Smith concentrated his army near Budowal. He now had with him more than 10,000 men and 30 guns, of which 22 were horsed. Brigadier Cureton commanded his two cavalry brigades, which numbered about 3,000 sabres.* He also had three European and eight native infantry regiments. Two of these were battalions of Gurkhas, virtually the first ever to see action under the British.

*   *   *

On 28 January Sir Harry, learning that the Sikh force, numbering perhaps 18,000 men, with nearly 70 guns, was about to move towards Jagraon or Ludhiana, attacked and totally defeated it near Aliwal. The enemy infantry occupied a curved line of shallow entrenchments, with his guns in front of them. His right rested on the village of Bhundri, and his left on the village of Aliwal. Behind him was the Sutlej, over which in case of defeat he hoped to be able to cross by fords and boats. This, of course, was the weakness of an otherwise sound position.

* *1st Brigade* (Brigadier MacDowell, 16th Lancers): 16th Lancers (530); 3rd Bengal Native Cavalry (372); 4th Bengal Irregular Cavalry (398).

2nd Brigade (Brigadier Stedman): Governor-General's Bodyguard (351); 1st Bengal Native Cavalry (422); 5th Bengal Native Cavalry (402). Attached to this brigade were 630 men of the Shekhawati cavalry. These were part of an irregular corps of cavalry and infantry which had been raised in 1835 to keep order in the Shekhawat country near Jodhpur.

Aliwal, 1846

Starting from Budowal at first light, Sir Harry came across the enemy after a march of six miles. Emerging from sandy desert on to a large flat plain of hard grass-land, perfect for the manoeuvring of all arms, especially cavalry, which formed a semi-circular apron in front of the Sikh position, he 'ordered the cavalry to take ground to

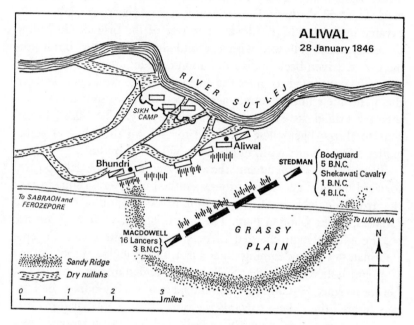

Map 13

the right and left by brigades', and deployed his infantry. This process looked to Trooper Pearman, who had got himself attached to the horse artillery, like the slow opening of

'a lady's fan. . . . The sun', he reported, 'was bright and clear. . . . Our Army came into line as steady as a field day. . . .
'It sounded "Advance", and on we moved. I could see the skirmishers of the 16th Lancers were firing their carbines, and at 10 minutes to 10 a.m. the first shot, about a 9-pounder, passed over our heads. It sounded "Skirmishers in" and back they came at a trot. At about 700 yards from the enemy, the Colonel shouted: "Action! Front! Unlimber and prepare for action!" . . . "Bang" went our guns. About the third shot I saw was making holes in the ranks.'[54]

Almost at once Smith launched two infantry brigades against the enemy's left at Aliwal and then sent others against the centre. After severe fighting the village was taken. The Sikh commander perceiving that his left was about to be turned brought forward his cavalry to try to re-establish it. These were at once charged by part of the right-hand cavalry brigade, commanded by Brigadier Stedman. This was the first of at least eight separate charges made by the cavalry in the battle of Aliwal. The rest of the brigade, including the Bodyguard, followed with a second charge, and the Sikh horsemen were driven back in disorder upon their infantry. Smith, seeing that if he continued to press the enemy's left he could get between them and their line of retreat across the fords, brought up another infantry brigade to support Stedman's cavalry. The Sikhs, forced thus to throw back their left, tried to re-form their line at right-angles to the river pivotting upon the village of Bhundri.

To cover this movement, the enemy commander again pushed forward his cavalry. Against these Smith at once sent a squadron of the 3rd Bengal Native Cavalry, supported by another of the 16th Lancers, under Captain Bere. The 3rd, it is said, wavered;* but not so the 16th, which charged in fine style without them. Trooper Pearman saw them 'coming on at a trot, then a gallop. I took off my Cap and hollered out. . . . Such cutting and stabbing I never saw before or since.'[55] Crashing into the mass of enemy horse, the Lancers hunted the enemy towards the river. Bere then rallied his men for the return, only to find his way barred by Sikh infantry. These were part of the finest regular battalions in the Khalsa, known as the Avitabile Corps from the Italian general who had trained them. They at once threw themselves into squares, or rather equilateral triangles, which were the Sikh equivalents.

'We went at them', wrote a trooper in Bere's squadron, 'and

* There is no traceable first-hand evidence for this accusation, though it is repeated in more than one account. In fact the native troops of all arms seem to have behaved with much more steadiness at Aliwal than at Mudki and Ferozeshah. This was almost certainly due to the fact that they were fresh and well fed, and already knew that the Sikhs were not invincible. Smith goes out of his way to commend in his despatch the 1st and 3rd Bengal Native Cavalry and 'the 8th Irregulars' (probably a mistake for the 4th). 'It is my duty', he wrote, 'joyfully to report the manner they contended for the glorious prize of victory, in the many charges they this day delivered.' He also says that the Bodyguard (which suffered no casualties except in horses) and the 5th Bengal Native Cavalry 'well did their duty'. (*Hardinge and Gough*, 76; Hodson, Maj. V. C. P. *Historical Records of the Governor-General's Bodyguard*, 1910, 139.)

on coming within 40 yards they gave us a volley, a ball from which struck the chain of my lance-cap just over the left cheekbone. They then threw away their muskets, and, taking their large shields, came at us sword in hand.'[56]

Of this charge Corporal Cowtan wrote that this troop

'moved on like a flash of lightning, clearing everything before us, guns, cavalry and infantry. As for myself, I went through cavalry and infantry squares repeatedly. At the first charge I dismounted two cavalry men, and on retiring we passed through a square of infantry, and I left three on the ground killed or wounded. . . . My comrade on my left, just as we cheered before charging, had his heart torn from his side by a cannon-ball, but my heart sickens at the recollection of what I witnessed that day. The killed and wounded in my squadron alone was 42.

'After the first charge self-preservation was the grand thing, and the love of life made us look sharp, and their great numbers required all our vigilance.

'Our lances seemed to paralyse them altogether, and you may be sure we did not give them time to recover themselves. There was no quarter given or taken. We did spare a good many at first, but the rascals afterwards took their preservers' lives, so we received the order to finish everyone with arms.'[57]

After a short tussle the infantry gave way and two horse artillery guns which had followed closely behind the 16th opened fire on the retreating enemy.

Almost simultaneously with this charge, Captain Fyler's squadron, which, with Bere's, formed the left wing of the regiment, was ordered to attack another mass of Avitabile's infantry. This charge, too, was successful and Fyler rejoined Bere. Before he had done so the two remaining squadrons, which formed the right wing of the 16th, were sent against

'a battalion of the enemy's infantry and a battery of 9 and 12-pounder guns. . . . We had a splendid man for commanding officer, Major Rowland Smyth,' wrote Sergeant Gould of C Troop. 'He was six feet in height and of most commanding appearance. At the trumpet note to trot, off we went.

'"Now", said Major Smyth, "I am going to give the word to charge, three cheers for the Queen." There was a terrific burst of cheering in reply, and down we swept upon the guns. Very soon they were in our possession. A more exciting job followed. We had to charge a square of infantry. At them we went, the bullets flying round like a hailstorm. Right in front of us was a big sergeant, Harry Newsome. He was mounted on a grey charger, and with a shout of "Hullo, boys, here goes for death or a commission", forced his horse right over the front rank of kneeling men, bristling with bayonets. As Newsome dashed forward he leant over and grasped one of the enemy's standards, but fell from his horse pierced by 19 bayonet wounds.

'Into the gap made by Newsome we dashed, but they made fearful havoc among us. When we got out on the other side of the square our troop had lost both lieutenants, the cornet, troop-sergeant-major, and two sergeants. I was the only sergeant left. Some of the men shouted, "Bill, you've got command, they're all down." Back we went through the disorganised square, the Sikhs peppering us in all directions. . . . We retired to our own line. As we passed the General he shouted "Well done, 16th. You have covered yourselves with glory." Then noticing that no officers were with C Troop, Sir H. Smith enquired, "Where are your officers?" "All down", I replied. "Then", said the General, "go and join the left wing, under Major Bere." '⁵⁸

Bere's squadron now made yet another assault against a square and broke it. Finally the whole regiment, supported by nearly all the rest of the cavalry present, charged triumphantly forward for the last time. The infantry followed in close support and carried the village of Bhundri by the bayonet. Immediately in their rear came the horse artillery. Avitabile's men fought desperately as they approached nearer and nearer to the river. At one point a large body of them 'rallied under a high bank of a nullah', but the infantry (to use Sir Harry's word) 'unkennelled'⁵⁹ them for the guns to smash into at 300 yards' range. Soon 'the enemy, completely hemmed in, were flying from our fire, and precipitating themselves in disordered masses into the fords and boats, in the utmost confusion and consternation.'⁶⁰

By their own admission the Sikhs lost 3,000 men. Sixty-seven of their guns were taken, and enormous quantities of stores of all kinds. By the standards of Mudki and Ferozeshah, the British casualties were not high. 589 officers and men were returned as killed, wounded and missing – 245 from the cavalry. Of these no less than

141 came from the 16th Lancers (88 killed and 53 wounded), more than a quarter of the total casualties of the army. The regiment's achievement, no less than its loss, is by any standards remarkable.

The fire of the disciplined Sikh infantry, wrote Lieutenant-Colonel Maude in 1903, was 'in the opinion of the survivors of the Peninsula and Waterloo . . ., both better delivered and better aimed than that of the Napoleonic infantry . . . Even when broken, these men fought to the death as no other infantry, except the Russians at Zorndorf, [1758], have ever done before or since.'[61] The breaking of the squares at Aliwal should rank with Le Marchant's larger scale feats at Salamanca and with Bock's smashing of the perfectly formed square at Garcia Hernandez (see p. 55). Indeed Sir Harry described Aliwal as 'a little sweeping second edition of Salamanca – a stand-up gentlemanlike battle, a mixing of all arms and laying-on, carrying everything before us by weight of attack and combination, all hands at work from one end of the field to the other'.[62]

After the battle Sir Harry told the men of the 16th Lancers that when they had been in Lahore in 1837 Ranjit Singh had thought them 'all gentlemen'. Had he survived to see them at Aliwal, he would have proclaimed them all devils, 'for you charged their ranks more like them than anything else'. With 'tears in the poor old man's eyes', wrote Trooper Eaton, Sir Harry left them with the words: 'God bless you, my brave boys; I love you.'[63]

When the exhausted survivors paraded next day it was seen that the red and white pennants of their lances were so coated with dried blood that they appeared to have been starched. From that day onwards it became the regimental custom to crimp all the 16th's pennants in memory of the battle. The tradition is still preserved in the three which flutter at the present time outside the regimental headquarters. To what extent the 16th used their lances or had confidence in them is debatable. Captain Nolan stated in 1853 that it was

'well-known that, in battle, lancers generally throw them away, and take to their swords. I never spoke with an English lancer who had been engaged in the late Sikh wars that did not declare the lance to be a useless tool, and a great incumbrance in close conflict.'[64]

From Pearman's 'such cutting and stabbing I never saw before or since' (see p. 262) it would seem that sabres were used at least as freely as lances, for cutting is not an operation easily performed with the lance.

The supposed last survivor of the 16th Lancers who fought in the battle died in 1906 'at an advanced age'. He was Private James Fuller, who was commissioned as quartermaster of the 16th in 1860, given the honorary rank of Captain in 1870 (and placed on half-pay), and retired in 1881.[65]

The commander of the cavalry at Aliwal was Brigadier Charles Robert Cureton. To him Sir Harry and others gave the chief credit for the successful use of the mounted arm, not only at Aliwal, but also during the tricky manoeuvring before the army was concentrated, especially at Budowal. Cureton's career had been a strange one. Born in 1789, the son of a Shropshire squire, he had obtained a commission in the local Militia in 1806. His extremely extravagant habits soon forced him to flee from his creditors. For this purpose, leaving his uniform on the beach to simulate accidental drowning, he made for London disguised as a sailor. There he enlisted as a private in the 14th Light Dragoons under the *nom de guerre* of Robert Taylor. Quickly rising to the rank of sergeant, he went through the Peninsular War with distinction, being thrice wounded. In 1813, he was recognised by Lord Fitzroy Somerset (later Lord Raglan), one of Wellington's staff officers, 'who had known him at home'[66] and before long he was given an infantry ensigncy without purchase. In 1819 he entered the 16th Lancers. As assistant-adjutant-general of the cavalry he was the first man to enter Kabul in 1839 (see p. 218). At Maharajpur, four years later, he commanded a cavalry brigade (see p. 239). Sir Harry Smith wrote of him, after Aliwal, that he was 'one of those officers rarely met with; the cool experience of the veteran soldier is combined with youthful activity – his knowledge of outpost duty, and the able manner he handles his cavalry under the heaviest fire, rank him among the first cavalry officers of the age'.[67] He was killed at Ramnagar in 1848 (see p. 275), aged fifty-seven.

Two of his sons attained distinction in the cavalry. The elder, E. B. Cureton (1822–94), who became a lieutenant-general, was severely wounded in the 3rd Light Dragoons at Mudki, and served with the 12th Lancers in the Kaffir War of 1851–3. The career of the younger, who became General Sir Charles Cureton (1826–91), was entirely in the Bengal army. He was present at Aliwal as aide-de-camp to his father. In 1858 he raised Cureton's Multani Cavalry and commanded it with distinction in the Great Mutiny. Another son was killed at Chilianwala in 1849 (see p. 282).

*   *   *

As a result of Smith's victory at Aliwal Gough's communications were secured and the safe arrival of his siege-train was assured. Further, the Sikhs were at once compelled to evacuate all their bridgeheads south of the Sutlej with the exception of their main one at Sobraon.

This which was extremely formidable was strongly and skilfully fortified. It was defended by some 20,000 troops and 67 guns. Behind it was the river and on the far shore were more guns, infantry and

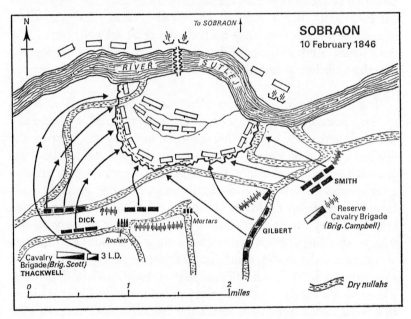

Map 14

cavalry in support. At dawn on 10 February, with an army now 15,000 strong, Gough launched his assault. There followed what Sir Harry Smith called 'a brutal bulldog fight'.[68] For the first two hours, until the heavy guns' ammunition ran out, the British artillery played upon the entrenchments. 'Such a cannonade and noise', wrote Trooper Pearman, 'no thunder was ever equal to. . . . The firing appeared like practice in Woolwich Marches.' As the big guns became gradually silent, Gough sent in a series of massive infantry attacks. 'Oh, what a sight to sit on your horse,' exlaimed Pearman 'to look at those brave fellows as they tried several times to get into the enemy's camp; and at last they did, but, oh, what a loss of human life. God only knows who will have to answer for it.'[69]

Though Gough had at his disposal ten regiments of cavalry, commanded by Sir Joseph Thackwell, there was little scope for their use at Sobraon. Nevertheless, at one of many critical moments, Thackwell himself led two squadrons of the much reduced 3rd Light Dragoons, followed by the 4th and 5th Bengal Native Cavalry, in single file into the enemy's position within sixty yards of its extreme right. He had found, for this purpose, one of the 'dams' left by the defenders 'at intervals across the ditch for their own convenience.' Gough's despatch says that the sappers had made 'openings in the entrenchments' but Thackwell specifically denies this.[70] 'It was a miracle we were not properly riddled', wrote Thackwell, 'but . . . the guns had so sunk in the sand that the gunners could not depress the muzzles sufficiently, and therefore most of the grape went over our heads.'[71]

'It was now our turn,' Trooper Pearman wrote in his diary. 'It was given: "Forward, 3rd King's Own Light Dragoons", an order the Colonel used when he was in a good temper. On we went by the dead and dying, and partly over the poor fellows, and up the parapet our horses scrambled.'[72] The squadrons were now formed, one after another, within the entrenchments. A number of charges followed which much facilitated the entry of the infantry. Some years later Sir Harry Smith remembered Thackwell 'shoving in your unwinged shoulder [he had lost his left arm at Waterloo] into the gap at Sobraon – the most gallant "go" of you and the 3rd Dragoons I ever witnessed.'[73]* Thackwell complained that the official despatches did not do him and the 3rd sufficient justice for this attack. He claimed that he had done more than Smith and Gilbert who commanded the right and centre infantry divisions 'for it was my attack which enabled those two divisions to get into the Sikh entrenchments from which Gilbert's division, as well as Smith's, had been driven back twice with great loss.'[74]

The Sikhs's resistance had been dogged and their counter-attacks on occasion resulted in the recapture of their guns, but before noon

---

* One authority says that one squadron of the 3rd Light Dragoons, 'under Captain Cookes, with the 5th L.C., were ordered to create a diversion in favour of Sir H. Smith on the right . . . . Lieutenant E. Roche, 3rd Dragoons, D.A.Q. M.G. of the Cavalry Division, accompanied this charge, and saved the life of Captain J. W. Ryley, Adjutant, 5th L.C., killing a Sikh chieftain, who attacked him from behind.' The same authority states that the 4th B.N.C. had come up on the Sikhs' extreme right 'where the enemy's Horse were, . . . where they entered (the outworks) and, charging down, assisted in clearing them'. (Stubbs, III, 147.)

they were totally defeated. All their guns were taken and thousands of men perished in the swollen waters of the Sutlej. The British casualties were high: 320 killed and 2,063 wounded. The cavalry's share was negligible, the 3rd being virtually the only sufferers. They lost five men killed, and five officers and twenty-two rank and file wounded. The total losses of the regiment in the First Sikh War were 289 men and 364 horses.

Cureton's brigade (16th Lancers, 3rd Bengal Native Cavalry and 4th Bengal Irregular Cavalry) was not present at Sobraon, as it had been detached some miles to the east to create a diversion by simulating an attempt to cross the river.

Another brigade, consisting of the 9th Lancers, the Bodyguard, a wing of the 2nd, and the whole of the 8th and 9th Bengal Irregular Cavalry, and possibly some other native regiments, was in reserve and not called upon to take part. This brigade was commanded by Alexander Campbell, the senior lieutenant-colonel of the 9th Lancers. On the morning of the battle he was palpably drunk and incapable. Major James Hope Grant of the regiment (of whom a great deal more will be heard in later volumes) took the bold step, after the battle, of asking the second lieutenant-colonel to place Campbell in arrest. This he refused to do. Consequently Hope Grant himself went to Campbell next day and said:

'"You know you were very drunk yesterday, sir, when you led us into action. I have come to tell you that if you do not at once undertake to leave the regiment, I shall now put you in arrest and report your conduct."

'"Will you, indeed," said the colonel in great anger. "Very well, I will be beforehand with you, and I now place you in arrest for bringing a false and insulting accusation against your commanding officer," and I went to my tent in arrest.'[75]

Gough ordered an enquiry at the end of which Hope Grant was returned to duty. Campbell retained command of the regiment, although no one had seriously contested the fact that he had been totally incapable during the battle. What effect this lenient treatment of an acting brigadier's intemperance in the field must have had upon the rank and file is hard to imagine. If an 'other rank' had appeared drunk in action, the consequences would have been harsh indeed.

Hope Grant was later induced to apologise, not for charging his colonel with drunkenness, but for telling him that he should leave the regiment. Hope Grant was a poor man, one of the few who had received his commission without purchase (see p. 158). The risk he took in acting as he did was a very real one. Had it not been for Gough's well-known fairness, he might have been turned out of the army and lost the value of his commission – perhaps £5,000. It is significant that Gough's Sobraon despatch, though including an inordinately lengthy list of specially mentioned officers, does not include the name of Lieutenant-Colonel Alexander Campbell.

*   *   *

The battle of Sobraon effectively finished the First Sikh War. The Khalsa was humbled and its famous artillery had been captured: 200 guns in all. The Sikh state was prostrate. By the Treaty of Lahore 9 March 1846, the army was limited to 12,000 cavalry and 20,000 infantry. Certain areas were ceded to the British, and an indemnity of £500,000 exacted. This solution, as will be shown, was far from being final. In the event, outright annexation would have saved much trouble, bloodshed and money; but at the time the expense and difficulty were thought to be too great.

'Lord Gough . . . all honour and nobleness of heart. . . . Were his military genius as great as his heart, the Duke [of Wellington] would be nothing in comparison.'

SIR CHARLES NAPIER[1]

(ii)

India: the Second Sikh War, 1848–1849

Gough, though not Hardinge, had always realised that a second instalment of the war against the Sikhs was unavoidable. The nation and the Khalsa had been humbled but not destroyed. Ironically it was almost certainly the excellence and speed of the reformist exertions of Henry Lawrence, the Resident at Lahore, which hastened the Second

Sikh War. That great man's attacks on unjust taxes, cruel punishments, female infanticide and *sati* (widow-burning), were heard by
the masses with gladness, but the *sardars* 'muttered in private and
bided their time'.[2]

In April 1848 an isolated local revolt took place at Multan. By
the end of the summer it had turned into a rebellion of the whole
Sikh nation against the paramount power. To meet the crisis there
was a new governor-general, the Earl of Dalhousie. The commander-
in-chief was still Gough, who had received a Barony after Sobraon.
He insisted, as soon as war was seen to be inevitable, that he required
no less than 24,000 men with 78 guns for a successful invasion of the
Punjab. For four months Dalhousie resisted Gough's demands; but,
convinced at last of the need, he gave way. The formation of 'The
Army of the Punjab' speedily followed.

While the troops were being collected, Gough dispatched Cureton with a mixed force which included four cavalry regiments* to
the north of Lahore so as to cover the capital. On 2 November it en-
camped at Parhal having crossed the River Ravi. Gough followed with
a large part of his army. He was anxious to attack the Sikhs as soon
as possible, so as to prevent their concentrating too large a force
against him. At dawn on 22 November, Cureton's cavalry division,
three batteries of horse artillery and an infantry brigade under Brigadier Colin Campbell came up to Ramnagar, near the south bank of
the Chenab.

At about 8 a.m. the enemy's outposts were sighted to the south of
the river. These were scattered about on the hard plain between
Ramnagar and the river bank. The main Sikh force, perhaps 16,000
strong with 28 guns, was in position to the north of the river with
easily negotiated fords in its front.

Gough was anxious to discover the strength of the enemy opposed
to him. At the same time he 'deemed it necessary to attack the force
[on the south of the river] before it could get across the Chenab.'[3] To
these ends the 3rd Light Dragoons (about 690 strong) were first sent
to drive in the enemy outposts. The 8th Bengal Native Cavalry
seems to have followed the 3rd. The regiment suffered a few casualties. One of those killed was a subadar-major, aged seventy-eight. He
had seen nearly sixty years' service with the regiment.[4]

'It sounded "Trot",' wrote Trooper Pearman of the 3rd, 'and

* 3rd Light Dragoons, 8th Bengal Native Cavalry and 12th Bengal Irregular
Cavalry. The 14th Light Dragoons joined next day. The force had with it one
infantry brigade, three troops of horse artillery and one light field battery.

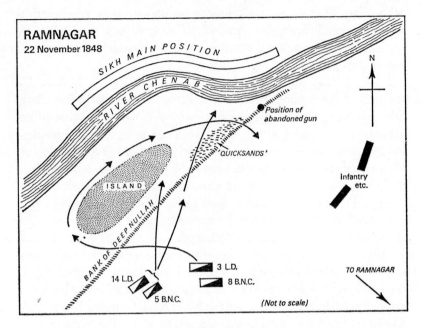

Map 15

we had to jump a *nullah* [one of the dry watercourses which intersected the plain], and then down a steep bank. It then sounded "Gallop", and at them we went, but they showed us their backs. . . . They took the ford and joined their army, which lay quiet enough but was soon on the alert. We halted on the bank of the river, about half a mile from the enemy. . . and waited some time until the remainder of the division came up. General Cureton came with them. He gave the order for our first squadron ['about 130 strong',[5] under Lieutenant Ouvry] to break ranks and gallop up [along] the bank of the river to see how many guns the enemy could bring to bear on us. . . . So off we went, broke up like a lot of sheep, only farther apart. We had not gone far when "bang!" went their guns at us as we galloped for about 3 miles. . . . We had 6 or 7 horses cut down, but the men were not hurt. . . . [At one time] we were riding over quicksands, and some of the horses got set fast up to the belly. The men had to leave them.'[6]

While this squadron was going to work, the horse artillery guns

26. (*Left*) A prosperous Sikh cavalry-man, *c.* 1839

27. (*Below*) A poor Sikh cavalryman, *c.* 1839

28. (*Left*) 'A Scene on morning after Mood (Mudki): One of the 3rd Dragoons bringing in headless body of his broth

29. (*Below*) 'Capt Code the 3rd Dragoons, cut pieces between the gun the wheel, probably Mudki.'

16" Lancers at play
a Seck gunner

30. Men of the 16th Lancers killing a Sikh gunner after Aliwal.

31. Viscount Hardinge

32. Viscount Gough

33. Sir Harry Smith

34. Sir Charles Napier

were ordered forward, some say so as to cover the withdrawal of Ouvry's squadron. As they came close to the water's edge they, like the 3rd, found the ground soft and muddy. After several rounds of shot, they limbered up and retired to a better position. In so doing one of the guns got stuck. After nearly an hour's ineffectual struggle, all the while under fire from the Sikh artillery concealed on the river's high north bank, the gun had to be abandoned. This, and the apparent retreat of Ouvry's squadron, so excited the Sikhs that they recrossed the fords with considerable numbers of cavalry and infantry, and even, it is thought, brought some of their guns on to a prominent 'island' between two dry watercourses.

The battle, wrote Pearman, now

'began in right earnest. . . . We [the 3rd] sat for nearly an hour, their infantry firing at us. They didn't do us much harm. . . . The right of the regiment now fell back . . . to try to draw out the enemy, but no go. They kept to the nullah. We again formed line and made two feint charges, but could not get them out. We now went back . . . again, as we saw the 14th Light Dragoons coming down, their horses being fresh, not having done anything but the steady march in the morning.'[7]

It is impossible to say exactly what happened next. That it was unnecessarily calamitous there can be no doubt. Gough later wrote to his son that he had 'intended having as little to do with the reconnaissance as you'. But when he was told about the stranded gun, he rode forward to see if it could be extricated, 'and it was a considerable time before I met Cureton, who commanded the reconnaissance. He was at the time in front of the 14th Light Dragoons, and not under fire.' The commanding officer of the 14th, William Havelock,* now rode up to Cureton 'and asked permission to charge a body of the Enemy's Cavalry, which appeared to be close. . . . The number of the enemy was much less than the 14th, [who went into action with about 645 sabres]. Leave was given him. . . . To my astonishment,' wrote Gough, 'Havelock took his Regiment, with a portion of the 5th Light Cavalry, in Column of Troop, right down

---

* William Havelock (1793–1848) acquired fame at the age of twenty when he inspired a Spanish force to defeat the French at Vera in 1813. He had taken at one bound a formidable *abattis* which had checked the Spaniards. From that day on he was known as 'el chico blanco' (the fair boy), the name with which the Spaniards cheered on their blond leader.

to the river, when he wheeled into line, and charged along the whole face of the Sikh Batteries at the opposite side.'[8]

This is Gough's very much telescoped description of what happened. 'One who was present' told William Havelock's more famous brother Henry that Gough himself had told William: 'If you see a favourable opportunity of charging, charge.'[9] Captain Apthorp, the 14th's Adjutant, had no doubt that 'Havelock thought this almost tantamount to an order', since Gough, according to Havelock, had said to Cureton that he could not understand 'a dry nullah stopping cavalry'.[10] Havelock, leaving one squadron in reserve, set off 'happy as a lover'[11] with the other three.* 'They came on', wrote Pearman, 'in pretty style, so steady and straight.'[12]

Cureton had been told by Brigadier White, who had charged with the 3rd, about the dangers of the nullah and the 'quicksands' beyond it. He was horrified, therefore, to see that Havelock, having speedily driven back the enemy horse in his first advance, did not do as the 3rd had done and resist the temptation to go further. Indeed, according to Pearman, Brigadier White 'called out "Havelock! Havelock!" and pointed to the nullah, but on they went. Then came a Volley and smoke.'[13] The 14th were followed into the trap by part of the 5th Bengal Native Cavalry.†

Gough thought that Havelock had lost 'the direction of the body of Ghorchurras which General Cureton had sanctioned his attacking', and had charged in error 'across an arm of the river, under the bank of which numbers both of infantry and cavalry were concealed'.[14] Cureton, appalled at the blunder about to be committed, exclaimed, it is said: 'My God! This isn't the way to use cavalry!'[15] He at once rushed forward, with a small escort of the 5th Native Cavalry, to try

* At the moment when the 14th was ordered to advance the men were dismounted 'in a turnip field eating turnips. A sergeant named Clifton had just peeled one when the trumpet sounded to mount, he placed it in his shako, his horse was shot under him, he was surrounded and the top of his shako cut to shreds and the turnip to slices without touching his head, and he escaped with a few slight scratches on his shoulders.' (27 Dec. 1848, Tookey, 35.)

† 'The relations between the European and the native troops were of the most cordial character. In particular, the attachment between the 14th Light Dragoons and the 5th Light Cavalry was so warm, that when Gough presented the latter with Rs. 500 in token of his approbation of their behaviour, they spent it in giving a dinner to their European comrades. In his diary Lord Dalhousie adds the following facts and comment: "Their religion forbade their partaking of it themselves, but they stood by, superintending the feast, and literally dispensing their hospitality to their guests. When such is the feeling, troops will do anything and everything."' (Lee-Warner, I, 205; see also Thackwell, 183–4.)

to stop Havelock, but he had gone only a short distance when he himself was shot dead by a matchlock ball. Havelock and fourteen of his men were killed, and five officers and twenty-two men wounded. The 5th suffered twenty-three casualties.

The general concensus of opinion is that Havelock lost his head. 'It was natural', wrote his brother, 'that an old Peninsular officer, who had not seen a shot fired since Waterloo, should desire to bleed the noses of his young dragoons.'[16] On the other hand if it is true that Gough 'pooh-pooed'[17] White's and Cureton's advice about the dangers of the nullah and the 'quicksands' — and it would seem to have been in character for him to do so — the commander-in-chief was guilty of inciting Havelock to rashness. This would have been especially reprehensible since not more than six or seven of the 14th had ever seen action before.

Henry Havelock summed up the mistakes of 22 November thus: the Sikh horse, 'pushed forward on the left [south] bank, were intended to bravado and decoy, and should have been simply let alone, or cannonaded when convenient and possible, by guns out of reach of those of the enemy.'[18] Certainly Gough's intention of clearing the south bank had been achieved, and considerable numbers of the enemy had been killed, but at a ridiculously high cost. The death of Cureton, the foremost cavalry commander in India, was a real tragedy.*

* * *

Cureton's place at the head of the cavalry was taken by Sir Joseph Thackwell. He was also made second-in-command to Gough. On 2 December, with a large detached force, Thackwell crossed the Chenab unopposed near Wazirabad. The commander-in-chief intended him to march down the north bank of the river and to attack the left of the Sikh position at Ramnagar, while Gough held the enemy's attention with an artillery barrage. The plan miscarried and Thackwell fought a minor and inconclusive action at Sadulapur on 3 December. The Sikhs that night retired northwards. Gough and Thackwell followed at leisure and formed camp at Helan. There they

* Gen. Thackwell's son says that Cureton 'was the only officer in the army who carried to the scene of war air-cushions, articles of great comfort, and the alleviators of pain to wounded men. . . . We were present at the sale of the lamented officer's effects, therefore can vouch for the truth of this story.' (Thackwell, 45.)

stayed inactive till 9 January under a prohibition against a further advance imposed by Dalhousie. The long delay was connected with questions of supplies, supports and communications, with doubts as to whether the army was strong enough for the task ahead and with the siege of Multan. This, which had been carried on intermittently since September, was tying up a mixed force of Bengal and Bombay troops which would have been useful to Gough. Yet before the eventual fall of Multan on 22 January and before, therefore, any considerable reinforcements could reach Gough, other considerations induced Dalhousie to give the commander-in-chief the go-ahead.* Chief among these was the fact that considerable reinforcements were about to reach the Sikhs, including troops from Afghanistan sent by Dost Muhammad. With every week of delay not only did the enemy's strength increase but so also did his self-confidence.

* * *

On 13 January Gough advanced to Chilianwala between which village and the broad River Jhelum the main Sikh army was known to be arrayed in a strong entrenched position. He intended to encamp near the village that day 'with a view to reconnoitre', as he wrote in his diary, 'or to fall across the Sikhs should they attempt flight'. From a mound about three miles from the enemy's entrenchments he surveyed the scene. 'As it was one o'clock before I fully satisfied myself of his position', he wrote, 'I determined to postpone the attack until the following morning, and the Quartermaster-General was in the act of arranging the formation of the camp when the enemy brought forward some guns to bear upon Chilianwala.' Gough at once ordered forward his heavy artillery to dislodge them. This was soon accomplished, but, in reply, the Sikh artillery opened up 'from nearly their whole line, evidently thrown much in front of their different positions'.[19]

Realising that the enemy had advanced from their entrenchments to the edge of the jungle, Gough decided to attack at once. He took this decision in spite of the lateness of the hour (not much before 2 p.m.), and aware that his troops would have to attack through 'a belt of rather dense low jungle, not forest, but a mixture of thorny mimosa bushes and wild caper'.[20] It was certain that he could not

* Some authorities state that Gough was in entire agreement with the policy of delay, and that he would have preferred to wait even longer for the reinforcements from Multan. This, however, seems unlikely.

encamp under the fire of the Sikh guns. It was equally certain that if
he retired the Sikhs would advance. Further, there was no water to
be had except at Chilianwala. He had no alternative but to fight the
battle of Chilianwala there and then. This is Gough's story. Some

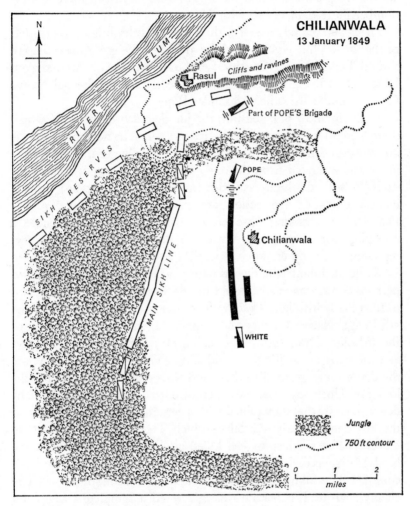

Map 16

authorities believe that there was no need to fight that day and that
the arrival of a few rounds 'in the direction of the Staff and Lord
Gough', in the words of Trooper Pearman, 'got the old man's Irish
out'.[21]

The battle was largely an infantry affair opened, as was customary, by the artillery. The nature of the ground precluded the extensive use of the cavalry. The enemy line, spread thinly over six miles, greatly outflanked Gough's at both ends. In it were some 30,000 men with over 60 guns. Its right was unassailable, being placed at Rasul among steep cliffs and numerous ravines. The British force did not number more than 14,000 with 66 guns.

Thackwell placed himself with White's cavalry brigade on the left of the line. White commanded the 3rd Light Dragoons and the 5th and 8th Bengal Native Cavalry. On the right of the line were the 9th Lancers,* 14th Light Dragoons and the 1st and 6th Bengal Native Cavalry, under Brigadier Alexander Pope.

As the infantry plunged into the jungle, each brigade (of which there were four in line and one in reserve), 'lost its neighbour', as the governor-general wrote to the Duke of Wellington. 'Every regiment was separated from the one next to it, and fought a battle for itself.'[22] Both the high casualties (mostly in the infantry) and the indecisiveness of the action are partly explained by Trooper Pearman's penetrating observation that 'the enemy had chose a rare place for us to work. We could not combine one [infantry] regiment to the other, so close was the jungle in places.'[23]

While the infantry battle was raging, a large force of Sikh cavalry, perhaps 800 strong,[24] advanced from the enemy's right in an attempt to turn the British left. Thackwell at once ordered five troops of the 5th Bengal Native Cavalry and Captain Unett's 'Grey' squadron of the 3rd Light Dragoons to charge. This they did, in line, as fast and as coherently as the jungle would allow. The 5th failed to penetrate the dense mass opposed to them and wavered in the face of matchlock fire. Unett says that they 'ran away to a man', but there is evidence to show that they rallied with a certain degree of steadiness on the 8th Bengal Native Cavalry, which Thackwell had held in reserve.[25] (The 5th lost sixteen killed and fourteen wounded in the battle).[26] Nevertheless Unett was forced to go on 'alone, as hard as I could'.[27] The Sikhs then closed around his valiant squadron. 'The enemy', wrote Trooper Pearman, 'formed a complete wedge, and we had to cut our way through them for quite a hundred yards before there was any clear ground.'[28] The lieutenant commanding Unett's right-hand troop states that the Sikh horsemen now 're-

* The 9th Lancers, like the 16th in the First Afghan War (see p. 215), had with them in India, as Captain Delmar wrote in December 1848, 'a bobbery pack of hounds . . . .There are seven couples, and I am the huntsman. We have great sport of a morning hunting Foxes and Jackals.' (24 Dec., 1848, Delmar, 107.)

formed their line on nearly the same ground on which we had just
charged through them.'[29] Unett and his two fellow officers collected
what men they could lay hands upon, and charged back again. This
time the enemy 'did not offer so much opposition, but opened out,
and abused us as we passed . . . . On our re-forming they retired off
the field.'[30]

Unett's squadron had twenty-four men killed and sixteen wounded
(including Unett and another officer). On re-forming there were seen
to be only 48 men in their saddles, out of 106 who had charged. This
dashing action of the 'Grey' squadron of the 3rd, which caused panic
and dismay on the Sikh right, has been overshadowed by what was
happening at about the same time on the extreme right of Gough's
army.

Here Brigadier Pope, seeing a considerable force of Sikh horsemen
on the hills threatening his right, detached eight guns and five squadrons to keep them off. These, except for protecting the right flank,
played only a subsidiary part in the battle. They nevertheless had
quite a tussle, the horse artillery firing many rounds so as to repulse
a number of charges. Part of the two detached squadrons of the 9th
Lancers must also have seen some action, for an officer of one of them
wrote home that 'the enemy were almost impervious, from the shields,
armour and wadded clothes they wore – the men of the 9th Lancers
often failed to pierce them'. And again: 'Our men ran their lances
so far thro' the Sikhs, they could not pull them out again, and were
obliged to leave them. A cut from these Sikhs is most awful – it leaves
a dreadful gash.'[31]

As the infantry on Pope's left advanced, he ordered his remaining
nine squadrons to mount and deploy. This they did, two squadrons
of the 9th on the right, three squadrons of the two native regiments
in the centre and the four squadrons of the 14th on the left. They
advanced in one long line with ten horse artillery guns between them
and the infantry. Captain Thompson, commanding the second
squadron of the 14th, relates what occurred next:

'Having previously drawn swords, the brigade was now
ordered to advance at a trot, without a skirmisher or "scout"
in front, or a man in support or reserve in rear, through
broken, jungly ground, where some of the enemy's horsemen
were seen to loiter, watching our movements. Brigadier Pope
himself led the line in front of the native cavalry, forming the
centre by which we had been ordered to dress and regulate our

pace, when insensibly its "trot" dwindled to a "walk", and then came to a dead halt at the sight of a few Sikh horsemen peering over the bushes. Of course the flanks of the brigade had to do the same, being guided by the fluctuations of the centre which were not always clearly visible in the thick jungle, but were conformed to more by sound than by sight. I then saw Colonel King, commanding the 14th Light Dragoons, gallop to the Brigadier in front, energetically pointing with his sword towards the enemy position and evidently urging an attack, which the other seemed unable to make up his mind to order. The Sikhs seeing the hesitation, a handful of their horsemen, some forty or fifty in a lump, charged boldly into the thick of the native cavalry, who instantly turned with the cry 'threes about', and disappeared for the rest of the day – at least I saw none of them.'[32]

The experience of Hope Grant commanding the 9th Lancers on the right was much the same. In his official report, which was extremely frank, he says:

'The squadrons were going along with the line steadily, and no hesitation was evinced; on the contrary, the flank-men were engaged with some of the enemy, and doing their duty, when the whole line checked and went about from the left [i.e. from the centre of the line which was to Grant's left], and my squadrons, certainly without a word from me, turned round too; but the jungle and the dust might make some excuse for the men, as it was difficult to hear, and in many cases to see. The dust upon this movement became very great, and the men of my regiment got mixed up with the [native] regiments; and though I did all in my power to stop them, ordering them to halt and front, and many of the officers in the regiment did the same, it was useless. They would not turn round; they appeared, after having gone about, to have got panic-struck.'[33]

The blame for this débâcle rests with those responsible for appointing Pope to his command. In his younger days he had acquired a reputation for bravery (see p. 200), but in 1849 he was so ill and enfeebled that he had to be lifted into the saddle. As the historian of the 9th Lancers puts it, 'the sight of his huddled figure in its padded coats and wrappings . . . was not one to inspire confidence'.[34] He was a comparatively junior lieutenant-colonel of native cavalry, who had never commanded more than a squadron in the field before. It remains a mystery why he was given command of a brigade which contained two 'crack' British regiments, 'whilst' to quote Thackwell's son 'his seniors, such active, experienced and distinguished officers as Colonel John Scott, of the 9th Lancers, were left unemployed, to fade away in the solitude of a deserted cantonment in the rear.'[35]

It seems that even when bringing his brigade on to the field before the battle, Pope's irresolute inefficiency had been manifest. When he formed his nine squadrons in a single long line, leaving not a squadron in support, all confidence in him must have finally ebbed away. A more foolish formation, especially in a jungle with numerous obstructions, can hardly be imagined. Before the brigade had gone many yards, the unwieldy line began to get in front of the guns, and effectively to mask them. For a time it even overlapped the infantry to the left of the guns. It was because of this, no doubt, that the line was brought first to a walk and then to a halt.

When it became clear that a battle would have to be fought that day an alteration of the front of the British line had become necessary. 'The left', says General Stubbs, 'had to be brought up, and line was formed from the right Horse Artillery, Pope's Brigade of Cavalry not changing front, so that its direction crossed the line of fire of the guns.' Stubbs's authority for this is the official plan of the battle. If it is correct it shows that Pope's masking of the guns when he advanced was an extension of his initial failure to conform with the general alteration of front.[36]

Who, if anyone, gave the order 'threes about' will never be known. It has been suggested that Pope, in an effort to shift the line to the right, away from the masked guns, gave, or meant to give, the order 'threes *right*'; that, at that very moment, the small body of Sikh horse charged and that the word of command, as then passed on, became 'threes *about*'.[37] At the time of the earlier halt, according to the testimony of some of the native cavalrymen, their British officers were some fifty yards in advance of the troops. When the enemy horsemen were sighted these officers were ordered to return. The men, seeing their officers galloping back, wavered and some unauthorised person shouted out 'threes about'.[38] It is interesting to compare this explanation of what happened to Pope's brigade with the flight of the 2nd Bengal Light Cavalry at Parwandara in the First Afghan War (see p. 222).

Whatever really happened, it is certain that the sudden disappearance of the cavalry left the horse artillery guns wholly unprotected.

They tried to retire with the cavalry but were given too little time to limber up, and the panic soon communicated itself to the gunners. Many of the cavalrymen 'rode slowly to the rear'.[39] Some, regrettably, broke into 'a reckless stampede'.[40] John Hearsey, who commanded the troops guarding the baggage (which covered more than four squares miles!), says that 'many of the men of the 14th sought shelter with the rear-guard, shouting out that the army was defeated and in full retreat. I dismounted them and bade them hold their peace, telling them they were quite safe with me.'[41] Since there were no cavalry supports upon which they could rally, some of the 14th attempted to halt and re-form upon two of the horse artillery guns, but these, too, moved off.[42] The Sikh horsemen, exultantly following up, cut down some of the teams, carried off four guns, two wagons and numerous horses and put out of action most of the remaining six guns. Eventually two of them seem to have managed to draw up, unlimber and with a few shots effectively scatter the Sikh horsemen.[43] Pope himself was mortally wounded in the retreat, but the cavalry casualties were shamefully few.

The 14th only lost one officer (a son of Cureton's) and one trooper killed; one officer and fourteen men wounded, and two men missing. Only eight horses were lost. In the whole of Pope's brigade seventeen men were killed and thirty-nine wounded. The governor-general, who most unfairly wrote to Wellington that Gough's conduct of the battle was 'beneath the criticism even of a Militiaman like myself',[44] wished to place some 'petty indignity' upon the four regiments of Pope's brigade. Gough protested. Dalhousie replied to him: 'If you, whom the unanimous voice of all your countrymen has long since pronounced to be brave among the brave, shall tell me that you think I had better not put the slight I have threatened on these four regiments, I shall readily submit to your judgement on this point.'[45]*

Thackwell much regretted that he had not placed himself on the British right, as had been his original intention. He presided over a court of inquiry into the conduct of Pope's brigade after the battle. His verdict was that 'their retrograde movement originated more from mistake than a fear of encountering an insignificant enemy'.[46]

The right-hand infantry brigade, finding their flank totally exposed as a result of the débâcle, had a hard time of it but eventually

---

* Compare the fact that none of the regiments concerned suffered any sort of punishment, with the disbanding 'with ignominy' of the 2nd Bengal Native Cavalry after Parwandara in the First Afghan War (see p. 222).

by skill and good luck extricated itself from a perilous position. The battle came to an inconclusive end sometime after darkness fell. The total British losses were 602 killed, 1,651 wounded and 104 missing. An interesting sidelight upon these figures (the size of which much horrified contemporary opinion) is thrown by Gough's biographer. The proportion of killed, he states, was about 5 per cent of the whole force; of wounded about 12 per cent. Only 72 of the 1,651 were permanently disabled, while of the 624 wounded Europeans, 156 had returned to duty a fortnight after the battle.[47]

At the battle's end, the Sikhs retreated into the hills on their left, but Gough 'could not pursue from want of daylight, and he could not hold his ground from want of water'.[48] After bringing in as many of the wounded as possible,* but leaving his spiked guns for the enemy to collect, he retired to Chilianwala. The Sikh casualties were said to be high.

That Pope's fiasco prevented a positive victory is a possibility. The officer commanding all the artillery had 'no doubt from what we saw of the Sikh cavalry afterwards at Goojerat (see p. 288), that had [our cavalry] charged and the Horse Artillery been allowed to open . . . the left of the Sikh line would have been turned, their retreat . . . would have been cut off, and the result would probably have been as effective as at Goojerat.'[49]

'Our Cavalry must have lost their prestige in the eyes of the Sikhs', wrote Lieutenant Ouvry. 'The whole thing has been most disastrous, and all through wretched generalship and the panic of our Cavalry on the right of our line.'[50]

Lieutenant-Colonel King of the 14th, who had tried unsuccessfully to urge Pope to attack (see p. 280), committed suicide in July 1850. Trooper Pearman was present when Sir Charles Napier, who succeeded Gough, reviewed both the 3rd and the 14th. After unconditional praise for the 3rd, Sir Charles

'turned to the 14th and said: "14th Kings Own! I am proud to see you . . . and if you had been properly handled on 13th January [at Chilianwala] the disgrace that now hangs over the regiment could not have taken place." At this, a young trumpeter,

* Gough, it is said in most accounts, in spite of the raging thirst of his army, declared: 'I'll be damned if I move till my wounded are all safe.' Writing home on 15 January, however, a captain of the 9th Lancers says: 'We were not able to recover our dead and wounded till yesterday morning, on account of the night coming on.' (15 Jan. 1849, Delmar, 117.) Many of the wounded who were left were killed and their bodies mutilated by the Sikhs.

by name John Springate, about eighteen years old, rode up to the General and said: "General, our Colonel is a coward." General Napier said: "Make that man a prisoner." Which was done, and after a little more talk we were dismissed to our tents. About an hour after this, as we sat in our tents, we heard the report of a pistol, and in a few minutes came the report that Colonel King had blown out his brains, which was true. We were all very sorry that he did that, as we got no explanation as to what made the regiment retire in the way it did. However John Springate was released from being a prisoner. He afterwards died from the effects of drink.'[51]

In September 1850, an anonymous trooper of the 14th wrote to the full colonel of the regiment to vindicate King. He blamed the suicide upon three troopers, one of whom was Springate, whose 'false words' about their commanding officer preyed upon his mind.[52] Henry Havelock goes out of his way to show that King 'did all that the bravest of men could do to rally his panic-stricken men'[53] at Chilianwala, and it is generally agreed that at Gujrat he was far from cowardly.

* * *

The news of Chilianwala when it reached Britain caused extreme consternation. This was not lessened by Dalhousie's hysterical despatches. To supersede Gough, Sir Charles Napier, reluctantly consenting, was at once bundled off to India. But long before he arrived, the commander-in-chief had gloriously vindicated his reputation by ending the war with one decisive blow.

The day after Chilianwala, Gough intended to pursue his advantage, such as it was, but heavy rain made any sort of move impossible. The Sikhs, meanwhile, received considerable reinforcements in their entrenched position at Rasul. These included some Afghan horse, Dost Muhammad having succumbed to the temptation to have a crack at the British by allying himself with the Sikhs. Gough wisely decided, before continuing the struggle, to await the arrival of his own reinforcements, which, after the fall of Multan on 22 January, were hastening towards him. Among these was the Scinde Irregular Horse, the only cavalry regiment from the Bombay Presidency to serve under Gough in the war.

The enemy, meanwhile, tried everything possible to induce Gough to fight a pitched battle but he would not be drawn. He knew that the Sikhs could not long subsist in the barren country around Rasul and that they would soon be compelled to take up a less impregnable position. 'By a careful exploration of the ground and by a series of masterly movements', as Lord Lawrence has justly put it, Gough prepared the way 'for as crowning a victory as ever smiled upon our arms in India.'[54]

By the time the Multan troops had joined him, five weeks after Chilianwala, the Sikhs had placed themselves in an unentrenched position on an open plain at Gujrat, near the Chenab, which was precisely what Gough wanted. Further, he had at last an army of almost exactly the size which he had long ago stipulated as necessary for the conquest of the Punjab. Early on the morning of 21 February, he brought on to the field some 20,000 men with 88 guns of which 18 were heavies. The enemy, though they may have had between 35,000 and 60,000 men, could produce only 59 guns. Thus, for the first time Gough possessed a marked superiority in artillery. This he used with great effect.

The battle opened with a massive gun duel which lasted from 9 a.m. till 11.30 a.m. The infantry then went in and, after some severe fighting, the Sikh army broke. Soon after 1 p.m. it was in headlong flight. 'We stood two hours in hell', said one Sikh, 'and after that we saw six miles of infantry.'[55] On Gough's flanks were three cavalry brigades. White commanded that on the left, overseen by Thackwell, who, as second-in-command of the army, took charge of all the troops to the left of centre. Brigadier John Hearsey commanded his own and Lockwood's brigades on the right.* Throughout the battle large numbers of the enemy's cavalry tried to turn the two flanks. Hearsey, by skilful use of his horse artillery and cautious handling of his cavalry, kept them off on the right. On one occasion, as Hearsey reported, 'a regiment of [Sikh] regular cavalry moved round by a circuitous route, and got completely into our rear.' Three guns, a squadron of the 14th Light Dragoons and the 9th Irregulars drove them off without the necessity for a charge.[56] A daring body of these same

* *Left*: Brigadier White: 3rd Light Dragoons; 9th Lancers; 8th Bengal Native Cavalry; part of Scinde Irregular Horse; two troops, horse artillery.
Right: Brigadiers Hearsey and Lockwood: 14th Light Dragoons; 1st Bengal Native Cavalry; 3rd Bengal Irregular Cavalry (Tait's Horse); 9th Bengal Irregular Cavalry (Christie's Horse); part of 11th, 13th and 14th Bengal Irregular Cavalry.
The Guides Cavalry was also engaged in the battle and in the pursuit. The 5th and 6th Bengal Native Cavalry guarded the baggage.

Sikhs actually penetrated behind the heavy guns and approached the commander-in-chief and his staff. His personal escort, a troop of the 5th Bengal Native Cavalry, immediately charged and cut them to pieces.

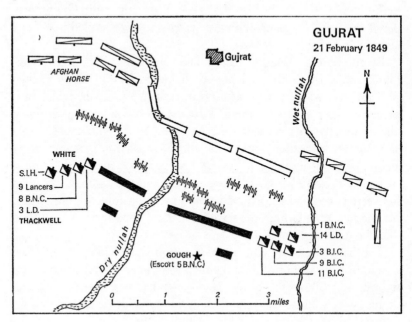

Map 17

On the left White's brigade was confronted by some 4,000 horsemen of which 1,500 were Afghans. These made a wide sweep in an effort to turn the British flanks. Thackwell in person ordered Lieutenant Malcolm, commanding the Scinde Irregular Horse (only 243 strong) to bring his 'right shoulders forward and charge the Afghan Cavalry'.[57]* 'It was indeed a splendid sight', wrote an eye-witness, 'to behold the Irregular Horsemen of Scinde . . . rushing upon the enemy with fiery speed, yet close as the blades of a field of corn,

* Malcolm says that Thackwell added: 'You will be supported by a squadron of the 9th Lancers.' Thackwell afterwards said (and indicated in his despatch) that he had ordered the fourth squadron of the 9th to charge, too, and that they had indeed done so. Malcolm categorically denied this. There followed an acrimonious correspondence between Malcolm and Captain Campbell, commanding the squadron of the 9th. It seems likely that in fact the Scinde Irregular Horse bore the brunt of the charge alone, but that Campbell's squadron did also charge on their right, unseen by Malcolm. (*S.I.H.*, 290–3.)

driving everything before them, their sabres circling and flashing in the sun.'[58]

As the Sikhs in the centre gave way, Captain Delmar of the 9th Lancers saw our troops

'driving them before them like so many sheep . . . their cavalry galloping away in all directions. . . . The whole line pursued them, cutting them down right and left. Every village about and beyond Goojerat was filled with Sikh infantry, and the slaughter was fearful. Our infantry march'd in, and bayonetted every man of them. . . . Our cavalry and horse artillery were pursuing their cavalry and artillery who were retreating before us and yelled most dreadfully. . . . We at last came upon a number of their guns which they in the hurry of their flight had left . . . for our possession. . . . [We] overtook numbers of their infantry who were running for their lives – every man of course was shot. . . . We pass'd over acres of wheat crops, which were two feet in height, and we detected three or four Sikhs scattered in every field, who had thrown themselves down for the purpose of hiding themselves, until we had passed them – their object being to escape altogether or to shoot at us *as we passed*. . . . They jumped up and prayed for mercy, but none was granted them. . . I never saw such butchery and murder! It is almost too horrible to commit to paper – there were our own men sticking their lances into them like so much *butter*, but the way in which this sticking business took place, was truly shocking – fancy a man piercing you thro' the head and body, and, after all this, shooting you by way of a finish. . . . But besides all this *ground* shooting, there was an immense deal of *tree* shooting. . . . Every tree that was standing was well searched, and two or three Sikhs were found concealing in almost every tree we passed – this afforded great *sport* for our men, who were firing up at them, as at so many rooks. . . . Down they would come like a bird, head downward, and bleeding most profusely.'[59]

This was the first time in either of the Sikh wars that the cavalry had an opportunity for a sustained chase of a broken enemy. The regiments had received orders before the battle began 'not to draw rein until their horses drop in the pursuit'.[60] The whole division, perhaps 5,000 men, joined together north of Gujrat to take part in it. Some of the regiments covered up to seventeen miles before being re-called. Some did not return to camp at Gujrat till 10 p.m. They had been in the saddle for fifteen hours. In fact most of the enemy's cavalry got clean away, nor were the casualties in their other arms very great. The pursuit was not ordered, it seems, as soon as it might have been. 'The reason given', according to Malcolm, 'was that Lord Gough thought Goojerat still occupied.'[61]

Throughout the battle the cavalry was employed, except in the case of the charge of the Scinde Irregular Horse, with considerable caution. The commander of the infantry brigade adjoining the cavalry of the left, 'could not understand what Thackwell was about in not driving away the rabble he had in his front.'[62] The adjutant of the Scinde Irregular Horse wrote to John Jacob, his commandant: 'the splendid Cavalry Division was thrown away, for what reason I know not; they must have expected a trap or something. Sir J. Thackwell is a good man; I would swear that he must have mistrusted his men.'[63]

It is indeed likely that after Ramnagar and Chilianwala both Gough and Thackwell were reluctant to depend too much upon their mounted arm. On the other hand, it played its part sufficiently well and incurred no unnecessary casualties. Indeed it is arguable that it was more judiciously handled at Gujrat than in any of the battles of the two Sikh wars with the exception of Aliwal.

Gujrat was the first of Gough's battles in which he placed all his irregular, or *silladar*, regiments in the line. It is significant that he put two regular regiments (the 5th and 6th Bengal Native Cavalry) in charge of the baggage, rather than some of his irregulars.

The failings of the Bengal regulars had become manifest in the actions of both the Sikh wars, while the relative, potential excellence of the irregulars was beginning to be recognised. The arrival of the Scinde Irregular Horse in Gough's army and its brilliant action at Gujrat caused a sensation among the European and Bengali cavalrymen. Two men of the 9th Lancers exclaimed to Malcolm after the charge: 'By God, Sir! They are splendid fellows – I would go to the devil with them.'[64] Nothing astonished the adjutant of the Scinde Irregular Horse 'more, than after the action, fellows coming up and congratulating us on our conduct. . . . They surely did not expect us to run away!'[65]

Items of equipment of the Scinde Irregular Horse were the envy of cavalry officers of other regiments, particularly the steel chains sewn along the outside of the troopers' coat-arms and breeches, and along their snaffle-reins, for turning sword-cuts (see p. 253).

The officers of Gough's cavalry had devised, in the course of the campaign, all sorts of expedients for protecting their heads from the Sikh's deadly sword cuts. These included rolls of linen wrapped around their shakos. Had they worn polished metal helmets like those of the Scinde Irregular Horse, they would not have needed to resort to such improvisations.

General Stubbs remarks that the regulation sabres of the regular cavalry were often 'blunted by too close an acquaintance with the steel scabbard.' The regular trooper 'could not deliver a cut as efficiently as the Sikhs; the guard and point was the best for the Dragoon.'[66] Gough recognised the deficiency of the issue swords three days before Gujrat when he directed that men of the light cavalry 'who are so inclined' might 'arm themselves with their own Tulwars (which they are understood in general to possess) in lieu of the Government sabres they at present carry'.[67]

* * *

The total British casualties at Gujrat were 96 killed and 706 wounded. The cavalry lost only three men killed (of which two were from the Scinde Horse), and forty wounded. Fifty-three guns were taken and a number of colours.

The battle effectively ended the war. The climax of the struggle for British supremacy in India was past. The Sikhs surrendered unconditionally. Dalhousie, on his own responsibility, for he could get no intelligible guidance from London, decided upon full annexation of the Punjab. Thereby he added an enormous frontier tract to the domains of the Company.

EPILOGUE

'That's the reason they're called lessons,' the
Gryphon remarked; 'because they lessen from
day to day.'

Alice in Wonderland

Though the thirty-five years covered by this volume are usually
thought of as a period of stagnation in the British army, they did in
fact witness some useful social reforms. Yet even in that sphere, and
especially in training and tactics, progress was sluggish in comparison with the last half of the nineteenth century. In the cavalry, as
has been shown, this was particularly evident.

In 1850, as in 1816, officers were still 'attached more closely to
their class than to their profession'. Only at the very end of the
period, for example, were the first examinations for men wishing to
buy commissions instituted and these were very elementary. Few
inducements had been given to the poorer man to become an officer.
Virtually the only new regulation for the welfare of officers had been
the establishment in 1833 of pensions for distinguished service.

Though pay for all ranks had remained unchanged, reforms
affecting the living conditions of the non-commissioned officers and
men were surprisingly comprehensive. They ranged from the abolition of enlistment for life, through the introduction of reading and
coffee rooms, to the third obligatory daily meal, radical pension reform, good-conduct pay and badges and drastic reductions in the
severity of floggings.

In the late 1840s army education was beginning to be taken seriously, but the illiteracy rates half-way through the century were
probably much the same as they had been at its beginning. Barrack
room conditions and the lot of soldiers' wives had improved hardly
at all.

*   *   *

In India the first glimmerings of concessions to the climate were to
be seen, yet the European troops' rations were still unsuitable and

Epilogue

typically English. This they remained for many years to come.
Trooper Pearman speaks of salt rations being served out on the
march in 1845,[1] while Lance-Corporal Tookey's rations two years
later consisted of '1 lb of bread, do. of meat, 4 ozs rice, with coffee
for breakfast and tea at night, sugar, salt and pepper.' In the following year he wrote home that he had drawn the rations for '42 men:
1 lb each. It took a sheep and a half to make up that quantity, so
you may think what sort of meat it is.' Goat sometimes replaced
mutton and beef. Tookey's Christmas dinner in cantonments consisted of 'ducks, fowls, roast beef, plum pudding, green peas and
young potatoes, besides cracking a bottle of wine each.'[2] With his
spare money when he had any the soldier could supplement his
rations by buying eggs and chickens which were much cheaper in
India than at home.

As for clothing it was, and remained for a long time to come, of
much the same type and weight as that worn in England.

'A man's kit in India in quarters', wrote Pearman in 1846, 'is
6 prs of white trousers, 6 prs of draws, 3 flannels, 6 shirts, 4
white jackets, 4 puggerees [light turban-type headdress], 6 pr
socks. . . . For watering order: 2 prs blue clothern overalls, one
blue stable jacket, 1 dress coat, 1 shako, one cloak, 2 prs boots.'[3]

Little distinction was made between the clothes worn in the hot
and the cold seasons. Most of the East India Company's native regulars were encased in equally inappropriate uniforms. The example
of wearing loose-fitting, lightweight clothing set by some of the
irregular cavalry regiments was not to be followed till much later.

Neither in India nor at home had there been any but the most
marginal improvements in the care of the sick and wounded. Typical
of the primitive nature of the medical arrangements is Tookey's
description of what happened in the 14th Light Dragoons after a
four days' peacetime march in Northern India in August 1848. The
hospital quickly became full. In one end of the barrack room, therefore, lay

'12 men, and the Dr went from one to the other and bled them
all in both arms and left them bleeding till they fainted. No
attempt was made to catch the blood so that the floor was
covered with it. The barbers were there cutting their hair and
the beasties or water carriers were putting water on their heads
whilst we were employed rubbing their hands and feet. Our
exertions were crowned with success and they all recovered.'[4]

Epilogue

The very high mortality figures in all regiments show that these particular victims of the hot weather season were unusually fortunate.

*　*　*

It is impossible to claim that either training or tactics underwent any material change during the thirty-five years after Waterloo. As has been shown, the military thinking which informed the commanders in the nine Indian campaigns described in this volume differed hardly at all from that displayed in the Napoleonic Wars.

The lessons which ought to have been learned seldom were. The employment of senior officers in commands clearly beyond their capacity or state of health (and in India this last was an especially important factor) continued unabated. Men of the decrepitude of Elphinstone at Kabul and Pope at Chilianwala were still commanding at all levels from regiment to army at the outbreak of the Mutiny.

The obvious need to cut to a minimum the vast and unwieldy army of followers which made speedy manoeuvre impossible and tied up so many men in guard duties may have been recognised but all attempts to fulfil it were frustrated. The first important success in this respect did not come till Robert Napier's Abyssinian campaign of 1868.

Indian campaigns, it was for ever being made clear, required a larger proportion of highly mobile troops, particularly cavalry, organised for preference into permanent flying columns. Yet when the suppression of the Mutiny in 1857 and 1858 demanded as never before just such bodies, they did not exist.

It took the terrible shock of the Mutiny, too, to make clear what ought to have been seen much earlier, that for many purposes the native *silladar* cavalry was superior to the native regular.

One comparatively minor lesson which was learned concerned the use of horse artillery unsupported. This had happened with unhappy results at Mehidpur in 1817. The error seems seldom if ever to have been repeated.

*　*　*

Throughout the period at home, since no European campaigns were demanded of it, the army was subject as usual to parliamentary parsimony. Training in 1850 was much as it had been in 1816. There was no increase whatever in the incidence of manoeuvres above regimental level. The first divisional 'camp of exercise', an experiment proposed by Wellington just before his death, did not take place till 1853. The numerous lessons learned from it could not, alas, be implemented in time for the Crimea.

In the cavalry the major training and tactical reforms instigated by such men as Nolan and Valentine Baker lay in the future. Improvements in methods of teaching riding and horsemastership were yet to materialise; the stiff, insecure cavalry seat, for instance, was still in fashion in the early 1850s. Veterinary skill and recognition of its importance had shown little advance and were not to do so for years to come.

No important change in cavalry arms or equipment had occurred, except the reintroduction of the lance and this was thought by some to be a retrograde step. The revolution which had taken place in the speed, accuracy and range of infantry small arms and of artillery, had had as yet not the slightest effect on cavalry thinking, tactics or training.

It was to take the traumatic experiences of the Crimean War and the Great Indian Mutiny to shatter the complacency of British arms. How these two critical events affected the British cavalry and the improvements which stemmed from them, culminating in the Cardwell reforms of the early 1870s, will be examined in the second volume of this work.

APPENDIX

1. *European and native mounted troops raised in India between 1672 and the beginning of the nineteenth century.* (See Prologue, p. 65.)

The very earliest cavalry in the British service in India was a troop of fifty Englishmen raised in 1672 in Bombay. The island of that name had passed to the Crown as part of the dowry of Catherine of Braganza ten years before. In 1668, the Crown granted it to the East India Company. The troop existed for only six years. Shortly before 1720, a troop of European Dragoons was formed, took part in the Angria expedition of 1721, and was reduced in 1728. The first native cavalry in Bombay consisted of a single troop raised in 1804. This was the nucleus of what became in 1817 the 1st Bombay Light Cavalry. (For the origins of the Poona Horse, see p. 189.)

In Bengal, the first native horsemen to be organised in the service of the British were two troops of Mogul Horse, entirely officered by natives. Raised in Patna in 1760 they were disbanded in 1772. In January 1761, a 'Troop of Horse' had been raised in England for service in Madras. On arrival it was transferred to Bengal.[1] Some of its personnel probably entered a small European bodyguard for the Governor which was raised in 1762 and disbanded in 1772. The following year the nucleus of what remained to the end of British rule in 1947 as the Governor-General's Bodyguard, was formed under the name of 'The Governor's Troop of Moguls'.

In 1776 two British-officered regiments were raised by the Nawab of Oudh. These were transferred to the Company in the next year and disbanded in 1783. They formed the first cavalry brigade in the Bengal army together with what later became the 1st Bengal Light Cavalry, raised at Oudh in 1777 as the 3rd. This regiment was converted into a regular unit in 1796. After a career of good service it was one of those which mutinied in 1857. What later became the 2nd Bengal Light Cavalry was raised in 1778, also at Oudh, as 'The Kandahar Horse'. The origin of this title is obscure, but it seems that the regiment was composed almost exclusively of Pathans. It was disbanded in 1841 for misconduct (see p. 222). At Dinapore, in 1796, the 3rd Bengal Native Cavalry was raised and at Moneah in 1797 the 4th Bengal Native Cavalry.

In 1800, at Ghazipur, the 5th and 6th Bengal Native Cavalry were raised. All four were disloyal in 1857, the 4th and 5th being disbanded in 1858.

294

Appendix

Numbers of irregular cavalry regiments were raised in 1796. Among these was De Boigne's bodyguard 'a corps of 600 chosen cavaliers, of Persian nationality, superbly armed, equipped and mounted, and attended by 100 camel-riders and four light field-pieces'.[2] This had been offered to Sindhia by De Boigne, but the price demanded was too high, and it was eventually acquired for the Company by Cornwallis, who paid three-and-a-half lakhs of rupees for it, and gave liberal terms of engagement to the men. It became Lieutenant-Colonel Bruce's 'Independent Regiment of Cavalry' and seems to have been incorporated in Major Frith's 'Hindustani Independent Regiment'. This was an irregular body formed in 1803 at Ghazipur and reduced at the end of the Maratha War in 1805. This was the first of a number of irregular units similarly reduced once the war was over. In 1803, Captain James Skinner raised Skinner's Horse (see p. 187), which after a distinguished career became, in 1861, the 1st Bengal Cavalry. In 1805 the 7th and 8th Bengal Native Cavalry were formed. The 7th mutinied at Lucknow in 1857, and the 8th was disbanded in 1858 for disaffection.

At Delhi in 1809 Major W. L. Gardner raised Gardner's Horse (see p. 186), which after eighty-one years of distinction became in 1890, the 2nd Bengal Lancers.

In 1815 three regiments were raised in Rohilkhand: the 1st, 2nd and 3rd Rohilla Cavalry, of which only the 1st survived very long. It became the 3rd Local Horse in 1823 and in 1840 the 3rd Irregular Cavalry, and was known as 'Tait's Horse' until 1851. In 1857 part of it mutinied and four years later it was disbanded. The 2nd Rohilla Cavalry, raised by Captain George Cunningham, was disbanded after the Third Maratha War. The 3rd, raised by Captain W. C. Baddeley, was transferred in 1819 to the service of the King of Oudh.

In 1815, Skinner raised two further regiments, the 2nd and 3rd Skinner's Horse (see p. 188). The 3rd was disbanded in 1819 but the 2nd became, in 1861, the 3rd Bengal Cavalry. In 1818 'Sneyd's Frontier Horse', which became for a short time the 4th (Sneyd's) Rohilla Cavalry, was raised. At about the same time the 1st, 2nd and 3rd Regiments of Rampoorah Local Cavalry started their short careers. These were the first entirely native corps of the Company to be commanded by a Royal officer, Major Bunce of the 24th Light Dragoons.

In Madras the earliest mounted force consisted of a troop of thirty Europeans raised in 1748. This, augmented in numbers and with a further troop of 'foreign hussars', existed in one form or another until 1779. For the last eight years of its existence it was known as the 'H.E.I.C.'s Troop of Dragoons'. Various native levies were raised from time to time until, in 1784, four native regiments were taken directly into the Company's service. What later became the 4th, or Prince of Wales's Own, Madras Light Cavalry and the 5th Madras Light Cavalry were raised in 1785, fol-

Appendix

lowed in 1787 by another regiment, which evolved into the 1st Madras Light Cavalry. The Bodyguard was first formed in 1778, and disbanded in 1808. Between 1799 and 1804, the 5th, 6th, 7th and 8th Madras Cavalry were raised.

2. *Cavalry regiments which were disbanded between 1816 and 1822.* (See p. 75.)

23rd Light Dragoons, 1817; 20th Light Dragoons, 1818 (reformed as 2nd Bengal European Light Cavalry, 1858; became 20th Hussars, 1861); 24th and 25th Light Dragoons, 1819; 21st Light Dragoons, 1820 (reformed as 3rd Bengal European Light Cavalry, 1858; became 21st Hussars, 1861, and Lancers, 1897); 22nd Light Dragoons, 1820; 18th (King's) Light Dragoons, 1821 (reformed as 18th Light Dragoons (Hussars), 1858) – Field-Marshal the 1st Marquess of Drogheda, who had raised the regiment (Drogheda's Light Horse) in 1759, survived until 1821 the year of its disbandment. He died of heartbreak, it is said, at the loss of his beloved creation, aged ninety-one; 19th Lancers, 1821 (reformed as 1st Bengal European Light Cavalry, 1858; became 19th Hussars, 1861).

3. *The establishment of irregular regiments.* (See p. 184.)

These varied widely. In the 1840s the native strength of a typical Bengal regiment of eight troops was:
Native commissioned officers:
   4 risaldars (senior troop commanders)
   4 russaidars (junior troop commanders)
   8 naib risaldars (deputy troop commanders)
   8 jemadars (lieutenants)
   1 wordi major (assistant to the adjutant).
N.C.O.s:
   8 kote duffadars (troop sergean-majors)
   64 duffadars (sergeants)
   8 nishanbardars (standard bearers)
   4 trumpeters
   4 nagarchis (kettle drummers)
   640 sowars (troopers).
   The original (1809) establishment of Gardner's Horse was: six troops:
European officers:
   1 commandant
   1 other officer
   1 adjutant

Appendix

Native commissioned officers:
  6 risaldars
  6 naib risaldars
  6 jemadars
N.C.O.s:
  6 kote duffadars
  30 duffadars
  6 nishanbardars
  6 vakils
  6 bhistis
  1 writer
  1 nakib (herald)
  600 sowars (troopers).

(Jacob, 4; Whitworth, 3)

4. *Gardner's Horse.* (See p. 186.)

In 1823 the regiment was renamed the 2nd (Gardner's) Local Horse. In 1840 it became the 2nd Irregular Cavalry. On the reorganisation of the Bengal Army in 1861, it became the 2nd Bengal Cavalry; in 1890, the 2nd Bengal Lancers, and in 1903 the 2nd Lancers (Gardner's Horse).

5. *The 2nd and 3rd Regiments of Skinner's Horse.* (See p. 188.)

The 2nd Regiment became in 1823 the 4th (Baddeley's) Local Horse; in 1840 the 4th Irregular Cavalry; in 1861 the 3rd Bengal Cavalry and in 1903 reverted to the title of 3rd Skinner's Horse. In 1922, together with the 1st Skinner's Horse, it became the Duke of York's Own Skinner's Horse.

The 3rd Regiment was disbanded in 1819 at the end of the Third Maratha War.

6. *The Poona Horse.* (See p. 189.)

The regiment became the Poona Irregular Horse in 1847; the Poona Horse in 1860; successively the 4th and 5th Silladar Horse and the 1st and 2nd Regiment Poona Horse in 1861, reverting in 1862 to the title of the Poona Horse. In 1885 it was renamed the 4th Bombay Cavalry (Poona Horse); in 1903 the 34th (Prince Albert Victor's Own) Poona Horse and in 1921–22 it joined with the 3rd Regiment of Light Cavalry to make the 17th Queen Victoria's Own Poona Horse.

Appendix

7. *The Gujarat Irregular Horse.* (See p. 189.)

Raised by Major Roberts from men of the Bombay Presidency, the Gujarat Horse was primarily a civil corps and figured for only a short time in the Army List. It performed useful service in the great Mutiny of 1857. In 1861 it was renamed, first, the 6th Gujarat Silladar Horse, and then the Gujarat Irregular Horse. It was disbanded in 1865. The 2nd Gujarat Horse was raised in 1860, renamed the 7th Gujarat Silladar Horse in 1861, and disbanded in the same year.

8. *The Southern Mahratta Horse.* (See p. 189.)

In 1858 the regiment became the 1st Southern Mahratta Horse, in 1861 the 12th Southern Mahratta Silladar Horse and in 1862 reverted to the Southern Mahratta Horse. It was disbanded in 1865. From it was formed in the same year the Governor of Bombay's Bodyguard, later renamed the Governor's Body Guard, Bombay. In 1858 the 2nd regiment was raised becoming in 1861 the 13th Southern Mahratta Silladar Horse and in 1862 reverting to its original title of 2nd Southern Mahratta Horse. It was disbanded in 1862. The 3rd regiment was raised in 1860 becoming the 14th Southern Mahratta Silladar Horse in 1861 and was disbanded in 1862.

9. *The Mysore Silladar Horse.* (See p. 201.)

These horsemen, it seems, were raised at Bangalore by Diwan Purnea in 1799 from the remnants of Tipu Sultan's army after the capture of Seringapatam. At some unknown date they were renamed the Mysore Lancers, becoming in 1892 part of the Imperial Service Troops, and in 1922 of the Indian States Forces. (*Indian States Forces Army List*, 1944. See also Cambridge, Marquess of, 'Notes on the Armies of India, Part III', *J.A.H.R.*, XLVII (1969), 195.)

10. *'Shah Shuja's Force'.* (See p. 215.)

The cavalry element consisted of the 1st Shah's Cavalry, known as 'Christie's Horse' after its commander, Captain J. Christie of the 3rd Bengal Light Cavalry, and the 2nd Shah's Cavalry, commanded by an officer of native infantry. From 'Christie's Horse' the 9th Irregular Cavalry was formed in 1844. It was disbanded in 1861. The 2nd Shah's Cavalry did not survive the First Afghan War. In 1842 Captain (later Field-Marshal Sir) Neville Chamberlain of the 16th Bengal Native Infantry was given temporary command of Christie's Horse with which he distinguished himself. The regiment was, consequently, sometimes referred to as 'Chamberlain's Horse'.

11. *The Scinde Irregular Horse.* (See p. 220.)

The regiment was founded in 1839. A second was raised in 1846. On the reorganisation of 1861 the two regiments became the 8th and 9th Silladar Horse, and almost immediately afterwards the 1st and 2nd Scinde Horse. In 1888 the 1st became the 5th Bombay Cavalry (Scinde Horse), and the 2nd became the 6th Bombay Cavalry (Jacob's) Horse. In 1903 the two regiments were renamed the 35th Scinde Horse and the 36th Jacob's Horse, and in 1921–22 they were joined together to make the 14th Prince of Wales's Own Scinde Horse. A third regiment was formed in 1857. In 1858 it became Macaulay's Horse; in 1861 the 10th Scinde Silladar Horse and then in the same year the 3rd Scinde Horse. It was disbanded in 1882. A fourth regiment was formed in 1860, became in 1861 the 11th Scinde Silladar Horse and was disbanded in 1862. In 1885 there was formed the 7th Bombay Cavalry (Jacob-Ka-Risallah). In 1886 it became the 7th Bombay Cavalry (Baluch Horse), in 1890 the 7th Bombay Lancers (Baluch Horse), in 1903 the 37th Lancers (Baluch Horse) and in 1921–22 was joined to the 15th Lancers.

The Royal Regiments (

	1816	1817	1818	1819	1820	1821	1822	1823	1824	1825	1826	1827	1828
Household Cav. (1660)	H	H	H	H	H	H	H	H	H	H	H	H	H
1st D.G. (1685)	F/H	H	H	H	H	H	H	H	H	H	H	H	H
2nd D.G. (1685)	F	F	F/H	H	H	H	H	H	H	H	H	H	H
3rd D.G. (1685)	F/H	H	H	H	H	H	H	H	H	H	H	H	H
4th D.G. (1685)	H	H	H	H	H	H	H	H	H	H	H	H	H
5th D.G. (1685)	H	H	H	H	H	H	H	H	H	H	H	H	H
6th D.G. (1685)	H	H	H	H	H	H	H	H	H	H	H	H	H
7th D.G. (1688)	H	H	H	H	H	H	H	H	H	H	H	H	H
1st D. (1661)	H	H	H	H	H	H	H	H	H	H	H	H	H
2nd D. (1678)	F/H	H	H	H	H	H	H	H	H	H	H	H	H
6th D. (1689)	H	H	H	H	H	H	H	H	H	H	H	H	H
3rd L.D. (1685)	H	H	H	H	H	H	H	H	H	H	H	H	H
4th L.D. (1685)	H	H	H	H	H	H	H/I	I	I	I	I	I	I
7th L.D. (H.) (1690)	F	F/H	H	H	H	H	H	H	H	H	H	H	H
8th L.D. (H.) (1693)	I	I	I	I	I	I	I	I/H	H	H	H	H	H
9th L.D. (L.) (1715)	H	H	H	H	H	H	H	H	H	H	H	H	H
10th L.D. (H.) (1715)	F/H	H	H	H	H	H	H	H	H	H	H	H/P	P/H
11th L.D. (H.) (1715)	F	F	F/H	H/I	I	I	I	I	I	I	I	I	I
12th L.D. (L.) (1715)	F	F	F/H	H	H	H	H	H	H	H	H	H/P	P/H
13th L.D. (1715)	F/H	H	H	H/I	I	I	I	I	I	I	I	I	I
14th L.D. (1715)	H	H	H	H	H	H	H	H	H	H	H	H	H
15th L.D. (H.) (1759)	F/H	H	H	H	H	H	H	H	H	H	H	H	H
16th L.D. (L.) (1759)	H	H	H	H	H	H	H/I	I	I	I	I	I	I
17th L.D. (L.) (1759)	I	I	I	I	I	I	I	I/H	H	H	H	H	H
18th L.D. (1759)	F	F	F/H	H	H	D							
19th L.D. (1759)	C	C/H	H	H	H	D							
20th L.D. (1759)	H	H	D										
21st L.D. (1759)	A	A/H	H	H	D								

Key: A: South Africa   F: France or Flanders   P: Portugal
      C: Canada   H: Home (i.e. U.K.)
      D: Disbanded   I: India

Cavalry: Stations from 1816–1850

1833	1834	1835	1836	1837	1838	1839	1840	1841	1842	1843	1844	1845	1846	1847	1848	1849	1850
H	H	H	H	H	H	H	H	H	H	H	H	H	H	H	H	H	H
H	H	H	H	H	H/C	C	C	C	C	C/H	H	H	H	H	H	H	H
H	H	H	H	H	H	H	H	H	H	H	H	H	H	H	H	H	H
H	H	H	H	H	H	H	H	H	H	H	H	H	H	H	H	H	H
H	H	H	H	H	H	H	H	H	H	H	H	H	H	H	H	H	H
H	H	H	H	H	H	H	H	H	H	H	H	H	H	H	H	H	H
H	H	H	H	H	H	H	H	H	H	H	H	H	H	H	H	H	H
H	H	H	H	H	H	H	H	H	H/A	A	A	A	A	A/H	H	H	H
H	H	H	H	H	H	H	H	H	H	H	H	H	H	H	H	H	H
H	H	H	H	H	H	H	H	H	H	H	H	H	H	H	H	H	H
H	H	H	H	H	H	H	H	H	H	H	H	H	H	H	H	H	H
H	H	H	H	H/I	I	I	I	I	I	I	I	I	I	I	I	I	I
I	I	I	I	I	I	I	I	I/H	H	H	H	H	H	H	H	H	H
H	H	H	H	H	H/C	C	C	C	C/H	H	H	H	H	H	H	H	H
H	H	H	H	H	H	H	H	H	H	H	H	H	H	H	H	H	H
H	H	H	H	H	H	H	H	H/I	I	I	I	I	I	I	I	I	I
H	H	H	H	H	H	H	H	H	H	H	H	H	H/I	I	I	I	I
I	I	I	I	I/H	H	H	H	H	H	H	H	H	H	H	H	H	H
H	H	H	H	H	H	H	H	H	H	H	H	H	H	H	H	H	H
I	I	I	I	I	I	I	I/H	H	H	H	H	H	H	H	H	H	H
H	H	H	H	H	H	H	H	H/I	I	I	I	I	I	I	I	I	I
H	H	H	H	H	H	H/I	I	I	I	I	I	I	I	I	I	I	I
I	I	I	I	I	I	I	I	I	I	I	I	I/H	H	H	H	H
H	H	H	H	H	H	H	H	H	H	H	H	H	H	H	H	H	H

ABBREVIATIONS USED IN THE
FOOTNOTES AND IN THE
SOURCE NOTES

Only those sources which occur more than once
in the footnotes or source notes are included in this list.

Adams   Adams, W. J. *The Narrative of Private Buck Adams, 7th Dragoon Guards . . . 1843–1849*, (ed.) Gordon-Brown, A., 1941

Anglesey   Anglesey, Marquess of *One-Leg, the Life and Letters of the 1st Marquess of Anglesey, 1768–1854*, 1961

Anglesey: *Pearman*   Anglesey, Marquess of (ed.) *Sergeant Pearman's Memoirs . . .*, 1968

Anglesey: *Hodge*   Anglesey, Marquess of (ed.) *Little Hodge*, 1971

Arthur   Arthur, Sir George, bt. *The Story of the Household Cavalry*, 2 vols., 1909

Atkinson   Atkinson, C. T. *History of the Royal Dragoons, 1661–1934*, 1934

Bajwa   Bajwa, F. A. *Military System of the Sikhs*, 1964

Baker   Baker, Valentine *The British Cavalry: with remarks on its practical organisation*, 1858

Barrett   Barrett, C. R. B. *The 7th (Q.O.) Hussars*, 2 vols., 1914

Benson Freeman   Benson Freeman, Eng.-Com. *The Yeomanry of Devon*, 1927

Bewick   Bewick, T. *Memoirs . . . by himself*, 1924

Blacker   Blacker, Lt.-Col. V. *Memoir of the Operations of the British Army in India during the Mahratta War of 1817, 1818 and 1819*, 1821

B.M.   British Museum papers

Bolitho   Bolitho, H. *The Galloping Third*, 1963

Bonham-Carter   Bonham-Carter, V. *Soldier True*, 1963

Broadfoot   Broadfoot, Maj. W. *The Career of Major George Broadfoot, C.B.*, 1888

Bruton   Bruton, F. A. 'The Story of Peterloo', *Bulletin of the John Rylands Library, Manchester*, V (1918–20)

Burton: *M & PW*   Burton, Lt.-Col. R. G. *The Mahratta and Pindari War*, 1910

Burton: *SW*   Burton, Lt.-Col. R. G. *The First and Second Sikh Wars*, 1911

Cannon   Cannon, R. *Historical Record of the Third Light Dragoons*, 1847

Abbreviations

Cardew	Cardew, Lt. F. G. *A Sketch of the Services of the Bengal Native Army to the year 1895*, 1903
Churchill	Churchill, W. S. *History of the English-Speaking Peoples*, 4 vols., 1957
Clode	Clode, Charles M. *The Military Forces of the Crown; their Administration and Government*, 2 vols., 1869
Coley	Coley, James *Journal of the Sutlej Campaign of 1845–1846 . . .*, 1956
Cumming	Cumming, Capt. John, 80th Foot, to his father, 30 July 1846, 'The Night of Ferozeshah, 21st–22nd of December, 1845', (ed.) Oman, Sir Charles, *Orkney Herald*, 1910, reprinted in *Army Quarterly*, XXXIII (1936–1937)
Delmar	Delmar, Capt. C. A. to his family: MS book of extracts from his letters, 1848–49, the property of F. M. Delmar, Esq.
Denham-Cookes	Denham-Cookes, Lt. G. to his brother, quoted in Bolitho
Durand	Durand, Sir H. M. *The First Afghan War and its Causes*, 1879
Evans	Evans, Maj.-Gen. R. *The Story of the 5th Royal Inniskilling Dragoon Guards*, 1951
Forrest	Forrest, G. W. *Life of F-M Sir Neville Chamberlain*, 1909
Fortescue	Fortescue, J. W. *A History of the British Army*, 13 vols., 1899–1930
Fortescue: *17L*	Fortescue, J. W. *A History of the 17th Lancers*, 1895
Fortescue: *Canteens*	Fortescue, J. W. *A Short Account of Canteens in the British Army*, 1928
Graham	Graham, H. *History of the 16th Light Dragoons, 1759–1912*, 1912
Graham: *Wilts*	Graham, H. *Annals of the Wiltshire Yeomanry*, 1886
Gough & Innes	Gough, Gen. Sir C., VC, and Innes, A. D. *The Sikhs and the Sikh Wars*, 1897
Halévy	Halévy, Elie *A History of the English People in the Nineteenth Century* (2nd English ed.), 1949
Hamilton	Hamilton, Col. H. B. *Historical Record of the 14th (King's) Hussars*, 1901
Hansard (C)	*Hansard's Parliamentary Debates*, House of Commons
Hansard (L)	*Hansard's Parliamentary Debates*, House of Lords
Hardinge & Gough	*Despatches of . . . Viscount Hardinge . . . Lord Gough. . . .*, 1846
Hardinge	Hardinge, Charles, 2nd Visc. *Viscount Hardinge*, 1891
H.E.I.C.	Hon. East India Company papers in I.O.L.
Henderson	Henderson, R. *The Soldier of Three Queens*, 1866
Hodge Papers	The unpublished diaries & letters of Col. E. C. Hodge, 4th Dragoon Guards, in the possession of F. R. Hodge, Esq.
H.O.	Home Office papers in B.M. or P.R.O.
Hough	Hough, Maj. W. *A Narrative of the March and Operations of the Army of the Indus, 1838–1839*, 1841

Abbreviations

Humbley	Humbley, Capt. W. W. W. *Journal of a Cavalry Officer*, 1854
I.O.L.	India Office Library
Jackson	Jackson, Maj. E. S. *The Inniskilling Dragoons*, 1909
Jacob	Jacob, J. *Papers on Silladar Cavalry as it is, and as it might be*, 1848
J.A.H.R.	*Journal of the Society for Army Historical Research*
Jolliffe	Jolliffe, W. J. Hylton to Estcourt, T. G. B., 11 Apr 1845, in Pellew, Hon. G. *Life and Correspondence of 1st Viscount Sidmouth*, 1847
J.U.S.I.	*Journal of the (Royal) United Service Institution*
Kaye	Kaye, Sir John W. *History of the War in Afghanistan*, 3 vols (3rd ed.), 1874
Knollys	Knollys, H. (ed.) *Life of General Sir Hope Grant*, 2 vols, 1894
Lambrick	Lambrick, H. T. *John Jacob of Jacobabad*, 1960
Lambrick: *SIH*	Lambrick, H. T. 'The Scinde Irregular Horse in its earliest days', *Journal of the Sind Historical Society*, V, 1941
Latimer	Latimer, J. *The Annals of Bristol in the 19th Century*, 1887
Lawrence, G.	Lawrence, Sir G. *Forty-Three Years in India*, 1874
Lawrence, H.	Lawrence, Sir H. *Essays, Military and Political*, 1859
Lee-Warner	Lee-Warner, Sir W. *Lord Dalhousie*, 2 vols 1904
Lowe	[Lowe, Capt. A. C.] *Diary of an officer of the 16th (Queen's) Lancers, 1822–1840* (privately printed), 1894
Lucas	MS 'Autobiography of Private (later Sergeant) William Lucas, 7th Dragoon Guards, 1830–1865', the property of E. A. Lucas, Esq.
McGuffie	McGuffie, T. D. (ed.) *Peninsular Cavalry General (1811–1813)*, 1951
Mackinnon	[Mackinnon, D. H.] *Military Service and Adventures in the Far East: including sketches of the campaigns against the Afghans in 1839, and the Sikhs in 1845–6, by a Cavalry Officer*, 2 vols, 1847
MacMullen	MacMullen, J. *Camp and Barrack Room; or the British Army as it is, by a late Staff Sergeant of the 13th Light Infantry*, 1846
Marshall	Marshall, H. *Military Miscellany*, 1846
Marshall: *Pun*	Marshall, H. *A Historical Sketch of Military Punishments*, [c.1840]
Marshman	Marshman, J. C. *Memoirs of Sir Henry Havelock*, 1860
Mather	Mather, F. C. *Public Order in the Age of the Chartists*, 1959
Maude	Maude, Lt.-Col. F. N. *Cavalry: its Past and Future*, 1903
Mole	[Mole, Edwin] *A King's Hussar, being the Military Memoirs for 25 Years of a Troop Sergeant Major of the 14th (King's) Hussars* (ed.) Compton, H., 1893
Moyse-Bartlett	Moyse-Bartlett, H. *Louis Edward Nolan and his influence on the British Cavalry*, 1971

Abbreviations

Murray   Murray, Rev. R. H. *The History of the VIII King's Royal Irish Hussars, 1693–1927*, 2 vols, 1928

Napier   Napier, Lt.-Gen. Sir Charles *Lights and Shades of Military Life*, 1851

Napier   Napier, Sir William *Life of Sir Charles Napier*, 4 vols., 1857

Nolan   Nolan, Captain L. E. *Cavalry: its History and Tactics*, 1853

Norman   Norman, Lt.-Col. W. W., 22nd Cavalry (Frontier Force) 'The Native Cavalry of India', *Cavalry Journal*, II (1907)

Oatts   Oatts, Lt.-Col. L. B. *I Serve: Regimental History of the 3rd Carabineers. . . .*, 1966

Oman   Oman, C. *The Art of War in the Middle Ages*, 1885 or 1924

Ouvry   Ouvry, Col. H. A. *Cavalry Experiences and Leaves from My Journal*, 1892

Paget   Paget, Gen. Lord George *The Light Cavalry Brigade in the Crimea*, 1861

Parry   Parry, E. G. *Reynell Taylor*, 1888

Parry & Freeman   Parry, Col. Ll. E. S. and Freeman, B. F. M. *Historical Records of the Denbighshire Hussars Imperial Yeomanry, 1795–1906*, 1909

Pearse   Pearse, Col. H. *The Hearseys*, 1905

Pomeroy   Pomeroy, Maj. Hon. R. L. *The Story of the 5th Princess Charlotte of Wales' Dragoon Guards*, 1924

P.R.O.   Public Records Office papers

Queen's Regs   *The Queen's Regulations and Orders for the Army, 1844*, (3rd ed.), 1855

Rait   Rait, R. S. *The Life and Campaigns of Hugh, Viscount Gough*, 2 vols, 1903

Scott Daniell   Scott Daniell, D. *4th Hussar: The Story of the 4th Queen's Hussars, 1685–1958*, 1959

Seaton   Seaton, Maj.-Gen. Sir Thomas *From Cadet to Colonel* [1866]

Shakespear   Shakespear, Capt. C. M. J. D., RHA, Unpublished 'Diary of events and observations during the Turkish campaign of 1854, being an account of what I saw, heard and thought,' the property of Mrs L. S. Bickford

Sheppard   Sheppard, Maj. E. W. *The Ninth Queen's Royal Lancers, 1715–1936*, 1939

Siborne   Siborne, H. T. (ed.) *Waterloo Letters*, 1891

S.I.H.   [Anon.] *Record Book of the Scinde Irregular Horse* ('printed for private and confidential Regtl. use only'), 2 vols., 1856

Smith   Moore Smith, G. C. (ed.) *The Autobiography of Sir Harry Smith*, 2 vols, 1901

Smith   Smith, Maj.-Gen. Sir Frederick *A History of the Royal Army Veterinary Corps 1796–1919*, 1927

Smyth   [Smyth, Charles Carmichael], *A Rough Sketch of the Rise and Progress of the Irregular Horse of the Bengal Army by an old Cavalry Officer*, [1847]

Abbreviations

Somerville	Somerville, A. *The Autobiography of a Working Man* (ed.) Carswell, J. [1848]
Spear	Spear, Percival (Smith, V. A.) *The Oxford History of India*, Part III, 1964 ed.
Stanley	Bruton, F. A. (ed.) 'Bishop E. Stanley's account of Peterloo', *Three Accounts of Peterloo*, 1921
Stubbs	Stubbs, Maj.-Gen. F. W. *History of the Organisation, Equipment, and War Services of the Regiment of Bengal Artillery*, 3 vols, 1877–95
Teichman	Teichman, Maj. O. 'The Yeomanry as an aid to civil power, 1795–1867, II, 1831–1867', *JAHR*, XIX (1940)
Thackwell	Wylly, Col. H. C. *The Military Memoirs of Lieut.-Gen. Sir Joseph Thackwell, GCB, KH . . .*, 1908
Thackwell	Thackwell, E. J. [son and ADC to Sir Joseph] *Narrative of the Second Seikh War in 1848–1849*, 1851
Thomson	Thomson, Col. Anstruther *Eighty Years' Reminiscences*, 1904
Thomas	Thomas, Hugh *The Story of Sandhurst*, 1961
Tookey	MS letters of George Tookey, 14th L.D., 1846–1848, in typescript only, the originals being lost. The property of 14/20 King's Hussars
Trotter	Trotter, Capt. L. J. *The Life of John Nicholson*, 7th ed., 1898
Tylden	Tylden, Maj. G. *Horses and Saddlery: an account of the animals used by the British and Commonwealth Armies from the 17th century to the present day with a description of their equipment*, 1965
Unett	Walter Unett Papers, MS, property of Lt.-Col. W. H. Unett
Webster	Webster, P. C. G. *Records of the Queen's Own Royal Regiment of Staffordshire Yeomanry*, 1870
Wellington (D)	Gurwood, Lt.-Col. (ed.) *The Dispatches of Field Marshal the Duke of Wellington . . ., 1799–1818*, 1837–8
Wellington (SD)	Wellington, [2nd] Duke of (ed.) *The Supplementary Despatches, Correspondence and Memoranda of Arthur, Duke of Wellington*, 1858–72
Wellington (D:NS)	Wellington, [2nd] Duke of (ed.) *Despatches Correspondence and Memoranda of Arthur, Duke of Wellington (New Series)*, 1867–80
White	White, Lynn, jr. *Medieval Technology and Social Change*, 1962
Whitworth	Whitworth, Capt. D. E. *History of the Second Lancers (Gardner's Horse)*, 1924
Whyte	Whyte, Col. A. C. T., VC *The Story of Army Education, 1643–1963*, 1963
Williams	[Williams], H. J. *The 1st King's Dragoon Guards*, 1920
Wilson	Wilson, Lt.-Col. W. J. *History of the Madras Army, 1746–1826 . . .*, 4 vols., 1888

Abbreviations

W.O.	War Office papers
Wolseley	Wolseley, Gen. Visc. 'The Army', in Ward, T. H. *The Reign of Queen Victoria*, 1887
Woodward	Woodward, E. L. *The Age of Reform, 1815–1870*, 1938
Wylly	Wylly, Col. H. C. *XVth (The King's) Hussars, 1729 to 1913*, 1914

SOURCE NOTES

PROLOGUE (p. 25–70)

(i)

1   Gordon, D. H. 'Swords, rapiers and horseriders' *Antiquity*, XXVII (1953), 75. See also White, where exhaustive studies of other important equine inventions, such as the nailed horseshoe, occur
2   White, 28
3   Oman, 16
4   Fortescue, I, 13
5   Nolan, 13
6   Oman (1885), 96
7   Dimock, F. (ed.) Giraldus Cambrensis *Itinerarium Kambrine*, 1868, 54
8   Oman (1924), 136
9   Machiavelli, N. *Art of War*, Farnesworth ed., 1775, 62
10   Fortescue, I, 207

(ii)

1   Robson, Eric 'The Armed Forces and the Art of War', *New Cambridge Modern History*, 1957, VII, 166
2   Carlyle, Thomas *History of Friedrich II of Prussia*, 1905 ed., III, 300
3   Savory, Lt.-Gen. Sir Reginald *H.B.M.'s Army in Germany during the Seven Years' War*, 1966, 171

(iii)

1   Fortescue, IV, 243
2   Oman, C. *A History of the Peninsular War*, I, 1902, 536
3   Fortescue, VII, 162
4   Cornet F. Hall 'Peninsular Recollections', *J.U.S.I.*, LVI (1911), 1935
5   Fortescue, VIII, 175
6   MS Journal kept by an officer of the Royals, quoted in Atkinson, 279
7   *Wellington (D)*, IX, 238
8   Atkinson, 279
9   Boswell, J. *The Journal of a Tour to the Hebrides with Samuel Johnson*, 1785 ed., 313
10   Le Marchant, J. G. *The Rules and Regulations for the Attainment and Practice of the Sword Exercise*, 1796
11   Grattan, W. *Adventures with the Connaught Rangers*, 1847, II, 62
12   Beamish, N. L., *History of the King's German Legion*, 1832, II, 82

(iv)

1   Wood, E. *Cavalry in the Waterloo Campaign*, 1895, 49
2   Uxbridge's account in Siborne, 8
3   Uxbridge's account in Siborne, 9–10
4   Capt. A. K. Clark's account in Siborne, 72
5   Capt. A. K. Clark, quoted in Atkinson, 308

(v)

1   Fortescue, VII, 598
2   Fortescue, VII, 596

CHAPTER I (p. 71–94)

(i)

1   Burghley, W. C. *A Memorial for Thomas Cecil* (1962 ed.), 11
2   Fortescue: *Canteens*, 16
3   Fortescue, XI, 55
4   McDowell, R. B. *Public Opinion and Government Policy in Ireland, 1801–1846*, 1952, 185
5   Mole, 130. This seems to have derived from a verse by Thomas Jordan (1612–85):

'Our God and the soldier we alike adore.
  'When at the brink of ruin, not before.
'The danger past, both are alike requited;
  'God is forgotten, and our soldier slighted.'

Another version was written by Francis Quarles (1592–1644). Its wording is slightly different from that of Jordan. Both may have sprung from the medical rendering of the epigrammatist John Owens (1560?–1622):

'God and the Doctor we alike adore
  'But only when in danger, not before;
'The danger o'er, both are alike requited,
  'God is forgotten, and the Doctor slighted.'

The most poetical interpretation of the same sentiment is the late nineteenth-century poem 'Tommy' by Rudyard Kipling, of which two of the choruses are:

'O it's Tommy this, an' Tommy that, an'
  '"Tommy, go away";
'But it's "Thank you, Mister Atkins," when
  'The band begins to play'.
          *   *   *
'For it's Tommy this, an' Tommy that, an'
  '"Chuck 'im out, the brute!"
'But it's "Saviour of 'is country" when the
  'guns begin to shoot.'

Source notes (pages 73–83)

6   Halévy, I, 94
7   W.O. 33/32, 5–8
8   Fortescue, XI, 92
9   Wolseley, I, 155–6; H.O. 50/16 (1840); Sir William Molesworth's speech, *Hansard (C)*, XCVII, 1848, 1173–4
10 Baker, 62
11 Evidence before the Finance Commission, 1828, 4, quoted in Clode, I, 320
12 Pomeroy, I, 161
13 Williams, 13
14 Wylly, 258
15 Scott Daniell, 132; speech of Sir R. Peel, *Hansard (C)*, XXXII, 1816, 922
16 Evans, 64
17 Barrett, II, 3–31

(ii)

1   Journal, 15 Aug 1839, *Napier*, II, 73
2   Codrington, Col. G. R. 'Yeomanry Cavalry', *J.A.H.R.*, IX (1930), 138
3   Mather, 156
4   Clode, I, 316
5   Fortescue, XI, 43
6   Gladstone, E. W. *The Shropshire Yeomanry*, 1953, 34
7   *Smith*, I, 338
8   Teichman, 136; Parry & Freeman, Appendix I, 'The Flintshire Yeomanry Cavalry, 1797–1838', viii
9   H.O. 41/13; H.O. 41/17
10 P.R.O., W.O. 3/250/51–56; W.O. 3/179
11 Earl Grosvenor (father of 1st Duke of Westminster) to Lord John Russell, Parry & Freeman, Appendix I, 'The Flintshire Yeomanry Cavalry, 1797–1838', xi
12 Peel to Wellington, 24 Aug 1842, *Peel Papers*, B.M. Add. MSS, 40, 459
13 Leary, F. *The Earl of Chester's Regiment of Yeomanry Cavalry . . . 1797–1897*, 1898, 241
14 Webster, 63, 65
15 Bewick, 154–5
16 Cobbett, W., quoted in Bryant, A. *The Age of Elegance, 1812–1822*, 1950, 381
17 Graham: *Wilts*, 97
18 Graham to the Vice-Lieutenant of Staffordshire, Jul 1842, H.O. 41/17
19 *Hansard (C)*, XLII, 1838, 651
20 Napier to Under-Secretary, Home Office, 11 May 1839, *Napier*, II, 32
21 Napier to Lord de Grey, 8 May, 1839, *Napier*, II, 30
22 *Smith*, I, 331
23 Mather, 147
24 'Affray at Newtownbarry – Capt. Graham', 16 Apr 1832, *Hansard (L)*, 3rd Series, XII, 499–537
25 Jackson, 151
26 Benson Freeman, 46

27   Webster, 80–82; Wylly, 272
28   Graham: *Wilts*, 110
29   Sheppard, 100–101
30   Hamilton, 195

(iii)

1   Arthur, II, 625
2   Jolliffe, III, 254
3   *Manchester Observer*, 20 Apr 1822; Hunt, H. *Address to the Radical Reformers*, 29 Oct 1822, 13–16
4   *Stanley*, 14
5   Bruton, 279
6   *Stanley*, 15
7   *Stanley*, 18
8   J. Tyas's report in *The Times*, 19 Aug 1819
9   Jolliffe, 256
10   Bruton, 286
11   Jolliffe, 256–7
12   *Inquest on John Lees*, 1820, 180, quoted in Thompson, E. P. *The Making of the English Working Class*, 1963, 686
13   The best modern account of Peterloo is Read, Dr Donald *Peterloo – the 'Massacre' and its Background*, 1958. The fullest of all, but biased, is Walmsley, Robert *Peterloo: The Case Reopened*, 1969
14   Hamilton, 193
15   Latimer, 169
16   The account of the Bristol riots in this chapter is largely based upon Latimer, 146–84; Teichman, 130–4 and Hamburger, Joseph *James Mill and the Art of Revolution*, 1963, 161–81. I am grateful to Mr David Large of the Department of History, University of Bristol, for much assistance
17   Lord Chief Justice Tindal, quoted in H.O. 41/14 (1839)
18   *Select Committee on Railways, 1844*, 5th report, 144–5
19   Redford, A. *Labour Migration in England, 1800–1850*, 1926
20   *Napier*, II, 16
21   Mather, 173, quoting *The Times*, 19 Aug 1842; H.O. 45/264.

CHAPTER II (p. 95–113)

(i)

1   Nolan, 279
2   *Queen's Regs*, 371
3   Moyse-Bartlett, 91
4   Moyse-Bartlett, 91
5   Thomson, I, 43
6   Nolan, 106–7
7   Robson, Brian 'The British Cavalry Trooper's Sword 1796–1853', *J.A.H.R.*, XLVI (1968), 105

(ii)

1   Quoted in (Anon.) 'Lancers', *Cavalry Journal*, XII (1922), 111
2   Sumner, Rev. P. 'Uniforms and equipment of the Light Dragoons (Hussars) 1800 to 1813', *J.A.H.R.*, XVI (1937), 168
3   Granville, Castalia, Countess (ed.) *Lord G. Leveson Gower, private correspondence, 1781–1821*, II, 421
4   Drouville, Capt. *On the Formation of British Lancers*, 1813
5   Montmorency, Lt.-Col. R. H. de, *Proposed Rules and Regulations for the Exercise and Manoeuvres of the Lance, compiled entirely from the Polish system . . . adapted to the Formations, Movements, and Exercise of the British Cavalry . . .*, 1820
6   Evans, 64
7   Mercer, Gen. C. *Journal of the Waterloo Campaign . . .* (ed.) Fortescue, Sir J., 1927, 192–3
8   Wall, C. C. 'La Reine des Armes Blanches' *Cavalry Journal*, XVIII (1928), 264
9   *Essex Standard*, 26 Sep 1834
10 Luard, Capt. J. *History of the Dress of the British Soldier*, 1852, 192; Boulderson, Maj. S. 'The Armament and Organisation of Cavalry . . .', *J.U.S.I.*, XXII (1878), 378
11 Nolan, 126
12 Nolan, 124
13 Jacob, 45

(iii)

1   Nolan, 217
2   Nolan, 97, 150
3   Nolan, 147

(iv)

1   Baker, 2

(v)

1   Henderson, 191
2   Sworder, Capt. J. C. C. 'The Wood', *Royal Artillery Journal*, LXXXIV (1957), 209
3   Henderson, 199
4   Henderson, 197
5   *Queen's Regs*, 378
6   Pennington, W. H. *Sea, Camp and Stage*, 1906.

(vi)

1   Quoted from a lecture given by Veterinary Surgeon G. Fleming at Aldershot in 1889, Tylden, 1
2   Tylden, 48

3 Nolan, 164
4 Smith, Maj.-Gen. Sir F. (in a lecture at Aldershot in 1891), *Animal Management*, 136
5 Baker, 17
6 Tylden, 3
7 Tylden, 46
8 Smith, 98
9 Addington, Maj. Hon. R. A. 'Notes on the Recruiting of the Madras Cavalry in the days of the Company Bahadur', *Cavalry Journal*, XVII (1927), 80 and 'Remounting of the Madras Cavalry in the days of the Company Bahadur', *Cavalry Journal*, XIX (1929), 580
10 Lecture by General Rimington, 1904, quoted in Tylden, 62
11 Quoted in India: Army HQ: Intelligence Branch *Frontier and Overseas Expeditions from India*, Vol. III 'Baluchistan and the First Afghan War', 1910, 309 (Outram, 77)
12 *Report of Board of General Officers*, April 1796, P.R.O., W.O.4/164, 286
13 War Office memo. to P.V.S., 1846, quoted in Smith, 120
14 *The Veterinarian*, Sept, 1830
15 Percivall, John, article in *The Veterinarian*, Nov, 1828
16 P.R.O., W.O. 43/107730
17 Smith, 119
18 Smith, 17
19 *Queen's Regs*, 373
20 Tylden, 230
21 Anon. article in *Edinburgh Medical and Surgical Journal*, No. 335, 1838
22 Moyse-Bartlett, 134

CHAPTER III (p.114–151)

(i)

1 Whyte, 38
2 Mole, 33
3 MacMullen, 311
4 Stanhope, Earl of *Notes of Conversations with the Duke of Wellington*, 1889, 18
5 Adams, 5
6 Clode, 211
7 Somerville, 108–9

(ii)

1 Napier, 52
2 McGuffie, 20–21
3 P.R.O., W.O. 1/660/307–8.
4 Somerville, 127
5 From Col. the Hon. H. Murray's pocket-book: 'Record of Men', Malet, Col. H. *The Historical Memoirs of the XVIIIth Hussars*, 1907, 203
6 Speech of Capt. Layard in Army estimates debate, 27 Feb., 1843, *Hansard* (C), LXVI, 1370

(iii)

1   Dibdin the Elder, Charles *Songs*, 1841, 59
2   Marshall, 68, quoting Wade, Dr *History of the Middle and Working Classes*
3   Henderson, 208, 249
4   Wylly, 263
5   Marshall, 65, 71, 74–5; Clode, 30–31; 10 & 11 Vic. c.37, 1847
6   *Commission on Military Punishments*, 1836, 306; *Pension Regulations*, 1863; see also, Clode, II, 290–1
7   [Anon.] *Six Months in the Ranks or The Gentleman Private*, 1890, 18
8   McGuffie, 21
9   Lucas

(iv)

1   Nolan, 115
2   Nolan, 115
3   Nolan, 103
4   Lowe, 46

(v)

1   MacMullen, 16
2   Adams, 6, 7

(vi)

1   Adams, 16
2   Halévy, 71
3   Whyte, 19
4   Clode, I, 225
5   Speech of Lord Ebrington, *Hansard (C)*, 11 May 1858, 478
6   Henderson, 197
7   *Hansard (C)*, LXVII, 1842, 324
8   Lucas
9   Wolseley, 164
10 Bonham-Carter, 11
11 Adams, 11, 12
12 de Watteville, Col. H. *The British Soldier: His Daily Life from Tudor to Modern Times*, 1954, 131
13 Wolseley, 164
14 Anglesey: *Pearman*, 25
15 Anglesey: *Pearman*, 60
16 Coley, 51
17 Henderson, 208; Anglesey: *Pearman*, 60
18 Fortescue, XI, 10
19 Adams, 13
20 Wylly, 267
21 Henderson, 208

Source notes (pages 133–152)

(vii)

1 Kincaid, J. *Random Shots from a Rifleman*, 1835, 47
2 Bryant, A. *The Age of Elegance*, 1950 331
3 Marshall: *Pun*, 240; Ritchie, C.I.A. 'A Nineteenth-century 2nd Dragoon's Account Book', *J.A.H.R.*, XXXIX (1961), 160, 219
4 [Ryder, Cpl. John] *Four Years' Service in India*, 1853, 28–9
5 Knollys, I, 114, 115, 116
6 Marshall, 111
7 Wolseley, I, 172
8 Gough to Sir H. Hardinge, 14 Apr 1845, quoted in Rait, I, 356
9 Mole, 48–52
10 Marshall: *Pun*, 204
11 Lucas
12 Thomson, I, 40

(viii)

1 *Wellington (D:NS)*, V, 594
2 Tookey, 27 Nov, 1847
3 Speech of Colonel Lindsay in canteens in barracks debate, 5 Mar. 1847, *Hansard (C)*, XC, 952
4 Tookey, 30 Jul, 1848
5 Anglesey: *Pearman*, 61, 63
6 Wylly, 277
7 Tookey, 13 May 1847
8 *Parliamentary Papers* (1888) LXVII (245), 807
9 Tookey, 30 Jan 1848
10 Tookey, 13 May 1848
11 Broughton, Lord, *Recollections of a Long Life*, 1909, I, 237
12 Barrett, 20
13 Woodward, 256
14 Marshall, 77–8, 106
15 Thomas, 32–3
16 Whyte, 18–38
17 Adams, ix
18 Woodward, 260
19 Mole, 37

(ix)

1 Quoted by Wolseley, 209
2 Fortescue: *Canteens*, 20, 21

CHAPTER IV (p. 152–178)
(i)

1 Swift, J. *The Grand Question Debated*, 1732, 7
2 Halévy, I, 87

3   *Parliamentary Papers* (1870), XXIV, (C.25), 20g
4   Fortescue, XI, 33
5   Fortescue, XI, 33, fn
6   *Hansard (C)*, XXXIII, 93 (7 Mar 1816)
7   Wylly, 352

(ii)

1   Craig to Sir Hew Dalrymple, 12 Oct. 1794
2   Mockler-Ferryman, Maj. A. F. *Annals of Sandhurst* . . . , 1900, 23, 24, 27, 32
3   Dickens, Charles *Dombey and Son*, I, X
4   Thomas, 22, 23, 86, 87, 96, 97, 118
5   Lambrick, 7

(iii)

1   14 Jan 1855, 11 June 1856, Hodge Papers
2   Evidence of Mr Hammersley of Cox & Co., army agents, before the *Royal Commission on Purchase*, 1857
3   Shakespear, Capt. C. M. J. D., RHA, quoted in Hibbert, C. *The Destruction of Lord Raglan*, 1961, 8
4   Fonblanque, de, *Money or Merit*, 1857, 12
5   *Parliamentary Papers* (1857) XVIII (c.2267), 293
6   Scott, Sir W. 'Character of the Duke of York' (from *Edinburgh Weekly Journal*) *Annual Register*, 1827, 461
7   Douglas, Sir G. (ed.) *The Panmure Papers*, 1908, II, 492
8   *Report from Select Committee on Army and Navy Appointments, 1833*, 274
9   Thomson, I, 76
10 Fortescue, XI, 31–2
11 Speech of George Trevelyan, *Hansard (C)* 19 May 1868, 525
12 28 May 1871, BM, Add. MSS, 44119 (*Gladstone Papers*)

(iv)

1   [Bromley, W.] *Letters from a Father to his Son on entering the Army*, Carmarthen, 1833, 36
2   *Evidence before the Royal Commission on Army & Navy Appointments*, 1833; Clode, II, 116
3   Parkyn, Maj. H. G. 'A letter Book of General Sir James S. Denham . . .' *Cavalry Journal*, XII, 146
4   Thomson, I, 46
5   W.O. 27/387; Murray, I, 400
6   Fortescue, XI, 35
7   *Queen's Regs*, 380
8   Capt. W. Unett to his father, 18 Jun 1842, *Unett*, 61
9   Stocqueler, J. H. *The British Officer* . . ., 1851, 33–65.

(v)

1   Journal, 4 May 1839, *Napier*, II, 24
2   Blakeney, Robert *A Boy in the Peninsular War: Services, Adventures and Experiences*, 1899, 240–1
3   Anglesey, 311
4   Evans, 64
5   Loftus, Capt. Charles *My Life from 1815–,1849* II, 118–20
6   Scott Daniell, 159–60
7   Oatts, 122
8   Evidence before the *Royal Commission on Military Punishments*, 1836
9   Anton, Sgt. J. *Retrospect of a Military Life*, 1841, 241
10   *The Times*, 8 March 1855
11   Smyth, Sir J. *In This Sign Conquer: the story of the Army Chaplains*, 1968, 62

(vi)

1   Verner, Col. Willoughby (ed.) *A British Rifleman*, 1899, 277

(vii)

1   'Memorandum on the Mutiny at Barrack-poor', 10 Oct 1825, *Wellington (SD)*, II, 528
2   Lambrick, 14
3   Seaton, 56

CHAPTER V (p. 179–189)

(i)

1   Quoted in Norman, 423
2   Smyth, 2
3   Trower, Capt. C. F. *Hints on Irregular Cavalry . . .*, 1845, 22
4   Jacob, 8
5   Lambrick, *S.I.H.*, 35
6   Whitworth, 211
7   Wallis, Capt. H. J. K. 'Indian Silahdar Cavalry' *Cavalry Journal* (reprinted from *J.U.S.I.*), VI (1911), 205
8   Quoted in Norman, 423
9   Malcolm, Sir John *The Government of India*, 1833, Appx E, 234–5
10   Marshall, 99
11   See O'Donnell, Maj. B. H. 'The Indian Cavalry Group System', *Cavalry Journal*, XX (1930), 266

(ii)

1   Sheppard, 119
2   [Anon.] 'Sketches of Remarkable Living Characters in India', *The Asiatic Journal*, October, 1844

3   Smyth, 8–9
4   15 July 1817, quoted in Anderson, M. H. & E. S. J. *The Poona Horse ...*
1817–1931, 1933, I, 180
5   11 Nov 1817, *MS Journal of Lieutenant J. Macleod, 1816–21*, I.O.L., 295
MSS Eur. B. 7, p. 94

CHAPTER VI (p. 190–211)

(i)

1   Fortescue, XI, 354
2   Fortescue, XI, 6
3   Fortescue, XI, 354
4   Moira to Bathurst, 10 Nov 1814, I.O.L., C.O. 77/34
5   Pemble, John *The Invasion of Nepal: John Company at War*, 1971, 148.
The quotation is from a letter signed 'Parry' to the editor, *East India
United Services Journal*, VIII (1836), 274–6
6   Murray, I, 372

(ii)

1   Burton: *M & PW*, 110
2   Spear, 575
3   Macaulay, T. B. *Essay on Lord Clive*, 1840, 13
4   *Asiatic Journal*, 1819, vii, 174–83
5   Wilson, IV, 14
6   Wilson, III, 372
7   Fortescue, XI, 172; Wilson, IV, 4
8   'Autobiography of Sir John Hearsey' in Pearse, 247–60.
9   Hearsey, John letter to *Delhi Gazette*, 2 July 1845, quoted in Pearse, 325
10   Including Blacker, 113; McNaghten, Lieut. R. A. *A Memoir of the
Military Operations of the Nagpore Subsidiary Force ... from ... 1816
to ... 1819 ...*, 1820; Clarke, Lieut. M. *Summary of the Mahratta and
Pindarree Campaign during 1817, 1818 and 1819 ...*, *chiefly embracing the
operations of the Army of the Deckan ...*, 1820 (who writes that Scott
'disapproved of the proposal and returned a positive refusal to Capt.
Fitzgerald with a peremptory injunction not to attempt anything of the
kind at the hazard of his commission. Capt. Fitzgerald observed ... "If it
is only at the hazard of my commission, here goes" ...'), and Marshman,
J.C. *The History of India ...*, 1842 (who writes that 'contrary to the impassioned protest of his faint-hearted commander, Fitzgerald rushed with
irresistible fury...'). See also 'Peter's Finger', 'History As She is Wrote',
J.A.H.R., XVI (1937), 110
11   Stubbs, II, 79; Blacker, 120
12   Fortescue, XI, 206
13   Gov.-Gen. to Madras Govt., 8 Apr 1819
14   Adjt.-Gen. MS return, quoted in Wilson IV, 512
15   Fortescue, XI, 215
16   Burton: *M & PW*, 61

17 Stubbs, II, 98
18 Stubbs, II, 96
19 Pearse, 278–80
20 There is an almost total lack of first hand, personal accounts, such as diaries, letters and autobiographical narratives of cavalry officers engaged in the Pindari and Maratha War. Sir John Hearsey's autobiography and statement of services which are included in Pearse, are the sole example which I have been able to discover. The chief authority on the war as a whole is Blacker. The official history, Burton: *M.&P.W.*, follows Blacker (who as a cavalry officer is not entirely objective when discussing that arm) pretty closely, but gives more information about the actual formations engaged. Princep, H. T. *A Narrative of the Political and Military Transactions of British India under . . . the Marquess of Hastings, 1813 to 1818*, 1820, contains some additional information of interest, as does Fitzclarence, Lt-Col. [Munster, 1st Earl of], *Journal of a Route across India, through Egypt to England in the latter end of the year 1817, and the beginning of 1818*, 1819. Gupta, Pratul C. *Baji Rao II and the East India Company, 1796–1818*, 1939, is of interest concerning the Peshwa and his armies. Wilson, IV, is invaluable for the operations of the Army of the Deccan. Cardew adds little to the other authorities. Many nuggets of interest are to be found in Stubbs, II

(iii)

1 Fortescue, XI, 368
2 Diary of Capt. Thomas Hooke Pearson, quoted in Graham, 85
3 Biddulph, H. 'The Era of Army Purchase', *J.A.H.R.*, XII (1933), 230

CHAPTER VII (p. 212–227)

(i)

1   Mackinnon, 115
2   Churchill, IV, 65
3   Despatch, Secret Committee, Directors, H.E.I.C., 25 Jun 1836
4   Spear, 598
5   *Thackwell*, 118
6   Holdsworth, T. W. E. *The Campaign of the Indus* (priv. printed), 1840, 21–2
7   Lawrence, G., 10; Hough, Appx 58–73
8   Hay, Capt. B. 'The First Afghan War, 1838–1842', *J.U.S.I.*, Feb 1911, 201
9   Lawrence, G. 7
10 Graham, 85
11 *Thackwell*, 126, 129
12 Lawrence, G., 10, 11
13 Lowe, 342
14 Graham, 85
15 Hough, 96
16 Hough, 75

17   *Thackwell*, 127, 130–1
18   Lawrence, G., 10
19   Hough, 92
20   Havelock, Capt. H. *Narrative of the War in Afghanistan in 1838–9*, 1840, 270
21   Lowe, 336–7
22   Scott Daniell, 147
23   Quoted from an undated letter to an anonymous correspondent in Kaye, I, 363–4, See also, Colebrooke, Sir T. E. *Life of the Hon. Mountstuart Elphinstone*, II, 373–4
24   Spear, 605
25   Hough, 262
26   Graham, 93
27   Fortescue, XII, 132
28   Lawrence, G., 44–8
29   E.g. Durand, 292–3; Fortescue, XII, 137–8
30   Hearsey, J. Letter to *The Delhi Gazette*, 2 Jul 1845, quoted in Pearse, 333

(ii)

1   Quoted in Lunt, James *Bokhara Burnes*, 1969, 198
2   Churchill, IV, 65
3   Bolitho, 142–3
4   Greenwood, Lieut. (31st Foot) *Narrative of the late victorious campaign in Afghanistan under General Pollock*, 2nd ed., 1844, 221–2
5   Cardew, 190
6   Kaye, III, 327–8
7   [Currie, Maj. A. P.] *Historical Record of . . . the 3rd (Queen's Own) Regiment of Bombay Light Cavalry* [1877], 4–5
8   Bolitho, 144
9   Strachey, L. and Fulford, R. *The Greville Memoirs, 1814–1860*, 1938, V, 70

CHAPTER VIII (p. 228–242)

(i)

1   *Napier*, II, 269
2   Journal, 7 Oct 1842, *Napier*, II, 218
3   Sir C. Napier to Capt. J. Jacob, 25 Feb 1844 [Jacob, J.] *Papers regarding the first campaign against the Predatory Tribes of Cutchee in 1839–40, and affairs of the Scinde Frontier*, 1853
4   Fortescue, XII, 289
5   Quoted in Lambrick, 86–7
6   *S.I.H.*, I, 23
7   Napier, Sir William *The History of Gen. Sir Charles Napier's Conquest of Scinde*, 2nd ed., 1857, 233
8   Lambrick, 95
9   *Napier*, II, 350

10 18 May 1844, *Punch*, VI, 209. The chief and most reliable sources for the conquest of Sind are the works of H. T. Lambrick, C.I.E. (*Sir Charles Napier and Sind*, 1952; *John Jacob of Jacobabad*, 1960; 'The Sind Battles, 1843', *Sind Historical Society's Journal*, VII, 1943). Upon these this section is largely based

(ii)

1 *Smith*, II, 136
2 *Smith*, II, 127
3 General Orders, 4 Jan 1844, *Govt. Gazette*, 1; (Enclosures to Secret Letters from India, Vol. 95. Enclosures 65 and 66 E Secret Letter No. 7 of 1844)
4 Gough to Duke of Wellington, 17 Dec 1843, Rait, I, 312
5 Gough to his son, 20 Jan 1844, Rait, I, 311
6 Gough's Despatch, 4 Jan 1844, *Govt. Gazette*, 3
7 Gough's Despatch, 4
8 Gough's Despatch, 4
9 Gough's Despatch, 4
10 Gough to his son, 13 Nov 1844, Rait, I, 329
11 *Thackwell*, 184
12 Corporal E. Cowtan (later adjutant), to his father (n.d.), Graham, 100
13 29 Dec 1843, Forrest, 174

CHAPTER IX (p. 243–289)

(i)

1 1967, Introduction, 25–6.
2 Spear, 612
3 Lawrence, H., 262–3
4 Sir H. Hardinge to Maj. Broadfoot, June 1845, quoted in Burton: *SW*, 15
5 Denham-Cookes, 148
6 William Hoff to his brother in Reeves-Brown, G., 'Moodkee and Ferozeshah, 1845. A Camp Follower's Account', *J.A.H.R.*, XIII (1934), 41
7 Denham-Cookes, 148
8 19 Dec 1845, *Hardinge & Gough*, 29
9 Denham-Cookes, 150
10 Parry, 52
11 Denham-Cookes, 150–1
12 Despatch of Brig. M. White, 19 Dec. 1845, Cannon, 127
13 *Hardinge & Gough*, 30
14 Gough to his son, 19 Dec. 1845, Rait, I,I 7
15 Gough and Innes, 79
16 E.g. Gough and Innes, 70
17 Cumming, 276
18 Intercepted letter quoted in Capt. Nicolson's diary, Broadfoot, 388
19 Parry, 61, 62
20 Hardinge, 90
21 Stubbs, III, 124
22 Despatch of Brig. M. White, 25 Dec 1845, Cannon 129

23 Ley, Capt. A. E. H. 'The 3rd Light Dragoons at Moodkee and Ferozeshah', *Cavalry Journal*, VI (1911), 466

24 Denham-Cookes, 153–4

25 Humbley, 132

26 Stubbs, III, 129

27 Gough and Innes, 94; *Calcutta Review*, VI, 276

28 Taylor to his father, 17 Jan 1846, Parry, 61

29 Cumming, 278

30 Marshman, 154

31 Marshman, 156

32 Cumming, 278–82

33 *Hardinge & Gough*, 39

34 16 Jan 1846, Rait, II, 28

35 Lt.-Col. the Hon. Thomas Ashburnham to Marquess of Sligo, 30 Jan 1846, Leslie, Lt.-Col. J. H. 'The First Sikh War, 1845–6', *J.A.H.R.*, XI (1932), 71

36 [Bunbury, T.] *Reminiscences of a Veteran*, 1861, III, 288

37 Denham-Cookes, 155

38 Innes, Lt.-Col. P. R. *The History of the Bengal European Regiment . . .*, 1885, 389–90

39 Fortescue, XII, 367. See also Broadfoot, 397

40 Hardinge, 99

41 Gordon, Sir J. J. H. *The Sikhs*, 1904, 143

42 Revised figures, Cardew, 210

43 Fortescue, XII, 368

44 Fortescue, XII, 368

45 McGregor, W. K., MD *The History of the Sikhs . . .*, II, 114

46 Steinbach, Lt.-Col. *The Panjab*, 1845, 97; Griffin, L. P. *Ranjit Singh* (Rulers of India Series), 1911, 134; 'H.M.L.' *Some Passages in the Life of an Adventurer in the Panjab*, 1842, 44

47 Coley, 20

48 22 Feb 1848, Foreign Dept. Secret Proceedings, I.O.L., 42

49 Cummings, 284

50 Trotter, 55

51 Smith, II, 186

52 Letter of Cpl. F. B. Cowtan (n.d.), Graham, 112

53 Anglesey: *Pearman*, 36–7

54 Anglesey: *Pearman*, 43

55 Anglesey: *Pearman*, 45

56 Letter of 'a private' (n.d.), Graham, 113

57 Letter of Cpl. F. B. Cowtan (n.d.), Graham, 113

58 Letter of Sgt. Gould (n.d.), Graham, 111

59 Sir H. Smith to Lt.-Col. Alexander, RA (n.d.), Stubbs, III, 139

60 Sir Harry Smith's despatch, 30 Jan 1846, *Hardinge & Gough*, 73

61 Maude, 181

62 Sir H. Smith to Sir J. Kempt, 24 Feb 1846, *Smith*, II, 194

63 Letter of 2 Feb 1846 from Tpr. Eaton *Cambridge Independent Press*, 4 Apr 1846

64   Nolan, 127
65   *Yorkshire Post*, Nov 1906
66   Mackenzie, Col. R. H. 'Brig.-Gen. C. R. Cureton, C. B.' *Cavalry Journal*,
     VII, 1912, 205
67   *Hardinge & Gough*, 75
68   Sir H. Smith to Sir J. Kempt, 24 Feb 1846, *Smith*, II, 194
69   Anglesey: *Pearman*, 52, 53
70   *Hardinge & Gough*, 101; *Thackwell*, 214
71   Thackwell's letter home, 26 Mar 1846, *Thackwell*, 213–14
72   Anglesey: *Pearman*, 55
73   Sir H. Smith to Sir J. Thackwell (n.d.: 1850s?), *Thackwell*, 214
74   Thackwell's letter home, 26 Mar 1846; *Thackwell*, 213
75   Knollys, I, 86

(ii)

1   *Napier*, IV, 185
2   Spear, 618
3   Gough's Despatch, 23 Nov 1848; Thackwell, 287
4   Cardew, 228
5   Ouvry, 48
6   Anglesey: *Pearman*, 71–2
7   Anglesey: *Pearman*, 73–4
8   Gough to his son, 18 Mar 1849, Rait, II, 186–7
9   Memo. by H. Havelock, 1849, Marshman, 178
10   Capt. R. P. Apthorp to Col. H. B. Hamilton, 14 Feb 1899, Hamilton,
     571
11   Marshman, 178
12   Anglesey: *Pearman*, 75
13   Anglesey: *Pearman*, 75
14   Ld. Gough to Ld. Fitzroy Somerset, 26 Nov 1848, Rait, II, 183
15   Rait, II, 183
16   H. Havelock to Col. Birch, 7 Dec 1848, Marshman, 176
17   Apthorp, Hamilton, 570
18   Marshman, 175
19   Gough's diary, 13 Jan 1849, Gough & James, 293
20   Forrest, 210
21   Anglesey: *Pearman*, 85
22   Dalhousie to Duke of Wellington, 22 Jan 1849, Lee-Warner, I, 207
23   Anglesey: *Pearman*, 89
24   Lt. MacQueen's account, *Thackwell*, 294
25   Gough & Innes, 294
26   Statement by Maj. Wheatley, C.O. of the 5th, Stubbs, III, 207
27   Unett to his father, 15 Jan 1849, *Unett Papers*
28   Anglesey: *Pearman*, 91
29   MacQueen, *Thackwell*, 294
30   Unett's account, *Thackwell*, 293
31   Delmar, 120, 131
32   Thompson, Gen. C. W., Oct 1895, *J.U.S.I.*, XXXIX, 1021
33   Knollys, I, 137

Source notes (pages 280–295)

34 Sheppard, 117
35 Thackwell, 132–3
36 Stubbs, III, 200
37 *Thackwell*, 302
38 Stubbs, III, 205
39 Testimony of some of the artillery officers, quoted in *Thackwell*, 302
40 Gough, Sir Charles 'Reflections on Chilianwala', *J.U.S.I.*, Mar 1895, 245–6
41 Pearse, 361
42 Visc. Chetwynd, the serrefile of the 2nd Squadron of the 14th, to his squadron commander, 5 Jul 1896, Oct 1895, *J.U.S.I.*, XXXIX, 1026
43 Stubbs, III, 206
44 Lee-Warner, I, 208
45 Dalhousie to Gough, 19 Feb 1849, Rait, II, 260
46 *Thackwell*, 303–4
47 Rait, II, 238
48 Fortescue, XII, 457
49 Sir J. Tennant, K.C.B., in a private letter, Stubbs, III, 206
50 Ouvry, 67
51 Anglesey: *Pearman*, 109
52 Thackwell, 140–5
53 Marshman, 185
54 Quoted in Rait, II, 270
55 Rait, II, 274
56 Hearsey's despatch, Thackwell, 352
57 Malcolm to Capt. Pratt, A. A.-G., Cav. Div., 17 Mar 1849, *S.I.H.*, I, 290
58 Thackwell, 223–4
59 Delmar, 141–5
60 [Sandford, D. A.] *Leaves from the Journal of a Subaltern*, 1849, 147
61 Malcolm to J. Jacob, 26 Feb 1849, *S.I.H.*, I, 283
62 Brig.-Gen. H. Dundas to Malcolm, 16 Mar 1849, *S.I.H.*, I, 289
63 Lieut. H. Green to J. Jacob, 1 Mar 1849, *S.I.H.*, I, 285
64 Malcolm to J. Jacob, 26 Feb 1849, *S.I.H.*, I, 283
65 Green to J. Jacob, 1 Mar 1849, *S.I.H.*, I, 285
66 Stubbs, III, 197
67 Thackwell, 57

EPILOGUE (p. 290–293)

1 Anglesey: *Pearman*, 28
2 Tookey, 27 Sep 1847; 28 June 1848; 19 Jan 1847
3 Anglesey: *Pearman*, 60
4 Tookey, 29 Aug 1848

APPENDIX (p. 294–299)

1 H.E.I.C. Court Minutes, 69,300, vol. 70,9: I.O.L. 'Letters received from Madras', vol. 1A
2 Cardew, 79

INDEX

BATTLES, REGIMENTS and WARS appear under these headings

Index

Index

Index

James I (1566–1625), 106
James II (1633–1701), 35
Jarry, Gen. Francis (1733–1807), 156
Johnson, Dr Samuel (1709–1784), 23, 54
Jolliffe, Lt, 15 LD, 86–7
Junot, Andoche, Duc d'Abrantès (1771–1813), 48

Kehilans (Arab horse), 106
Kempt, Gen. Sir James (1764–1854), 58
Khalsa, the, 102, 243–4, 254, 257, 262, 270
khudaspas, 181
King, Lt-Col. John Wallace, CB, 14 LD, at Chilianwala, 1849, 280, 283–4; commits suicide, 284
Knipe, Capt. Robert, 14 LD, 52

Lahore, Treaty of, 1846, 270
Lake, Gen. Gerard, 1st Viscount (of Delhi and Leswarree) (1744–1808), 65, 66, 67, 186, 187, 188, 195
Lancaster, Thomas Earl of (1277?–1322), 82
lance, the, 25, 29, 30, 34, 98–101, 265
lancers, 98–101, 265; English, first armed with pistols, 1599, 30; Fairfax's, 33; Polish, 'of the Vistula', 53, 98, 99
Lawrence, Gen. Sir George St Patrick (1804–1884), 157, 218, 221–2
Lawrence, Brig.-Gen. Sir Henry Montgomery (1806–1857), 145, 244, 270–1
Lawrence, John Laird Mair, 1st Baron (1811–1879), 257, 285
Lefebvre-Desnouettes, Gen. Comte Charles (1773–1822), 50
Le Marchant, Lt-Gen. John Gaspard (1766–1812), 53, 54–5, 97, 146, 265; killed at Salamanca, 54–5; founds RMC, 156
Leon, Cornet Baron, 98
L'Estrange, Lt-Col. Guy, 85–7
Ligonier, F-M John, 1st Earl (1680–1770), 40
Littler, Lt-Gen. Sir John Hunter (1783–1856), 245; at Ferozeshah, 1845, 251–252, 255
Lloyd, Capt. J. Arthur, 77
Lockwood, Col. Sir George Henry (1804–1884), 285
Long, Lt-Gen. Robert Ballard (1771–1825), 51, 117, 122
Louis XIV (1638–1715), 36
Lucan, George Charles Bingham, 3rd Earl of (1800–1888), 161
Lucas, Tpr William, 122–5, 130, 140
Luddite riots, 56

Lumley, Capt. J. R., at Ferozeshah, 1845, 255–6
Lunatic Asylum Protector Insurance Company, 83
Lushington, Gen. Sir James Law (1779–1859), 197
Luxembourg, Marshal François Henri de Montmorency-Bouteville, Duc de (1628–1695), 35, 36

Macan, Col., 66
Macaulay, Thomas Babington, 1st Baron (1800–1859), 148, 194
MacDowell, Lt-Col. George James MacDowell, 16 L, at Aliwal, 1846, 260–1
Machiavelli, Niccolo (1469–1527), 31; his *Art of War*, 30
Mackinnon, Lt David Henry, 16 L, 213
Mackworth, Maj., in Bristol riots, 1831, 88, 90
Macnaghten, Sir William Hay, bt (1793–1841), 214, 215, 219, 223
M'Shee, Tpr, 9 L, 135
Madras Mutiny, the, 1809, 69
Maidstone Cavalry Depot, 100, 104, 105, 129
Malcolm, Lt, Scinde Irregular Horse, at Gujrat, 1849, 286, 288
Manchester, 79, 84, 92, 165; St Peter's Fields, 85; the, 'Reformers', 85
Mansel, Brig. Gen., 45, 46
Mar, Donald, 12th Earl of (1293?–1332), 29
Marlborough, John, 1st Duke of (1650–1722), 36, 38, 47, 48, 146
Marmont, Marshal Auguste Frédéric Louis Viesse de, Duc de Raguse (1774–1852), 54
Martel, Charles (689?–741), 26
Martin, Lt, Bengal Cavalry, 248
Masséna, Marshal André (1758–1817), 51, 52
Maude, Lt-Col. F. N., 265
Mawdsley, Sqn Sgt-Maj., 8 H, 193
Maxwell, Col., 66
Mercer, Gen. Cavalié (1783–1868), 100
Metropolitan Police, the, 72
military savings banks, 148
Minto, Sir Gilbert, 1st Earl of (1751–1814), 190
Mole, Sgt-Maj. Edwin, 14 H, 137, 149
Monmouth, James Scott, Duke of (1649–1685), 35
Monro, Lt, RHG, 176
Moorcroft, William, 108
Montecuculi, Count Raimund (1609–1680), 98
Montmorency, Maj. Reymond Hervey de, 9 L, 99

330

Index

Moore, Gen. Sir John (1761–1809), 48, 49, 50
Muy, Gén. de, 43

Napier, Lt-Gen. Sir Charles James (1782–1853), 86, 92, 117, 171, 237, 270; commands Northern District of England, 79, 81; conquers Sind, 228–236; succeeds Gough as C-in-C, India, 283–4
Napier of Magdala, F-M Robert Cornelis, 1st Baron (1810–1890), 157, 292
Napier, Gen. Sir William Francis Patrick (1785–1860), 234
Napoleon I (1769–1821), 19, 38, 46, 48, 49, 50, 65, 98, 114, 190; at Waterloo, 58
Naval and Military Bible Society, 119
'necessaries', 118
New English School of Cavalry, 33
New Model Army, 33, 34, 35
Newsome, Sgt, 16 L, 264
Newtownbarry, affray at, 1832, 82
Ney, Marshal Michel, Prince de la Moskova and Duc d'Elchingen (1769–1815), 58, 61, 62
Nicholson, Brig. Gen. John (1821–1857), 245
Noailles, de, Marshal Louis (1713–1793), 39
Nolan, Capt. Lewis Edward (1820?–1854), 95, 96, 97, 100, 101, 102, 103, 106, 125, 126, 265
non-silladar (regular) Indian cavalry, 184
Northern Horsemen, the (16th c.), 31
Nott, Maj.-Gen. Sir William (1782–1845), 224, 226, 227

Ochterlony, Maj.-Gen. Sir David, bt (1758–1825), 192, 193, 209
Otto, Gen. [Austrian], 44
Oudh, the King of, 295
Outram, Lt-Gen. Sir James, bt (1803–1863), 109, 230
Ouvry, Lt, 3 LD, at Ramnagar, 1848, 272–3; at Chilianwala, 1849, 283

paga horse, the, 180–1
Palmerston, Henry John Temple, 3rd Viscount (1784–1865), 73
Palmer, Tpr, 9 L, 133–5
Panmure, Fox Maule, 2nd Baron (11th Earl of Dalhousie) (1801–1874), 163
Parlby, Col. William, 10 H, 160
Pattle, Lt-Col. William, 233, 236
pay, officers', 168, 290
pay, other ranks', 119–20, 290
Peace Preservation Force, Ireland, 72

Pearman, Tpr John (1819–1908), 3 LD, 131, 143, 259, 265, 283, 291; at Aliwal, 1846, 261–2; at Sobraon, 1846, 267–8; at Ramnagar, 1848, 273–4; at Chilianwala, 1849, 277–8
Pedlar, Capt., Bombay army, 197
Peel, Sir Robert, bt (1788–1850), 72, 79, 176, 258
Peniston, Lt, 78
Pennington, Pte, 11 H, 105
pensions, officers', 170
pensions, other ranks', 148–9, 290
Perron, Gén., 187
Pescara, Fernando Francisco de, Marqués de (1489–1525), 30
Peshwa, the, Baji Rao II (d. 1852), 186, 189, 195, 197, 203, 204; defeated at Seoni, 1818, 206–7
Peterloo, the 'massacre' of, 1819, 85–7
Peter I of Russia (the 'Great') (1672–1725), 37
Pettit, Lt, 78
Picton, Lt-Gen. Sir Thomas (1758–1815), 57, 58
Pitt, William, 1st Earl of Chatham (1708–1778), 41
Plymouth, Other Archer, 6th Earl of (1789–1833), 78
Pollock, F-M Sir George, bt (1786–1872), 224
Ponsonby, Maj.-Gen. Sir Frederick Cavendish (1783–1837), 99
Ponsonby, Maj.-Gen. Sir William (1772–1815), 58
Pope, Brig.-Gen. Alexander, 200, 292; at Chilianwala, 1849, 278–83
purchase system, 155, 158–67
Purnea, Diwan of Mysore, 298

Queen's Riding House, Pimlico (Cavalry Riding Establishment), 99, 104

'Race of Castlebar', the, 1798, 48
Raglan, Lord Fitzroy James Henry Somerset, 1st Baron (1788–1855), 266
Ranjit Singh (1780–1839), 101, 214, 216, 243–4, 265
Rawlinson, Sir Henry Creswicke, bt (1810–1895), 183
reading rooms in barracks, 144, 290
Reform Bill riots, 79, 144; at Bristol, 1831, 87–91
regimental schools, 147

REGIMENTS (Titles, where possible, as at 1850)
  1st Life Guards, 35, 36, 56, 74, 75, 82, 111, 173–4; at Genappe, 1815, 57; at

331

Index

Index

Index

Index

Index